D1598738

# PAL JOEY

## THE BROADWAY LEGACIES SERIES

Geoffrey Block, Series Editor

*Series Board*

*"South Pacific": Paradise Rewritten*
Jim Lovensheimer

*Pick Yourself Up: Dorothy Fields and the American Musical*
Charlotte Greenspan

*To Broadway, to Life! The Musical Theater of Bock and Harnick*
Philip Lambert

*Irving Berlin's American Musical Theater*
Jeffrey Magee

*Loverly: The Life and Times of "My Fair Lady"*
Dominic McHugh

*"Show Boat": Performing Race in an American Musical*
Todd Decker

*Bernstein Meets Broadway: Collaborative Art in a Time of War*
Carol J. Oja

*We'll Have Manhattan: The Early Work of Rodgers and Hart*
Dominic Symonds

*Agnes de Mille: Telling Stories in Broadway Dance*
Kara Gardner

*The Shuberts and their Passing Shows: The Untold Tale of Ziegfeld's Rivals*
Jonas Westover

*Big Deal: Bob Fosse and Dance in the American Musical*
Kevin Winkler

*"Pal Joey": The History of a Heel*
Julianne Lindberg

# PAL JOEY

## The History of a Heel

JULIANNE LINDBERG

# OXFORD
UNIVERSITY PRESS

Oxford University Press is a department of the University of Oxford. It furthers
the University's objective of excellence in research, scholarship, and education
by publishing worldwide. Oxford is a registered trade mark of Oxford University
Press in the UK and certain other countries.

Published in the United States of America by Oxford University Press
198 Madison Avenue, New York, NY 10016, United States of America.

Library of Congress Control Number: 2019040681
ISBN 978–0–19–005120–4

1 3 5 7 9 8 6 4 2

Printed by Sheridan Books, Inc., United States of America

*For Isabel and Amelia.*

# CONTENTS

• • •

# FOREWORD

* * *

*"Pal Joey": The History of a Heel* by Julianne Lindberg explores the conception, creation, and afterlife of a pioneering theater work. The title role is Broadway's first conspicuous antihero, who unconventionally ends up unredeemed, unrepentant, and losing, not just the momentary object of a mutual adulterous lust, but a second understanding and potentially suitable partner. *Pal Joey* (1940) possessed a fine set of lyrics by Lorenz Hart and an exceptional musical score by Richard Rodgers that included the perennial song hit "Bewitched, Bothered and Bewildered." The choreographer was Robert Alton, who finally gets his due in Lindberg's history of a heel. In large part because his work was not preserved, Alton has been eclipsed by the memory of a young Gene Kelly, just twenty-eight, as the charming scoundrel "Pal" Joey Evans in his first and only starring stage musical role before becoming one of the all-time great male dancers in Hollywood. In the 1957 film adaptation, which also receives a chapter of its own in this volume, readers will learn how and why the role of the dancing Joey metamorphosed into a singing Frank Sinatra, who, unlike the Broadway Joey, gets to run off into the sunset with the younger ingénue.

The trail-blazing *Pal Joey* was based on a collection of John O'Hara short stories in epistolary form that had recently appeared in the *New Yorker*. O'Hara had already exposed the downside of the country-club set in his first novel, *Appointment in Samarra* (1934), and the sordid lives of café society in his second, *BUtterfield 8* (1935). Although he had some help from the legendary producer and director George Abbott and Hart, O'Hara was also given sole official credit for the show's book.

*Pal Joey* was the earliest show to appear in the Broadway musical director and author Lehman Engel's exclusive list of twelve excellent shows from 1940 to 1973 in his influential critical history *The American Musical Theater* (1975), and from its time to ours *Joey* has been widely acknowledged as Rodgers and Hart's greatest achievement among several dozen fine shows. *Babes in Arms* may have the most hit songs; *On Your Toes* can boast the extended jazz ballet "Slaughter on Tenth Avenue"; and *The Boys from Syracuse*, the first significant musical adaptation of a Shakespeare play and like its source, *A Comedy of Errors*, a perfect farce, is probably the most revived Rodgers and Hart show. For most musical theater historians and aficionados, however, none of these shows match the dramatic power and originality of *Pal Joey*, which might be one of the earliest musical comedies that directors confidently revive without making notable changes to its book or score.

Even Rodgers himself asserted late in life that "*Pal Joey* was the most satisfying and mature work that I was associated with during all my years with Larry Hart." It was a musical that refused to compromise and give us mainly likable characters, and its gritty realism remains modern and timeless. Surprisingly, despite its iconic importance and the universal esteem it has received for its precociously sophisticated presentation of provocative themes, its historical significance, and its overall artistic quality, *Joey* has not received the attention it deserves. Lindberg's most welcome book, her first, will admirably fill this lacuna.

Lindberg's comprehensive and jargon-free study of *Pal Joey* covers the evolution and transformation from short story to script and the working relationships within the musical's creative team, not only the songwriting team work of Rodgers and Hart but also the artistic and personal rapport between O'Hara and Hart. In the second part of her book Lindberg takes readers inside "the world of *Pal Joey*," the clubs and clubbing, the "book numbers" (i.e., the nondiegetic songs without dance), and the diegetic dance numbers directed by Alton that take place, first in Mike's seedy club in act 1 and then in the glitzy nightclub *Chez Joey* purchased by Joey's wealthy older mistress in act 2. Rounding out Part II is a jargon-free chapter on the women of *Pal Joey* and issues of gender. The third and final part of the book first considers the acclaimed and popular first revival, inspired by an extremely successful studio recording, which, after the 1942 revival of *Porgy and Bess*, was only the second major revival to surpass its original run. Lindberg then focuses on the 1957 film adaptation, which despite its sanitized approach to its unsavory stage predecessor and its often unpersuasive plot revisions, disputed musical deletions, and questionable choices of interpolated songs, for good or ill remains the *Pal Joey* most people know and merits the rigorous and balanced discussion it receives here.

*"Pal Joey": The History of a Heel* joins other Broadway Legacies volumes that focus on a single classical musical of the Golden Age: *Show Boat* (1927), *On the Town* (1944), *South Pacific* (1949), and *My Fair Lady* (1956). In his review of *Pal Joey*'s Christmas Day opening, the *New York Times* drama critic Brooks Atkinson ended with a famous question: "Although *Pal Joey* is expertly done, can you draw sweet water from a foul well?" After reading Julianne Lindberg's first major history of Broadway's first major heel, I believe that readers will answer Atkinson's question in the affirmative.

Geoffrey Block
*Series Editor, Broadway Legacies*

# TIMELINE: FROM SHORT STORY TO MUSICAL COMEDY

• • •

| | |
|---|---|
| October 22, 1938 | John O'Hara's first Joey story appears in *The New Yorker* |
| Early 1940 | George Oppenheimer approaches O'Hara about securing option for stage rights; this comes to nothing |
| Early 1940 | O'Hara pens letter to Richard Rodgers, suggesting a collaboration on a musical based on his *New Yorker* stories |
| | Rodgers responds to O'Hara's suggestion enthusiastically |
| March 1940 | O'Hara writes letter: "I am going to write the book for a musical comedy to be produced next fall in New York. Also, probably around the same time I am going to bring out a collection of the pieces, in a book."[1] |
| April 1940 | O'Hara finishes work on *Down Argentine Way* (in Los Angeles) |
| May 1940 | O'Hara begins writing book for *Pal Joey*, the musical |
| July 1940 | George Abbott agrees to produce *Pal Joey*, the musical |
| July 13, 1940 | *The New Yorker* publishes its final Joey story (the twelfth in the series; O'Hara would go on to write an additional two stories) |
| July–August 1940 | Auditions are held for *Pal Joey*, the musical: "A half dozen auditions were held in July and August. For the role of Joey, they saw Gene Kelly—and didn't bother to see anyone else. Vivienne Segal, Leila Ernst and Jack Durant were cast sight unseen."[2] |
| August 1940 | Principals are chosen |
| October 1940 | Duell, Sloan & Pearce publish O'Hara's Joey stories as a collection (fourteen in total, including the two previously unpublished stories), titled *Pal Joey* |
| October 1940 | George Abbott begins work on *Pal Joey* |
| Late October 1940 | Chorus calls for *Pal Joey*, the musical |
| November 11, 1940 | Rehearsals begin at the Biltmore and Longacre Theatres |
| November 1940 | June Havoc's initially small role is expanded |
| December 11–22, 1940 | Tryouts for *Pal Joey*, the musical, at the Forrest Theatre, Philadelphia |
| | "Love Is My Friend" (eventually titled "What Is a Man?") added for Vivienne Segal |
| | "I'm Talking to My Pal" is dropped |

| | |
|---|---|
| December 25 | Broadway premiere of *Pal Joey* at the Ethel Barrymore Theatre |
| September 1, 1941 | *Pal Joey* moves to the Shubert Theatre |
| September 7, 1941 | Gene Kelly gives his final performance of Joey |
| September 9, 1941 | Georgie Tapps takes over the role of Joey |
| October 21, 1941 | *Pal Joey* moves to the St. James Theatre |
| November 29, 1941 | *Pal Joey* closes at the St. James Theatre |

# ACKNOWLEDGMENTS

• • •

While writing this book, my first, I was struck by how an often solitary process was least solitary when it mattered most.

Thank you first to Geoffrey Block, who is among the most generous scholars I've ever met. Beyond the wealth of writings he's gifted us all, he was also attentive to my own writing, reading numerous drafts of my work (even those I am now embarrassed to have sent him). His encouragement helped lead me down the research path that now forms my career. I am so thankful for his support and guidance.

Norm Hirschy is, frankly, a gift. Thank you, Norm, for your enthusiastic support of work in musical theater, for your musical and editorial expertise, and for your uncommon patience, especially with a rookie like me.

I've been charmed by a life full of generous, brilliant mentors. David Ake, Susan McClary, Raymond Knapp, Mitchell Morris, and Olivia Bloechl, especially, have helped shape the way I see the world, and through their example have encouraged me to blur the line between academic and civic practice. Likewise, my graduate school cohort—Marianna Ritchey, Elizabeth Morgan, Joanna Love, Phil Gentry, Marcie Ray, and Jessica Bissett Perea, in particular—provided, and still provide, commiseration, friendship, and a much-needed levity as we work to find balance in our lives and careers.

Thank you to Helen Gallagher for granting a timely interview, and for reminding me that first-person accounts are often the most vibrant sites of history. Thanks to Norton Owens (Jacob's Pillow) and Laurence Maslon for generously answering my written queries. Special thanks to Paul Christman for his extensive work on reconstructing the score of *Pal Joey*.

My unending gratitude to all of the wonderful staff and librarians at the libraries and archives I consulted, especially those at the Library of Congress (Mark Eden Horowitz), the New York Public Library for the Performing Arts, and the Rodgers and Hammerstein Organization (Ted Chapin, Wayne Blood, Rob Shapiro, and Nicole Harman). Thank you also to the staff at the Margaret Herrick Library (Academy of Motion Picture Arts and Sciences), the Special Collections division at Penn State, and the Rare Book Library at Emory University. I would also like to thank the General Publications Fund of the American Musicological Society, supported in part by the National Endowment for the Humanities and the Andrew W. Mellon Foundation, for granting a generous subvention for this book.

Thank you to the College of Liberal Arts and the School of the Arts at the University of Nevada, Reno, through which I was able to secure funding for vital research trips. I'm lucky to have a supportive workplace. Special thanks to the wonderful administrative staff in the Department of Music at UNR (Vicki Bell, Cynthia Prescott, and Neva Sheehan), and to my brilliant and supportive colleagues.

Without the numerous conferences that provided a platform to present the work that appears in this book, I wouldn't have had the nerve to publish it. Thank you to Dominic McHugh, Dominic Symonds, George Burrows, John Graziano, Ian Sapiro, Ashley Pribyl, Daniel Fister, and Caleb Boyd for generously hosting. Thank you too to the three blind reviewers of my book manuscript, who challenged me in productive ways and saved me from a number of embarrassing mistakes and omissions. Extra thanks to the friends (and family!) who read drafts of all or parts of the book (Louis Niebur, Raymond Knapp, David Ake, Melissa Lindberg, and David Perez).

Closer to home, I'd like to thank Larry Engstrom, friend and former Director of the School of the Arts at UNR, who provided unwavering and crucial support for this book, and more generally my career. Without Louis Niebur I would never have finished the book. Our daily writing sessions, and his friendship, expertise, and encouragement got me through some very challenging periods. Thank you too to Ruthie Meadows, who rounds out our ethno/musicology trio, and whose enthusiasm and constant good cheer are restorative. Kate and Greg Pollard, excellent friends and fellow parents, facilitated a one-week writing retreat, without which I wouldn't have made it to the finish line.

Love and appreciation for my parents, Roberta and Harold Lindberg, who have always been supportive of me and my career. Love, too, to my mother-in-law Connie Dinneen, who loves and supports me unconditionally. Thank you to my brother Steven, who was the first person to challenge me to listen to music closely. I love and miss my grandfather, Don Perez, an avid listener who first introduced me to the American songbook. I am so lucky to have a sister, Melissa Lindberg, who is both my best friend and a generous, smart, and kind reader.

Finally, I am deeply grateful for my family. Thank you to my husband, Peter Epstein, who offered love and support as we weathered the storm of the last three years. This book is dedicated to the loves of our lives—our daughters Isabel and Amelia—who surprise us every day and challenge us to be better versions of ourselves.

One of the more daunting realizations I had as I wrote this book is that it could, like any book, manifest itself in countless ways; the version you hold is just one document of the rich histories and archives that I consulted. As I tell my students, books are part of a larger conversation, never the end of one. Still, deadlines are deadlines, and you eventually have to submit your manuscript. Thank you, reader, for your patience.

# INTRODUCTION

• • •

## "A FOUL WELL"

On December 27, 1940, two days after *Pal Joey* premiered on Broadway, an inter-office report was sent to the Motion Picture Producers and Distributors of America on behalf of one of its departments, the Production Code Administration (PCA). Taking on the form of a theater review, the report ended with the following note:

> This show contains:
> (1) an adulterous affair between two leads; (2) much vulgar, suggestive, double-meaning dialogue and singing; (3) some profanity and obscenity; (4) some vulgar dancing and costuming; (5) some drinking; (6) portrayal of Chicago Police Commissioner as the pliant tool of the misbehaving wife of a prominent business leader; (7) attempted blackmail.[1]

The preliminary report was written a little over a month before Columbia acquired the screen rights for *Pal Joey*. The February after the Broadway premiere, Columbia sent the script to the PCA office; when Joseph Breen, head of the PCA, had the chance to read the script in full, his objections were more specific. In a letter to Harry Cohn, the head of Columbia Pictures, Breen objected to the "references to sex perversion," the "references to loose sex on the part of your hero with various women," and the "entirely unacceptable" lyrics to "Happy Hunting Horn," "Bewitched," "Zip," and "Den of Iniquity."[2] Breen's complaints were based on a strict code of censorship specific to Hollywood. John O'Hara, the author of the source material and book for *Pal Joey*, recalls that after watching the premiere of the preview in Philadelphia, a "story editor of one of the major film companies" exclaimed "George Abbott better take his loss on this one, and stay out of New York. A middle-age broad and a young pimp?"[3] Theatrical experimentation, however, was not anathema to Broadway, and songwriters, directors, and producers could get away with far more than they could in Hollywood. *Pal Joey*, however, pushed even Broadway's limits.

Objections such as Breen's have become part of the lore surrounding the creation and reception of *Pal Joey*, the brilliant, famously adult show with music by Richard Rodgers and Larry Hart. Directed by George Abbott and based on an unflinchingly realistic book by John O'Hara, the eponymous lead of the show

*Pal Joey*. Julianne Lindberg, Oxford University Press (2020). © Oxford University Press.
DOI: 10.1093/oso/9780190051204.001.0001

is a scoundrel, a womanizer, a third-rate nightclub singer, and a first-class heel. He would be hard to redeem, had the creators of the show had any intention of redeeming him. Joey uses women for sexual and material gain. He thinks nothing of singing a tender, lyrical, seemingly sincere ballad to the ingénue Linda—a testament to both Joey's charms and Rodgers and Hart's musical alchemy—only to speak a completely different vernacular when addressing Vera, the wealthy benefactress who uses Joey for sex, and in return funds his dream club. Joey revels in the tawdry underworld that he helped to create, and in the penultimate song of the show, the two women he wronged are positively gleeful at moving past him. *Pal Joey* challenged audiences to question their preconceptions about musical comedy, and ignited new possibilities for theater producers hungry for quality books. It was bold, it was smart, and it blazed an entirely new trail in musical theater.

***

## THE STORY

*Pal Joey* opened at the Barrymore Theatre on Christmas day, 1940. Just a few blocks north and an avenue east, an eighty-eight-foot tall Norway spruce stood proudly at Rockefeller Center, twinkling with the cheerful contentment of the season. The first-nighters were not exactly primed, then, for O'Hara's grim naturalism. The story follows the exploits of Joey, a charismatic, womanizing, small-time nightclub entertainer who hopes to make it to the big time. At the center of the story are his ambitions—his ambition to "score" with any attractive woman he comes across, and his more desperate ambition to perform in and even own his own swanky nightclub. The curtain opens on Joey (Gene Kelly) in audition for the job of emcee at a seedy nightclub in the South Side of Chicago ("Chicago"). The book establishes straight away that *Pal Joey* is not for the morally high minded: page one alone of the opening-night script references alcohol abuse, cocaine, and homosexuality, all framed as vices. Mike (Robert J. Mulligan), the club owner, soon ferrets out Joey's true vice: women. Soon after Joey's successful audition the chorus dancers enter, dominated by Gladys (June Havoc), the tough-talking featured performer at Mike's club. After some banter with the girls, which solidifies Gladys's and Joey's mutual dislike for each other, Joey performs a jaunty dance number with the chorus ("You Mustn't Kick It Around"). In the next scene, set outside the window of a pet shop, Joey first meets Linda (Leila Ernst), the show's naive ingénue. Joey charms her, telling a whopper of a lie about his status as a formerly rich playboy, and they sing a duet ("I Could Write a Book"), which begins as a disingenuous pickup line.

Back at the nightclub, the chorus girls perform a few numbers that establish both the tackiness of the club and Gladys's ability to comically bump and grind ("Chicago"; "That Terrific Rainbow"). In between numbers, Joey emcees the evening. Joey is smarmy, but his audience loves him. It's in this scene that Joey first meets Vera (Vivienne Segal), a rich married woman who is "slumming" it along with a group of her highbred friends. Vera calls Joey over to her table and, in an attempt to avoid the false flattery that she's used to, Joey flirts brazenly. She leaves, apparently offended. Mike is furious, but Joey makes a deal with him: if Joey can get Vera back to the club in two nights, he can keep his job. In the following scene Joey calls Vera and tells her to "go to hell" for costing him his job, a deliberate gamble on his part. After Joey hangs up, Vera responds by calling her other paramours to cancel their plans; she is eager to embark on a fresh man-shaped diversion ("What Is a Man?" [originally "Love Is My Friend"]). In the next scene, Vera visits Joey after hours at the club and invites him home. Joey celebrates his "conquest"—although, truly, it seems more Vera's conquest—by performing the number "Happy Hunting Horn."

The next scene, set in a tailor shop, illustrates what Joey's life as a kept man is like. Here he is fitted for a new wardrobe, and he tells Vera how much he enjoys being pampered. Joey momentarily exits and Vera sings "Bewitched," revealing her surprising obsession with Joey. Directly afterward, Joey returns and riffs a bit on what his life will be like when he's the emcee at his very own swanky club, soon to be funded by Vera. Vera begins to reveal that she's a bit insecure over Joey's womanizing, and gets jealous when she sees Joey interact with Linda, who is working as a secretary for the tailor. While Joey is busy with the tailor, Vera concocts a lie to hurt Linda, involving the idea that Joey's a gangster and that Vera is his moll—Linda bursts into tears, she tells Joey off, and Joey is left alone on stage, confused and a bit defiant. Frustrated, he declares that he doesn't need a woman to realize his ambitions ("What Do I Care for a Dame?"). The song segues into the act 1 closer, the dream ballet ("Joey Looks into the Future"). Through some impressive stage magic, the cheap club is transformed into the club of Joey's dreams.

Act 2 opens on Chez Joey, the club that Vera has bankrolled for Joey. While the backdrop and some of the props remain from the transformation that occurred at the end of act 1, the reality of Joey's new club falls far short of his fantasy. The scene begins with the stage crew struggling to set up the club before opening night, complete with offstage hammering; the chorus rehearses "The Flower Garden of My Heart," an old-fashioned Ziegfeldian spoof number performed in deliberate bad taste. The number features a moony-eyed tenor (Nelson Rae) singing a treacly ballad to Gladys, who is called upon to dance *en pointe* while singing at the top of her range. Gladys fails miserably at portraying herself as an elegant, high-class performer, but succeeds in getting some of the biggest laughs of the show.

Later in the scene Joey sits for an interview with Melba (Jean Casto), a straight-shooting journalist reporting on the soon-to-be-opened club. Joey botches the interview—he again lies through his teeth, claiming that he's from old money and went to "Dartmouth College." Melba doesn't buy it. Somewhat shaken, Joey exits. Melba follows up their interview with the song "Zip," a showstopping mock striptease channeling her most fascinating interviewee, the burlesque star Gypsy Rose Lee. After Melba exits, Ludlow Lowell (Jack Durant), a wise-guy con artist and friend of Gladys, enters. With help from Gladys, Ludlow convinces Joey to take him on as his agent. After Joey exits, Lowell performs a high-energy, swinging dance feature—"Plant You Now, Dig You Later"—featuring Gladys and the chorus.

The next scene, set in the apartment that Vera funds for Joey, is an intimate look at Joey and Vera's now-established domestic situation. Joey is sore over his opening-night notices, which focus more on the club's social scene (including Vera and her fashionable friends) than on the quality of his show. Vera placates him, changing the subject, and comments that she likes Joey's apartment because there, if nowhere else, it's just the two of them. They sing a mock-innocent duet cataloging the best features of their "little cozy nest" ("In Our Little Den"), ironically acting the part of the wholesome starry-eyed lovers, even as they drop more sordid references, such as the "ceiling made of glass."

Back at Chez Joey, Ludlow and Gladys are scheming, finalizing their plan to blackmail Joey, Vera, and Vera's husband for cash (they plan a "two-way blackmail," whereby Lowell will extort Vera's husband separately from Vera and Joey). Linda, on an errand for the tailor, overhears their conversation. After she exits, Ludlow is featured in "Do It the Hard Way," an acrobatic dance number. Back at Joey's apartment, Joey is fitted for yet another jacket as Vera looks on. Linda arrives, and asks to speak to Vera alone. Linda warns Vera of the impending blackmail scheme, and after a pause, Vera calmly suggests that Linda has feelings for Joey. Linda quickly denies her feelings, but it's obvious to all that Vera is right. As a kind of exorcism, Linda begins to sing the song "Take Him"; Vera soon joins in, confirming that Joey is simply not worth the effort involved. Oblivious, Joey dances a cocky tap-tango as they sing in harmony. After Linda and Joey exit, Vera calls in a favor to her friend, Deputy Commissioner O'Brien; soon afterward Joey returns. Gladys and Ludlow then arrive, ready to con their way into Vera's bank account. During the encounter Ludlow knocks Joey out cold, and Vera is left to feign surprise at Gladys and Ludlow's scheme. To Gladys and Ludlow's great surprise, Commissioner O'Brien then arrives, apprehending the two crooks. After they leave Joey regains consciousness, and Vera very gently gives him "the brush off." Vera offers to let Joey keep the club, but he ruins it by insulting her. Their final exchange (JOEY: Blow. VERA: Yes dear.) precedes the reprise of "Bewitched," in which Vera declares that she's "wise at last" and that her heart is "antiseptic" now that Joey has "moved out of there."

After Vera exits, Joey is left to deal with his new reality: the apartment manager tells him he needs to be out of the apartment by 6 p.m., his account at Chez Joey is now frozen, and he doesn't even get to keep his new clothes. Linda returns during this scene, and Joey quickly lies that he's headed to New York because he's been offered a part in a musical comedy. Linda invites him for dinner at her sister's house, and Joey agrees. The finale to the show occurs after dinner, in front of the pet shop as Joey and Linda are parting. Although they are affectionate with each other, it's clear that Joey is truly leaving town. They say their goodbyes, both a bit wistful at what might have been, and she exits. Joey sings a chorus from "I Could Write a Book" (reprise), and then he too begins to exit. He starts to follow

Linda offstage but a pretty woman passes by in the opposite direction; after a moment of hesitation, he changes course and follows this potential conquest offstage, accompanied by the orchestra swelling to a climactic finish. Joey remains as he ever was, a heel through and through.


## RECEPTION

*Pal Joey*'s book marked a first in musical comedy history. Its title character was a louse. The characters and situation were depraved. The setting was caustically realistic. Its female lead was frankly sexual and yet not purely comic. With help from a narratively driven dream ballet that closed the first act, it begged audiences to take seriously the inner life and desires of a confirmed heel. In the end, Joey learns no lessons; the only moral to the story, apparently, was to avoid getting mixed up with a Joey type. Given the sheer audacity of the book, which challenged the easy narrative resolution and morally simplistic universe of most musical comedies—where wrongs are righted and scoundrels get their due—it's startling to find that it was so well received, and perhaps even more surprising that it didn't prompt a spate of similarly naturalistic shows in the period immediately following its premiere. Along with other challenging shows that appeared during the same period, including the political satires of the 1930s and the Freudian *Lady in the Dark* (which premiered less than a month after *Pal Joey*), *Pal Joey* was poised to truly change the face of Broadway, pointing out new avenues in both form and content.

Featuring one of musical comedy's first antiheroes, *Pal Joey* challenged audiences to identify with, or at least tolerate, characters who would otherwise be flattened out into stereotypical villains. The show, which ran for 374 performances, was a success, and most critical reactions were positive. Sidney B. Whipple (of the *New York World-Telegram*) praised its "rich characterizations," Richard Watts Jr. (of the *New York Herald Tribune*) called it "an outstanding triumph," and Wolcott Gibbs (of the *New Yorker*) made the bold statement that "[m]usical comedy took a long step toward maturity" the night of *Pal Joey*'s premiere.[4] Still, the most memorable review of the show, then and now, was also its most negative. Brooks Atkinson, of the *New York Times*, penned one of the most infamous lines in theater history when he wrote: "Although 'Pal Joey' is expertly done, can you draw sweet water from a foul well?"[5] He called the story "odious" and Joey a "rat infested with termites," finally concluding that *Pal Joey* "offers everything but a good time."[6]

Atkinson's review prompted a number of think pieces on the show, most of which challenged his idea that the storyline wasn't appropriate for a musical comedy. Sidney B. Whipple, for instance, compared the audience's sympathy for Joey to the sympathy for Casanova (another interesting "rascal"), as well as another "depraved and amoral character" then featuring on Broadway—Jeeter Lester, the ignorant, desperate patriarch in the stage adaptation on Erskine Caldwell's

*Tobacco Road.*[7] Louis Kronenberger of *PM Weekly* found it surprising that "one or two critics"—obviously referencing Atkinson—"found John O'Hara's forthright treatment of a bunch of low-lifes shocking and distasteful."[8] After all, he argued, Joey wasn't new to theater at all:

> Indeed, our greatest classic in the musical-comedy field deals with thieves and sluts and is riddled with the most shameless cynicism. It contains, at the same time, tunes as gay and delightful as any of Richard Rodgers's. When it comes to low life, *Pal Joey* isn't a patch on *The Beggar's Opera*.[9]

If we put aside musical comparisons, Kronenberger was right that both stories revel in their respective underworlds, featuring characters who despite being mostly despicable are in the end somewhat sympathetic. Consider Macheath, who takes on a more sinister role in Kurt Weill and Bertolt Brecht's *Threepenny Opera*: he's a thief and a womanizer at best, and a rapist and murderer at worst. And yet, by the end of the show he's set free.[10] Joey is given a similar free pass by the end of act 2 in *Pal Joey*, although his crimes are petty in comparison. Henry T. Murdock called Joey "a male Becky Sharp," referencing the scheming lead character in Thackeray's *Vanity Fair*; Joey certainly has more in common with the everyday wickedness of Becky than he has with Macheath.[11] As Joey sings in the song "I'm Talkin' to My Pal," which was cut during tryouts, "I'm a descendent of quite a family of heels."

Wolcott Gibbs wondered if Atkinson's problem was mostly an aesthetic one:

> There have been some complaints [. . .] about the taste of presenting a musical comedy whose hero is a chaser, a gigolo, and an all-round louse, the New York *Times* going so far as to employ the curiously vehement word "scabrous." Apparently a tradition is involved here: amoral people are all right on the stage so long as they're not accompanied by popular music.[12]

Gibb's comment stresses the fact that *Pal Joey* had a genre problem: musical comedy had not seen a character like Joey before. Certainly, Depression-era musical comedies previous to *Pal Joey* had addressed serious themes and had even featured "amoral" types: the 1930s and early 1940s were rife with musical comedies that included scathing political commentary, for instance, including the satirical *Of Thee I Sing* (1931), the pro-union *Pins and Needles* (1937), the Federal Theatre Project (FTP)–funded *The Cradle Will Rock* (1937), the antiwar *Hooray for What!* (1937), and the Huey Long satire *Louisiana Purchase* (1940). Rodgers and Hart, with Moss Hart and George S. Kaufman, joined in with their FDR satire *I'd Rather Be Right* (1937), starring George M. Cohan. Even Cole Porter, who was softer in his commentary, wrote his share of political songs and shows (see "Love for Sale," from *The New Yorkers*, 1930, or his show *Red, Hot and Blue*, 1936). To be sure, Porter, more than anyone in the 1930s, pushed the envelope as far as "adult" themes and sexual innuendo were concerned. Where he was sly and sophisticated, however, *Pal Joey* was brutal and frank.

As Alisa Roost has argued, shows from the 1930s frequently experimented with form and especially with content.[13] Most musical theater histories have dismissed the 1930s and early 1940s as a period of theatrical frivolity, even while acknowledging the glittering brilliance of its songwriters.[14] *Pal Joey* is usually exempt from censure of this kind, and considered a precursor of the so-called integrated era to come. More historically accurate, however, is to acknowledge *Pal Joey* as one in a series of culminations of increasingly bold theatrical experimentation in musical comedy, especially in the realm of satire. The idea, however, of presenting a story that so upended the conventions related to the audience's comfort—the happy ending, the likable leads, and the redemption afforded the flawed characters—was undoubtedly new. It was also virtually unheard of for the title character to be the amoral one. Understanding *Pal Joey* as an extension of, rather than simply a break with, the musical comedies of the 1930s helps situate the show as innovative even within a time of theatrical innovation.

Perhaps the most original aspect of *Pal Joey*'s script was how its satirical elements were balanced by a theatrical realism usually seen only in straight theater. In this way the show resembled straight comedy, including George Abbott's own *Broadway* (1926), a play set in a criminal underworld featuring gangsters, bootleggers, and their chorus-girl girlfriends. The question raised by Atkinson's review was whether or not the musical comedy stage was ready for the kind of realism that was already seen in straight theater, and that had become the defining feature of American literature during this same period. Eugene O'Neill, Upton Sinclair, and a bit later F. Scott Fitzgerald, Ernest Hemingway, William Faulkner, and John Steinbeck—the latter four direct contemporaries of John O'Hara—were all concerned in one way or another with American social realism, and would help shape American fiction in the twentieth century. In straight theater, playwrights Lillian Hellman, Richard Wright, Elmer Rice, and Clare Boothe Luce, in addition to Erskine Caldwell, would help bring literary realism into the mainstream. These plays and novels featured everyday evil and weak or unredemptive characters. Like these stories, the mundanity of *Pal Joey* was a central part of its realism. Its characters, as opposed to the larger-than-life heels like Casanova, were drawn from real life.

*Pal Joey* was both praised and criticized for its proximity to straight comedy, a feature that could be seen in both John O'Hara's script and George Abbott's direction. One critic, from the preview production in Philadelphia, said, "Despite generally rave reception here there are some who think the show goes a little overboard on 'book.' That applies particularly to the second act when, after a whirlwind song-and-dance start, tempo changes completely and story assumes straight dramatic aspects that recall 'Burlesque' and 'Broadway.' "[15] Some, including Robert Sensenderfer of the Philadelphia *Evening Bulletin*, saw this characteristic as an asset: "It is in the conversation pieces of the play that "Pal Joey" rises right out of the usual musical comedy class. The company has expert comedians [who] all play up to straight light comedy standard."[16] Kronenberger, in his opening-night review, agreed:

> As a fast, tough, lowdown story of people you'd rather not meet, *Pal Joey* provides one of the few musical comedy books that has ever been able to stand on its own feet. [. . .] The highest praise that can usually be bestowed on the book of a musical comedy is to call it "literate." It is

a pleasure to announce that *Pal Joey* is superbly illiterate, full of rich and gamey spade-calling.[17]

Gibbs praised the realism of the book, optimistically stating that "[e]quipping a song-and-dance production with a few living, three-dimensional figures, talking and behaving like human beings, may no longer strike the boys in the business as merely fantastic."[18]

The preoccupation with the quality of the book (whether appreciatively called literate or, also in admiration, illiterate), paired with the use of the term "maturity" to describe the show, helps situate *Pal Joey* as a transitional piece. Many musical comedy producers of the time were looking for more thoughtfully crafted books; this attitude is apparent, for instance, in the books for *Cabin in the Sky*, by Lynn Root, and *Lady in the Dark*, by John LaTouche, both of which ran during the same season as *Pal Joey*. The unsentimental or even anti-sentimental quality of *Pal Joey*'s book, however, was not immediately influential. This reaction might have been due to the cultural moment during which it was born.

The year 1940 was, in retrospect, a dividing line between the last great rupture in American history—the Great Depression—and the next: the US engagement in World War II. While the unemployment rate had recovered from the high of 25% in 1933, the height of the Depression, it was still at 15%, and Broadway shows were produced at less than half the rate of a decade before.[19] *Pal Joey*'s setting was the product of this depressed economic condition as well as changes in contemporary nightlife in the United States, where cheap clubs proliferated after the repeal of Prohibition in 1933. Experimenting with grittily realistic and anti-sentimental themes was not, as it would be considered in some quarters a year later, a threat to national morale in a time of war.

The year 1940 also marked the height of a conflict between the American Society of Composers, Authors, and Publishers (ASCAP) and radio broadcasters over rising licensing fees. The broadcasters, represented by the National Association of Broadcasters (NAB), reacted to a demand from ASCAP for fully double the royalty fees they had previously required by forming Broadcast Music Incorporated (BMI), a new music licensing agency. In the words of Laurence Maslon, BMI "hired arrangers, offered favorable rates to songwriters whose contracts with ASCAP expired, cultivated relationships with new songwriters, and lured away music publishers from the ASCAP fold."[20] Just a few days after *Pal Joey*'s premiere, the radio broadcasters officially rejected ASCAP's licensing hike, boycotting all music by ASCAP songwriters; as Maslon puts it, "more than one million ASCAP songs vanished from the airwaves overnight."[21] ASCAP members, who included nearly all of Broadway's biggest songwriters, including Rodgers and Hart, wouldn't hear their songs on the radio for nearly all of 1941. This change was devastating for *Pal Joey*; by the time the broadcasters made a deal with ASCAP, the freshness of *Pal Joey* had already worn off. Unless they were lucky enough to see the show live, American audiences didn't get to know *Pal Joey* until nearly a decade later. After the tryouts for *Pal Joey*, John O'Hara predicted that his "hard-boiled and cynical" approach to the book was "bound to have some effect on the output of musical shows in the immediate future."[22] Surely, on the basis of the show's critical reception, he had every reason to believe this. Yet *Pal Joey*'s naturalistic, unsentimental style—so tied to Depression-era experimentation—wouldn't be felt on Broadway books for decades.

## CANONS IN MUSICAL THEATER

The quality of *Pal Joey*'s book, however, if not its substance, had an immediate influence on the books of Broadway shows. The legacy of *Pal Joey* is tied to a cultural movement that began mid-twentieth century and extends, in part, to the present day. Arguments over American identity and native art forms—who we are, where we came from, and where we're going—have always been fraught with the legacy of racism in this country, as well as an uneasy relationship with European imports. The notion that musical theater could be considered "artistic" dates back to the origins of the form. Artistry and craftsmanship—terms that center care and process—are not so different from each other, after all. The semantic differences between those two terms and capital-A art are, however, pronounced. This difference can be seen in the way that writers situated *Pal Joey* in retrospect.

Lehman Engel, veteran Broadway music director, composer, and commentator, counted *Pal Joey* among fifteen musicals that "represent [. . .] theater in its most complete and mature state."[23] Engel considered only two of Rodgers and Hart's shows—*Pal Joey* and *The Boys from Syracuse*—to be revivable.[24] He felt that *Pal Joey*, chronologically the first on his list, was a model of excellence," and that "despite many differences among them in subject matter, style, and invention," all fifteen shows "are surprisingly similar in technical accomplishment and artistic form."[25] According to Engel, good "artistic form" depends on excellent "music, lyrics, and librettos" that "hang upon [. . .] the characters and action they have been created around."[26] This language connects directly to that loaded word "integration," which was used regularly from the 1940s on to evaluate musical theater works. With the use of such criteria, what Geoffrey Block calls a "a small musical museum" formed between *Show Boat* and *West Side Story*, made up of shows that "have enjoyed long runs (at least for their time), are regularly revived, and [are] favorably regarded by critics and historians as well as theater-goers."[27] Most recently, John O'Hara's book for *Pal Joey* has been canonized in *American Musicals: The Complete Books and Lyrics of 16 Broadway Classics, 1927–1969*; complied and edited by Laurence Maslon, this collection holds special importance because of its publisher, Library of America. The nonprofit press claims a kind of populist consensus on culture and in their words "champions our nation's cultural heritage by publishing America's greatest writing in authoritative new editions and providing resources for readers to explore this rich, living legacy").[28]

Engel's widely read opinion and Maslon's edition notwithstanding, *Pal Joey* lives uneasily in the canon. It's not a popular classic. *Pal Joey*'s flawed characters aren't loveable (like those in *My Fair Lady* and *Guys and Dolls*), it doesn't signal the virtue of its creators (like *Show Boat* and many of Hammerstein's shows with Rodgers), it doesn't allow for the celebratory nationalism of *Oklahoma!*, and its tougher themes aren't made more palatable through aesthetic distancing, as they are in *West Side Story*. Compared to these shows, *Pal Joey*'s subject matter doesn't appeal as widely to a mainstream audience, and for this reason it is not as frequently part of the repertoire of regional repertory companies or summer-stock productions. Despite its entry in the previously mentioned collection, its book has been both praised and criticized; Moss Hart and Arthur Laurents had reservations over the book, and the latter even refused to have his work published in the Library of America volume if *Pal Joey* was also included (the collection, which includes Laurents's *Gypsy*, was published posthumously).[29] Revivals of the show, while very successful between 1952 and 1963, had mixed results thereafter, including two spectacular flops in the 1970s. The show had a controversial start, and it remains difficult to situate it within the legacy of musical theater.

## HISTORY OF A HEEL

The impetus for this book lies at the meeting place between my two great loves: music and teaching. Like most people—save those lucky enough to see one of the revivals of the show—I was introduced to *Pal Joey* through the Columbia film with Frank Sinatra, Rita Hayworth, and Kim Novak. As I incorporated *Pal Joey* into my musical theater survey course, I found that not only were the sources for the show limited, but also the most well-known source—the film adaptation—said little about the more beguiling, and even aggravating, elements of the original stage show. Further, people familiar with the film see Joey as a charming, Playboy-approved crooner and Vera as a sexy bombshell, rather than as the decidedly more complex characters they were in the stage production. On stage Vera was a complex, self-invested, and in the end sympathetic older woman. From the moment that I heard Vivienne Segal's recording of "Bewitched"—with her simpering, self-mocking interpretation of the line "and now I'm like sweet-seventeen a lot"—it was clear that there was more to the character Vera than was allowed for in the Columbia film. As I began to pull this thread, I unraveled a truly fascinating moment in musical theater history, and began to feel strongly that *Pal Joey* worked best as a theater piece during those periods when it encountered the most critical pushback.

This book chronicles the life of *Pal Joey*, from John O'Hara's brilliant initial idea to the afterlife of the show on both stage and screen. Part I, "Making *Pal Joey*," follows the genesis of the show; Chapter 1 looks at Joey's first appearance in the pages of the *New Yorker*, connecting the origins of Joey to author John O'Hara's personal vices. The chapter also explores O'Hara's fraught working relationships and his distinctive writing style—featuring slang, contemporary pop culture references, and flawed characters—underscoring how centrally important his writing approach was to the effect of the musical. Chapter 2 looks at Rodgers and Hart's enthusiastic involvement with the show, connecting their drive to innovate with their desire to collaborate with O'Hara. Chapter 2 also acknowledges the significance of signing on George Abbott, a veteran of straight theater and a by-then frequent collaborator with Rodgers and Hart, as director. Special attention is paid to the process by which the script and musical numbers were transformed from page to stage.

Part II, "Chez Joey," explores the sordid, naturalistic world of Pal Joey, focusing on the uncommon attention its creators paid to characterization and narrative cohesion. Chapter 3 examines both the "cheap club" of act 1, set in the South Side of Chicago, and Chez Joey, Joey's attempt at a classy joint (and the setting for much of act 2). Rodgers and Hart's club numbers are bitingly satirical, full of clever class commentary; through both imitation and parody, these numbers show a close understanding of the aural demarcations of class and respectability, a skill Rodgers and Hart developed early on in their career. Chapter 4 looks at the narrative impact of the book songs, including "I Could Write a Book" and "Bewitched," by far the best known numbers from the show. Rodgers and Hart's book songs are never sentimental but are unusually attentive to complex character types, especially in regard to Vera. Chapter 5 explores the characterization and cultural relevance of two women from the show—Vera and Melba—who partially encapsulate the show's ambivalent attitude toward women. Chapter 6 considers the importance of dance to the immediacy of Pal Joey, outlining the reception and legacy of its original choreographer (Robert Alton), its first Joey (Gene Kelly), and the chorus of dancers. Finally, Part III ("Reviving Pal Joey") outlines the history of the celebrated revival of 1952 (the first significant revival to surpass the run of the original), the legacy of the 1957 screen adaptation, and the success and failures of significant stage revivals up to the present day. Pal Joey has weathered the intervening years since its premiere like the hardy, Depression-era relic that it is. Although born of its time, the show has continued to find relevance in later eras and for new audiences.[30]

# MAKING *PAL JOEY*

• • •

# 1

## O'HARA, THE HEEL

• • •

## FROM SHORT STORY TO SCRIPT

John O'Hara (1905–1970), the author of the source material and book for *Pal Joey*, the musical, was regarded as a difficult man. He had a quick temper, he was often "nasty, curt, churlish" and, as one critic said, he was "so utterly sure of his own worth that he set one's teeth on edge."[1] Although he could be wonderfully generous with his friends and those he considered loyal, O'Hara was famously bitter about his status in the eyes of critics and his place in the institutions that they patrolled, causing him to have, as Richard Rodgers (1902–1979) once called it, "occasional attacks of persecution-mania."[2] These "attacks" were often followed by bouts of alcohol-fueled self-loathing.[3]

O'Hara's character Joey Evans was born from one of these benders.[4] At some point in October 1938 O'Hara, who narrated this story to *New York Post* columnist Earl Wilson, had been drunk or passed out for four days straight when remorse finally set in:

> I asked, "What kind of a god damn heel am I? I must be worse'n anybody in the world." Then I figured, "No, there must be somebody worse than me—but who?" Al Capone, maybe. Then I got it—maybe some night club masters of ceremonies I know.[5]

He proceeded to write what he would later call "a bit of autobiography" "about a night-club heel in the form of a letter."[6] The *New Yorker*, for which he'd written extensively by that point, bought the story that same day and commissioned a handful of others. O'Hara insisted to Wilson that he was "perfectly sober" when he actually sat down to write the first Joey story, and that it was "the only good thing I ever got out of booze."[7]

From the beginning, then, Joey was inextricably bound to O'Hara's own personal vices. One of O'Hara's leading biographers, Matthew Bruccoli, remarked that he "was regarded as a difficult drinker at a time when inebriety was a national pastime."[8] Like Lorenz (Larry) Hart's, O'Hara's biographers underscore his intemperance, his mercurial work habits, and his personal insecurities, which often extended to his work. O'Hara's brand of antihero, seen throughout

*Pal Joey*. Julianne Lindberg, Oxford University Press (2020). © Oxford University Press.
DOI: 10.1093/oso/9780190051204.001.0001

his novels and short stories, was written with unflinching, and often unflat-tering, realism in mind. O'Hara's use of slang and musical references—central to his brand of realism—are coupled by a kind of personal, autobiographical insight: despite his infamous defensiveness, O'Hara was quick to own his per-sonal faults. This trait can be seen in his antiheroes, whom he never champi-oned, but gave ample time to speak. As one reviewer put it, "there they are [. . .] crummy, but alive."[9] Joey is a quintessential antihero, a product of his time, a product of the kind of literature developing in the United States during this period, and, perhaps, a product of O'Hara's tense relationship to his own literary status. A look at the life and career of O'Hara helps explain how Joey came to be, and how central O'Hara's aesthetic was to the effect of *Pal Joey*, the musical.

## O'HARA: A DIFFICULT MAN

O'Hara's relationship with Richard Rodgers is a good example of his hypersensi-tivity. While Rodgers and O'Hara were good friends for over a decade, from the time of their work on *Pal Joey* in 1940 to just before the premiere of the revival in early 1952, their friendship soured. Although Rodgers mentions in his auto-biography a "long correspondence" with O'Hara during the production of *Pal Joey*, only a few pieces of correspondence between the two men have survived.[10] One of them is the letter sent from O'Hara to Rodgers that proposed the musi-cal version of *Pal Joey*, confirming that the project was O'Hara's idea.[11] Rodgers's enthusiastic telegram back reveals his excitement for the project. Other extant letters are held in the Richard Rodgers Papers at the New York Public Library (NYPL).[12]

One of these is a very funny parody letter written in the style of a jealous Joey to a successful friend (this mimics the style of Joey's letters, described later on in this chapter). Here O'Hara begrudgingly congratulates Rodgers on selling the rights for *Annie Get Your Gun* to a "big moving picture company for $650,000."[13] He also narrates a fictional day in 1944 when O'Hara supposedly gave Rodgers the idea for the musical and its brassy lead. In O'Hara's words:

> We were having dinner (just to refresh your memory, that is) at the sidewalk cafe, and a young girl went by, probably a student at the nearby Washing [sic] Square College of NYU, and she was carrying some books in the one hand, and over her shoulder, her left shoulder, she had slung a Winchester .22 pump gun. She reminded me of a plot that I had been toying with and I asked you if you would like to hear it and you said of course. [. . .] I would not have given the matter another thought if Louis Nizer, of Phillips, Nizer, Benjamin & Krim, had not called me up the other day from his law offices in the Paramount Building, asking me if I had read about your good fortune. He said he thought I ought to write and congratulate you.[14]

The letter ends by chronicling O'Hara and his family's fictional ailing health, and is topped off by disingenuous well-wishing:

> We are all doing as well as can be expected. Belle has had all her teeth out owing to lack of dental care and our little daughter's belly is all swelled up which the visiting nurse says is on account of her not getting the right things to eat, like milk, but we can't complain so long as we have so many good friends. [. . .] Best wishes to your beautiful well dressed wife and happy well fed children. You can always reach me at this address unless we are evicted next week, or you can get in touch with me through Louis Nizer, of Phillips, Nizer, Benjamin & Krim, Paramount Building, Times Square, New York City.[15]

Rodgers purportedly treasured this letter, which was obviously sent in a playful spirit. O'Hara and his family were quite comfortable at this point in his career.

A later letter from O'Hara to Rodgers, however, shows a less flattering, more suspicious, and more easily offended side of O'Hara's personality. In this letter, dated June 10, 1951, O'Hara references an "extraordinary document which makes it appear that you control all rights to PAL JOEY," and tacitly accuses Rodgers of making a deal behind his back. He ends the letter with the following frustrated lines: "For God's sake, let's get this straightened out. I distinctly recall writing the stories and the libretto of the show."[16] Rodgers's response—which stands out as an unusually frank, frustrated letter amidst his usually graceful, generous correspondence (seen in so many of his other letters, to collaborators and fans alike)—is to the point:

> I am very unhappy about your June 10th letter, which you obviously wrote in a disturbed condition. I have no idea what mysterious "document" you refer to concerning PAL JOEY nor do I know why you neglected to identify it [. . .] I have acknowledged your participation and ownership in PAL JOEY too often in print, and even under my own name on the back of the recent Columbia album for there to be any question about my feelings.
>
> I hope that you will unravel this mystery by return mail because I would hate to have these occasional attacks of persecution-mania come between us permanently after all these years of close friendship.[17]

In the next paragraph Rodgers brings up and chastises O'Hara for another misunderstanding. O'Hara was planning to name a soon-to-be-published short novel "A Small Hotel," in admiration of Rodgers and Hart and in reference to their song from *On Your Toes*. O'Hara called up Rodgers to tell him this news and Rodgers, perhaps pedantically, told O'Hara that the full name of the song was "There's a Small Hotel." O'Hara was purportedly insulted by what he saw as a lack of enthusiasm for the gesture, and his hurt feelings got back to Rodgers. Rodgers's reply expresses his exasperation:

> While I am at it, our mutual friend Bennett Cerf reports that you are deeply incensed because I did not express enthusiasm over your suggestion that you use "Small Hotel" as the title of your new book. You are a much better reporter

than that, John. You should have told him that not only did I like the idea, but I felt you should use the whole title, "There's A Small Hotel," so there could never be any question as to its source. I was flattered by the idea, and told you so.[18]

Still, O'Hara was wounded by this interaction, and changed the name of the novel to *The Farmers Hotel* (published in November1951). Their friendship continued to sour after this point.

O'Hara's difficult personality is chronicled by many other collaborators, including George Cukor, who in 1954 was slated to direct the film version of *Pal Joey* for Columbia (a film that was eventually directed by George Sidney). In a letter from O'Hara to Cukor, who had requested a meeting with O'Hara related to the project, O'Hara boldly states that "for such consultation I believe I ought to be paid a fee, since I no longer participate in the financial glory of the picture. Advice that costs nothing is usually worth just about that."[19] Cukor was not used to this kind of suspicious, combative response from an author. In a letter to Harry Cohn (head of Columbia), Cukor states,

> In a long career, man and boy, I've never heard of an important author behaving as idiotically as O'Hara has. I am enclosing a copy of the note he sent me. I think we had better forget this gentleman.[20]

Many anecdotes like the preceding ones show the degree to which O'Hara's difficult personality got in the way of his collaborative projects. This side of his nature may be another reason that he never had much success, outside of *Pal Joey*, in theater, where collaboration is essential.


## O'HARA AND HART

One of the few collaborators that O'Hara did get along with was Larry Hart. Hart and O'Hara were cut of the same cloth: they both suffered from personal insecurities, they both were alcoholics (although later, after the death of his second wife, O'Hara became sober), and they both reveled in the more unsavory corners of New York nightlife. Arguably, Hart's closeted homosexuality was at the root of his famous self-loathing (playwright Jerome Lawrence called him the "poet laureate of masochism"), and from early on O'Hara knew that his Irish Catholic background and his once-respected family's loss of fortune set him apart in significant ways from the "class" society around him. Beyond their personal lives, O'Hara and Hart's respective work seemed to hum with a kindred energy.

Many preview and opening-night reviews for *Pal Joey* comment on this point. Waters remarked that in *Pal Joey* "Hart seems especially happy working along the O'Hara lines," while Richard Watt Jr., of the *New York Herald Tribune*, stated that the

> spiritual kinship between Hart and O'Hara [is] something to be applauded. Of the two it is rather surprising to find that Mr. Hart is somewhat the rowdier,

but they do work together with wonderful success, so that the prose of one and the verse of the other seem delightfully complementary.[21]

O'Hara's Joey stories seemed tailor made to Hart's talents as a lyricist: both writers wrote with a sometimes cynical edginess, and both were comfortable with confronting feeling and emotion, though often from a tough distance. They both tended toward disreputable characters, or at least helped craft characters who were out of sync with the world around them.

In a retrospective piece on Hart, published with the *New York Times* in February 1944 (just a few months after Hart had died), O'Hara fondly remembers his time and collaboration with Hart; says that Hart was a "delightful, inspired, and inspiring co-worker"; admits to the reader that both he and Hart were apt to forego work for a "stimulant"; and comments that Hart was a gentle, cultured, and sweet man.[22] O'Hara further muses, in a comment that could have been made only about someone who was already dead, upon the somewhat curious dissonance between the smooth, sophisticated lyrics of Hart, and the man himself:

> Nice but non-professional people, meeting Larry for the first time, usually got a bit of a shock. One I know seemed to have expected someone on the physical lines of Tyrone Power, not realizing that the incidence of manly beauty among the men who write our American love lyrics is, I suppose, lower than that to be found in any other occupation [. . .] [T]he sad thing was that Larry knew better than anyone else that he was a disappointment to the lady admirers who had counted on swooning.[23]

O'Hara also recounts the time that Hart came to his home to persuade him to come back to the theater during *Pal Joey* rehearsals. According to O'Hara, he was avoiding the theatre in order to "not be that perennial Broadway nuisance, The Author."[24] Apparently, O'Hara had hurt "George's [George Abbott's] feelings," and Hart was performing the duty—waking O'Hara from a drunken stupor in order to get him back to work—that Rodgers often had to perform for Hart. This scenario reveals that O'Hara and Hart understood each other, and O'Hara ends the anecdote by saying that he wouldn't have tolerated anyone else but a man like Hart—truly, like himself—waking him up in such a fashion.

Compared to his other collaborators, O'Hara's easy relationship with Hart was an anomaly. O'Hara's early life might help illuminate some of his lifelong insecurities, the root of much of his combative behavior. For one, he was born into a wealthy Pennsylvania family, under a father who liked to show off his wealth (via the tony street they lived on, the collection of horses they maintained, the large number of cars they owned, and the upper-crust company they kept). O'Hara came to appreciate the finer things in life and, significant to his eventual profession, became keenly aware of all the little markers of class, from dress to accessories to school pedigree. When O'Hara was just twenty his father died, and his death eventually took its financial toll on the family wealth. Many scholars pin this turn of events—and O'Hara's ensuing inability to attend Yale, which was a lifelong dream—to his insecurity, his frustration with his place in society and the literary establishment, and his tendency to be easily offended by his peers and by critics. He surely felt his loss of status keenly, and many of his fictional characters, including Joey, are both apt to criticize and mock the habits of high society, all the while aspiring toward it.

## O'HARA THE REALIST, O'HARA THE REPORTER

O'Hara was a contemporary of F. Scott Fitzgerald, Ernest Hemingway, John Steinbeck, and William Faulkner, all authors who have since become central to the American literary canon. Though O'Hara placed himself among these now canonic writers, and had many aesthetic aims in common, his work was met with mixed reviews. Despite a handful of high-profile supporters, including Hemingway, his critics were often quick to dismiss him. O'Hara felt particularly undervalued by the literary establishment; he felt this slight most keenly in the fact that he never won the Nobel Prize in literature, a prize he believed he deserved.[25] He is today perhaps not remembered as well as he should be; his novels are so specific to their era that they can appear dated. For the historian, however, this characteristic makes O'Hara's writing a valuable source.

Much of the spirit of the American novels of this period is steeped in the climate of their era: the heady, overextended vibrancy of the 1920s, and the weary scrappiness of the 1930s. *Pal Joey* is, essentially, a 1930s story with an era-appropriate nostalgia for the 1920s: Joey and his circumstances are a product of economic depression, the repeal of Prohibition, and the diversification of nightlife that accompanied both. The realism that characterizes many novels of the period reflects the world in which it was written. O'Hara was proud of this realism: in an interview from 1961, when asked to provide a critical quotation that would characterize his career thus far, he said, "Better than anyone else, he told the truth about his time."[26] This remark was subsequently written on his tombstone.

The realism so central to O'Hara's work often comments directly on issues of class, causing some scholars to categorize his work within the genre of the "novel of manners."[27] O'Hara was concerned with and highly observant of social interactions, conduct, and cultural products related to class. This viewpoint came out hypercritically in some of his novels, and was revealed in extended descriptive passages, and, crucially, in dialogue, especially in the use of the vernacular. His multiple references to music—to contemporary songs, songwriters, and bands— were frequently made to create an atmosphere, to help develop a character (as seen in the Pal Joey stories), or, very likely, to show off his vast and detailed musical knowledge. O'Hara's musical references are in keeping with his reference to other cultural products, like cars, clothing, and brands, and help situate his characters within a hierarchical world specific to time and place.

The realistic grittiness seen in O'Hara's Joey stories is present in O'Hara's other writings as well. This quality can be seen in his first novel, *An Appointment in Samarra* (1934), which brought him widespread notoriety, and his other significant novels, including *BUtterfield 8* (1935), *A Rage to Live* (1949), *Ten North Frederick* (1955), and *From the Terrace* (1958). O'Hara specialized in the antihero; all of the protagonists in the previously mentioned novels are deeply flawed, and suffer from an incongruity with the society around them. Julian English (from *Appointment in Samarra*) is a destructive alcoholic; Gloria Wandrous (*BUtterfield 8*) goes against the sexual mores of the day by behaving like a man; Grace Caldwell's (*A Rage to Live*) sexually violent past affects her relationships in the present; Joe Chapin (*Ten North Frederick*) is a failure in the eyes of his wife, and eventually an alcoholic.[28] In a tribute article written after O'Hara's death, writer and critic Charles Champlin noted,

> At times his characters were almost too predictable—sex-haunted, abrasive, etched by fault lines, doomed either to die by the hand of an indifferent fate or to go on living a life that was worse than death in its posturing hollowness or echoing despair.[29]

O'Hara's Joey is equally flawed, and, like most of O'Hara's protagonists, never finds lasting satisfaction or redemption. These flawed character portrayals sometimes polarized critics: some saw them as realistic portraits drawn from life, while others remarked that O'Hara simply didn't know enough virtuous people.

O'Hara's Joey stories, in format and style, were not without precedent. Ring Lardner's *You Know Me Al* stories (the first one published in the *New York Post* in 1914, and the entire set as a book in 1916) were written in the form of letters from a pro baseball player to his hometown friend. Lardner's protagonist, baseball player Jack Keefe, gets the opportunity to play for the big leagues, and his letters to his friend Al (alternately addressed as "Friend Al," "Old Pal," or some combination of these) are refreshingly casual, full of misspellings, idiomatic slang, and lack of punctuation. Jack Keefe, like O'Hara's Joey, is a bit of a braggart, and like Joey, he doesn't develop in any moralistic way—he remains a braggart, confident in his abilities, even if most of his success can be attributed to luck. It's in these features that one can immediately see Lardner's stories as a predecessor to O'Hara's Joey stories.

O'Hara was a fan of Lardner's work, which he first discovered when he was a young man growing up in Pottsville, Pennsylvania. In a letter to his friend F. Scott Fitzgerald, responding to a heartfelt tribute Fitzgerald wrote about Lardner upon his death, O'Hara called himself a "frank imitator of Lardner." 95.[30] O'Hara, in a foreword to a later edition of his *Appointment in Samarra*, stated that Lardner taught him that

> if you wrote down speech as it is spoken truly, you produce true characters, and the opposite is also true: if your characters don't talk like people they aren't good characters. It's a point, or rather two points, that most critics do not appreciate when they speak so airily of the Good Ear, the Rhythms of American Speech.[31]

Though the Joey stories are indebted in many ways to Lardner, their style is also similar to that of Damon Runyon, another short-story writer who specialized in chronicling the exploits of society's supposed lowlifes: mobsters, hoodlums, and others associated with Manhattan nightlife in the Prohibition era. Bruccoli posits that the association with these writers (Runyon, especially) earned him a "Broadway wise-guy" reputation, and "almost certainly impeded the proper recognition of O'Hara's major work."[32] Regardless, the reading public loved this style of writing. Both Lardner and Runyon (and some of O'Hara's other early influences, including Sinclair Lewis) worked extensively in the newspaper business, which almost certainly honed their ear for dialogue.

Much of O'Hara's gritty realism has been attributed to his own early days as a newspaper reporter. Born in 1905 in Pottsville, Pennsylvania, O'Hara began his career as a reporter at the age of nineteen, first working for the *Pottsville Journal*, and later for the *Tamaqua Courier*.[33] In 1928 he moved to New York City and soon began work at the *New York Herald Tribune*; within a few years he was reporting for *Time*, the *New York Daily Mirror*, the *New York Morning Telegraph*, and the *New Yorker*. Most biographers note O'Hara's realistic dialogue and his exacting observational prose—present in his novels and short stories—both qualities that very likely derive from his days as a reporter, and situate his work within the literary trends of the 1920s and 1930s. O'Hara himself stated that his years as a newspaperman taught him "economy of words. It makes you write faster. When you're on rewrite as I was, you can't fool around at half-past nine trying to write beautiful lacy prose."[34]

## THE *NEW YORKER* STORIES

Though O'Hara wrote extensively for newspapers as a reporter, he was also a prolific short-story writer. Bruccoli makes the revealing observation that while Hemingway published 50 short stories, Faulkner around 70, Lardner 115, and Fitzgerald 160, O'Hara published an astounding 374 stories during his life; he wrote more than 30 in his first year and a half with the *New Yorker* alone.[35] Upon O'Hara's death in 1970, Charles Champlin declared that O'Hara and Hemingway "were the two best short story writers in America in this century. They were much alike in their ability to convey complicated relationships and subtle emotional states—and a great deal of information—largely through dialogue and a notably sparse minimum of objective detail."[36]

The bulk of O'Hara's short stories were published with the *New Yorker*: he wrote his first story for them in 1928, and his 247th and last story in 1967.[37] At the time that O'Hara first published with the *New Yorker* he was in his early twenties, and had moved to New York only a few months earlier, first working as a reporter at the *New York Herald Tribune*. While in New York he worked with and actively supported many young writers, including Dorothy Parker, Robert Benchley, and Wolcott Gibbs, all of who were already working at *The New Yorker*, and all associated at some point with the so-called Algonquin Round Table—a bohemian collection of writers, critics, publishers, and wits. Parker would become one of his good friends, a first reader of his work, and an influence on his writing.

In October 1938 O'Hara submitted his first "Joey" story, which was published on October 22 of that year (see Table 1.1). By mid-1940, he had written thirteen more, twelve of which, in total, were published in the *New Yorker* (the final two were published as part of the novel/story compilation in 1940). O'Hara's Joey stories are written as letters from Joey, a cut-rate nightclub entertainer with lofty aspirations, to his friend Ted, an established, successful bandleader. Though he treats Ted as an old friend, Joey makes clear throughout the stories that he's jealous of Ted's position in the world. Like many of O'Hara's characters, Joey is keenly aware of class and where he lies in the hierarchy. Because Ted has "made it," so to speak, Joey struggles with his relationship to his friend, and Joey regularly overcompensates, playing up his "class" gigs and associations. Most of the letters are boastful accounts of Joey's sexual conquests, his cons, and his pipe dreams, or are just colorful portraits of a local character.

The Joey stories were eventually published in a single volume by Duell, Sloan & Pearce in October 1940. O'Hara's plans to publish them in book form were connected to the larger project of the musical, which he had been thinking about as early as late 1939. In a letter to his editor at the *New Yorker* from very early 1940, O'Hara states that he was planning "(a) a book of [Joey stories] and (b) a play based on Joey."[38] He goes on to say,

> As I have told you before, but do not object to telling you again, these damn things are the most successful things I've ever done for the NYer. I beat my brains out writing fine, sensitive prose, careful streams of consciousness, lean spare sharp exposition, accurate shots of dialog and what do I get yet? [. . .] [I]n O'Brien. Then one morning at the Pierre, with a roaring hangover and no sleep and a wife thinking I am in Philadelphia, I knock out a bit of autobiography and the literary people discover me.[39]

The book was released in November 1940 to mostly positive reviews; naturally, O'Hara had a pre-made audience in his *New Yorker* readers. The publishers of the novel self-consciously tied O'Hara's Joey stories to the great American storytelling tradition; in a press release they described them as "[a]n American characterization, classic as those of Mark Twain or Ring Lardner."[40] In a review of the book from the *New York Herald Tribune*, Joey is described

> as unmitigatedly and authentically cheap as any of Mr. O'Hara's earlier heroes. Mr. O'Hara has an ear for sidewalk speech, and a gift for establishing a shoddy character. You never doubt that Pal Joey exists, precisely as he paints himself in this series of letters to his old friend Ted.[41]

This review ends with the following reservation, anticipating some of the Broadway reviews to come: "A little of it is amusing, and a lot of it is monotonous. I wish Mr. O'Hara could meet some part-way decent people sometime,

Table 1.1 Complete list of O'Hara's Joey Stories, including the date/place of publication, and story outline

| Story Title<br>In the order they appeared in the *New Yorker* and in the published collection by Duell, Sloane & Pierce (1940) | Date of Publication in the *New Yorker* | Story Outline[1] |
| --- | --- | --- |
| "Pal Joey" (1) | October 22, 1938 | Letter to his Pal Ted (a successful bandleader), from Ohio; brags about his position in a hotel bar and ballroom (which he acquired with the help of a connected "mouse" named Nan). Mentions his exploits with a "society" girl named Jean Spencer. |
| "Ex-Pal" (2) | November 26, 1938 | Registers his anger at "Pal Ted" for adding to his reputation as a womanizer (which Ted apparently innocently reinforced after meeting the Nan of the previous story). Jean finds out about Joey's exploits and threatens to end it; his hotel job is also at risk. |
| "How I Am Now in Chi" (3) | April 1, 1939 | Forgives Ted with regard to the incidents of the previous letter. Chronicles his newest exploits, which involve an argument with Jean, a fight with her father, and the loss of his hotel job; he's eventually run out of town, and ends up in Chicago, where he is "singing for coffee and cakes at a crib on Cottage Grove Ave" (45). |
| "Bow Wow" (4) | May 13, 1939 | Tells Ted all about his encounter with a "mouse" in front of a pet shop; he feigns "an interest in the dog kingdom" in order to attract her (53). Names the dog they observe through the pet shop window "Skippy."[2] Joey makes up an elaborate, and fictional, story about his supposedly high-class upbringing. He knows the girl won't catch on, because he is a keen observer of class: "I had cased this mouse and she was pretty but I knew she was no society debutante. Probably a stenog out of work but very cute" (56). Joey characterizes her as naïve. |

| "Avast and Belay" (5) | October 7, 1939 | Tries to convince Ted that it would be to his/their advantage to start a military-affiliated dance band, as it seemed like the United States was on the brink of war; according to Joey and an accountant named Charley, this could be a way to "pick yr. spot" rather than get drafted, and to make lots of money besides. Joey's enthusiasm for the project is clearly grounded in fantasy (68). |
| "Joey on Herta" (6) | November 25, 1939 | After a lengthy intro, tells the story of meeting a woman named Herta Gersdorf, who wants to be a singer; turns out she's a fair singer, and Joey decides to take her under his wing. He gives her advice and free lessons, and even becomes her "agent." He gets her a singing job at the club (though he takes $25 a week, and gives nothing to her, as he considers his "lessons" to her unpaid). She later wants the payment, and a fight ensues between Joey and Herta's boss. Joey almost gets into a fight with the boss by accusing him of an affair with Herta, even though he's married. Herta ends up negotiating $50 a week, and Joey is out. |
| "Joey on the Cake Line" (7) | December 23, 1939 | Tells Ted that he's broke (on "the cake line" [98]: i.e., a little better than the bread line). Explains how the club he sings at burned down; he talks with the "front men," who say "this was an act of god, so your contract is void" (Joey didn't have a contract, but the mobsters think he's being nice; give him his week's pay, $125, anyway). Sings around town ($50 a week). Also, cons a tailor. |
| "The Erloff" (8) | February 3, 1940 | Joey goes "slumming" with the college/society set. Description of the Club (112)—Irish joint run by an older guy named Paddy Dunlin. Dunlin keeps making a comment about "the erloff" ("what do you think of the erloff"), which confuses Joey. Eventually Paddy Dunlin reveals that he knows who Joey is, and talks about the sort of clubs Joey sings in. Turns out that Dunlin owns the "joint" that Joey currently sings in. |

(continued)

*Table 1.1* Continued

| Story Title In the order they appeared in the *New Yorker* and in the published collection by Duell, Sloane & Pierce (1940) | Date of Publication in the *New Yorker* | Story Outline |
| --- | --- | --- |
| "Even the Greeks" (9) | March 2, 1940 | Describes how cold it is in Chicago. The club that caught fire is back up and running. Tells the story of a restaurant proprietor named Nick and a guy named Pete who works in the kitchen ("pecular [sic] local people" [122]). Finds out that Pete went through a traumatic event (his wife left him, with the kids, for another man). Became a drunk, got in a fight, suffered some sort of brain damage, and hasn't been the same since. Pete was a short-order cook, but after the accident Nick hired Pete as a janitor (because he knew Pete from the "old country"), and every so often, he thinks he hears Nick order something (hence free food for Joey). |
| "Joey and the Calcutta Club" (10) | March 30, 1940 | Meets a British woman named Jean Benedict (actually from Buffalo); the woman is a con artist, a fact that Joey doesn't get for a while—the joke comes about that all the men who fall for her line (parents in London, interests in India) should call themselves the "Calcutta Club." |
| "Joey and Mavis" (11) | May 4, 1940 | Begins the story with a colorful account of a sailor working as a doorman or bouncer, and then gets into meeting Mavis (who gets her foot slammed in the door by the sailor; she gets a settlement, in part because of Joey, who then gets fired from the club). While in the hospital Mavis tells Joey her life story: her husband killed himself (she has kids), and she moves to Chicago. |

| "A New Career" (12) | July 13, 1940 | Another proposition for Ted. . . . First sets up the story: his mobster boss is cheap, and Joey can tell he wants to fire him, so Joey goes looking for other work. He happens to hear a busboy singing a Mexican-inspired tune, and Joey writes it down. He then tries to make a deal with Ted, whom he wants to play it and get a deal for Joey: "see if you think it has possibilities and if so maybe you can get Johnny Mercer or somebody to write some lyrics for it" (167). Joey is dreaming of his future career as a songwriter: "I have a lot of ideas along this line and only need a little encouragement. My tune can be played as either a rumba or conga, fox trot or waltz. If I could get a good Ascap [sic] rating this year I would quit this business in a minute" (168). |
|---|---|---|
| "A Bit of a Shock" (13) | Not published In the New Yorker | Singing in a room, for "gorills" in the Loop district. Puts down the girls who are dancing (he belittles their dancing ability, etc.). Melba comes in to interview him about the club. He describes her in exceedingly negative ways (plays up her masculine qualities). Thinks she's a lesbian. When he realizes she's a reporter he tries to play cool and makes up stories about his classy upbringing (they lost their fortune in the crash). Mount "Holy Oak" mix-up. She knows he's bluffing, and tells him so. She goes into the back, and comes out dressed like a dancer. Joey is pleasantly shocked. She is a knockout. He hits on her; she rejects him (notes her husband, who "played football for Dartmouth").[3] |

(continued)

*Table 1.1* Continued

| Story Title In the order they appeared in the *New Yorker* and in the published collection by Duell, Sloane & Pierce (1940) | Date of Publication in the *New Yorker* | Story Outline |
| --- | --- | --- |
| "Reminiss?" (14) | Not published In the *New Yorker* | Final Joey letter to Ted; lonely; reflects on his life thus far; recalls nostalgically some unsavory events that Ted also partook in (paying a doctor for an abortion for a girl Ted also went around with). Drops some interesting info about his (and Ted's) class position. Reminisces about all the bands he played with and musicians he's met. This story reads like O'Hara showing off to the reader his in-depth knowledge of bands and personnel. Lots of specific references to bands of the 1920s and 1930s. Interesting section on Chicago musicians (including Bix Beiderbecke). Joey never mails this letter to Ted.[4] |

1 All page numbers correspond to O'Hara, *Pal Joey* (New York: Duell, Sloane & Pierce, 1940).

2 This story directly corresponds to the "Pet Shop" scene in the musical (act 1, scene 2). The dog doesn't exist as a character in the musical (just the location of the pet shop). He does, however, come back as a character in the 1957 Columbia film (featuring Frank Sinatra as Joey), though his name is changed to "Snuffy."

3 Roughly corresponds to the "Reporter" scene featuring Melba Snyder (partway through act 2, scene 1). In the musical, this scene features the song "Zip."

4 The tone of the letter alternates between nostalgia, love for his pal Ted, and extreme jealousy of Ted's secure position in the entertainment biz.

or that some part-way decent people might attract his writing attention."[42] Like O'Hara's other protagonists, Joey is sometimes difficult to sympathize with. Unlike with many of his other characters, however, Joey's imperfections are comic, rather than tragic. His characterization as a louse is meant to provoke laughter, and is tied directly to his class position as a low-class nightclub entertainer, one that audiences would have recognized and felt comfortable laughing at.

## JOEY'S VERNACULAR AND THE QUESTION OF HIPNESS

Joey's most distinctive feature is his style of speech: the casual slang that O'Hara uses in his stories was intentionally rough, and evocative of well-worn street talk. Just like Lardner's "Friend Al" letters, O'Hara intended for Joey to speak realistically, from his geographic location, class position, age group, and subcultural position as an entertainer at mostly cheap nightclubs. Since O'Hara's Joey stories are in the form of letters, some features of Joey's communication style—such as his use of casual abbreviations and his frequent misspellings—are found only in the stories, and couldn't practically translate to stage dialogue.[43] What did translate to the stage was his free and playful use of language.

Though his speech is rough, Joey has no problem expressing himself—he uses widely adopted slang terms like "a buck" and "play ball," but also sprinkles in his own expressions (as when he says that he thinks he bungled an opportunity, or, rather, "tho't I plumbered it").[44] It's worth considering whether or not Joey's slang, in combination with his frequently misspelled words, is the product of a poor education, a deliberate rejection of rules, or a creative deconstruction of language. It seems likely, especially knowing what we do about O'Hara's desire to create a unique character through realistic language, that Joey's vernacular reflects all three of these elements, indicating both his class position and the way that he navigates social hierarchies. The question of hipness—the calculated distance from a perceived-to-be hum-drum, status quo way of life—is certainly at stake here, and might help decode the impulse behind these Joeyisms.

Richard McRae has explored the origin of the type of slang common in jazz communities and clubs in the first half of the 20th century, and links it to a rebellious nonconformity first associated with African Americans in urban communities. As McRae explains it, this "jive language" was, like jazz, uniquely American, and, quoting H. L. Menken, "an amalgam of Negro-slang from Harlem and the argots of drug addicts and the pettier sort of criminals, with occasional additions from the Broadway gossip columns and the high school campus."[45] The explicit connection between urban underworlds and the slang common in jazz communities, and beyond, relates to how O'Hara wanted the reader to understand Joey: he lives on the fringes of society, and his rebellious connection to the Chicago demimonde comes with a certain subcultural cachet. Though O'Hara took credit for many of the slang phrases included in his writing, McRae points out that beginning as early as 1934, glossaries and dictionaries of "jazz slang" found their way into print.[46] Being the voracious consumer of pop culture that he was, O'Hara was likely aware of these sources.

Still, O'Hara was both proud of his use of slang, and frustrated when his editors questioned it. Harold Ross, the editor-in-chief of the *New Yorker*, frequently aggravated O'Hara with his editorial queries, which were usually delivered through O'Hara's editor at the time, William Maxwell.[47] Letters between Maxwell and O'Hara during this period show O'Hara's irritation with Ross. In one, he bemoans the fact that Ross doesn't seem to understand his "use of the vernacular":

> Ross ought to know that crib is a derogatory term for a night club, like flea-bag for hotel. I wish to hell there would be an end to this quibbling about my use of the vernacular. Even if people don't get it at first, they will. I was the first person ever to do a piece about double talk, and God knows a lot of people still don't know what it is, but that was several years ago that I did the piece [. . .] and several things in that piece have become established slang. It is a point of artistry with me. I'm afraid to put in anything more recent that you tell em casket, I'm coffin.[48]

While O'Hara states that Ross "ought to know" what he means by his slang terms, he also emphasizes the fact he himself is, to use another piece of slang, "in the know."[49] As Phil Ford has said, "*hip*, in its original meaning, means to be aware [. . .] [T]he hip gesture is therefore a shortcut to meaning, a signifier of shared understanding."[50] In many ways, it seems that O'Hara was seeking the same sort of hipness that he bestowed upon Joey.

Joey's vernacular is mirrored in many of O'Hara's personal letters. Ford's definition of "hip" applies well to O'Hara: he was keen to show just how aware he was of subcultural signs and their signifiers, and was apt to "code switch" in letters. For example, O'Hara ends a letter to Joseph Bryan III (an editor at the *Saturday Evening Post*), by writing, "I'll buy you a powder at the crib soon, I trust."[51] The character of this line is a deliberate contrast from that of the rest of the letter, which is somewhat casual, but absent of this sort of slang. In one linguistic gesture, O'Hara marks himself as "in the know"—as hip—a phrase that in turn renders him, as opposed to Joey, a social chameleon: he is able, or rather tries to demonstrate that he is able, to navigate from both inside and outside of polite society.

## O'HARA THE JAZZ AFICIONADO

Since Joey lives and breathes the entertainment world of the late 1930s, O'Hara peppered his Joey stories with references to real songs, musicians, entertainers, and venues (see Table 1.2). Most of the songs mentioned in the stories are contemporary to the late 1930s, written by still-active songwriters, including Jerome Kern, Irving Berlin, Cole Porter, Johnny Mercer, and Hoagy Carmichael. Some of the songs are nostalgic throwback references, meant to either characterize the age of a person Joey's talking about, or his own nostalgia: these songs include "Swanee" (1919), "Everybody Step" (1921), "Oh, You Beautiful Doll" (1911), "My Buddy" (1922), and "Me and My Shadow" (1927). O'Hara/Joey also makes reference to numerous swing musicians, including well-known names like Artie Shaw, Tommy Dorsey, and Benny Goodman. More interestingly, however, O'Hara also mentions many real-life musicians whom Joey supposedly crossed paths with, and who are now generally unknown: these include guitarist Dick McDonough—who died in 1938, which Joey references in a letter—clarinetist Fud Livingston, vocalist Al Rinker, guitarist Carl Kress, trumpeter Manny Klein, drummer Chauncey Morehouse, and drummer Dave Tough. O'Hara is clearly flexing his jazz knowledge in these spots, both setting an atmosphere for the reader and proving his own jazz credentials.

Some of the Joey stories are more centered on music than others. In the third story, "How I Am Now in Chi," Joey discusses buying vocal arrangements (from his "guy" for $50 apiece), underscoring that it was common for vocalists to commission original arrangements.[52] Joey even accepts money from one of his dates to buy an original arrangement of "You Go to My Head" (though Joey instead pockets the money and uses an old arrangement). In the fourth story, "Bow Wow," Joey explains how he keeps up with new recordings, and how he cobbles together new arrangements when he's out of funds to buy them:

> I happen to drop in at this store as I do every week to hear the new recordings. You know me, Ted. Strictly larceny when it comes to listening to those arrangements but I cant [sic] afford to buy any new arrangements of my own right now so I have to get them from the recordings and take the best of this one and that one.[53]

Joey references arrangements yet again in the sixth story, "Joey on Herta." In this letter, Joey claims that while listening to the radio he heard a couple of new arrangements by Phil Harris and his band, and decided to "crib" them:

> One night I happen to get a small slice of Phil Harris broadcasting from Los Angeles and happen to tune in when he was polishing off Hold Tight. I said this can not be the guy that formerly I use [sic] to consider a road company Richman but it was. I knew there would be no trouble at all so I polished off his Hold Tight and practicly [sic] over nite I was the one man attraction of this joint. Then I caught Harris again one nite doing Fishes and from then on I and the Joint were but set.

Joey's surprise over what he sees as a worthwhile tune played by what he had previously considered to be a corny comic is surely extra-textual commentary made by John O'Hara himself.[54] The dig at Richman in the previous quotation is echoed in O'Hara's preliminary script for the "Flower Garden of My Heart" number in act 2

*Table 1.2* References in O'Hara's Pal Joey stories to songs, songwriters, and performers

| Joey Story | Songs Referenced, Origin | Songwriter/ Performers Referenced |
|---|---|---|
| "Pal Joey" | "Everybody Step"; Irving Berlin, *Music Box Revue*, 1921<br>"Swanee"[1]; George Gershwin and Irving Caesar, 1919<br>"Jerry Kern Medley"[2] | Jerome Kern (1885– 1945)<br>Hoagy Carmichael (1899– 1981)<br>Maxine Sullivan (1911– 1987) |
| "How I Am Now in Chi" | "You Go to My Head"; J. Fred Coots and Haven Gillespie, 1938[3]<br>"Jeepers Creepers"[4]; Harry Warren and Johnny Mercer, 1938 (for film *Going Places*) | Artie Shaw (1910– 2004)<br>Fred Waring (1900– 1984)<br>Chink [Martin] (1886– 1981)<br>Mort [?]<br>Joe Venuti (1903– 1978) |
| "Bow Wow" | "Hong Kong Blues"; Hoagy Carmichael, 1939 | Fred Waring (1900– 1984)<br>Dick McDonough (1904– 1938)<br>Fud [Livingtson] (1904– 1938)<br>Tommy Dorsey (1905– 1956) |
| "Avast and Belay" | "Stars and Stripes Forever"; John Philip Sousa, 1896<br>"Shine Little Glow-Worm"[5]; Paul Linke and Lilla Cayley Robinson | James Reese Europe (1880– 1919)<br>John Philip Sousa (1854– 1932)<br>Rudy Vallee (1901– 1986) |
| "Joey on Herta" | "Deep Purple"[6]; Peter DeRose, 1933<br>"Hold Tight"[7]; Sidney Bechet and Leonard Ware, 1938<br>"Three Little Fishes"[8]; Saxie Dowell, Josephine Carringer, and Bernice Idins)<br>"Day in, Day Out"<br>Rube Bloom and Johnny Mercer, 1939 | Artie Shaw (1910– 2004)<br>Benny Goodman (1909– 1986)<br>Arturo Toscanini (1867– 1957)<br>Al Rinker (1907– 1982)<br>Brooke Johns (1893– 1987?)12<br>Phil Harris (1904– 1995)<br>Harry Richman (1895– 1972) |

*Table 1.2* Continued

| Joey Story | Songs Referenced, Origin | Songwriter/ Performers Referenced |
|---|---|---|
| "The Erloff" | "The Lamp Is Low"[9]; Peter DeRose, Bert Shefter, and Mitchell Parish | Frank Parker (1903– 1999) Bing Crosby (1903– 1977) |
| "Joey and the Calcutta Club" | | Bing Crosby (1903– 1977) |
| "Joey and Mavis" | "Oh, You Beautiful Doll"; Nat Ayer and Seymour Brown, 1911 "Begin the Beguine"[10]; Cole Porter, for *Jubilee*, 1935 "My Buddy"; Walter Donaldson and Gus Kahn, 1922 | |
| "A New Career" | | Irving Berlin (1888– 1989) |
| "A Bit of a Shock" | | Maurice Chevalier (1888– 1972) Katharine Hepburn (1907– 2003) Lionel Barrymore (1878– 1954) Sheila Barret (1909– 1980?) |
| "Reminiss?" | "Me and My Shadow"; Billy Rose, Dave Dreyer, and Al Jolson, 1927 "Jazz Me"[11]; Tom Delaney, 1921 "Farewell Blues"; Paul Mares, Leon Roppolo, and Elmer Schoebel, 1922 | Fred Astaire (1899– 1987) Bing Crosby (1903– 1977) Fred Waring (1900– 1984) Jack Jenney (1910– 1945) Carl Kress (1907– 1965) Manny Klein (1908– 1994) Bobby Hackett (1915– 1976) Horace Heidt (1901– 1986) Bix Beiderbecke (1903– 1931) Chauncey Morehouse (1902– 1980) Dave Tough (1907– 1948) Jack Gallagher (?) Frank Trumbauer (1901– 1956) |

1 Originally performed by Muriel de Forrest in the revue *Demi Tasse*, the song was popularized by its publication in 1919 and subsequent performance and recording by Al Jolson (who incorporated it into his revue *Sinbad*); it was Gershwin's first international hit.

(*continued*)

*Table 1.2* Continued

2 Referred to as one of "a couple of old numbers." John O'Hara, "Pal Joey," *Pal Joey* (New York: Duell, Sloane & Pierce, 1940), 13.

3 The song reached number three on the pop charts in 1938.

4 Makes reference to the version performed by "Vanuti," a characteristically—for Joey—misspelled reference to the jazz violinist Joe Venuti.

5 Also known as "The Glow Worm"; the original German lyrics of "Das Glühwürmchen" were by Heinz Bolten- Backers, for the operetta *Lysistrata* (1902); in 1907, they were translated to English by Robinson for the show *The Girl behind the Counter*. In 1952 the lyrics were reworked by Johnny Mercer.

6 Originally a tune for piano, the song was recorded by Paul Whiteman's group in 1934, and became so popular that lyrics, by Mitchell Parish, were added in 1938.

7 Also titled "Hold Tight, Hold Tight (Want Some Sea Food, Mama?)"; later recorded by the Andrews Sisters. In O'Hara's story, the piece is performed by Phil Harris.

8 The recording by Kay Kyser and His Band was a number- one hit in 1939.

9 The song is based on Ravel's *Pavane pour infant défunte*; it was popularized by Mildred Bailey, and was soon followed by recordings by Kay Kyser and his Orchestra, Glenn Miller and his Orchestra, Jimmy Dorsey and his Orchestra, Connee Boswell, and Harry James (featuring Frank Sinatra), among others.

10 The most popular dance- band version was recorded by Artie Shaw in 1938.

11 Very likely a reference to "Jazz Me Blues"; a popular recording was made by the Original Dixieland Band in 1921.

12 O'Hara had Joey misspell the vaudevillian's name as "Brooks John," because this was "the kind of error Joey would make. The fellow's real name was Brooke Johns. Played banjo for Ann Pennington, and is now, I understand, running a chicken farm in Maryland. You will find me never making the errors I occasionally come upon in New Yorker reviews of 'swing' records." O'Hara, letter to William Maxwell, 1939 (John O'Hara Papers, Penn State, Box 1, folder 23).

of the stage version of *Pal Joey*, when he refers to the Ziegfeldian burlesque as "Richman corn."[55]

Joey also references the quality of entertainment in the clubs he sings at (generally poor), the types of songs requested (including "Begin the Beguine"), and his own musical abilities, of which he is very confident. He is sometimes self-deprecating, as when he refers to himself as "the poor man's Bing Crosby," but generally believes that his talents warrant better jobs than he typically secures.[56] Joey is obviously not a trained musician, and O'Hara makes clear that this isn't necessarily a bad thing. At one point Joey says,

> Well you know how I am. Like Berlin. I can fake a tune in one key so that the next couple days I was down at the joint in the afternoon playing it on the piano till I had it all mastered.[57]

Like Joey, the performer, O'Hara, the listener, was a true autodidact, and took a certain amount of pride in his ability to discern "good" music from the rest.

O'Hara was a follower of popular music, and considered himself an aficionado of the jazz and swing dance bands of the 1920s and 1930s. O'Hara was, first and foremost, an avid listener. In a story he wrote in 1941 for *Newsweek* (where he was, for a time, their regular entertainment columnist), O'Hara compares his knowledge of jazz bands and records to a baseball aficionado's knowledge of stats and batting averages. After an introduction in which O'Hara discusses the type of friend who is "able and more than willing to tell you offhand how far Bullet Joe Bush smacked the apple in an exhibition game between the Athletics and Pottsville [. . .] in 1911," he goes on to say,

> Now all this about baseball is by way of showing that even though the statisticians and their figures bore me, I have a certain understanding of their malady, because I have pretty much the same thing about jazz musicians and composers, and can be just as boring about the date of a tune, who wrote it, the true words of the lyric, and what band made the best recording of it.

O'Hara grew up in a musical household—his mother was a pianist—and though he never took formal lessons, as a young man he picked up the banjo and even played publicly with a group called the "Jolly Trio." He regaled others with his knowledge of jazz and often went to hear and dance along to the major dance bands of the period when they came through the Pennsylvania coal-mining region of O'Hara's youth (including his hometown of Pottsville, and elsewhere in Schuylkill County). Some of the venues he frequented also appear in the Joey stories; these clubs include Maher's in Shenandoah and Lakewood Park near Mahanoy Plane, both of which are mentioned in the final Joey story, "Reminiss."[58] In O'Hara's youth, these venues featured well-known celebrity acts, including Paul Whiteman and his band, as well as regional favorites like the Scranton Sirens (which introduced the Dorsey brothers, who at the time O'Hara heard them were not yet international stars).

O'Hara developed an ear for music, and was forceful in his musical opinions. He was a fan of Whiteman, and the Rhythm Boys (a vocal trio who performed frequently with Whiteman, and included Bing Crosby), and was critical of the popularity of others, including Guy Lombardo.[59] When he moved to New York, some of his first articles for the New York *Herald Tribune* covered jazz and jazz artists.[60] Later in his career he would write reviews of books on jazz (including Frederic Ramsey Jr. and Charles Edward Smith's edited collection *Jazzmen* [1939] and Eddie Condon's biography *We Called It Music* [1947]).

O'Hara's early jazz-related pieces for the *Herald Tribune* are revealing. The first of these, an article titled "Saxophonic Fever" from 1929, describes a peculiar "tribe" of jazz aficionados, among whom he counts himself, whom he characterizes as "insane on the subject of dance orchestras and dance orchestrations." He calls these men—all men, and ostensibly all white—sensitive of ear, and frenzied by good arrangements (a term he uses interchangeably with "orchestrations"), performances, and performers. This "orchestra nut" might even stop listening to the conversation of his dancing companion if he's struck by something particularly novel in a performance.[61] In the article O'Hara drops all manner of names and terms to prove his insider status:

> You will hear [the "orchestra nut" say] such words as back time, Fletcher Henderson, dirty break, the-ending-of-Lady-of-the-Evening, Ben Bernie, bull fiddle, Emil Coleman, sarusophone, Rube Bloom.[62]

O'Hara goes on to say that he is one of the first to recognize the phenomenon of this "tribe" of listeners. He names Edward of Windsor, the Prince of Wales, as the "most prominent member" of the tribe; O'Hara calls the Englishman a "Whitemaniac," and one of the "aristocrats of orchestra insanity."[63] He contrasts these listeners/aficionados against the more "primitive school," who were fans of the decidedly "hotter" Ted Lewis and Red Nichols's bands. O'Hara's characteristic attention to detail is used here in the service of classifying dance bands and their listeners. Though he seems to distance himself from the "aristocrats," and from the "highbrows" who would have scorned "hotter" forms of jazz, O'Hara clearly likes a lot of the "sweeter" arrangements favored by this so-called collective.

It is revealing that O'Hara distanced himself from the types of audiences who, for instance, attended the opera. In a later article for *Newsweek*, he recounts the time he was assigned to report on a production of *Tosca* at the Met. O'Hara makes it quite clear that opera isn't his cup of tea, in large part because of the type of crowd who frequents it:

> So I stepped out, my dear, to breathe an at-mos-phere that simply reeked with class . . . Yes, for the first and unquestionably the last time this season, and maybe ever, I duded up my shirt front, put on my top hat and tails and went to hear "Tosca."[64]

This passage borrows liberally from the lyrics to Berlin's song "Top Hat, White Tie and Tails" from the film *Top Hat* (1935), originally performed by Fred Astaire, who was dressed in the manner of the song title (accompanied by dozens of identically dressed male dancers). Like some of O'Hara's other references to pop culture, this serves to differentiate him from the upper set. O'Hara's desire to exempt himself from a kind of musical snobbery reveals that he was aware of the role music played in creating and sustaining class hierarchies. Yet, like many ardent lovers of music, O'Hara never goes so far as to interrogate what his own musical tastes might indicate about his relationship to class structures— he tends to discuss his musical preferences in purely aesthetic terms. This tendency is somewhat surprising, given his typical awareness of exactly these relationships.[65]

While O'Hara was never a professional jazz critic, his writings contribute to debates related to music and middlebrow culture, and the ways that class and taste intersected these debates in the early 1930s. Though he resisted taking a definitive side in the debate, O'Hara's articles nevertheless reflect the contemporary discourse. While the conversation became much more widespread and heated in the 1940s—when the term "middlebrow," used pejoratively, was frequently invoked—the 1930s were an early breeding ground for mid-century arguments related to popular culture and its effects on society. Although O'Hara was never censorious of jazz in the way of critical theorist Theodor Adorno and others, his critiques of dance groups in the early 1930s echo some of the concerns of cultural critics like him.

For one, O'Hara spends a good deal of time in his article "The Decline of Jazz" bemoaning what he sees as the homogenization, or standardization, of dance band arrangements/orchestrations. This criticism echoes the contemporary idea that mass culture dilutes high culture, although O'Hara doesn't seem intent on defending the "highbrows" in any way (this defense would surely have undercut his "hip" credentials). John Howland has written about the shift in jazz criticism in the early 1930s, when "contemporary art music circles" began to lose interest in "jazz-styled concert music," like Gershwin's *Rhapsody in Blue*, at the same time as it became more mainstream.[66] Howland argues that the tradition of white symphonic jazz (of which Paul Whiteman was one of the earliest practitioners) was an easy target during this shift in criticism because of the earlier idea that this sort of music "elevated" jazz. And, indeed, John O'Hara struggles in his last jazz-related article for the *Herald Tribune*—titled "Sing Us the Old Songs"—to articulate his position within this discourse.

The article begins by reinforcing the sentiments expressed in his "Decline of Jazz" article by saying that "jazz has gone stale." He asserts that no good "jazz tunes" are being written anymore, so the old ones are being recycled.[67] Later in the article he seeks to identify an aesthetic sweet spot between the music of the "jazzophile" ("of which I am not quite") and that of the lover of Tin Pan Alley: he situates himself among these listeners.[68] He says that this sort of listener "definitely responded to a kind of jazz that may be described and cursed by calling it nicer." He goes on to say that this "nicer" music could be called "'white' jazz," as opposed to "Negro jazz" (though he admits that the music of Fletcher Henderson was one of the first to "recognize and embrace" this so-called white jazz). He reinforces old binaries by saying that this sort of music was "better organized, without losing much of the spontaneity in the solo work" and that it didn't exclude the songs of the major songwriters, including "Gershwin, Kern, Katscher, Caesar, Rose, Schwartz, Rainger, Bloom, Jones, Porter, Coward, Swift, Rodgers, Desylva, Brown and Henderson." O'Hara goes on to write that this music requires a certain amount of education from the listener: "a finer sense of tempo, an acquired or innate feeling for harmony, and at least a smattering (whatever that is) of musical knowledge." He contrasts these listeners with the "intelligentsia who preferred hot jazz," presumably targeting the new jazz critics of the period; he admits that his taste in jazz leans toward "the less strident form."

Though O'Hara never resolves what seems to be a tension between his musical preferences and his keen knowledge of classed cultural products and their affiliation with groups that he doesn't identify with, he does defend his ability to tune in, so to speak, to fine musical detail. If one detects a bit of grandstanding in the preceding articles, this posture is consistent with what we know about O'Hara: his writings on jazz show him to be a capable listener, but somewhat desperate to show his musical credentials.[69] As in his other writings on pop culture (including that on cars and clothing), O'Hara attempts to prove to his readers through his uncommon powers of observation that he's an insider. He name-drops, uses technical terms, and then self-consciously catches himself (". . . there I go getting technical"). In the end, O'Hara sets himself apart from mainstream listeners.[70]

## SONGWRITERS AND O'HARA

In addition to his love of jazz, O'Hara was also a vocal admirer of contemporary songwriters. O'Hara's most well-known piece of writing on music is undoubtedly his tribute to George Gershwin, written three years after the composer's death on the occasion of a concert in memoriam. His article includes the moving and frequently quoted line "George Gershwin died on July 11th, 1937, but I don't have to believe that if I don't want to."[71] This was the first article written for his regular column at *Newsweek*, where he was assigned to report on entertainment news. O'Hara praises Gershwin's artistry even as he acknowledges his ego ("everyone understood the mono-egomania, took it for granted, and considered it rather charming [. . .] [T]he truth is everyone knew George was good, and no one ever tried to keep it a secret from him"), but O'Hara can't help boasting as he chronicles the parties he attended at the Gershwin residence, and elaborates on his own musical credentials as a listener and aficionado.[72] In one particularly telling passage, O'Hara attempts to prove both his love of Gershwin and his ability to recall records with unusual accuracy:

> When I say that no layman knew and loved his work so well as I, I can almost prove it with an anecdote. One of those Saturday nights George was playing "Do Do Do," using an arrangement he had worked out for a phonograph record. When he came to the ending I said: "Why don't you play it the way you did on the record?"
> "I did," he said.
> "No, you didn't," I said.
> "Well now really, John, I wrote the piece. I ought to know."
> "Don't bet him!" said Ira to George.
> So I one-fingered the ending as it had been written in 1926, annoying George with a compliment, or what might have been regarded as a compliment but for my smugness and the fact that George rightfully enough considered himself the leading authority on his favorite subject, his music.[73]

O'Hara's Gershwin feature reveals an aspect of his personality that he was seemingly aware of—his smugness, and his eagerness to be seen as an authority, especially on music. This difficulty in O'Hara's personality might be compared with Gershwin's own difficult personality; as Joan Peyser points out, in her biography of George Gershwin, O'Hara's praise of Gershwin was tempered by his acknowledgment of his faults, particularly his ego, captured in the line "I am a little sorry now that I did not like George, that I was not his friend."[74] Although George Gershwin might have been difficult, it's worth noting that O'Hara's own ego would have potentially soured any friendship they might have had.

In another article for *Newsweek*, O'Hara praises Harold Arlen's *Americanegro Suite* (1940), which he heard performed by the composer himself. O'Hara describes Arlen as "one of the few white men who can sing with the tenderness, gayety, and exuberance of the Negro."[75] Arlen's suite never heard radio play during the time of its creation, very likely because of the widespread broadcasters' boycott of ASCAP artists, which began in January of 1941; O'Hara was strongly in favor of the interests of the ASCAP composers. In the same article he goes on to defend them: "It is my considered opinion that the radio broadcasters are entirely in the wrong, not only from the point of view of the composers, but from the point of view of the public, if only the public could be interested in taking a point of view."[76] Although it was not mentioned in the article, O'Hara had a financial and an artistic interest in the debate: *Pal Joey*, the musical, premiered in December 1940, and none of its hit tunes—including "Bewitched, Bothered and Bewildered" and "I Could Write a Book"—saw radio play until later on. These two songs, especially "Bewitched," were widely recorded in the late 1940s, a factor that might have contributed to the popularity behind the Columbia recording, released in February of 1951, which in turn influenced the mounting of the revival in 1952.

Later in his career O'Hara attempted to write more musical scripts.[77] O'Hara worked on over fifteen plays between 1940 and 1970 (both straight and musical). Besides *Pal Joey*, none of the musical scripts he worked on made it to Broadway, though some were in advanced stages of production when they failed. Some of these projects, especially in the years following *Pal Joey*, were announced in the *New York Times* as prospective pieces. These include another projected Rodgers and Hart collaboration (the *Times* wrote that "the action is set 'somewhere in Florida,' and that's about all Mr. O'Hara would divulge, except to concede that he has a 'gentleman's commitment' with Rodgers and Hart for them to do the songs"), a potential collaboration with Rodgers and Hammerstein about Toulouse-Lautrec ("Next season's backlog already includes [. . .] a play John O'Hara has promised to let them see as soon as completed"), and a production with Robert Alton, the choreographer, and possibly Elia Kazan ("the idea for the show, according to Mr. Alton, was relayed to him by Mr. O'Hara about a year ago. They feel it would be something Mr. Kazan might be willing to stage"; O'Hara said that the musical would be "much straighter than the average musical").[78] None of these scripts survive: none of them seem to have made it very far past the idea phase. One play that was written with music by Irving Berlin in mind, however, is extant.

The play *The Way It Was*, included in O'Hara's collection *Five Plays*, was initially intended as a musical. The play itself is set in both the Pennsylvania coal-mining country of O'Hara's youth and New York City in the 1920s. O'Hara felt that this was an appropriate book for Berlin because it was "about a time that he knew," and, besides, he was "fond" of the songwriter.[79] O'Hara approached Berlin, and they met in January 1957 to discuss the possibility of a collaboration. O'Hara wrote about the meeting in the preface to his published *Five Plays*. He claims that Berlin came to the meeting prepared with a title song. O'Hara recalls the encounter:

> He told me he had already written the title song for *The Way it Was*, and he handed a couple of sheets of music to a pianist and began to sing. He had not sung three notes before I pricked up my ears. He finished the song and looked at me for my reaction. I said, "Irving, do you mind if he plays the melody, and I'll sing the words?
>
> "No, go right ahead. Go right ahead," he said.
>
> So the pianist began to play, and I sang the lyric. But it was not the lyric he had created for *The Way it Was*. It was the lyric for *Butterfly*, as he had written it forty years ago. I knew it word-perfect.
>
> "You son-of-a-bitch," said Irving. "I was warned about you. That song was never a hit. How did you know the lyric?"
>
> Well, I know a lot of song lyrics, and everybody knows Berlin lyrics. But he was embarrassed, a bit ashamed, I think, to be caught trying to pull a fast one. I honestly didn't mind; *Butterfly* or *The Way it Was*, it's a pretty tune; but I knew I had lost Irving Berlin.[80]

Like the anecdote O'Hara recalls in the Gershwin article for *Newsweek*, here O'Hara once more proves his prodigious talent for recalling a tune. In a phone interview with Bruccoli in 1975, Berlin denied that he was upset by O'Hara's recall—to be sure, it wouldn't have been unusual for Berlin to recycle old songs in order to help establish what kind of mood would permeate the show. He wasn't embarrassed to reuse an old song; he was simply surprised that O'Hara knew the song at all. Instead, Berlin said he was troubled by some of the elements present in the book (including the suicide of one of the characters, and the unhappy ending), and didn't see O'Hara as willing to make any changes, or to truly collaborate on the project.[81]

Most literary critics who commented on O'Hara's inability to work well with others characterize him as an important writer of novels and short stories, who just wasn't cut out to write for the theater. While *Pal Joey* was undoubtedly a success, lightning didn't strike twice for O'Hara. Of the plays published as *Five Plays*, only two made it to summer stock. He would never have another theater success like *Pal Joey*.

## CONCLUSION

While working on *Pal Joey*, O'Hara wrote a handful of draft scripts. Three draft scripts of *Pal Joey* are currently extant. The earliest is currently held by the Rodgers and Hammerstein Organization (it appears to have been written before Rodgers and Hart wrote the songs), and the other two can be found in the John

O'Hara Papers at Penn State. The exact dates of these drafts are unknown, but they were all written in 1940, sometime between O'Hara's initial letter to Rodgers early in the year, and the start of rehearsals in November. The second and third draft script were written sometime after Rodgers and Hart began writing the songs, some of which are indicated in the draft. It is reasonable to suggest, then, that O'Hara was working on these scripts in the fall of 1940. While there are a few key differences between the final script and that of the drafts—including song placement, the addition of "What Is a Man?," the development of the character Gladys, the unredemptive ending, and a number of other small changes—the general story outline is largely the same.

O'Hara's temperament, love for music, and attraction to disreputable places and characters inform the distinctive flavor of *Pal Joey*, the musical. The show is so closely connected to O'Hara's characteristic style, his desire to create realistic portrayals of characters, and his focus on the antihero, that his contribution can't be overstated. His close attention to musical detail in his novels and short stories should pique the interest of music scholars, who are perhaps typically less inclined to take seriously a novelist's insight into music. Chapter 2 will address the working relationship between O'Hara, Rodgers, and Hart, as well as the creative input of George Abbott and Bob Alton. Examining O'Hara's preliminary, rehearsal, and final scripts in relation to the placement and impact of Rodgers and Hart's songs, Bob Alton's choreography, and George Abbott's direction of the narrative highlights a detailed, complex, and often-unacknowledged collaborative process.

# 2

# RODGERS AND HART'S BOLDEST VENTURE

• • •

## WORKING RELATIONSHIPS AND COLLABORATIVE PROCESSES

Dear Dick:                                                    Thursday [n.d.]
I don't know whether you happened to see any of a series of pieces I've been doing for The New Yorker in the past year or so. They're about a guy who is master of ceremonies in cheap night clubs, and the pieces are in the form of letters from him to a successful band header. Anyway, I got the idea that the pieces, or at least the character and the life in general could be made into a book show, and I wonder if you and Larry would be interested in working on it with me. I read that you two have a commitment with Dwight Wiman for a show this Spring but if and when you get through with that I do hope you like my idea.

All the best to you always. Please remember me to the beautiful Dorothy and say hello to Larry for me. Say more than hello, too.

Faithfully,
John O'Hara[1]

Rodgers received O'Hara's letter sometime in early 1940.[2] Rodgers apparently sent a telegram to O'Hara soon after; both he and Hart were enthusiastic about the prospect of "doing a musical without a conventional clean-cut juvenile in the romantic lead."[3] Many, including Rodgers, remarked that Hart was particularly excited at the prospect because it concerned an environment that he knew well: "he had spent thousands of hours in exactly the kind of atmosphere depicted in the stories and was thoroughly familiar with the Pal Joeys of this world."[4] There was no question that Hart was up to the task of writing lyrics that met the cynical, adult tone of the source material. For his part, Rodgers relished the idea of doing something completely different from what had been done on the musical comedy stage before.

Rodgers called *Pal Joey* "the most satisfying and mature work that I was associated with during all my years with Larry Hart," and it was purportedly also

*Pal Joey.* Julianne Lindberg, Oxford University Press (2020). © Oxford University Press.
DOI: 10.1093/oso/9780190051204.001.0001

Hart's favorite show; as Rodgers would later say, "few things ever gave Larry as much pleasure in his entire life as the original production of 'Pal Joey.'"[5] Even critics who found fault in the story were impressed with Rodgers and Hart's score. Brooks Atkinson said the score was written "with wit and skill."[6] Henry R. Murdock, in a review of the previews, said that *Pal Joey* "has a Rodgers and Hart score that ranks among the team's best. Larry Hart, in particular, has surpassed all previous efforts with his clever lyrics."[7] Sidney Whipple agreed, remarking upon the memorable lyrics "that sometimes skirt dangerously close to the risqué and sometimes plunge right into it—but always wittily."[8] Richard Watts Jr. praised the duo, commenting that "[t]he combination of Rodgers and Hart has always been a virtually perfect one, and now it is happily discovered that O'Hara fits in with them splendidly."[9] Despite Atkinson's reservations (see Introduction), the show was generally regarded as one of Rodgers and Hart's best.

By the time *Pal Joey* made it to Broadway, Rodgers and Hart had written twenty-six stage musicals together (including their London productions), had written the songs for five Hollywood films, and had standardized their songwriting process. Geoffrey Block has argued that the period between 1935 and 1943 might be called the "Rodgers and Hart era," during which no other songwriter or songwriting team had a successful book show running on Broadway every single year during that period, despite the slowdown in production during the Depression.[10] At this point in their career they had endured both spectacular failures (*Chee-Chee*, and to a lesser extent, *Betsy*) as well as admirable successes (*Connecticut Yankee*, and all save one of their shows after 1935). Although some of their work in film was innovative, their three-year tenure in Hollywood—a period marked mostly by frustration and a pervading ennui—purportedly taught them the value of the creative freedom that Broadway afforded them, especially because they now had, for the most part, the confidence of financial backers.[11] To be sure, by the time of *Pal Joey* Rodgers and Hart were Broadway veterans, established and well respected despite being only in their thirties and early forties, respectively. Their post-Hollywood stage musicals were some of the most successful shows of their career, and demonstrate a shared interest in stretching the bounds of artistic expression on Broadway.

This is not to discount their early collaborations. Even early on, Rodgers and Hart were interested in challenging conventions related to storytelling and genre. Their innovations date back to at least the *Garrick Gaieties* (1925 and 1926). The two installments of the revue included burlesques on current events and contemporary shows, a practice that reaches back to the earliest forms of stage entertainment in the United States. What was different here was the youthful, vibrant energy they brought to their travesties and especially Hart's witty, sophisticated, learned lyrics. These shows put Rodgers and Hart in the spotlight, and paved the way for other innovative shows. Another early innovator was *Chee-Chee* (1928), which O'Hara singled out as one of his favorites. Most of the literature on *Chee-Chee* emphasizes its now-offensive storyline, and how distasteful the subject and characterizations are (there is rampant orientalism and misogyny in the show). Recent work by Dominic Symonds, however, has shown that the failure of the show might well have been related more to producer/book writer Lew Fields's lack of confidence in it.[12] The importance of the show, in retrospect, was the degree to which it was integrated: Rodgers and Hart's big experiment on this show was that it featured a nearly continuous musical score, weaving the music in with the action. Other inventive early shows include the historical drama *Dearest Enemy* and the Freudian *Peggy-Ann* in 1926 and the Twain-inspired *Connecticut Yankee* (1927)—perhaps not innovative in the same way as *Pal Joey*, but boundary breaking nonetheless. In his autobiography, Rodgers makes the case that the guiding philosophy in his career with Hart was one of innovation, in meeting difficult, worthy artistic challenges, rather than simply churning out conventional fare.[13] As Rodgers said after the spectacular failure of the Ziegfeld-produced *Betsy*, "we knew we would have to be particularly careful of our future commitments. Being careful, however, did not mean playing it safe; if anything, it meant being careful not to."[14] A *Time* cover feature from 1938 summed up Rodgers and Hart's approach this way: "The one possible formula was: *Don't Have a Formula;* the one rule for success: *Don't Follow it Up.*"[15] They saw their greatest achievements in their greatest risks.

Their innovations were always tempered by the medium—they were writing for Broadway, a venue that welcomed a certain degree of artistic experimentation, certainly more than Hollywood, so long as it was entertaining and commercially viable. In the same *Time* article mentioned above, Rodgers and Hart are credited with having a "commercial instinct that most of their rivals have apparently ignored."[16] Through their early tutelage under Lew Fields, especially, Rodgers and Hart learned how to balance the seemingly conflicting ideals of innovation and commercial appeal.

This chapter traces the progress from bold idea to finished score, with attention paid to revisions, additions, and other subsequent changes as the score moved from sketch, to previews, to the Broadway premiere. Special attention is paid to the all-important collaborative process, giving due credit to the other members of the show's creative team, including John O'Hara, producer/director George Abbott, and choreographer Robert Alton.


## COLLABORATION


The unmarked graves and the whitened bones along Broadway belong to men who suffered delusions of grandeur, who thought that they did it alone when they only watched it being done.[17]

—George Abbott

Rodgers and Hart's innovations were, however, not simply their own. Like all songwriters on Broadway, they owed much of their artistic and commercial success to the indispensable collaborators who pitched projects, funded them, wrote their scenarios, rehearsed their stage realizations, directed them, promoted them, produced them, starred or otherwise played in them, and contributed essential nonmusical artistic elements to them (including dance, and set and costume design). Collaboration on the level of the score, even, was common practice; Rodgers, for instance, used orchestrators and dance arrangers to realize his admittedly mostly developed ideas. Still, as Dominic McHugh has argued, it would almost always be more truthful to refer to composers of Broadway musicals as "composer-collaborators," a term that would serve to not only give credit where credit is due, but to help resist the unquestioned authority that typically accompanies the term "composer."[18] Certainly, in opera histories the composer gets more credit than, say, the librettist, arrangers, musicians, or the director. In a field as interdisciplinary and so tied to commercial pursuits as musical theater, it's much more appropriate to credit the multiple collaborators responsible for the total effect of a show. The "composer-collaborator" configuration helps draw these relationships into the foreground.

For one, the word "collaborator" implies process, which by definition dislodges the idea that a musical is a museum object. Revision and adaptation are nearly always central to the production of Broadway shows, as they were for Rodgers's shows. The term also helps put Hart on equal footing with Rodgers. Although Hart is a celebrated figure, the fascination with the perennial Rodgers and Hart question—"which came first, the music or the lyrics?"—often seems to be one of authorship, whereby Hart is seen as artistically secondary to Rodgers. Most accounts of Rodgers and Hart state that Rodgers wrote the music first, and Hart then supplied the lyrics. Some scholars, including Block, have countered that claim by citing Rodgers's own words, showing that the arrangement wasn't always so straightforward: in 1939, Rodgers himself said that "there is no set procedure whatsoever," and that Hart "often hands me a completed lyric to be set to music."[19] However, as Rodgers continued, "More often I have a tune ready for him to work on."[20] As Block acknowledges, "no source convincingly documents a single specific instance in which a Hart lyric (other than a verse) preceded a Rodgers melody."[21] Still, sometimes a song title would be chosen (by Rodgers or Hart) before Rodgers wrote the music (Rodgers acknowledges as much in the 1939 article cited previously), and "since titles typically appear in prominent places within a song, such as the opening or closing, the presence of a title also means that, at least in one important sense, the lyrics do in fact come first." [22] This might have, in fact, been the case for the song "Bewitched" (see Chapter 4).

Another narrative, which Rodgers contributed to, was that he had to lock Hart in a room to get anything out of him, attributing much of the creative energy to Rodgers himself. In the introduction to *The Rodgers and Hart Songbook* (published in 1951, eight years after Hart had passed), Rodgers said, "There was the never-ceasing routine of trying to find him, locking him up in a room, and hoping to fire his imagination so that actual words would get down on paper."[23] Rodgers repeated the idea over fifteen years later: "Working with [Hart], however, did present problems since he had to be literally trapped into putting pen to paper—and then only after hearing a melody that stimulated him." [24] While Rodgers undoubtedly had his difficulties with Hart, these two quotations by Rodgers downplay Hart's creative involvement in the score. Rodgers, to be sure, was a monumental talent; nevertheless, he couldn't have done what he did without Hart. McHugh's term "composer-collaborator" also brings to mind other essential collaborators on the show. Documentation related to *Pal Joey* makes clear that George Abbott, Robert Alton, and John O'Hara, especially, played central creative roles and contributed a great deal to the process of building the show.

## BUILDING A SHOW: FROM CASTING TO REHEARSALS

Rodgers and Hart's ninth post-Hollywood show (including the atypical circus spectacular *Jumbo*), *Pal Joey* was much anticipated by the press. The newly launched magazine *PM Weekly*, which had just debuted in June 1940, featured an article titled "How a Musical Is Made," published on December 22 between the Philadelphia tryouts and the Broadway premiere. Written by Robert Rice, the son of playwright Elmer Rice, the article is unusually detailed, including information on the show's finances, the audition process, and other particulars of production. According to Rice, the show was the product of "eight months of time, the efforts of at least 100 skilled workers and a cash outlay of $80,000."[25] The gossip columns from that year confirm most of the details from the story: Abbott was associated with the project as early as April 1940, although he didn't officially commit until a few months later, and the first actors to be considered were Vivienne Segal, Gene Kelly, and Leila Ernst.[26] Segal, who had just played the part of Countess Peggy Palarffi, sister to the male lead in Rodgers and Hart's Wiman-produced *I Married an Angel* (1940), was cast without an audition (she didn't officially sign on until November).[27] *I Married an Angel* was Segal's first show with Rodgers and Hart and signaled a significant shift in her career, which up to this point was dominated by ingénue roles in operettas. It also proved that she had comedic range; for Hart especially, Segal was a perfect choice for Vera. She was reportedly his favorite actress, and they grew to be good friends.

Kelly made his debut on Broadway in 1938 when, at the age of twenty-six, he won a spot in the chorus for Cole Porter's *Leave It to Me*. After performing in a featured spot in Nancy Hamilton's intimate ensemble revue *One for the Money* (1939), he got his first real break in a play by the Armenian-American playwright William Saroyan. Rodgers recalls seeing Kelly in Saroyan's *The Time of Your Life* (1939); he played the part of Harry the Hoofer, a melancholy out-of-work vaudevillian whose only wish is to make people laugh. Kelly devised his own dances for the show, and later expressed that this was the show in which he finally made the connection that dance could express character. Rodgers claimed that "the stage was aglow with life whenever [Kelly] appeared, and his dancing was superb"; Rodgers told O'Hara that he'd found their Joey.[28] Rodgers then reportedly called John Darrow, Kelly's agent, and asked whether or not he could sing. Kelly's thin tenor needed work, and Darrow immediately hired a singing coach to help Kelly prepare for an audition. At the audition only Rodgers, O'Hara, and Abbott were present; the absence of Hart was a blow to Kelly, who felt Hart would be his only "friend at court."[29] Kelly worked up two songs: Rodgers and Hart's "I Didn't Know What Time It Was" (from *Too Many Girls*, 1939), and "It's the Irish in Me," which he told Clive Hirschhorn he "used to do in the cloops."[30] The latter song might have appealed especially to the proudly Irish O'Hara; Kelly remembers him exclaiming, from the back of the theater, "That's it. Take him."[31]

Leila Ernst, eventually cast as the ingénue Linda, had recently played the part of co-ed Talullah Lou in Rodgers and Hart's college comedy *Too Many Girls* (1939), directed by Abbott. After leaving the show in February 1940, she headed to Hollywood to film her first movie, playing opposite Jackie Cooper in *Life with Henry* (released in 1941), the second of Cooper's two Henry Aldrich films.[32] Abbott reportedly thought of her first for the role of *Pal Joey*'s ingénue, and even successfully negotiated with Paramount to give her temporary release from her contract.[33] Jack Durant and June Havoc were cast a bit later, in September. Durant was chosen for his comedic talents and his skills as an acrobat, and at this point Havoc's role as the lead dancer in the *Pal Joey*'s cheap nightclub was still rather small (it would be expanded during rehearsals); Havoc's relationship to Gypsy Rose Lee, who was her sister, was already being mentioned in the press.[34]

O'Hara reportedly began writing the script in May 1940, although he might have started writing as early as March.[35] Most of Rodgers and Hart's score was done by September.[36] Chorus calls took place in late October. Alton was reportedly looking for "17 chorus girls and eight boys"; on opening night, nineteen women and nine men were listed in the chorus.[37] Jo Mielziner was signed on to design the sets in November.[38] Rehearsals began on November 11 at the Biltmore Theatre, where Abbott worked with the cast on the book, and the Longacre Theatre, where Rodgers and Alton worked on the music and the dances (June Havoc remembers that the latter was always "noisy and exciting").[39]

Rice notes that "George Abbott didn't agree to produce [*Pal Joey*] until early July [. . .] Then Abbott launched an ill-formed production known as *The White-Haired Boy*, and wasn't ready to start working on *Joey* until October."[40] *The White-Haired Boy*, which was in tryouts in Boston in late October, was a complete failure. A satirical spoof on the writing of William Saroyan, who had won a Pulitzer the previous year for *The Time of Your Life*, the play was called illogical and "esoteric" by the critics, and Abbott, who directed and produced it, pulled it after a one-week tryout.[41] Although Abbott had agreed to direct and produce *Pal Joey* months before the failure of *The White-Haired Boy*, it's a good example of Abbott's willingness to scrap a show, no matter how much work went into it, if he didn't think it was going to work.

And as it turns out, Abbott had his reservations about *Pal Joey*. *PM Weekly* reported that when Abbott read O'Hara's preliminary script, his first comment was that the show was "a straight comedy" (the article goes on to say that "Messrs. Rodgers and Hart songwrote him out of that belief").[42] Although most accounts of the show chronicle Hart and O'Hara's poor working habits, which led to much frustration in rehearsal, Rodgers was also worried about Abbott's attitude toward the production, at least early on in the process. Rodgers remembers in his autobiography that although they had previously worked on three shows together, this was the first one for which Abbott quibbled over Rodgers and Hart's royalties (as Rodgers states it, "he informed me that he felt Larry and I were getting too much of a royalty and that we should agree to take a cut.").[43] They eventually worked it out (Abbott agreed to the original terms), but Rodgers mentions two more instances that made him believe that Abbott was worried about the success of the show: (1) Abbott purportedly told Jo Mielziner to "spend as little money as possible on production costs" and (2) Abbott apparently denied Robert Alton's request for two extra dancers for the chorus.[44] This frugality led Rodgers to believe that Abbott had no faith in the show: "Perhaps because of the daring nature of our show he thought he was sticking his neck out a bit too far."[45] In an earlier interview, Rodgers says that Abbott was "afraid of it. But, like so many people, I think he was afraid to let it go, too. That was why he went through with it."[46] Abbott's account of his time on *Pal Joey*, written—like Rodgers's—decades later in his memoirs, makes no mention of this wariness, but does describe O'Hara's preliminary script as "a disorganized set of scenes without a good story line [that] required work before we would be ready for rehearsal."[47] Abbott's statement is a bit curious, as O'Hara's draft script is not drastically different (in idea, at least) from the script used at the premiere.

Abbott does describe the idea for the show as "a very daring one" and states that when rehearsals began, "[we were] unsure of what the total effect was going to be"; this statement perhaps highlights the inherent risk Abbott, as producer, took.[48] The daring qualities of *Joey*—its proximity to straight theater, its use of the vernacular, and its adult themes—are, significantly, the very elements that shaped Abbott's first smash success on Broadway, fittingly titled *Broadway* (1926). A handful of critics compared *Pal Joey* to *Broadway*, but the similarities perhaps warranted more chatter.

## MISTER ABBOTT

As with that other Broadway fixture, Irving Berlin (1888–1989), George Abbott's career spanned nearly the entire twentieth century: he was born in Chautauqua County, New York in 1887, and died in 1995 at the age of 107. A celebrated writer, producer, and director, Abbott was a significant force in directing the trajectory of both straight and musical theater in the twentieth century. Abbott worked with Rodgers and Hart on five shows, and his significant post–Rodgers and Hart musicals include *Best Foot Forward* (1941); *On the Town* (1944); *Billion Dollar Baby* (1945); *High Button Shoes* (1947); *Where's Charley?* (1948); *Call Me Madam* (1950); *Wonderful Town* (1953); *The Pajama Game* (1954); *Damn Yankees* (1955); *Once Upon a Mattress* (1959); *Fiorello!* (1959), for which he earned a Pulitzer Prize as well as a Tony; and *A Funny Thing Happened on the Way to the Forum* (1962), as well as a number of significant revivals (including the 1983 production of *On Your Toes*, for which he won a Drama Desk Award).

Abbott began his Broadway career as an actor—his debut performance, at twenty-six, was in the William Harris Jr. production *The Misleading Lady* (1913). He went on to perform in at least nine more Broadway shows before beginning his career as a writer with the play *The Fall Guy* (1925), which he wrote with Jimmy Gleason. From then on he was known for coauthoring, adapting, directing, and, importantly, "play doctoring" scripts. As one critic from 1939 put it,

> One of his chief assets is his experience and talents for shoring up tottering scripts. It is called "play doctoring," though Mr. Abbott objects to the term. Compares it rather with copy editing as practiced by city rooms. But it is an ability which has stood him in good stead and paid handsome dividends at the box office.[49]

Abbott rarely wrote an original script, and of those he wrote none of them were successful on Broadway. He realized the nature of his talent early on, and made a career of it:

> I was not a successful playwright until I took parasitical advantage of other people's ideas. All my success has been either in rewriting some piece which was created by another author, or in adaptations for a musical book of such standard works as *Charley's Aunt* and *A Comedy of Errors*.[50]

Abbott's comment downplays, clearly in the service of humility, the significance of adaptation and revision in stage productions. Abbott's jobs required an understanding of the genre conventions related to both straight and musical theater (as well as comedy and melodrama), a deft hand in translating prose to dialogue, and a keen sense of pacing. He often played a role in casting, sometimes calling upon actors who performed successfully in his earlier productions. Even in productions for which he was not credited with the book—like *Pal Joey*—he played an important role in the flow, pacing, and total effect of his shows.

Abbott's first big success was with the previously mentioned straight play *Broadway* (1926), originally written by Philip Dunning, but adapted for the stage with significant assistance by Abbott; Dunning and Abbott also directed the production. *Broadway* was billed as a "new play of New York Night Life," and was based on former actor Philip Dunning's "earlier experiences and observations in Gotham cabarets."[51] Like *Pal Joey*, its characters are hoofers, chorus girls, and gangsters. Because it premiered in 1926, it also featured bootleggers; in fact, minutes into act 1, one of the main characters—a smooth, bad-guy bootlegger named Steve Crandall—shoots his rival "Scar" Edwards dead. Also like *Pal Joey*, it was praised for its realistic attention to the details of setting, from set designs and costumes to slang and vernacular in the dialogue. The show ran for 603 performances, and established Abbott as an important new voice on Broadway. While he didn't have another smash success like *Broadway* until *Three Men and a Horse* (1935), which ran for 835 performances, he was hugely prolific and a highly respected figure in the "legit" theater.

Also in 1935 Abbott was contacted by Rodgers and Hart, recently back from their tenure in Hollywood. They were interested in having Abbott work on their upcoming production, *On Your Toes* (1936), to be produced by Dwight D. Wiman. In order to get his feet wet, Abbott says that Rodgers and Hart suggested he "break in" by first directing the book for *Jumbo* (1935), the Billy Rose–produced circus-musical spectacular at the Hippodrome.[52] *Jumbo* did include a story, but it was first and foremost an extravaganza, offering such stage spectacle as chorus girls and acrobats balancing high above the stage on suspended hoops, the daring acrobat Barbette, a sweet elephant (Big Rosie, playing the part of Jumbo), a bevy of other animal specialties, and a handful of stars (including Jimmy Durante and Paul Whiteman and His Orchestra); all of this featured in the impressive, vast space of the Hippodrome. The visual spectacle was accompanied by a Rodgers and Hart score featuring a number of hit songs (including "Little Girl Blue" and "My Romance"). The show was attended by "everybody who's anybody," in the words of one New York journalist, including the "Somebodies of Park Avenue" and the "big shots of Broadway."[53] *Jumbo* was a hybrid work, advertised as "Bigger than a Show—Better than a Circus."[54] Abbott's first experience on a musical comedy was thus atypical. Abbott recalls the success of the show, along with his relative unimportance as book director: "*Jumbo* was a beautiful spectacle, but in the vastness of the Hippodrome the book was almost lost."[55]

Abbott's other collaborations with Rodgers and Hart—*On Your Toes* (1936), *The Boys from Syracuse* (1938), *Too Many Girls* (1939), and *Pal Joey* (1940)—are among Rodgers and Hart's major successes, and were more in line with what would characterize Abbott's contributions to musical theater. His early experience in straight theater, and the values—including narrative cohesion—associated with it, allowed him to approach a musical comedy with a less conventional mindset. And it would be fair to say that this quality went both ways—the reason that Rodgers and Hart were interested in working with Abbott was that they thought he could bring something different to musical comedy, including a shared interest in theatrical innovation. By 1935, Abbott's "touch" was seen as an asset to any show, even if he had never worked on a musical comedy. Critic Arthur Pollock credited Abbott with the sophistication of *On Your Toes:* "Now, with George Abbott working in collaboration, the result is something as fresh as ever and at the same time suaver and more finished."[56] By the time *The Boys from Syracuse* premiered, Abbott was "Broadway's most prolific impresario."[57] And it was during the run of *The Boys from Syracuse* that Abbott made theatrical history: "For the first time, four productions, each a unique and distinct enterprise, have been tenanting four theaters simultaneously, filling four auditoriums nightly, all produced by one man, each directed by one and the same."[58]

*Pal Joey* was Abbott's fifth collaboration with Rodgers and Hart. Two critics from the preview production in Philadelphia commented on the similarity between *Pal Joey* and Abbott's earlier production *Broadway*. Another review compared it to Arthur Hopkins's straight play *Burlesque*, from 1927

> Despite generally rave reception here there are some who think the show goes a little overboard on "book." That applies particularly to the second act when, after a whirlwind song-and-dance start, tempo changes completely and story

assumes straight dramatic aspects that recall "Burlesque" and "Broadway." ("Pal Joey" is almost certain to be tabbed as "Broadway" with musical trimmings").[59]

It wasn't, but at least one other reviewer remarked on the similarity. Linton Martin, of *The Philadelphia Inquirer*, compared the characters, and the setting:

> The analogy between the two productions is obvious. For each has as its central character a not-too-nice night club hoofer and crooner, against a bawdy, bleary background of dizzy café life, with its line of capering chorus cuties and more or less melodramatic musical comedy goings-on. The current show might accurately be called the Repeal-time equivalent of its celebrated speakeasy period predecessor.[60]

Despite any reservations that Abbott had, his familiar touch helped characterize the show, paving the way for its success.


## ROBERT ALTON

Abbott was apparently not the only one worried: both Abbott and Rodgers remember that Bob Alton had reservations about his role in the production. According to Abbott, "Bob Alton thought the show was hopeless and wanted to quit, but Rodgers persuaded him to stick it out."[61] Rodgers couched Alton's reservations in different terms:

> We had our first rehearsal, which was a read-through, one morning at a theatre, and at the end of the rehearsal Alton came to me and said, " I have to quit this. I can't go with it."
>
> I asked him why. He said because there was nothing for him to do. I took him to lunch and talked him into staying with it. Of course, he did a brilliant job. There was plenty for him to do—things like "Happy Hunting Horn," the old "Flower Garden of My Heart"—you know, a lot of burlesque numbers.[62]

Rodgers's account of Alton's reservations—that he was worried that there was "nothing for him to do"—reveals another potential liability with the show, which was echoed by critics: was this show too much like straight theater? Would music and dance fit neatly into the show, or would the dances need to be so realistic as to be artistically frustrating? While the show—a backstage musical—might on the surface seem ideal for the inclusion of music and dance, Alton's comment shows that he too was concerned over whether the straight elements of the book would conflict with the expectations of a musical comedy.

Robert Alton's contributions to *Pal Joey* began at least during the rehearsal process. Although Alton is not typically remembered as a creative force in the development of the so-called integrated musical in the way of Agnes de Mille or Jerome Robbins, prominent critics such as *New York Times* dance critic John Martin, and mentees including Gene Kelly, remarked on his ability to create dance routines that are "virtually inseparable from the dramatic action."[63] Alton was, however, a showman, born and bred in musical comedy. Critics and scholars have tended to erect a divide between the artistic merits of musical comedies and the so-called musical plays or integrated musicals at the height of the Rodgers and Hammerstein era, thus downplaying the influence of musical comedy veterans' work on the musical plays.

Musical comedy choreographers, especially, have been left out of the story, not least because dance of the period is usually considered merely decorative: a pleasant, albeit nonessential, bit of fluff. Few have acknowledged that without the vibrancy—and corporeal immediacy—of dance, no one would have attended these shows in the first place. When a show is remembered only for its script and songs, as *Pal Joey* usually is, it is exceedingly easy to discount the total effect of the production, which one critic called the "dancingest show in town."[64] Like the popular operas of Gioachino Rossini a century earlier, musical comedy operated according to a value system that privileged immediacy, and was usually based on tried-and-true formulas that satisfied an audience's expectations. This value is in contrast to those of a later era, defined by the book musicals of Rodgers and Hammerstein, which are couched in terms of artistic transcendence, organicism, and innovation (note the values in common with the canonic European symphonic music of the nineteenth century). Despite these value systems, there was room for innovation within conventional forms; Alton's contributions fall into this category (see Chapter 6).

## THE PHILADELPHIA TRYOUTS

Despite the initial reservations of Abbott and Alton, they eventually threw themselves wholeheartedly into the production. After about a month of rehearsal, a two-week tryout opened in Philadelphia on December 11. As *PM Weekly* reported, "On the evening of December 8th and the morning of December 9th," the cast and crew set out from Penn Station to the Forrest Theatre in Philadelphia:

> There were 16 principals, 25 chorus boys and girls, the author, two songwriters, the dance director and two assistants, scenic designer and assistant, orchestrator [Hans Spialek], orchestra leader [Harry Levant], producer, stage manager [Jerry White] and assistant [Edison Rice], three freight cars full of scenery and lights, and a flock of stagehands and musicians.[65]

The three days of rehearsal in Philadelphia were frantic. The company rehearsed at the Erlanger Theatre while Mielziner's sets were put up at the Forrest. The pit orchestra musicians had just received their music and the company was singing and dancing with them for the first time. The lighting wasn't set up yet and rehearsals, which began around 11 a.m., would last until 3 or 4 a.m. There were rumors that Vivienne Segal "didn't like her part," which might have contributed to the addition of the song "Love Is My Friend" (which eventually became "What Is a Man?").[66]

Gypsy Rose Lee, sister to June Havoc, was in attendance at the opening-night preview show, and her presence made the affair all the more exciting. One reviewer put it this way: "Miss Lee was there to see her sister, June Havoc, acquit herself with distinction as the comedienne of the proceedings, rather than to investigate the travesty on her and her art of clothes peeling in the Zip skit."[67] Havoc remembers the pure joy that her sister felt upon seeing her stop the show twice (for "That Terrific Rainbow" and "Flower Garden of My Heart") in a musical that was sure to be a hit: "From my first entrance, Gypsy sobbed with such gusto that Dick Rodgers left his position at the back of the house, walked down the aisle quietly, and brought her back to stand with him."[68]

During the rehearsals and tryouts in Philadelphia, "the ending was tried half a dozen different ways and finally set."[69] O'Hara, in an interview with the society columnist Lucius Beebe (whose nickname—Luscious Lucius—Hart mentions in the lyrics for "Zip"), said that the hard-boiled ending, in which Joey walks away from Linda in pursuit of a new "mouse," was inspired by a night out on the town in Philly. Apparently O'Hara, Abbott, Rodgers, and Hart went to a local nightclub and realized "that the dingus was no exaggeration of the corny night life we were dealing with, but, if anything, an understatement."[70] This adventure, reportedly, inspired the team to go for a less sentimental and more realistic ending. Two different programs for the preview show (one dated December 11 and one dated December 16) reveal that the fifth and final scene of act 2 was added during the printing of the two programs. In the first version of the ending, Linda meets Joey in his apartment after Vera leaves him, and Joey and Linda walk off together to have dinner and, presumably, begin a relationship. The December 16 program shows an added scene 5, titled "The Way Things Looked at Dinner Time," which very likely reflects the scene in which Joey and Linda say goodbye to each other. The December 25 program—opening night on Broadway—shows that scene 5 is set outside the pet shop, and that Kelly sang a reprise of "I Could Write a Book," now clearly revealed as a cheap pickup line (see Table 2.1).

The notices for the tryouts were enthusiastic, despite what some remembered. O'Hara, writing retrospectively, claimed that "[i]t is simply not true that the show and the novel [Pal Joey] got off to rave notices."[71] They were perhaps not universally rave reviews, but the reviews for the opening night of tryouts were overwhelmingly positive. Arthur Bronson, of the *Philadelphia Record,* and J. H. Keen, of *Philadelphia Daily News,* "dispense[d] with the suspense" and called it a hit.[72] Henry T. Murdock, of the Philadelphia *Public Ledger,* said that the show "should be in the 'moola' for a long time. And deservedly, for among other things it is one of the brainiest tune-shows we have ever seen. (So help us, we never expected to use THAT adjective on a musical comedy!)."[73] Murdock goes on to say that "if we have any quarrel with an otherwise good adaptation, O'Hara lets his 'hero' down too gently in the climax," alluding to the early version of the ending. Robert Sensenderfer, of the Philadelphia *Evening Bulletin,* remarked on the

*Table 2.1* Last scenes of act 2, preview programs, December 11 and 16, 1940, Forrest Theatre, Philadelphia, PA; Broadway program, December 25, 1940, Barrymore Theatre, New York, NY

| Preview Program, December 11, 1940 | Preview Program, December 16, 1940 | Broadway Program, December 25, 1940 |
| --- | --- | --- |
| **Scene 4.** Joey's Apartment | **Scene 4.** Joey's Apartment | **Scene 4.** Joey's Apartment |
| "Take Him" . . . VIVIENNE SEGAL and LEILA ERNST | "Take Him" . . . VIVIENNE SEGAL and LEILA ERNST | "Take Him" . . . VIVIENNE SEGAL, LEILA ERNST and GENE KELLY |
| Reprise: "Bewitched" . . . VIVIENNE SEGAL | Reprise: "Bewitched" . . . VIVIENNE SEGAL | Reprise: "Bewitched" . . . VIVIENNE SEGAL |
| | **Scene 5.** The Way Things Looked at Dinner Time | **Scene 5.** Pet Shop Reprise, "Book" . . . GENE KELLY |

perfect balance between the show's satire and its realism: "Mr. Abbott gives this night club life just the right touch. The rehearsals for the floor show as burlesqued are a scream, and as seriously given a delight. They are mixed in just the right proportion, too."[74] Alton's dances, Mielziner's set design (which Murdock described as looking "so real that you expect the waiter with the water any minute"), and John Koening's costumes certainly contributed to this delicate balance.[75]

## O'HARA (AND ABBOTT'S) SCRIPT

Beyond the ending, discussed previously, the script was reworked in other important ways between rehearsals and the premiere. It is sometimes difficult to decipher what portion of the script was the result of edits made by Abbott. There is little reason to doubt Abbott's assertion that he ended up having to revise much of the script, given that he was by then a seasoned "play doctor" and that this was O'Hara's first musical. Abbott remembered that O'Hara "came to rehearsals very little":

> When I needed rewriting I would do it on set, and later he would drop into the theatre, look over what I had done, go to an empty dressing room, rewrite the new material and depart. I am sure that *Pal Joey* must have been very important to him; but I can never remember his demonstrating any approbation or enthusiasm—nor, on the other hand, any criticism. He seemed disinterested, but I am sure that this was just his manner.[76]

Abbott's recollection is supported by other accounts, including O'Hara's own. As O'Hara explains in the anecdote outlined in Chapter 1 (in which Hart convinced a hungover O'Hara to come back to the theater after a long absence because he was "hurting George's feelings"), he wasn't absent because he didn't care, but because he didn't want to be in the way.[77] As this was O'Hara's first time working on a show, he very likely wasn't totally clear on the expectations of a book writer for a Broadway show. Admittedly, O'Hara didn't take criticism well, and the reality of building a show, which centers critique and revision, was very likely difficult for him to endure. O'Hara eluded to this in his interview with Beebe:

> "Getting a musical together," [O'Hara] says, "is one long process of backing and filling, hedging and trimming. Other kinds of copy I have done and finished for the printer in a single draft. My short stories for the New Yorker never have taken me more than two hours to write, and 'Appointment in Samarra' was set in type from the original and only draft because the manuscript was three days late and there was not time to make a carbon. Writing clear copy is beaten into any one's technique by the urgency of newspaper work, and I have learned to edit my stuff before I put it down."[78]

The three extant typescripts for *Pal Joey* show an illuminating and sometimes subtle transformation from preliminary script to stage. The preliminary draft, which O'Hara probably began writing in May, was not the "disorganized set of scenes without a good story line" that Abbott called it. O'Hara had a good sense of character—both Joey and Vera were fleshed-out characters, and Joey's exploits remained, for the most part, as they were laid out in his earliest script. The preliminary script did, to Abbott's credit, require a good amount of revision before it went to rehearsal. O'Hara, although expert at writing dialogue for novels and short stories, was not familiar with translating dialogue to the stage. His lack of familiarity with spoken dialogue can be seen in some of the smaller revisions, presumably Abbott's, which include added punctuation for pacing and indications of other characters' reactions to the text. Aside from the ending, another difference between preliminary and rehearsal script is that the character Gladys wasn't fully fleshed out (see Chapter 3 for how Gladys's role was expanded). Finally, in the preliminary script the "mannish" reporter Melba is revealed to be conventionally attractive, just as she had in the short story her character originated in (see Chapter 5 for an in-depth look at Melba).

A handful of changes occurred during rehearsal, as can be seen in a comparison between the rehearsal script and what appears to be the opening-night script. The rehearsal script, most likely written and edited during rehearsals, includes much more dialogue than what would appear in the opening-night script. The subsequent cuts, presumably initiated by Abbott, are especially prevalent in act 2; the dialogue between the scheming Lowell and Gladys was initially much longer. Other significant changes between the rehearsal script and the opening-night script relate to song placement, character development and motivation, and pacing. The revisions are excellent examples of how the collaborative process, and the rehearsal process, prompted changes within the script.

One revision that seems to apply to the script as a whole was probably led by Abbott: throughout the script, O'Hara's wordy name-dropping is cut down. A feature of his writing, O'Hara's name-dropping served to set time and place by reference to contemporary people, places, and songs. Here is a typical passage, which occurs in the rehearsal script during Joey's stage banter during act 1, scene 3:

> [JOEY]: At two o'clock we have Beatrice Lille, Clifton Webb, Noel Coward, Gertie Lawrence and a whole mob coming down from a party at Ernie Byfield's. We—certainly—have. In addition to that Bennie Goodman and Artie Shaw will be here with their clarinets. They—certainly—will. Beatie and Clifton and Gertie and Noel, and Bennie and Artie will be here directly—notice that directly—after the management serves the free champagne.[79]

Although this passage is tongue in cheek—Joey is obviously kidding the club's patrons, letting them know that he knows exactly what class of club he's working for—O'Hara goes a bit overboard on the description. It reads, perhaps intentionally, as if Joey were showing off, naming all the "class" acts he can muster, showing that he's a social chameleon of sorts. And as we know from O'Hara's pop-culture criticism, this is a feature that O'Hara had in common with Joey. Abbott probably cut the second half of this passage, as well as other passages that made reference to show-business people like Noel Coward, Harry Richman, Al Jolson, "Freddie" Astaire, and "Ty" Power, mobsters ("Colosimo. O'Banion. Capone. O'Hara. Moran. And even Lingel [sic]"), and even a William Morris agent (Billy "Square Deal" Grady) known for his show-business hustle.[80] Another cut passage, which occurred late in act 2 between Joey and a salesman, featured one of O'Hara's favorite subjects: cars. Here Joey and the car salesman go on for over two pages, referencing speed ("this car has been electrically timed at 123 mph"), make and model (Lincoln Continental, "Darrin Packard") and cost ("a little over seven Gs").[81] Although meant to show just how far Joey has come up in life, the passage is a lag on the momentum of the scene. Perhaps Abbott felt that the overly wordy name-dropping and superfluous descriptions interrupted the flow of the scenes described previously. Or, perhaps, he felt that O'Hara was trying too hard to prove his knowledge of pop culture.

Act I, scene 3, the nightclub scene when Joey first meets Vera, was significantly revised for opening night. The rehearsal script begins with a lengthy exchange between Joey and Linda, who had met in the previous scene in front of the pet shop. Linda has come to watch Joey perform, and here they continue to flirt. An entire page of dialogue between Linda and Joey (which characterizes Linda as vulnerable and tenderhearted) was cut.[82] In a revealing stage direction, also cut, O'Hara (or perhaps Abbott) states, "it is obvious to us that [Joey] has been surprised by [Linda's] frankness and the naïve interest in him that she has revealed."[83] This statement shows an uncharacteristic awareness on behalf of Joey; in cutting the line, O'Hara and/or Abbott simplified Joey's emotional life, and gave Linda less time to express herself.[84]

Another change that occurred during rehearsals relates to the motivation behind Joey's interest in Vera. In the rehearsal script for act 1, scene 3, Joey notices Vera before he is told who she is.[85] As stated in the stage directions, Vera "studies" Joey in the same way that he studies women. Joey finds her manner interesting, and, though he very likely understands that she is a high-society "dame," he doesn't strike up a conversation because he wants her money. Instead, he seems to be interested in sex, pure and simple. In the revised opening-night script, Joey is told who Vera is before he first interacts with her, knowledge that changes his motivations from the start.

The placement of the song "Bewitched" is a good example of how revisions helped move the story along. The song, which reveals Vera's obsession with Joey, was initially included at the end of act 1, scene 4, right after the phone call in which Joey tells Vera to "go to hell." At this point, the only interaction that Vera and Joey had was their brief dialogue in scene 3, at Mike's club, when they size each other up, and Joey subsequently insults her. The creators of the show—probably Abbott and Rodgers, specifically—probably realized that Vera, the world-wizened cynic that she is, would not move so quickly from interest to obsession (which "Bewitched" encapsulates, both musically and lyrically). And "Bewitched" is not just a song about obsession—it's an expression of Vera's surprise that she could be so hung up on such an unimpressive specimen. Narratively speaking, "Bewitched" is a culminating point. It was thus smart to instead give Vera the song "Love Is My Friend" in act 1, scene 4, which shows that it's not just Joey that diverts Vera, but the idea of love in general. Even more shrewdly, Hart eventually changed the lyrics to reflect a more cynical perspective—with the revised title "What Is a Man?"—befitting a sophisticated, experienced woman like Vera, replacing Vera's interest in love more bluntly, and accurately, with men (see Chapter 4 for more on the song placement and impact).

One of the more surprising takeaways in a comparison of the two scripts is that—despite a few cut passages where O'Hara uses profanity or references sexual assault—Abbott's edits seemed to heighten, rather than lessen, the toughness of the script. In the end, Linda is made to be more naive and less sympathetic, Joey is unmoved by Linda's sweetness, Vera is more cynical and less sentimental, and Joey and Vera's relationship is a straightforwardly contractual one, based less on mutual sexual attraction and more on Joey's cynical grasping for money and fame. The other cuts and revisions in the show follow this logic.

## "I'M TALKING TO MY PAL"

One major cut—which took place sometime between previews prior to opening night—was the elimination of the song "I'm Talking to My Pal." This song was initially included in act 1, scene 6, right before the dream ballet, and segued into the song "Pal Joey/What Do I Care for a Dame?," which remained in the show for the Broadway premiere. The elimination of a major song was significant, even more so because this was a book song, and gave a particular view of Joey's inner world. Ethan Mordden describes the song as demonstrative of Joey's true self: he's "the perfect con artist, he cheats everyone and trusts none but himself."[86] Andrea Most considers the song "one of the saddest songs in the play," especially insofar as it critiques the American myth of self-reliance; she sees the song as tragically hopeful in the face of Joey's certain failure.[87] The song, however, isn't sad; instead, it's jaunty and charming.[88] Hart's lyrics to the verse are paired with a syncopated, swaggering motive by Rodgers:

> I'm independent.
> I'm a descendent
> Of quite a family of heels.
> I'm never lonely.
> I and I only
> Know how my pal Joey feels.
> Who else would pay for my meals?

The song is much more sophisticated, musically, than Joey's other songs. As Paul Christman notes, since the song originally segued into "Pal Joey/What Do I Care for a Dame?," which then transitioned into the dream ballet, the two songs take on a verse-chorus-trio format (much like "What is a Man?," from act 1, scene 4), where "What Do I Care for a Dame?" serves as the trio. The lyrics to the chorus reveal what an outsider Joey is:

> I'm talking to my pal,
> Myself, my closest friend.
> And that's the only pal
> On whom I can depend. (See web example 2.1.▶)

The last lyric of the chorus is particularly revealing of Joey's social deviance, and Hart's close understanding of Joey's psyche: "I can't be sure of girls, / I'm not at home with men— / I'm ending up with me again." Like the song "Take Him," the female-female duet sung by Linda and Vera near the end of act 2 (see Chapter 4), this song rejects conventional attitudes toward relationships, instead creating the space for a nonconforming version of intimacy (in this case, Joey's relationship with himself). Rodgers's melody at the chorus is smooth, mostly stepwise in construction, and, like other songs in the show, centered around a prominent half-step motif (see Figure 2.1). Block has posited that since half-step motifs feature prominently in a number of narratively significant songs (including "What Is a Man?" and "Bewitched"), Rodgers might have been working to musically integrate these songs.[89] Certainly, the melodic construction of "I'm Talking to My Pal" helps bolster his idea. Given the family resemblance to other songs in the show, and given the song's focus on characterization, it is perhaps surprising that the song was cut. Why it was cut remains a mystery. The song might have been seen by Abbott and Rodgers as out of character for Joey—it demonstrates a brand of self-awareness that belongs more to Vera. "What Do I Care for a Dame?"—a

*Figure 2.1* *"I'm Talking to My Pal," chorus*

simple, brutal song—is more in line with Joey's capacity for self reflection. Or, perhaps the act 1 closer was simply too long.

## RECORDS

*Pal Joey* was created during a transitional period in American musical-theater history, when musical comedies were valued for their immediacy and were not necessarily built to last. This transitory quality can be seen in Richard Rodgers own records for the original production, which are scant. After his initial collaborations with Hammerstein, Rodgers would be much more conscientious about keeping records. His scrapbooks, for instance, are comprehensive for his later shows; much more of Rodgers's production material (including written exchanges between Rodgers and his collaborators on the show) exists for the 1952 revival production of *Pal Joey* than for the original production. The notion of "durability"—of whether or not a show would survive and retain its relevance for future generations—was just beginning to be discussed when *Pal Joey* premiered.

Later in his career Rodgers, to be sure, was not just concerned with revivals but also with his artistic legacy. His archival collections at the Library of Congress (the Richard Rodgers Collection) and at the NYPL (the Richard Rodgers Papers) are carefully curated.[90] His papers at the NYPL include extensive correspondence with Oscar Hammerstein; no correspondence with Larry Hart is included. Rodgers's Collection at the Library Congress is more inclusive—most of Rodgers's work with Hart is represented in holograph scores—but the full orchestrations are absent (for comparison, the collection includes eight full Rodgers and Hammerstein scores).[91] Rodgers himself was much more vocal about his process, and the artistic significance of his work, during his years with Hammerstein than in his years with Hart. From 1951 to 1967 he wrote at least ten major articles reflecting on music (for comparison, between 1939 and 1950, he wrote one). This relative lack of information has meant that Rodgers and Hammerstein's work is far more extensively documented in secondary literature than that of Rodgers and Hart.[92] No matter how frustrating this relative lack of information is to the researcher, it is part of the story of Broadway at this moment in time. Just as Beethoven saved many of his compositional sketches and personal letters, Broadway songwriters of this transitional period were beginning to toy with the idea of their work withstanding the "test of time," no matter how self-fulfilling that concept is. But the records that songwriters keep are certainly not the only type of records. *Pal Joey*'s vibrant history is alive in oral accounts, critical reviews, holograph scores by Rodgers, musical paraphernalia from music directors and orchestrators, correspondence, photographs, and so on. The remaining chapters of this book attempt to give insight into this fascinating and, yes, sometimes bewitching classic of the Broadway stage.

## *CHEZ JOEY*

• • •

## THE WORLD OF *PAL JOEY*

# 3

# DIGGING FOR DIRT
• • •
## INSIDE THE CLUB

It's pretty unpleasant and tough, but of course that may be just the ticket.[1]

So ends a letter from John O'Hara to his editor at the *New Yorker*, William Maxwell. O'Hara was writing in reference to one of his short-story submissions (the Pal Joey story "Ex-Pal"), but he might as well have been describing the ethos of Joey's most frequent haunt: the cheap nightclub. The audience's first impression of Joey's underworld—and of the clubs he performs in—is reflected in O'Hara's opening stage explanation:

> Cheap night club, South Side of Chicago. Not cheap in the whorehouse way, but strictly a neighborhood joint.[2]

O'Hara pinpoints, with his characteristic brashness, the class of low-cost club that proliferated during the mid- to late 1930s in Chicago, New York, and other large urban cities in the United States. *Pal Joey* intentionally reflects a lurid, slightly worn environment and comically crafts an important distance between the audience and the characters onstage.

Jo Mielziner's set helped dictate the atmosphere. Mielziner, the prodigious talent who began working in scenic design and lighting in the mid-1920s, had since that time seen a steady stream of success in both straight and musical theater. He worked with Rodgers and Hart on most of their post-Hollywood shows, beginning with *On Your Toes* (1936), and, prior to *Pal Joey*, he designed the sets and lighting for *I Married an Angel*, *The Boys from Syracuse*, *Too Many Girls*, and *Higher and Higher*. Mielziner's set design for the seedy act 1 club featured copious amounts of red velour: the set steps, the band platform, the canopy top, and the revolving side walls were covered entirely in the stuff, sometimes topped with cellophane fringe, indicating the intimate, if slightly tacky, atmosphere. This decor is in contrast to his other sets, such as Vera Simpson's bedroom, which included Continental features like "French type" telephones and a copy of *Vanity Fair*, and the tailor shop, which featured a chaise lounge covered in "grey quilted satin trimmed with yellow silk moss edging."[3]

*Pal Joey*. Julianne Lindberg, Oxford University Press (2020). © Oxford University Press.
DOI: 10.1093/oso/9780190051204.001.0001

Mielziner's sets are one example of how *Pal Joey* vividly illustrated the trappings of class. Some of the time, as in Mielziner's sets, these class markers are placed in the background, subliminally setting the tone of a scene. Other elements of the show, including most of O'Hara's dialogue, are more overt in class-based satire. The musical numbers performed in the clubs-within-the-show belong to the latter category, and are particularly effective at capturing the seediness of Joey and company's environment. These songs—"Chicago," "That Terrific Rainbow," and "Flower Garden of My Heart"—best characterize the atmosphere of the club; the first two are performed in Mike's South Side Club, and the last in rehearsal at the aspirational Chez Joey. All three are excellent character numbers and are meant to reflect poorly on the performers who sing and dance to them. Rodgers and Hart here faced an interesting dilemma: how might one write an effectively "bad" song that's also entertaining in its own right? Fortunately, they were no strangers to social satire; their musical parodies date all the way back to their Varsity Show days at Columbia, where they burlesqued frat manners and the social conventions of college life; later on—seen in both of the *Garrick Gaieties*—Rodgers and Hart would parody the conventions of musical comedy, operetta, and the then overblown revues seen at the Winter Garden Theatre. The original meaning of the word "burlesque," defined by Armond and L. Marc Fields—descendants of the great vaudevillian-turned-producer Lew Fields—as "a satire or lampoon using grotesque exaggeration and comic imitation," was well understood by Rodgers and Hart, not least because they themselves were mentored by the elder Fields.[4] With help from O'Hara's scathingly satirical dialogue, they turned their keen and critical eye toward the manners of cheap nightclubs and their patrons, balancing aural realism with carefully crafted social commentary. Their efforts resulted in some of the funniest numbers in the show.

## THE CHEAP NIGHTCLUB

The club songs in *Pal Joey* appear in three different forms: (1) musical numbers that take place in the club but are not explicitly marked as diegetic, are thematically integrated into the narrative, and flow naturally from the dialogue (this form includes "Happy Hunting Horn" and "Do It the Hard Way"), (2) rehearsal numbers—including "You Mustn't Kick It Around" and "Plant You Now"—that are set up as diegetic, but are musically similar to the other integrated dance numbers, and (3) club numbers that are straightforwardly diegetic, and capture a kind of seedy nightclub authenticity.[5] Both the first and second type of club song feature dance, and will be examined in Chapter 5 ("Joey Dances"); the songs discussed in this chapter are of the third variety. These "character songs," as Ethan Mordden rightly calls them, all comically comment on issues of taste, class, and respectability.[6]

Rodgers was inspired by O'Hara's script and the innovative realism at its core, which relates directly to the authenticity he imparted to the nightclub numbers.

In *Musical Stages* Rodgers remarks that O'Hara's short stories excited him precisely because of their grittiness, and because they represented a kind of narrative authenticity not seen on the musical stage:

The idea of doing a musical without a conventional clean-cut juvenile in the romantic lead opened up enormous possibilities for a more realistic view of life than theatergoers were accustomed to.[7]

Later Rodgers explains how he and Hart relished the chance to write the nightclub songs:

Because of the night-club setting of most of the musical's action, Larry and I were able to have fun writing numbers burlesquing typically tacky floor shows. We had all our chorus girls parade around with little on except headdresses representing flowers (in "The Flower Garden of My Heart") and colors ("That Terrific Rainbow").[8]

It's relevant that only three of the nightclub tunes are full-out parodies: like the songs themselves, too great a percentage of realism in the show would have distracted from O'Hara, Rodgers, and Hart's satirical commentary. And since Rodgers wrote "scores and not isolated song numbers," he was careful about song placement and tone.[9] And they seems to have struck exactly the right balance. Nearly all of the opening-night reviews by the most prominent New York critics commented on how cleverly the show characterized the nightclub and their patrons. Richard Watts Jr., of the *New York Herald Tribune*, said,

The new show is not merely a picture of Joey. It is a bitter, satirical and yet strangely realistic account of the flora and fauna of the night clubs, done with such zest and scornful relish that it achieves genuine power.[10]

Burns Mantle, of the *New York Daily News*, remarked that "the satire on Chicago night club crudities is often screamingly funny."[11] Sidney B. Whipple, of the *New York World-Telegram*, commended Abbott's direction, and, along with the staging, praised Rodgers and Hart's ability to capture the authentic atmosphere of a cheap nightclub:

Mr. Abbott has staged the musical comedy with a seeming inside knowledge of the Grade C "clubs" that provide Mr. O'Hara with his background. He burlesques the managers, the hangers-on, the waiters, the dances and the songs that are seen and heard in a joint that is bound to be called Chez Joey. His costuming is in humorous keeping with the atmosphere. It is star spangled, gawdy [sic] and abbreviated. The lyrics of Lorenz Hart, to the music of Richard Rodgers, are equally brilliant in their reflection of the night club life—smoky and blue.[12]

The most effective satire lampoons contemporary life, and the type of club described by Whipple proliferated during this period. Further, this kind of club was a relatively new addition to the landscape of urban nightlife.

In a *Times* feature titled "Hi-De-Ho! The Night Clubs Turn 'Em Away" from March 1937, columnist Bosley Crowther posits that the repeal of Prohibition (in late 1933) legitimized nightclub life, and observes that by 1937, the economy had recovered enough that people began patronizing nightclubs in droves. He outlines the different classes of club, including the swanky Upper East Side spots, which featured "continental" entertainment "in the way of a few slick performers." He goes on to say,

> By far the most persistent type of after-dark club, so far as numbers is concerned, is the intimate, generally rowdy and innately fly-by-night affair of which several dozen are scattered about the city. These hey-hey places, with their hot bands and barrel-house atmosphere, work on the principle that the more a customer consumes in the way of powerful waters the more he wants to kick up his heels (and vice versa), the disposition most cordially encouraged is one of indiscretion [. . .] Entertainment is fast and flashy—hot-cha singers, fan dancers, strip-tease artists and the like—and acknowledges few inhibitions.[13]

The class of club just described captures the atmosphere, entertainment, and clientele seen in the clubs in *Pal Joey*. In his *New Yorker* stories O'Hara references multiple details that capture the atmosphere, including the characterization of typical audience members ("dopes that wouldn't know if I was Toscanini, Al Rinker, or Brooks John or myself. All they cared about was if I sang Deep Purple 75 times a nite"), the pay Joey received ("the joint where I am singing and m. c-ing in is satisfied with my work and it keeps me in coffee & cakes but not much more"), and the generally sleazy atmosphere ("Female lushes that they would stand right under me while their escorts were giving them a little going over and I and the band were not suppose [sic] to see it. Oh no, just dumb, is what we were").[14] Crowther's column reflects developments in urban nightlife felt in New York, Chicago, and other major urban areas; O'Hara's original *Joey* stories are born from these developments, and Rodgers and Hart capitalized on the contemporary relevance of the seedy nightclub.

## THE MUSIC

In Rodgers and Hart's long list of collaborations, there exists just one attempt at writing for a nightclub venue: the Billy Rose–produced *Fifth Avenue Follies* (originally titled *Billy Rose's Sins of 1926*), which premiered in January 1926.[15] Rose, with pressure from Hart's persuasive father, had previously provided Rodgers and Hart with $1000 toward *The Melody Man*. A persuasive man himself, Rose then approached Rodgers and Hart about writing the songs for a Broadway-style revue. The club itself—the 5th Avenue Club—was a new commercial venture for Rose, located on the posh corner of Fifth Avenue and 54th Street, and was dry, as opposed to Rose's earlier, and seedier, Backstage Club. Still, *Fifth Avenue Follies* was full of adult humor, sexual innuendo, and the devil-may-care attitude that characterized the jazz age. For an example, take Hart's line from the song "In the

Name of Art," originally performed by Cecil Cunningham, Doris Canfield, and Bert Hanlon: "Our show must please both movie stars / And ladies of virginity!/ It's proper to be dirty, / But it's dirty to be cheap!"[16] The number "Do You Notice Anything?" was used as a gag piece: the song was peppered throughout the revue, and with each reiteration the chorus girls had lost a bit of their clothing (unfortunately, the lyrics for this song have been lost). Despite these "naughty" elements, this was Rose's attempt at a classy production, and a far cry from the manufactured cheapness of the club tunes in Pal Joey.

## SETTING THE TONE: "CHICAGO"

The song "Chicago"—an upbeat, hokey number—appears in both the preview and opening-night programs during act 1, scene 3, directly after the Pet Shop Scene, when Joey and Linda first meet.[17] Lehman Engel once remarked that "Chicago" belongs "to the vulgar 'mammy-song' school associated with Al Jolson."[18] And, indeed, the corny overeagerness of the song is what makes "Chicago" an excellent character piece, marking Joey, the chorus girls, and the club itself as "tacky."

"Chicago" features the chorus girls, and marks the first time that they perform for an audience within the show. While the song captures the enthusiastic, if amateur, antics of the chorines, it is also pinpoints the atmosphere and class of the type of club where Joey feels most comfortable. Though seemingly reflective of the chorus girls, it makes a great deal of sense to connect this song to Joey; even though the title doesn't appear at act 1, scene 1 in the opening-night program, it's almost certain that the Broadway premiere opened with Joey singing this number, mid-audition, for the owner of the club where most of the show's action takes place.

In an annotation to the Library of America's edition of the script—included in the landmark collection of sixteen libretti, published in 2014—editor Laurence Maslon states that "what Joey sings as the curtain goes up is not specified in texts or the score of the 1940 Pal Joey."[19] The typescript that Maslon based the Library of America edition on sets the scene thus, without any indication of what song is sung: "MIKE the proprietor is sitting at a table stage left. JOEY has just finished singing."[20] While the song title doesn't appear in the program in act 1, scene 1 (in either the preview, premiere, or revival of the show), it does show up here in the published libretto of the revival (from 1952) and in the published piano-vocal score from Chappell (the published score refers to the act 1, scene 3 iteration as a "reprise").[21] While Maslon asserts that what Joey sings is not "specified [. . .] in the score of the 1940 Pal Joey," there is evidence to suggest otherwise. In both Harry Levant's conductor score and what appear to be the orchestral stand parts for the 1940/1941 production of Pal Joey (currently uncatalogued and housed in the theater library at the Rodgers and Hammerstein Organization), the song "Chicago" appears as the first number in the book, following the overture.[22] The number—a penciled-in "1"—suggests that there was some revision of the score (in all of the orchestral stand parts the "numbers" are penciled in), and this order may not reflect opening night. These parts were, however, used during the original run of the show. And the function of the song, even as it simultaneously acted as an up-tempo show opener, was dramatic.

Levant's score indicates that the full orchestra accompanied Joey as the curtains rose on act 1, scene 1, and then dropped out after sixteen measures, leaving the solo piano to finish out the form. Great care was taken with the orchestration to draw the audience into Joey's world, made evident by the smooth transition to what finally appears as diegetic piano, accompanying Joey's audition in the club.[23] It's possible that Spialek suggested this orchestration, but given its dramatic function, more likely that it originated with Rodgers and/or Abbott.[24]

Before settling on "Chicago," the creators considered other songs for Joey's audition. In the preliminary script, O'Hara suggested that Joey sing Rodgers and Hart's "Blue Moon," or a number like it ("a young man is singing; say the last few bars of 'Blue Moon'").[25] O'Hara perhaps suggested the song because of its popularity; it's the sort of song that Joey and Mike, as well as the audience, would have already known, and the type of song that a singer might audition on, reinforcing the dramatic context.[26] But "Blue Moon," it can be argued, doesn't have the dynamic vitality required of an opening number. In the rehearsal script (written after Rodgers and Hart began writing the songs, but before tryouts), the song indicated here is "You Mustn't Kick It Around."[27] This song might have been suggested by Rodgers, or perhaps by George Abbott, both of whom were at nearly every rehearsal, and who were invested in the dramatic impact of act 1, scene 1. In the opening-night script, "You Mustn't Kick It Around" appears later in the same scene and is, like "Chicago," a syncopated, mid-to-up-tempo song, full of contemporary jazz-inspired rhythms. "Kick It" is, however, much more sophisticated than "Chicago." Choosing "Chicago" over "Kick It" may indicate that Rodgers and Abbott were interested in opening the show with a song that captured the "tackiness," as Rodgers described it, of both Joey and the club he's trying to gain employment at. Further, O'Hara originally intended for Joey to feature in the act 1, scene 3, chorus version of this tune, too:

> JOEY sings song.
> REPRISE—First chorus Number
> He finishes it, and the girls come on and do a dance, while HE stands to one side, ogling, slapping, preening himself.[28]

"Chicago" is an entertaining, flashy show-within-the-show opener. The song is comprised primarily of a single rhythmic motif—a syncopated quarter note followed by an eighth note, bookended by another quarter—which expands, contracts, and adjusts emphasis over the course of the chorus (see Figure 3.1). The drum part calls for the drummer to emphasize the upbeats and pepper the tune with rimshots and other percussive effects. The rhythmic energy of the piece is appropriate to a large chorus number of this kind, imbuing the piece with an upbeat, fresh, youthful energy. O'Hara originally described the song that eventually became "Chicago" as "a real cheesy, razzamatazz chorus line affair with plenty

There's a great big town On a great big lake called Chi-ca-go

*Figure 3.1 "Chicago," chorus; syncopated motif*

of bumps and grinds."[29] The thirty-two-bar chorus reflects a standard AABA construction.

Scott Miller connects "Chicago" to other "empty city-songs," including Rodgers and Hart's own "Manhattan," which first premiered in the *Garrick Gaieties* of 1925, their first major professional show together.[30] "Manhattan" was a sincere, clever song in praise of their hometown—less "empty" than loving homage—while "Chicago" is much more generic, and the only nod to the actual specificity of place is the reference to that "great big town / on that great big lake." Dominic Symonds describes "Manhattan" as descriptive of the "insiders' New York, neither the city that trumpets its pretensions in big band stabs or dizzying skyscrapers, nor the 'helluva town' that is seen to the tourist."[31] In contrast, "Chicago" is so hollow that you can nearly take out the name of the city and replace it with any three-syllable locale.

Here Hart demonstrates his skill at writing the deliberately cheap knock-off lyric. The rhyme scheme is simple: the first two A sections of the chorus follow an abc/abc rhyme pattern, and there are no clever internal rhymes or interesting assonances. The rhythmic emphasis of the first two lines (There's a great big town / On a great big lake) falls, rather clumsily, on the repetition of the word "great." The "greatness" of Chicago is never precisely indicated: at the bridge Boston is dismissed as faux England, New Orleans as faux France, and New York as a characterless "anyone's." On the culminating lyric one is led to expect to hear something specifically special about Chicago. Instead, the audience is left with the line "But this great big town / On that great big lake / Is America's first / And Americans make / Chicago," punctuated with a flirty "hiya boys." Hart's lyrics are intentionally prosaic, save for a few clever references, including the reference to "ten cents a dance" (the title of a song from one of their earlier hits, *Simple Simon*), and his potential reference to the America First Committee.[32] In the 1952 revival, the chorus was instructed (presumably by Alton) to "salute" at the latter reference.

Rodgers's writing emphasizes the clumsiness of the lyrics. The contour of the chorus melody is comic: though in a singable range, the disjointed melody covers the span of an octave in just two bars, and requires comic effort from the untrained singers (sort of the aural equivalent of a cartwheel or a particularly difficult physical maneuver jammed into a dance routine for the sake of flashiness). The affect created—of trying too hard—is in direct opposition to the contained gentility of, for instance, a Ziegfeld number. In this context, effort equals coarseness, and is tied in part to the class of club "Chicago" is performed in. Just as the visible effort seen in many vaudeville acts was related to hard work and working-class identity, "Chicago" is reflective of the talent employed at a club of this kind. The apparent effort of the song is tied to inexperience, and perhaps to excess sexual energy (a topic parodied throughout *Pal Joey*), two elements that are connected to class and social position, and to the character of the girls who sing the song.

Beyond its disjunct construction, the melody also frequently aligns with the root of the chord on chord shifts, and always lands on the obvious resolution at cadences. This of course doesn't automatically make a song *bad*, but in combination with the disjointed contour of the melody, the static rhythmic idea, and the cut-rate lyrics, the tune is deliberately prosaic. Rodgers might very well have been parodying bad or amateur songwriting. The arrangement enhances this "bad" songwriting. The chorus girls sing in unison, appropriate to a chorus number, but in contrast to some of the more sophisticated chorus numbers, like "Plant You Now, Dig You Later" (with an interesting vocal arrangement by Hugh Martin). The rhythmic drive of the piece keeps the energy moving forward, typical of a throwaway razzmatazz number of this kind.

### "CHICAGO" ON VINYL

Depending on the recording, "Chicago" can lean toward the high, upbeat energy of a chorus line, or in a more sexually suggestive direction. Take, for instance, the cast recording from the 1952 revival (released by Capitol Records and featuring Helen Gallagher, who played Gladys in the stage revival, and chorus singers)—the tempo is between 144 and 152 beats per minute (bpm), and the orchestra is tight and upbeat, giving the impression of a line of chorus girls hurrying around in formation. At the dance break, the orchestra shifts affect every eight bars: for the first eight bars the full orchestra plays at full volume; in the next eight the rhythm section pulls back to a half-time feel, followed by another eight with full orchestra; in the last eight measures of the dance break the orchestra is underpinned by a "jungle-like" groove on the tom-toms, used frequently to denote ethnic otherness (as in the "jungle music" craze of the 1920s and early 1930s) and sexual excess (see Table 3.1, and web example 3.1 ▶). At the coda the performance loosens up considerably, shifting from a straight groove (which rides on the front end of the beat, thanks to the tight high-hat backbeat) to a swung, laid-back half-time feel, full of smeary trumpet interjections. This section is unabashedly sexual, perhaps indicating a shift in movement (or attire) on the part of the chorus line. Remember that O'Hara suggested in his draft script that this song feature "plenty of bumps and grinds." Beyond any hints at sexual suggestiveness of flirtatiousness (also present in the "Hi ya boys" line that caps off the number), this recording effectively highlights the amateur nature of the performers, and the parallel quality of the club. Significantly, the well-known Columbia recording omitted "Chicago," perhaps because it doesn't match the sophistication of the other tunes on the record, despite being important to the audiences' understanding of the chorus girls.

*Table 3.1* Graphic representation of the dance break in "Chicago," released by Capitol Records, 1952

| Eight measures: | Eight measures: | Eight measures: | Eight measures: |
| --- | --- | --- | --- |
| full orchestra at full volume (tempo shifts up to approx 160 bpm) | half-time feel; melody features brass | full orchestra; melody broken up between saxes and brass, which trade every bar | four measures with underlying "jungle groove," followed by four measures featuring chorus |

Commentary on the quality of the dancers can be traced to O'Hara's Joey stories, when Joey meanly mocks the abilities of the chorus girls, treating them quite differently from how he treats women of higher social classes. Here is a typical passage, from the short story "A Bit of a Shock":

> Well we are rehearsing and I am doing a patter with the kids in the line where they come up to me one by one and ask me what I want for Xmas and it is all the double entender [sic]. But it is the way I play it that is funny. I do not know exactly who to compare myself with but for illustraton [sic] Maurice Chevalier. I am having trouble with one of the mice because she is mugging even in rehearsal and as far as I could make out is doing her impresson [sic] of Kate Hepburn and any minute will go into her impresson [sic] of L. Barrymore. A poor man's Shiela Barret [sic]. In there punching and trying to crab *my* act. So I gave up in disgust.[33]

This passage demonstrates Joey's meanness, his characteristic vernacular, the bawdy routines typical of this nightclub, and his belief that he deserves better than his surroundings. These prose sentiments are made tangible by their translation into song. Though "Chicago" viscerally reflects the atmosphere of the club, it also reflect the world that Joey hopes to transcend.

## RED HOT MAMA: "THAT TERRIFIC RAINBOW"

"That Terrific Rainbow" appears in act 1, scene 3, shortly after the song "Chicago." In between "Chicago" and "That Terrific Rainbow" Joey plays emcee, flirting with Linda, telling ribald jokes, teasing the chorus girls, and kissing up to Vera and her party, whom he has just met. In one particularly revealing passage, Joey jokes bawdily about a supposed striptease performed by the character Valerie, and then continues with a joke about a male patron who was apparently more interested in the drummer than in Valerie. The overtly sexual tone of this passage—frankly joking about carnal lust and homosexuality—sets up the song to follow. "That

Terrific Rainbow," a raucous and sexually suggestive blues, features the character Gladys, the frowsy nightclub singer brought to life by June Havoc, an up-and-comer who was at the time most well-known for being the sister of Gypsy Rose Lee. Gladys is joined by the chorus girls and the character Victor (played by the then unknown Van Johnson).

Although initially just a background part, the character Gladys developed into one of Joey's primary antagonists, eventually teaming up with the capriciously named Ludlow Lowell to blackmail Joey and Vera. Gladys is also one of the more disreputable characters in *Pal Joey*: she's sexually experienced and she speaks in the rough vernacular of the club. Gladys isn't truly a villain, though—more than any other character, she represents the comically seamy world of the nightclub. June Havoc's rendition of Gladys was so appreciated by Abbot, O'Hara, and Rodgers that the role was greatly expanded. In her second memoir (*More Havoc*), Havoc remembers the rehearsal process for *Pal Joey* and her initially small role:

> *Pal Joey* began rehearsals in November. I was thrilled to vertigo as I received my contract. It said "As directed." We rehearsed in two theatres. On the stage of one the actors worked with Mr. A., as he was carefully called. The other stage was noisy and exciting. That was where Robert Alton worked with the dancers. At the first reading I had sat in the circle with Mr. A. and the actors. My part was very small. I didn't appear until the second act was well under way. That was at first.[34]

She reportedly befriended the production stage manager, Jerry Whyte, and began "prowling" between the two theaters, "burning for more to do."[35] Havoc says that she learned some of the dance numbers, and began a "crusade" to get Gladys into the first act.[36] She caught the notice of Alton, and eventually auditioned for a newly composed tune:

> A few days later, after rehearsal was over and the company had departed for the evening, I watched from my hiding spot in an upper box. Rodgers had brought in a new song. He played and sang. Everyone laughed. "Tomorrow," he said, "find a funny voice who can really move, okay?" Auditions were planned, the golden group departed. I emerged from my secret place, pouncing on Jerry Whyte. If he hadn't snagged a copy of "Terrific Rainbow" for me so I could work on it all that night, I could never have beat out my competitors at the auditions the following day.[37]

Though it is difficult to say how much Havoc's story is embellished, Abbott, O'Hara, and Rodgers were beguiled by Havoc, and what's more, the critics loved her. Burns Mantle called her a "comedienne with Fannie Brice tendencies"; Richard Watts Jr. observed that Havoc "reveals real comic gifts," and even Brooks Atkinson's famously negative review counted Havoc among the show's blessings, complementing her "broad, rangy style" and her "funny burlesques of nightclub routines and manners."[38] A staff writer for *Time* remarked that "Brazen little June Havoc, sister of Burlesqueen Gypsy Rose Lee, does a sidesplitting parody of all kinds of café singing and yields nothing to her sister in ability to make a rhinestone gown twitch with significance."[39] Havoc's skills as a vaudeville comedian greatly aided her in this particular tune, which called for (1) a knowledge of burlesque humor, (2) an intimate understanding of the boredom of a tacky floor show, and (3) the ability to convey both boredom and sexual suggestiveness through a comically tacky tune (see Figure 3.2).

If Havoc's account can be relied upon, "That Terrific Rainbow" was added during rehearsals. In the rehearsal script (written after Rodgers and Hart began writing the songs, but before Gladys's role was fully fleshed out), a section of the stage directions for act 1, scene 3 state, "the night club again, now inhabited. A GIRL is singing 'I'M BLUE' song and JOEY walks on during song."[40] Whether or not this title was a placeholder for a song yet to be written or a reference to "That Terrific Rainbow" is unclear. The 1940/1941 orchestral stand parts for "That Terrific Rainbow" are printed on heavier stock and in the hand of a different

*Figure 3.2  Van Johnson (Victor) and June Havoc (Gladys) in "That Terrific Rainbow";
NYPL Digital Collections, photo by Vandamm Studio, 1940*

copyist than that of most of the other songs in the show, potentially confirming Havoc's account that the song was added later in the creative process.

Whatever the case, the song appears to have undergone changes, either during rehearsals or during the course of its initial run. According to annotations to Harry Levant's conductor score (which possibly reflects the premiere of the show, but certainly its first run), the verse to "That Terrific Rainbow" was preceded by a bluesy instrumental rendition of the last sixteen measures of the chorus. The chorus/refrain is much more raucous than the verse, and this addition would have better set the mood for the performance to follow. Perhaps Abbott wanted to set the disreputable mood early on, rather than begin with the verse. The published piano-vocal score by Chappell reflects this revision.

After the bluesy introduction Gladys enters with the verse, which is cheekily coy and absent of any syncopated rhythms. The verse is dominated by a simple motivic idea (motif 1), rhythmically comprised of a quarter-note pickup on beat four, followed by another quarter note, and then punctuated by a half note; this simple rhythm repeats at measure 2 with descending instead of ascending pitches, creating a pleasant melodic arc (see Figure 3.3). The half-note emphasis on beats two in measures 1 and 2, however, corresponds clumsily with the lyrics, which emphasize, respectively, the words "had" and the second syllable of "color"—surely this ungainly text setting was intended by Hart, who rarely emphasized text that was so lyrically and thematically unimportant (later on the same musical passage corresponds with the equally unimportant word "have," and the second syllable of "duller"). Measure 3 propels motif 1 forward with a chromatic ascent up a minor third, from E to G, over a dominant seventh chord. This measure, punctuated as it is by the slinky chromatic line, is musically seductive. An innocent "bell" sounds on beat three of measure 4, punctuating, and comically contrasting with, the chromatic line (the "bell" part is indicated in Rodgers's holograph score for the piece, and in the published piano-vocal score). Although "That Terrific Rainbow" is not performed as a striptease act, the play between musical markers of innocence and seduction would have been familiar to those acquainted with burlesque acts.

The bridge of the verse inverts the contour of motif 1 (here measures 10 and 12), descending rather than ascending in pitch, over a string of secondary dominants ($D^7$–$G^7$–$C^7$). The text corresponding with the half notes highlights the third syllable of "resistance" in measure 10, and the third syllable of "existence" in measure 12, emphasizing the near rhyme. Measure 9 also introduces Hart's heavy-handed word painting on the word "weakened": the two syllables are matched by a descent down a fifth from A to D.[41] The last four measures return to the rhythm

Figure 3.3 "That Terrific Rainbow," verse

of motif 1, emphasizing perhaps the most hackneyed lyrics in the song: the half note occurs on the syllables "py" and "hap" of the line "I'm happy and unhappy too." This comically unoriginal line jars hilariously with the legacy of a lyricist who once rhymed "hero" with "queer ro-mance," also on a sequential motivic pattern. Whatever is lost in lyrical sophistication, however, is made up for in the rich characterization of Gladys: the chromatic flirtatiousness juxtaposed with the innocent bell motif, coupled with the hackneyed lyrics and obvious word painting, are rich in playful satire.

The contrast between the coy verse and the raucous chorus amplifies what Rodgers called a burlesque of "typically tacky floor shows."[42] The chorus is a syncopated, swung blues, and Rodgers's sketch for "That Terrific Rainbow" shows him playing around with the bluesy feel. In the final version of the song Rodgers marks the entrance of the voice with a syncopated quarter note on the upbeat of three, while his sketch indicates a dotted figure entering on beat four (see Figure 3.4). Three measures later in his sketch (corresponding to the lyric "I'm blue for you"), Rodgers ends the phrase with a quarter note on beat four, leading to a tied half note in measure 4. In the final version of the song the phrase ends with a syncopated dotted quarter note, followed by the same tied half note. It seems that in the end Rodgers opted for a harder swinging, more syncopated chorus. This rhythm would have emphasized the sex and heightened the comedy.

Of particular importance in the chorus is the sustained "blue" note featured in measure 3. In the published score the blue note is an E♭, the flat seventh of an F⁷ chord (typically understood as a I⁷ in a blues progression, but also acting as a dominant seventh, temporarily tonicizing B♭ in the fifth measure of the chorus). Idiomatically, the gesture is a clear reference to the blues, and the tempo marking indicated in the 1962 Chappell score reads "tempo di blues."[43] The call and response between Gladys and the brass section reinforces the idiom. Another of Rodgers's sketches (labeled "Color Me") shows that the lyrics—"I'm a red hot mama / and I'm blue for you"—were all-important: the blue note, rather obviously, aligns with the word "blue."

Beyond idiomatic gestures like the blue note and the swung, syncopated rhythms, the harmonic progression—especially the aforementioned harmonic shift in measure 5, which tonicizes the subdominant—clearly references the blues. Though not organized in a standard twelve-bar or sixteen-bar format, the first eleven measures of the thirty-two-bar chorus, excepting measure 12, follows a typical blues progression. Measure 12, the last measure of what would typically be the "turnaround" (leading to a repetition of the chorus), instead sets up a harmonic extension (measures 13–16), completing the first half of

Figure 3.4 Richard Rodgers's sketch for "That Terrific Rainbow," titled "Red Hot"; Box 12, folder 40, Richard Rodgers Collection, Library of Congress

the chorus. The second half of the chorus repeats the melodic figuration and harmonic progression of the first six measures of the chorus; the remaining ten measures act as another harmonic extension, using standard techniques like strings of secondary dominants, in addition to some spicy altered chords (like the $D^{alt}$ in measure 25), to bring Gladys home. In this way we can see that Rodgers adjusted a typical blues progression to satisfy the constraints of a standard thirty-two-bar song.[44]

In this context, the language of the blues is meant to signal disreputability. "That Terrific Rainbow" is a rendition of the "dirty" blues: slow, hard-swinging, full of brass growls, and deliberately sexual. Hart references an earlier era, and its frowsy nightclub singers, with the first line of the chorus, "I'm a red hot mama." The term "red hot mama" is rooted—like the idiomatic musical features of the song—in the 1920s. Cassell's *Dictionary of Slang* refers to the "hot mama" or "red-hot mama" as either a "flighty young woman" or a "large, hedonistic woman, often an habitué of saloons, bars and nightclubs."[45] The terms "large" and "hedonistic," in addition to the reference to singing and nightclubs, ties the "red hot mama" to the blues queens of the era, whose lyrics mimicked the slang inherent in the title. The chorus to Bessie Smith's recording of "Worn Out Papa Blues" (1929), for instance, contain the following lyrics: "I'm a red hot woman / Just full of flamin' youth. / I'm a red hot woman / Just full of flaming youth. / You can't cold me daddy, / You no good, that's the truth."

The object of Smith's song—the male partner who can't handle the sexual appetite of his woman—is a common blues trope. The sexual excess implied by these lyrics has long been coupled with blackness, following a long history of tying blackness to the body (and whiteness to intellect and the mind). The fact that "That Terrific Rainbow" is so exceedingly corporeal is intentional, and the disreputable nature of this kind of physicality is related, in part, to historical depictions of blackness. Still, the most iconic singer tied to the term "red hot mama" was white. Sophie Tucker, who was billed as the "last of the red hot mamas," might be considered one of the grandmothers of the frowsy white nightclub singer, and a direct ancestor of Gladys. Like Smith's, Tucker's song "Red Hot Mama" (1924), also plays with the idea that her sexual appetite is far too much for a mere man, ending the chorus with the lyrics "'Cause I'm a red hot mama, red hot mama, / But I'll have to turn my damper down."[46] Mae West's persona, although considerably more sexual, was cast in the same mold.

Hart's lyrics at the chorus of "That Terrific Rainbow" are connected to the sexual excess of the "red hot mama," but they're deliberately cheap, and rather than emphasize the sexually powerful blues queen, they play upon a theatrical gimmick: "I'm a RED hot mamma / But I'm BLUE for you /I get PURPLE with anger / At the things you do." With each mention of color, the lighting changed accordingly. This effect contributed significantly to the "tackiness" of the number, and Mielziner's "gelatin colors" (which survive in the Jo Mielziner Papers at the NYPL for the Performing Arts) reflect the clever lighting design. This device was purportedly well received. Whipple said this of the performance:

That Terrific Rainbow, sung by the terrific June Havoc with terrific color effects and terrific costumes, is a colossal, devastating commentary on the kind of a floor show that seems so magnificent after two drinks of Chez Joey's scotch.[47]

Whipple got the club wrong (by this point the audience has not yet been introduced to Chez Joey), but his comment neatly captures the importance of the lighting, costumes, and song to the central satire. Though conceived by Mielziner, this lighting effect has persisted in subsequent stage productions, most recently in the 2008 revival, in which it even becomes part of the comic dialogue: as Gladys, played by Martha Plimpton, sings, "But you burn my heart up / with an orange flame," a purple wash shines down on her, prompting her to yell "orange! Orange flame!" as an aside. In the 1957 film version of *Pal Joey*, this is one of the few club tunes that remain on the soundtrack, and the only one performed with lyrics. The lighting design in the film matches Mielziner's original concept, and is perhaps the only remaining visual remnant of the clever/cheesy color effect.

The corporeality of "That Terrific Rainbow" is present in both the music and the choreography. While the specifics of Alton's choreography for the original production seem to be lost (Alton himself stated that he never wrote charts or graphs), Max Meth's conductor score for the 1952 revival, also choreographed by Alton, includes movement cues, as well as cues for non-notated instrumental effects. Most of the penciled-in markings occur on the chorus—Meth indicates various "bumps" and "grinds," probably referring to drum and brass effects, though they might also relate to the dancer's movements (in this case, by Helen Gallagher and members of the chorus line). The word "shake" appears above the measure at the end of the line "but you're white and cold," which is reflected in the Capitol recording, when the chorus girls punctuate the line with a dramatic "brrrr!" that perhaps, on stage, was accompanied by theatrical shaking. Meth could have alternately been indicating a brass shake. When Meth writes "walk- arms out" over the third measure of the chorus, it probably indicates the chorus line, but the "walk" written over measure 5 is probably indicative of the walking bass line. While it is tempting to assign Meth's scribbles to the frustratingly absent choreography, perhaps the more important takeaway here is to acknowledge that this song is exceedingly corporeal. "Bump," "grind," "walk," "shake," "strut," "swing," "kick" and other terms scribbled on Meth's conductor score evoke the visual, the aural, and the corporeal planes of perception. The fact that some musical gestures evoke certain kinds of taboo movement (in this case associated with burlesque entertainment and striptease acts) is the very reason that this song would have sounded disreputable.

## "THAT TERRIFIC RAINBOW" ON VINYL

The available recordings of "That Terrific Rainbow" highlight the intentionally disreputable elements included in the score. The earliest commercially recorded version of the tune, sung by Barbara Ashley, appears on the Columbia record, released in 1951. The Columbia recording includes a stellar orchestra, up to the task of improvising in the idiomatic way of jazz musicians in a club setting. Take, for example, the clarinetist in the introduction (See web example 3.3 ▶). Spialek's original orchestration features two clarinets in the introduction, doubled for the most part at the third, but the performer on the Columbia recording glides easily in and out of the written notation (see Figure 3.5 for the written clarinet parts).

Most performances of the verse communicate the boredom of a nightclub chorine, a stark contrast to the virtuosic energy of the introduction. Hart's lyrics leave open multiple choices in performance; they could even be construed as sincere: "my life had no color / before I met you. / What could have been duller, / The time I went through?"[48] The manufactured tackiness of the lyrics paves the way for comic performance choices, as in the 1995 *Encores!* recording, when Vicki Lewis actually yawns on the word "duller." The affective shift at the chorus also opens the door for comic performance choices. The Capitol recording demonstrates this shift well. Helen Gallagher (Gladys in the revival and the Capitol recording) positively growls on the text "I'm a red hot mama," mimicking the trombones that precede her entrance (see web example 3.2 ▶).

It remains significant that "hotter" sounds, in this context, are related not only to sexual excess, but also to class, urban setting, and race. Marked as deviant, and allied with the thrill of visiting and viewing marginalized places and people, "That Terrific Rainbow" is perhaps most indicative of the sort of display expected by a nightclub slummer. As with "Chicago," Rodgers's music brings much of the comedy, as well as the authentic club feel, to the song. The affective distance between the mock-sincere sung introduction and the raucous chorus is intentionally wide. The chorus—featuring improvisatory instrumental interjections, a loose

Figure 3.5 *"That Terrific Rainbow," intro, Clarinets 1 and 2 (composite from Reed books 1 and 3; original stand parts)*

rhythmic feel, and comically rowdy choreography—marks the tune as both comic and deviant. The audience simultaneously laughs at the characters on stage while sampling the freedom associated with this sort of sexual display.

## A FAILURE OF TASTE: "FLOWER GARDEN OF MY HEART"

If "That Terrific Rainbow" was an indication of the cheap aesthetic taste of the club and the chorus of dancing girls, then "Flower Garden" is their, and Joey's, ill-informed interpretation of high-class entertainment. The song—a puffed-up, corny parody of a production number in an old-fashioned revue—appears shortly into act 2, scene 1, and is the audience's first look at the newly opened Chez Joey. The idea for the scene and song was entirely O'Hara's, who described the scene in detail in his preliminary draft script:

> It is late in the afternoon of the opening. The band in shirtsleeves. Vernon Macfarlane, or a reasonable facsimile, is screaming at someone on a ladder, and others are screaming at him to shut up. In this connection I have a song idea which is That Somewhat Different Idea. The song is Richman corn, the flower number kind of thing—every girl reminds me of a flower; here is a hydrangea, here is a crocus, etc. a YOUNG MAN stays in the spotlight, holding out a hand for Hydrangea, who is in silly nudish costume. He never quite lets her get all the way in the light, but hands her away with one hand as he reaches for Crocus with the other. He looks at the fannies etc in a way to make them ridiculous, and is mugging terribly, even in rehearsal.[49]

O'Hara's "Somewhat Different Idea" was apparently well received by George Abbott—the song was realized nearly exactly as O'Hara described it. "The Flower Garden of My Heart" is performed right after intermission, and is thus the first number after the act 1 dream ballet, in which the audience was introduced to the club of Joey's dreams. This number contrasts mightily with Joey's balletic fantasy, revealing just how far off Joey's aspirations are from reality.

"The Flower Garden of My Heart" features a Ziegfeldian tenor, the character Gladys, a specialty dancer, and chorus, a core of whom are fussily outfitted as different flowers; Cecil Smith and Glenn Litton called the number a "horticultural ballet."[50] Rodgers wrote a nostalgic throwback tune, punctuated here and there by sexually suggestive "hot" breaks of both the swing and Latin varieties. Hart's lyrics riff on the "moon/June" trope, with some clever double entendres, and the number features a recitation section for each of the flowers. The performers are meant to be out of their element. Their overwrought pretentiousness— signaled via set, costumes, music, lyrics, and choreography—is portrayed as a failure of taste, configured as a desperate, and ultimately laughable, display of their boorishness.

A particularly smutty sight gag, reconstructed via photos and prop lists, demonstrates this display well. A group of chorus girls, dressed as mild Bo Peeps, water their "garden" over a fence, constructed by the legs of male dancers (see Figure 3.6). Items from Mielziner's include "9 small hedges—brought on by boys" (who in photographs appear to be wearing them on their heads) and "8 small watering cans," used by the women, decorate the scene.[51] The overtly sexual innuendo of this scene—the hedges are encouraged to "grow" under the tender ministrations of their gardeners—is treated as a fumble: the chorus dancers are characterized as so inherently sexual that they don't know how to behave in polite company. This theme continues throughout the song.

In spite of, or more accurately because of, its aesthetic missteps, "Flower Garden" provided ample room for laughter. Cue sheets from the original production provide helpful information on how the song was laid out, and who was featured in each section. The song began with an instrumental introduction that was probably accompanied by dance (perhaps featuring the aforementioned human garden fence). Following the introduction, The Tenor, originally performed by Nelson Rae, enters with his saccharine ballad, comparing the various attributes of the flowers in his metaphorical garden to the object of his affection, performed by Gladys.[52] The chorus is followed by a dance break, which might have featured a specialty toe dancer, first performed by Shirley Paige, who also featured in the act 1 dream ballet. After the dance break the flowers are featured, each stepping forward to recite a short hokey rhyme specific to her flower type, which included Violet, Sunflower, Heather, Lily, Lilac, and finally the American Beauty Rose. After this comically hackneyed interlude, Gladys takes up the melody, comically out of

Figure 3.6 Chorus members water their garden, "Flower Garden of My Heart"; NYPL Digital Collections, photo by Vandamm Studio, 1940

depth, barely able to reach the high notes written at the close of the song.[53] June Havoc, as Gladys, ludicrously costumed in a fussy, flower-beladen gown by John Koenig (complete with toe shoes), was particularly skilled at burlesquing the out-of-her-element nightclub diva turned ingénue. As with "That Terrific Rainbow," Havoc hustled to win the part. As she tells it,

> Rodgers played them "Flower Garden of My Heart." It went over big, too. "Find a tatty soprano tomorrow."
>
> Auditions were set. That night, after blessing Jerry again, I blessed the vocal coach who had given me a few five-dollar lessons. That investment had liberated a high B-flat I hadn't known what to do with until now. As extra insurance, I sang in my high voice while on point. Oh, joy, I got the number.[54]

The comic image of a "tatty soprano" singing in her upmost range while balancing en pointe reflects the core effect of this song: it tries—devastatingly—too hard.

The published piano-vocal score for "Flower Garden" includes, like all of the extant musical material from the original run of the show, an instrumental intro-duction in D, a key far removed from the chorus, which is in E♭. No commercial recordings of the song, or the 2008 Broadway revival, include this introduction, and there is some question regarding its dramatic function. The twenty-eight-measure intro, which uses musical material from the verse to follow, is charac-terized by dotted figures, decorative triplets, and attractive part writing for the orchestra. A dominant seventh chord (A[7]) on the last measure of the introduction anticipates a cadence in D, but is instead followed by a deceptive arrival in B♭, the ♭VI of D. This deceptive cadence is accompanied by a change in musical character; the expressive marking in measure 29 is "Maestoso," and the meter broadens out to a dramatic $\frac{12}{8}$ ; the subdivisions here are stressed by the brass and percussion, while the upper strings execute a sweeping, ornamented, melodramatic phrase.[55] Though it is difficult to precisely reconstruct the action that took place during the instrumental introduction, it is reasonable to assume that any sharply con-trasting sections were created so for laughs.[56] It is possible that the "Maestoso" marked the entrance of either The Tenor, Gladys, or both (in promotional pho-tos, The Tenor and Gladys are seated on a bench together). Whatever the case, the lack of subtlety here was meant to reflect the coarseness of the performers on stage. Rodgers carefully exploited contrasting moods and musical ideas to accomplish this.

After the overwrought introduction, The Tenor entered with the verse, paro-dying starry-eyed Ziegfeldian tenors like John Steel, who in the 1920s introduced characteristic songs comparing women to music, flowers, and even flying insects.[57] The Tenor's melody is made up of short symmetrical phrases, and features long, grandiosely held-out notes. The verse is twenty measures long, organized into an A(eight) A(eight) B(four) pattern; the mostly stepwise melody is punctuated at the ends of phrases by triplet eighth notes in the woodwinds and violins (these cues are included in both the published piano-vocal score and the original stand parts). Hart's rhyme scheme is a very "on the nose" aab pattern, including lines such as the following: "I haven't got a great big yacht, / But I'm contented with my lot" and later, "I do not own a racing horse, / But that don't fill me with remorse." Hart's lyrics here mix slang ("my lot") and vernacular dialect ("that don't fill me with remorse") with grandiose imagery, relaying a comic mixture of pretentiousness and vulgarity that meshed perfectly with O'Hara's description of the scene.

A good deal of the humor in "Flower Garden" is derived from the contrast between Rodgers's melodramatically affected music and Hart's deliberately tacky lyrics, which are particularly hackneyed at the chorus. Here, Hart allows The Tenor to revel in the manufactured romance of some of the most corny lyrics he ever wrote: "In the flower garden of my heart / I've roses as red as your mouth / Just to keep our love holy I've got gladioli / And sunflowers fresh from the south" (later, Gladys sings the cleverly smutty double-entendre "Love is the archer and you are the dart / In the flower garden of my heart"). Rodger's melody at the chorus broadens out in an expansive melodramatic arch. The tune begins with a romantically overblown, arpeggiated major seventh tonic chord followed by two half notes and a sustained whole note. The smooth melodic arc is contrasted by the following four measures, which are characterized by an accented eighth note on beat two. These eighth notes (followed by a breathless rest), bring out The Tenor's description of his love's physical attributes: measures 5–7 read "I've got violets [rest] as blue as [rest] your eyes" while the corresponding phrase on the repeat reads "I've got roses [rest] as red as [rest] your mouth." According to the original stand parts, the vocal rests are highlighted by an ornamented oboe figure and bell accent on beat three, heightening the manufactured innocence of our romantic tenor (these cues don't appear in the published score). This same technique was used in the verse to "That Terrific Rainbow," though in that instance it contrasted mightily with Gladys's nature. Here, the orchestration plays up the "corny" affect—these little rests seem to emphasize the evidently innocent thrill felt by The Tenor, reinforcing his naive innocence, and comically contrasting him with the debauched flowers, who are soon to parade on stage.

The recitation of the flowers, which follows a dance break, is deliberately outrageous. John Koenig's costumes heightened the over-the-top effect: as each of the flowers in the garden is introduced (Violet, Sunflower, Heather, Lily, Lilac, and the American Beauty Rose), the dancers come forward in ridiculous outfits designed to both display their bodies and demonstrate a misguided attempt at sophistication. The American Beauty Rose, for instance, is dressed like a cigarette girl, and draped with a garland of roses; when she turned her back to the audience, a stylized cutout of Harry Richman appeared on her backside, complete with three-dimensional hands, each clutching a bouquet of roses (see Figure 3.7). Miles White's costumes for the 1952 revival were even more revealing (see Figures 3.8, 3.9, 3.10 and 3.11).

The flowers' recitation occurs over another iteration of the chorus. In both the original production and in the revival, the chorus is punctuated by commentary from the orchestra. As the first flower, Violet, finished her comically prudish recitation ("Violet—the flower dear old grandmother wore / Away 'way back in the days of yore"), the trumpets played her off with a swing figure. The swing figure is meant to be suggestive, related to jazz, hot-spot nightclubs, burlesque, and

*Figure 3.7  American Beauty Rose with Harry Richman detail, 1941; photo by Dmitri Kessel, The LIFE Picture Collection/Getty Images*

striptease. After the final flower (The American Beauty Rose) recites her lines, a syncopated rhumba rhythm plays her off. In one of the only known filmed excerpts from the 1940/1941 production (filmed on a handheld 8 mm camera, with no audio), the chorus dancer who plays the part of American Beauty Rose turns around and shakes her backside, presumably in time with the rhumba rhythm. Harry Richman, now facing the audience, shakes right along with her.

While none of the critics at the time commented on it, Rodgers and Hart had already tried their hand at spoofing Ziegfeldian excess. The *Garrick Gaieties* of 1926, the second installment of the revue, featured the song "American Beauty Rose" (alternately called "Say It with Flowers"), part of a show-within-the-show operetta parody entitled *The Rose of Arizona* (which in turn spoofed Friml's *Rose-Marie*, as well as Lew Fields/Victor Herbert's *The Rose of Algeria*). Like "Flower Garden," "American Beauty Rose" was a sendup of every overblown Ziegfeld show that featured a parade of chorus girls in ridiculous getups. The lyrics at the verse

Figure 3.8 Eleanor Boleyn as "Sunflower," c. 1952; courtesy of the Museum of the City of New York

read almost as a set of directions for "Flower Garden": **"Say it with flowers / If you're falling in love; / I've said it with flowers / To the one I'm dreaming of."**[58] At the chorus, Hart lists a handful of flowers and their corresponding countries—bluebells for Scotland, tulips for Holland, and so on—which come to represent women from all around the globe, who, the audience is made to understand, "can't compare" to the "American Beauty Rose." The title of the song (and the show-within-the show) might well have been referencing the song "Rose of the World" (by Victor Herbert, from the Lew Fields–produced *The Rose of Algeria* from 1908), a yearning, overdramatic duet. Rodgers described the lyrics in "American Beauty Rose" as "purposely horrible" (in reference to the "nonrhymes" "drizzle" and "Brazil," and so on); they are, like "Flower Garden," deliberately prosaic.[59] The fact that Hart also referenced the American Beauty Rose in the last part of the recitation section in "Flower Garden" is surely not coincidental—he, and perhaps Rodgers, were connecting the spoof number in *Pal Joey* not only to another Ziegfeldian parody, but also to what, by 1940, would have been a very out-of-date sort of production number. O'Hara, who dreamed up the scenario for "Flower

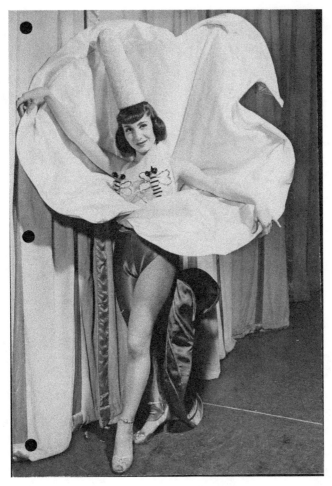

*Figure 3.9  Lynn Joelson as "Lily," c. 1952; courtesy of the Museum of the City of New York*

Garden," might have had Rodgers and Hart's earlier parody in mind. He was, after all, encyclopedic in his knowledge of music from the 1920s.

Although O'Hara's idea for "Flower Garden" was clever, it was not the first time that a musical comedy featured a number that was meant to be a dramatic failure within a larger show. Irving Berlin and Moss Hart's *Face the Music* (1932) included the production number "My Beautiful Rhinestone Girl," an overblown, saccharine song that also featured a sentimental tenor and chorus. As in "Flower Garden," the lyrics are comically corny, featuring such lines as "In your eyes there's a light divine / And like rhinestones they seem to shine. / Bless the miners who mine stones / That turn out to be rhinestones." The song is meant to provoke laughter, setting up the action to follow in act 2, where the song (and the show it comes from) is revised.[60] Although a failure of taste, the song is entertaining. Jeffrey Magee, in his analysis of the number, states that "Berlin succeeded in doing a rare

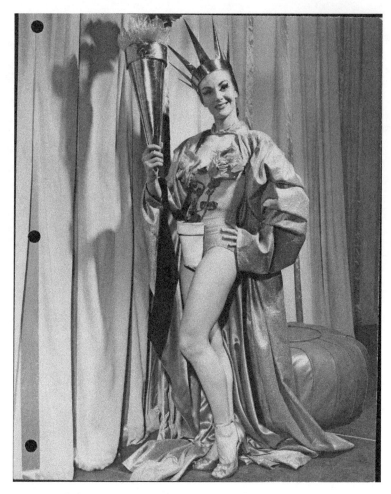

*Figure 3.10 Ethel Martin as "American Beauty Rose," c. 1952; courtesy of the Museum of the City of New York*

thing: writing a good exemplar of a bad song."[61] If critical reaction is any indication, Rodgers and Hart succeeded in kind.

## CONCLUSION

All of the numbers performed in the club—at either Mike's club or Chez Joey—satirize poor taste. Rodgers and Hart had to walk a fine line in the creation of these songs, crafting entertaining numbers that would also lampoon the genres in question. The Rabelaisian humor of the songs, particularly "That Terrific Rainbow" and "Flower Garden," descends from the genres that built Broadway,

*Figure 3.11 Helen Gallagher as "Gladys"/Toe dancer, c. 1952; courtesy of the Museum of the City of New York*

particularly vaudeville. More than that, though, some of the key creators of the show were exceedingly familiar with the types of club under scrutiny.

O'Hara and Hart, in particular, were known to frequent clubs of just this sort; according to O'Hara, Joey himself was modeled on "some night club masters of ceremonies I know."[62] Hart's exploits with Milton G. ("Doc") Bender, whom Samuel Marx and Jan Clayton call an "uninhibited swinger" and who was a lifelong friend to Hart, have become a part of Broadway lore; in the 1920s Hart and Bender frequented back-alley speakeasies as well as the more notorious variety, including Texas Guinan's hot spots.[63] Later, Gene Kelly remembers first spending time with Hart "not in Sardi's or the Stork Club or '21,' but the cheap saloons around Eighth Avenue and 45th Street."[64] Rodgers said that Hart was interested in *Pal Joey* because it was set in a world that he was familiar, and perhaps comfortable, with: "He had spent thousands of hours in exactly the kind of atmosphere depicted in the stories and was thoroughly familiar with the Pal Joeys of this world."[65] Hart, at his cynical best, was allowed free rein to include all of the adult innuendo, vernacular, and attitude of this environment. And Rodgers was encouraged to revel in tasteless clichés, exploiting the more disreputable sounds associated with nightclubs and with "hotter" jazz orchestras. Sidney Whipple's second review of the show, a psychoanalytic think piece from 1941, acknowledged Rodgers and Hart's success on this front:

> The very music contributed by Mr. Rodgers is a burlesque (beautifully contrived) of the rackety-bang, drum-busting technique of a hot-spot orchestra. The lyrics, which seem to have shocked a few people, are no more lurid than those the young people hear all the time in our Temples of Midnight Culture, and they are much cleverer.[66]

The explicit nature of the show might have been shocking in the context of the Barrymore, but not to one acquainted with the sights and sounds of some of the more disreputable night spots flanking Broadway. Frank Vreeland, remarking on the "predominantly masculine gender of audiences," brought everything back to the audience with the following remark:

> These audiences are quicker to respond than burleycue patrons, catching innuendoes on the fly even before the cast bat them out. We've often wondered whether burlesque performers are so lackadaisical because the audiences are so comatose, or vice versa. Certainly no such complaint can be leveled against players or spectators in [Pal Joey], and both sides of the footlights are quite unflagging in digging for dirt.[67]

No matter what perspective the audience took—that of the outraged social reformer, the titillated voyeur, or some angle in between—the realism inherent to the three diegetic club numbers was effective, drawing the viewers into the world that was being caricatured. Rodgers and Hart had to balance these comic sendups against the book numbers, which lent sympathy to characters who were, on the surface at least, exceedingly hard to sympathize with.

# 4

## I COULD WRITE A BOOK (MUSICAL)

• • •

## THE BOOK NUMBERS

It seems to me just possible that the idea of equipping a song-and-dance production with a few living, three-dimensional figures, talking and behaving
like human beings, may no longer strike the boys in the business as merely
fantastic.[1]

When Wolcott Gibbs, writer and sometimes-editor for John O'Hara at the
*New Yorker*, wrote the preceding statement, he wasn't particularly interested
in talking about the music in this unusual musical comedy.[2] Instead, he was
impressed that Joey, "the most single-minded character in contemporary fiction,"
"had been transplanted intact from print to stage."[3] Most critics, in fact, were
preoccupied with the literary qualities of the script, rather than how setting the
story to music might inflect a literary work. Yet the songs in *Pal Joey*, especially
the book songs, gave new life to O'Hara's characters.

Most secondary literature on *Pal Joey* focuses on its two hit songs: "I Could
Write a Book," and "Bewitched." Indeed, these two songs were recorded by a great
number of jazz and popular groups (see Chapter 7), and are now considered part
of the American songbook. Most recordings usually take the songs completely out
of their narrative context—"I Could Write a Book" and "Bewitched" have mostly
been interpreted as love ballads, or sometimes even torch songs (even by an artist such as Frank Sinatra, who was well aware of their original context). While
there is nothing unique about this performance practice—many of Rodgers and
Hart's songs, as well as Porter's, Berlin's, Kern's, and the Gershwins', have lost
their connection to their original contexts—*Pal Joey*'s songs were unusually cynical in their original setting, jarring with the best known recordings.

*Pal Joey* includes song-and-dance features, diegetic club songs, and the novelty
song "Zip"; the integrated book numbers, however, represent the greatest proportion of song type. Rodgers and Hart wrote six "book songs" for the show. By "book
song," I refer to songs that give a sense of the inner emotional life of a character;
relate directly to how we understand that character's relationship with others;
evoke sympathy from the audience; and do the important work of confirming,
foreshadowing, or changing direction in a narrative. In *Pal Joey*, the book songs
include "I Could Write a Book," "What is a Man?," "Bewitched," "What Do I Care

*Pal Joey*. Julianne Lindberg, Oxford University Press (2020). © Oxford University Press.
DOI: 10.1093/oso/9780190051204.001.0001

for a Dame?," "Den of Iniquity," and "Take Him" (see Chapter 6 for a discussion of "Dame"). These songs are both narratively and musically linked. The diegetic numbers burlesque specific musical styles and the dance features are more contemporary in feel; the book numbers, on the other hand, rely less on specific contemporary popular styles, and more on the equally idiomatic style of Rodgers and Hart. This type of integrated song was of course not new to Broadway, or to the shows of Rodgers and Hart. The degree to which these songs lend sympathy to hard-to-like characters, however—characters who might otherwise be dismissed as mere cutouts of pulp-fiction villains—is remarkable. These songs helped balance O'Hara's hard-boiled book, giving the audience the opportunity to identify with a group of character types they would otherwise be wary of associating with. The unconventional nature of many of the book songs, however, which critique, mock, and upend traditional musical comedy tropes, made way for a new critical discourse concerning musical theater.

## "I COULD WRITE A BOOK"

"I Could Write a Book," the first of the book songs to appear in the score, is usually understood to be a love duet. In the context of the story, however, it is a disingenuous pickup line offered by Joey, and taken seriously by Linda. The song takes place in act 1, scene 2, also called the Pet Shop Scene, so named for the setting where Joey and Linda face the audience, looking through the window of a pet shop (see Figure 4.1). The scene comes directly from John O'Hara's Joey story titled "Bow Wow," in which Joey first meets—or, as described in the original story, "cases"—Linda.[4] The scene remains very close to its original version—Joey, passing in front of a pet shop, stops upon noticing Linda and feigns interest in the puppies in the window. As in the original *New Yorker* story, Joey tells Linda an obviously fabricated tale about his dog Skippy, who was supposedly run over by Joey's family's Rolls Royce; that was before, as Joey tells it, his family lost their fortune in the crash.[5] Linda takes the bait, crying over the memory of the fictitious Skippy, and over Joey's supposedly tragic family history. O'Hara heightened the comedic effect of the dialogue by juxtaposing Joey's lies about his upper-crust upbringing with his Chicago wise-guy vernacular (i.e., "Yes, I never go by the house on Park Avenue without I have to laugh.").[6] In the stage version the audience isn't privy to Joey's inner monologue; O'Hara's original story, however, amplifies Joey's predatory nature by including the following line: "I had cased this mouse and she was pretty but I knew she was no society debutante. Probably a stenog out of work but very cute."[7]

"I Could Write a Book" is prompted, in true book fashion, by dialogue that relates directly to the lyrics in the song:

JOEY: I didn't mean to bore you with the story of my life.

MUSIC CUE

Figure 4.1 *Gene Kelly and Leila Ernst from act 2, scene 2 of Pal Joey, c. 1940; NYPL Digital Collections, photo by Vandamm Studio*

LINDA: Oh, I wasn't bored. I feel honored that you confided in me. I hope you tell me some more.

JOEY: I probably will. You inspire me. You know what I mean.

(SONG: I COULD WRITE A BOOK)[8]

The encounter between Linda and Joey is based on pretension and lies, on Joey's part, but the lyrics to Joey's first verse contradict his previous falsehoods. Here Joey expresses that he is in fact uneducated (despite attending, as he tells Linda, "Princeton College"):

> A B C D E F G,
> I never learned to spell,
> At least not well.

The last line of Joey's verse, "I'll strike while the iron is hot," shows how hungry he is for conquest. Common in Broadway love duets (then and now), this verse muddies the boundary between what is thought and what is spoken aloud: the vulnerable nature of verse allows for the illusion of intimacy between Joey and Linda. The tone of the song, accomplished primarily through Rodgers's music, is what makes the piece sound more like a love ballad than a pickup line.

Far from replicating Joey's bluster, "I Could Write a Book" instead gives the audience a taste of Joey's charm, seen through the eyes of Linda. Joey's opening verse has a meditative affect, featuring thirteen consecutive A♭ quarter notes, the

A  B  C  D    E  F  G  I   ne- ver  learned to   spell.   At   least  not   well.

Figure 4.2  "I Could Write a Book," verse

Figure 4.3  Rodgers's first sketch for "I Could Write a Book," chorus

simplicity of which might also be related to Joey's inner life (see Figure 4.2).[9]
Geoffrey Block sees the repeated pitches, paired with the recitation of the alpha-
bet (and, later, numbers) as indicative of a kind of "textual realism," in which
Hart's text matches Rodgers's music.[10] The song is not, however, a parody: it is
meant to beguile, rather than critique. Rodgers's clever use of a descending chromatic line (heard in the cellos and bassoons) creates an almost hypnotic effect,
effectively captivating the listener, just as Joey captivates his "mouse."

As opposed to the opening verse, the chorus of the song is plainly sung from
Joey to Linda, and is grand in musical and lyrical gesture. Mark Grant has argued
that the song is a "four-beat Broadway foxtrot"; the background rhythm of the
chorus certainly outlines the feel of a foxtrot, which is characterized by a slow-
slow-short-short pattern, here reinforced in the melody.[11] As Block has discussed,
Rodgers tried out three different versions of the opening chorus melody, unusual
for a composer who produced melodies, often in their final form the first time,
at an extraordinary rate. Specifically, Rodgers's sketches show different versions
of the all-important first four measures of the chorus, in which Joey seeks to
"hook" Linda. Rodgers's first sketch of the chorus melody is somewhat stagnant,
aligning it with the stasis of the verse, and does little to project the casual charm
of Joey (see Figure 4.3); the second full measure of the figure outlines a broken
tonic chord (over a V chord in the harmony), grounding the line, and approaching
the E in measure 3 by ascending stepwise motion. In the second sketch (labeled
"alt"), Rodgers shifts the repeated G up a step to A, allowing for more lyrical
movement, while also retaining the broken chord in measure 2; the jump down
a fourth between measures 2 and 3 in this version, however, is somewhat inel-
egant, undercutting the effortlessness of Joey's attempt at a casual pickup (see
Figure 4.4). Rodgers's third and final sketch (labeled "alt II") is very similar to the
final version of the figure; here Rodgers reaches up to a B in measure 1, and then

Figure 4.4  Rodgers's second sketch for "I Could Write a Book," chorus (labeled "alt")

follows by moving in stepwise descending motion for the following two beats (see Figure 4.5).[12] He also stays in the tonic here, not shifting to the dominant until the seventh measure of the chorus. Between the first and the third sketch, one can see Rodgers transform the opening melody from a fairly static figure to something much more dynamic, and, not accidentally, in keeping with Joey's seemingly suave exterior.[13]

Despite the charm of the melody, the form of the song is fairly simple and quite repetitive: Joey may be a cad, but he does not have a complex inner life (a lack that is also reflected in "What Do I Care for a Dame?"). The chorus—organized in a simple ABAB—is without significant lyrical or musical development. Graham Wood refers to the chorus of "I Could Write a Book" as an unusual manifestation of Rodgers's "parallel-period chorus," a frequently used form in the songs of Rodgers and Hart, especially their early work. A parallel-period chorus—typically thirty-two measures—is broken down into an even two-part structure where the first A section repeats after the first sixteen measures (in contrast to the also-typical AABA form, what Wood calls "lyric binary" form, where musical contrast, rather than repetition, appears after sixteen measure). This form can be organized into an ABAB or ABAC form—the defining feature is the return to A at the halfway mark. Wood considers "I Could Write a Book" to be unusual; Rodgers would usually create some kind of interest in the last four to eight measures of the chorus (what Wood calls the "final limb") by varying or adding to the previously stated musical material; he cites Rodgers and Hart's "Thou Swell"—where the last four measures of the last A section vary dramatically in both pitch and rhythm from the first A—as a good example of this variation. In "I Could Write a Book," however, despite the alteration of "some minor melodic and harmonic details" and a different cadence, Wood asserts that "the overall effect is one of sameness rather than difference."[14] This is especially true of the rhythm, which is identical in the "final limb" of the final A section. Further, Wood explains that "such relatively unmodified final limbs are quite rare for Rodgers."[15]

This relative narrative monotony may be what prompted Alec Wilder to say that the song is "curiously old-fashioned, much in the manner of Kern and really without any more than a well-shaped but, to me, uninspired melody."[16] If Rodgers was driven by character and situation in the creation of this song, what Wilder reads as shallowness is very much in tune, so to speak, with the scene: "I Could Write a Book" is not meant to be a moment of dramatic revelation, but a demonstration of Joey's depravity. To be sure, if Joey's pronouncement of love (his declaration that he loves Linda "a lot") were the dramatic point of the song, it wouldn't appear buried in the second A section of the first chorus. The dramatic function of the song is to demonstrate that Joey will say anything to make a

Figure 4.5  *Rodgers's third sketch for "I Could Write a Book," chorus (labeled "alt II")*

conquest. The fact that the song is charming is both in line with the scene, viewed through Linda's eyes, and a happy respite for the audience. These qualities do not mean that the song is not well crafted—it is intentionally well crafted—but it is by no means meant to be profound.

While there are no extant recordings Gene Kelly singing the song, a radio broadcast survives of Kelly reenacting the scene surrounding it, featured on November 19, 1945, on Paul Whiteman's Sunday broadcast *Your Radio Hall of Fame*.[17] Featuring Martha Tilton as Linda, the dialogue between Kelly and Tilton is based on O'Hara's short story rather than the Broadway script. Considering the other songs featured on the show, it is curious that they don't sing "I Could Write a Book." Kelly's Chicago wise-guy vernacular, however, is heard in full effect. Kelly overacts in his appreciation of the dogs in the window (affecting a kind of over-the-top baby talk), and is very solicitous of Linda; when he tells the tragic story of Skippy, his voice falters and takes on a wistful tone (see web example 4.1 ▶). One can see how Kelly's version of Joey was at once exasperating, ingratiating, and somehow forgivable. His methods of seduction are so transparent that it is hard to believe that Linda takes him at face value. Perhaps she is meant to be truly that naive or, as is hinted at in act 2, perhaps she likes Joey despite his obvious lies.


## "WHAT IS A MAN?"

"What Is a Man?," originally titled "Love Is My Friend," was added to act 2, scene 4 sometime during previews. Prior to previews (and reflected in the programs for the opening-night preview show on December 11) the song "Bewitched" was in its place. Apparently sometime during the tryouts Abbott realized that Segal needed a new number, "not because she was beefing," as *PM Weekly* stated, but "because the story needed it."[18] The song certainly adds to the motivation behind Vera's infatuation with Joey. The dialogue preceding the song is rather brutal. Joey makes a telephone call to Vera, who had in the previous scene stormed out of Mike's club after first meeting and then being insulted by Joey. He now tells her he lost his job and is thus leaving town because of her: "I just thought I'd tell you to go to hell before I leave."[19] In the story, this moment is Joey's big gamble: he treats her this way because he suspects she might appreciate it, as opposed to the typical flattery and false praise that marks her interaction with men. This exchange between Joey and Vera is almost identical in both the rehearsal and opening night scripts; the rehearsal script, however, follows with Vera's rendition of "Bewitched." The obsessive nature of the song, created by both music and lyrics, is surprisingly intense for this moment in the book. It makes little sense that Vera, who had met Joey only once, would fall so hard. Further, it was clear even early on that "Bewitched" would be a significant standout number—it called for a more dramatically significant spot in the show.

"Love Is My Friend," which would eventually replace "Bewitched" in this scene, didn't appear in the program until the Broadway opening. Although once thought to be lost, the original lyrics to "Love Is My Friend" have been recovered; the lyrics to the verse of "What Is a Man?" and "Love Is My Friend" are identical, but the chorus lyrics vary significantly (see Table 4.1).[20]

The original lyrics—which appear in O'Hara's opening-night script—are less sophisticated and less psychologically revealing. The change in lyrics signifies a shift from the idealized symbolic language of "love" to the earthy, decidedly carnal reality of "man." The culminating lines of the second chorus—"they're all alike / They're all I like / What is this thing called man?"—drives the point home. In this final line Hart reworks the title lyric of Cole Porter's hit song, "What is This Thing Called Love?" (from *Wake Up and Dream*, 1929). While the protagonist of Porter's song is haunted by love, Vera is more honest about the nature of her passion. Through a comparison between the two songs, the audience is encouraged to turn a more critical eye towards love songs in general. The revised lyrics are more frank, potentially more scandalous, and much more in line with Vera's actual desires, as seen through her relationship with Joey.

There is some question as to when, and more importantly why, the lyrics changed. As Dorothy Hart and Robert Kimball note in *The Complete Lyrics of Lorenz Hart*, the song title "Love Is My Friend" remained in the playbills from opening night until May 12, 1941.[21] It wasn't until May 19 that "What Is a Man?" appeared in the program. To further complicate things, neither Segal or Kelly remembered Segal singing the original lyrics.[22] In a gossip column in the *New York Times* from March 30, however, the columnist notes that "an entire new set of lyrics has been written for 'Love is My Friend' in 'Pal Joey.'"[23] The timing of this

*Table 4.1* Lyrics for the original version of the song (1940) and the revised version (1941)

| "Love Is My Friend," chorus | "What Is a Man?," chorus |
| --- | --- |
| Love is my friend— | What is a man? |
| Love always follows me, | Is he an animal, |
| Love keeps me cool, | Is he a wolf, |
| Love keeps me warm. | Is he a mouse, |
| Love brings the night to have fun in, | Is he the cheap or the dear kind, |
| Love lets the morning sun in. | Is he champagne or the beer kind? |
| Love is my guide, | What is a man? |
| Love is my chaperone. | Is he a stimulant, |
| Love starts my tears, | Good for the heart, |
| Love dries my eyes. | Bad for the nerves? |
| Love is my food, | Nature's mistake since the world began, |
| And I love to dine. | What makes me give, |
| Love can be mean, | What makes me live, |
| Love can be fine— | What is this thing called man? |
| Love is a friend of mine. | |

lyrical revision may indicate that Abbott, Rodgers, and Hart saw a new possibility in Vera, potentially stimulated by the positive critical reception of the character (see Chapter 5 for more on the reception of Vera).[24]

While the lyrics to the song changed, the music remained the same. The song is arranged as a musical scene: the song begins with a verse, followed by a chorus, followed by an interlude with underscore, and is capped off with a repetition of the chorus. This form, which emphasizes story and moves the drama forward, was typical in musical comedy of the time and would remain so through the 1950s. Traditionally, the interlude is called the "patter" or "trio" section; in the published score, Rodgers indicates "patter" at this section.[25] This passage underscores a series of phone calls; Vera calls her numerous paramours and cancels her plans with them, presumably to focus her attention on Joey. The patter section is twenty-eight measures long: twenty-four measures of dialogue with a four-measure tag, leading to another repetition of the chorus. While the patter section has pitches indicated for Vera—of a simple, sing-song nature—most recordings of this section are ad libbed. This interlude is very much in line with "change" music—it is vamp-like, is fast paced, and features busy upbeat accents. This section could, if Vera wanted, be extended for as long as her list of lovers is long.

The melodic construction of "What Is a Man?" helps add depth to Vera's character. As opposed to Joey, Vera has a complex inner life, full of contradictions. In the verse she laments, "It's just my foolish way. / What can I do about it? / I'm much too used to love to be without it." Between the words "my" and "foolish," Rodgers drops the melody down a fourth and unexpectedly shifts from the tonic A♭ to a c-minor chord (the function of which is to confound expectation), marking the word "foolish" as textually important: it affects a kind of musical mortification, wherein Vera reveals how aware she is of her weaknesses (see Figure 4.6). The chorus melody, motivically organized around a half-note-quarter-quarter pattern, and containing a half-step oscillation between E♭ and D (on the text "is a man"), mimics the pensiveness of

Figure 4.6 *"What Is a Man?," verse*

Figure 4.7 *"What Is a Man?," chorus*

the lyric (see Figure 4.7). Block characterizes the pervading half-step motif in the chorus as obsessive, and links it with the prominent half steps in the chorus of "Bewitched" (the latter an oscillation between the leading tone and tonic). Block posits that, through Vera's two prominent solos, Rodgers "helps establish the musical identity of a woman who has allowed herself the luxury of an obsession."[26] Significantly, the two songs also share another prominent motif—a rising sixth, which occurs in the chorus of both songs. In "What Is a Man?," the rising sixth (from E♭ to C on the first two syllables of "ornament") stands out in a melody mostly stepwise in construction. In both songs, the rising sixth reads as rather decadent; in "What Is a Man?" the sixth is a grand, striking gesture in an otherwise contained musical environment (see Figure 4.7). Hart's lyrics on the rising sixth—"animal," "stimulant," and later "ornament"—support this reading. All of these words are sensual, pointing respectively to base natures, chemical highs, and impractical indulgences. The chorus solidifies the characterization of Vera as a sexually mature woman, rather than a besotted schoolgirl. Changing the lyrics—from a rumination on "love" to a rumination on "man"—makes plain the object of Vera's obsession.

## "BEWITCHED"

"Bewitched" is by far the best-known song from *Pal Joey*. Along with being the song most referenced by critics after the premiere of the show, and it went on to become the most recorded song from the score. Rodgers, Hart, and Abbott certainly meant the song to play a prominent role: its melody is featured prominently in the orchestral accompaniment for the act 1 ballet, and it appears in a narratively significant reprise near the end of the show. After the premiere, it was clear that Segal would be called upon to sing encores of the song; many additional lyrics to the song are in circulation, and it's not always clear which lyrics appeared in the original run of the show, and which were added during the tour (by Hart) or during the revival (by someone else).[27]

As mentioned previously, the song was originally meant to be sung during act 1, scene 4; after tryouts, the song was moved to act 1, scene 6, in the tailor shop. At this point in the story Joey has already gone home with Vera, and he is playing at being a "kept" man. At the tailor shop, Vera sets Joey up with a new wardrobe; she chooses his clothes for him, since his version of "high-class" wear is the overwrought head-to-toe tweed of a preppy polo player. Joey admits that he likes being pampered and later exits with the tailor, presumably to finish being measured for his new clothes. In the rehearsal script, it's at this moment that Linda, working as a secretary for the tailor, enters. In the rehearsal script O'Hara suggests a musical number (annotated as "Duet about jealousy?") shortly after Linda's entrance.[28] Presumably, the duet would have been sung by Vera and Linda.

In the opening night script, Joey's exit is followed by Vera's rendition of "Bewitched."Since "Bewitched" is sung before Linda enters the scene, Vera's expression of obsessive desire is not precipitated upon jealousy. Instead, it is based on her previous exchange with Joey:

VERA: Stay as sweet as you are, dear.
JOEY: That's the way to do it.
VERA: Do what?
JOEY: Keep me as sweet as I am—pamper me a little.
VERA: Somebody started that a long time ago.
JOEY: Well, it got results.[29]

The lyrics to the verse, which directly follows this exchange, have been published in two different forms. One verse begins with the following text, which appears in the conductor score used during the previews:

> After one whole quart of brandy,
> Like a daisy I awake.
> With no Bromo Seltzer handy,
> I don't even shake.[30]

The lyrics included in the opening-night script, however, aren't as tough:

> He's a fool, and don't I know it—
> But a fool can have his charms;
> I'm in love and don't I show it,
> Like a babe in arms.[31]

The lyrics to the rest of the verse are identical, and both renditions of the verse were published in sheet music form in 1941. The second version, which is not in fact a bowdlerization of Hart's lyrics, as is often claimed, was also published with the script in 1952 (and with the piano-vocal score in 1962). The first version of the verse—complete with reference to Bromo Seltzer, an antacid and contemporary hangover cure—indicates that Vera is a serious drinker, perhaps even an alcoholic, and adds complexity to her already rich characterization. The second version of the verse, however, flows more naturally from the dialogue. Joey has, indeed, just proven himself to be a fool, and the latter verse makes more narrative sense than the former. The lyrics to the rest of the verse leave little doubt, however, as to Vera's extracurricular activities:

> Men are not a new sensation,
> I've done pretty well, I think;
> But this half-pint imitation
> Puts me on the blink.

Like "I Could Write a Book," the published piano-vocal version of "Bewitched" begins with a lilting four-bar violin melody (this time by a solo violin, rather than the section).[32] When the voice enters at the verse, a flute accompanies.

The articulation markings on the flute part are curious, and highlight one of the more interesting questions about the song: is it meant to be comic or torchy? The flute doubles the melody of the voice, but the pitches are meant to be performed staccato, countering a more legato interpretation of the verse. Only two commercially available recordings of the song—the City Center recording from 1995, featuring Patti Lupone as Vera, and a recording of the song by Frederica von Stade under the direction of John McGlinn—use this written articulation (both projects were based on the original orchestrations). The effect is a bit strange: Lupone's interpretation of the verse, for instance, is quite lyrical, and the staccato quarters in the flute war with her phrasing (see web example 4.2⊙). Segal's performance of the verse on the Columbia record, which omits the flute part in this passage, is less lyrical; rather than linger over the quarter notes, Segal pushes forward (see web example 4.3⊙). The effect here is less self-indulgent, and perhaps more self-aware. There's a good chance that Segal's interpretation was affected by the original orchestration. And perhaps the original orchestration was based on how Rodgers and Hart (and Abbott) felt about the character.

This small detail of orchestration might seem insignificant, but, along with the individual vocalist's approach to the song, it affected how audiences related to Vera. The critical reception of the song at the tryouts was warm: there was very little censure of Vera (Richard Watts Jr. called her "both believable and properly human"), and much praise for "Bewitched."[33] Robert Sensenderfer, of the Philadelphia *Evening Bulletin*, called the song "catchy" and Arthur Bronson, of the *Philadelphia Record*, called Segal's performance "snappy."[34] In his review of the premiere performance, Louis Kronenberger called the song "fetchingly humorous."[35] These descriptors run counter to the torchy interpretations of the song that have become the norm.

The chorus of "Bewitched," sung in the key of C major, is emblematic of Rodgers and Hart at their best, working in tandem to create a very particular effect, tied inextricably to character.[36] The first three lines of the chorus are Hart at his most textually clever (they contain an inner rhyme within a double-barreled three-part rhyme):

> I'm wild again!
> Beguiled again!
> A simpering, whimpering child again!

The word "again," the identical rhyme at the end of each line, undercuts any sentimentality that otherwise might be seen in the chorus: Vera has, to be sure, experienced this feeling before, and will probably experience it again. The repetition of these first three lines continues, and characterizes the A sections of the chorus. Rodgers music reflects the obsessive effect of the text: the leap in the first measure (E-B-C) highlights the minor sixth, the top note C of which is the dominant pitch for the first four measures of the chorus. Block has pointed out the significance of the leading-tone motif (the repetition of B-C), especially in its depiction of obsession. The pleasure of reaching up to the tonic (i.e., our "home" pitch) three times within the first four measures (preceded by what

might be read as a pleasurably tortuous detour through the leading tone) unde-
niably reflects musical desire, pleasure, and obsession, all things Vera indulges
in (see Figure 4.8). The close connection between lyrics and music here is
remarkable. As Block cogently notes,

> It is tempting to conclude that Rodgers's musical characterization of Vera's
> emotional state corresponds with uncanny accuracy to the lyrics. But since
> the lyrics apparently followed the music—in contrast to Rodgers's subsequent
> modus operandi with Hammerstein—it is more accurate to admire Hart's spe-
> cial sensitivity to Rodgers's music, which presents an equally repetitive musi-
> cal line.[37]

The repetition of the upward-reaching motif in the first four measures is
contrasted by the final four measures of the opening A section. These measures
conclude with a descending line, ending on an F in the voice, harmonized over
a D-minor chord (rather than a C-major chord, had the melody dropped to the
expected C).

The Richard Rodgers Collection at the Library of Congress includes two of
Rodgers's sketches for "Bewitched." One is a sketch of the melody of the first four
measures of the verse; it is identical in construction to the final version (except
for the key). The other sketch, however, is an alternate version of the closing four
measures of the A section, which aligns with the title lyrics (whether this is a
sketch for the first, second, or final A section of the chorus is unclear). The sketch
has a similar rhythmic character to the final version of the song, but it reaches
upward, rather than downward (see Figure 4.9). Since the title text is written
below the melody, Rodgers might have been sketched this out after the bulk of
the song was written. There is, though, the possibility that Rodgers sketched this
after he and Hart agreed upon a title for the song. If the latter was the case, the
music was potentially born of the title lyrics, which play prominently in capturing

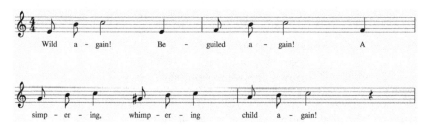

Figure 4.8 *"Bewitched," chorus*

Figure 4.9 *"Bewitched," sketch*

the mood of the song: the seed of the main motif of the song—the upward reaching line—was intact in this sketch, and the rhythm follows the rhythmic emphasis of the words. As Rodgers said in a "self-interview" in 1939,

> Sometimes we sit in a room and hate each other until we get a title; then I throw Larry out of the house and fool around until I get a satisfactory melody, inspired entirely by the title and not by nostalgia for Venice in spring.[38]

As Block argues, the title of a song is often significant to its musical construction, and here Rodgers seems to have been inspired by the text.

Many have characterized Rodgers and Hart's brilliance as an idiosyncratic combination of sweet, even sentimental music expertly balanced against cynical, self-aware lyrics; "Bewitched" is one of the best examples of this quality. Rodgers himself said, "[H]ere we tried something that I particularly effective in comedy numbers—the contrast of a flowing, sentimental melody with words that are unsentimental and self-mocking."[39] That Rodgers considered "Bewitched" a "comedy number" is telling; Lehman Engel would later say that the number was an example of a "short-joke" comedy song, in which multiple punch lines occur within a given chorus.[40] Despite the humor contained in the song, it is unlikely that most who know and love the song "Bewitched" would call it a comedy song. The song is such an effective portrait of the complex inner life of an older, witty, self-aware, still-sexual woman that it is hard not to see Vera as a direct precursor to, for instance, Joanne from Sondheim's *Company* (1970), and the song "Bewitched" as a less caustic version of "The Ladies Who Lunch." Certainly, the reprise of "Bewitched," the penultimate song of the show, can be seen as a triumphant moment of self-realization:

> Wise at last
> My eyes, at last
> Are cutting you down to your size at last.
> Bewitched, bothered and bewildered, no more.

Still, Rodgers and Hart couldn't help ending the song with a joke, perhaps revealing that there was a limit to how human Vera could appear:

> Romance—finis;
> Your change—finis;
> Those ants that invaded my pants—finis—
> Bewitched, bothered and bewildered no more.[41]

## "DEN OF INIQUITY"

"Den of Iniquity," Joey and Vera's act 2, scene 2 duet, is one of the more scandalous songs in the show. In this duet Joey and Vera are on the same page, so to speak. In Joey's duet with Linda (which was at best disingenuous, and at worst predatory), they were miles apart in terms of their sincerity. Here, Vera and Joey revel in their illicit affair; Rodgers's prim and proper music contrasts mightily with the scorching cynicism of Hart's lyrics. The piece is satirical, mocking typical love duets in typical musical comedies.

The song takes place in act 2, scene 2, in the apartment Vera funds for Joey, the day after they've spent the night together (O'Hara's stage directions in the rehearsal-script note that as she enters the scene, Vera should be "maybe rubbing her hands with lotion. Anyway doing something to show she has spent the night there.")[42] Joey is reading the reviews covering the opening of Chez Joey, and laments the fact that the papers focused more on the social set (including Vera) than on Joey or the entertainment. He's in a generally prickly mood, which Vera exacerbates by calling him "Beauty." It prompts the following reply from Joey: "I'm thinking that over. That Beauty. I'm not so sure I like it. I'm not exactly beautiful."[43] Vera appeases him by explaining that given her age (which she says is thirty-six), she knows "what's beautiful."[44] After a line that hints at Joey's roving eye, Vera and Joey have the following exchange, which leads directly into the song:

> VERA: Maybe not any place else—but here it's just you and I. While we're here I can be reasonably sure of you. That's why I'm really beginning to like this terrible apartment.
>
> JOEY: Terrible apartment? Why this is the <u>nuts</u>.

MUSIC CUE

> VERA: Yes, dear.[45]

The rehearsal script for the show depicts a very different exchange between Vera and Joey. Whereas in the opening-night script Vera is dispassionate about Joey's infidelities so long as he doesn't flaunt them, in the rehearsal script Vera is much more jealous. Nearly two pages of text were cut; here Vera grills Joey about his association with Gladys, who is now working at Chez Joey, and tells him to fire her.[46] Atypically, Joey is caught out in a moment of altruism. He begs Vera not to fire Gladys:

> JOEY: Gladys got this job without me knowing it. A whole bunch of 'em did. I may fool around with those kids in the chorus and bands, but I'm not that big of a heel that I'll get one fired. They have a tough enough time, and anyway they're a dime a dozen.[47]

This passage, which gives an entirely different sense of Vera and Joey's motivations, was almost certainly O'Hara's doing. As with the end of the preliminary draft script (where Joey shows signs of rehabilitation, and gets the girl), O'Hara was possibly conforming to musical comedy conventions in this passage, in which lead characters are at least somewhat sympathetic. The passage also shows a fondness for Joey, who comes across as an advocate for the "little people," adding perhaps more class commentary than Abbott was comfortable with (not because it was political, but because it was out of character). The passage also makes Vera look bad, portraying her as jealous and hectoring. Further, the passage presented a problem in relation to Gladys—in every other exchange with Gladys, Joey reveals that he despises her, and she him. The dialogue in the rehearsal script would have confused, or at least required further explanation of, the scenes to follow, in which Gladys and Ludlow blackmail Joey and Vera.

In the opening-night version of the scene, Vera is cooler and self-aware, and Joey is less noble. "Den of Iniquity" emphasizes both of these qualities. The song was received well by most critics, although many warned the "purists" that this was not a children's song.[48] Dramatically, the song served to amplify the "adult" aspects of the show while sending up the sentimental tropes it mocked. As Jeffrey Magee has argued, the song comments cynically on the "cozy cottage" trope so typical of Broadway and Tin Pan Alley songs.[49] These songs, the most famous of which might be the old-fashioned "Tea for Two" (1925), paint the picture of a "lover's oasis" far away from the hustle and bustle of the city. Often, as seen in both "Tea for Two" and "My Blue Heaven" (1927), the lover's oasis leads to a description of domestic bliss and babies. Rodgers and Hart themselves wrote a number of "cozy cottage" songs, including "Thou Swell" (from *A Connecticut Yankee*, 1927), which references a "hut for two" with "two rooms and kitchen," and "There's a Small Hotel" (from *On Your Toes*, 1936), which features "one room bright and neat" and "pretty window curtains made of chance."[50] As Magee explains, the "cozy cottage," configured in so many musicals of the 1920s and beyond, was often a reaffirmation of white, heteronormative, middle-class norms (the blueprint, as it were, of the "cozy cottage neighborhood" of American culture).[51]

In contrast, "Den of Iniquity" mocks the sentimentality of the these songs. As Magee explains,

> The verse begins in the conventional way, with a picture of "lovebirds all alone" in a "cozy nest" with a "secret telephone," but soon takes off in its own direction by replacing the usual pastoral imagery with "artificial roses" and substituting a "loving room" for the "living room." The second refrain gives more details about the "loving room," with its "canopy bed" and "ceiling made of glass," implying the sexual thrill of an overhead mirror.

These references—direct comments on the cozy-cottage song type—shake all the luster off typical descriptions of a love nest, instead rejoicing in more sordid environs. Stanley Donen remembers that on the line "knock on wood," Kelly knocked on Segal's "bum."[52] Hart's lyrics also include cynical asides, such as the reference to the apartment's chambermaid (who "always thinks we're so refined"—"Of course she's deaf, and dumb, and blind"). Near the end of the last chorus, Joey and Vera describe their separate bedrooms, which include "one for play and one for show." Magee also highlights the lyric where Vera describes her renewed joy in listening to the radio, after which she references either Ravel's *Bolero* or Tchaikovsky's *1812 Overture* (Hart wrote two versions). As Magee puts it,

It hardly matters which title the actors sing: both refer to pieces with a strong, throbbing pulse and an orchestrated crescendo to a massive climax. Neither sugar cakes nor children are the goals of *this* "tea for two."

To be fair, 1812 is the more explosive of the two; the lyric that precedes the reference to these classical warhorses ("now when it is dark and late") may indicate that Vera enjoyed that the music was loud enough to cover up any other sounds coming from their cozy cottage. Regardless of the exact meaning, Hart was clearly making a sexual allusion.

As in many of Rodgers and Hart's songs, Rodgers's music contrasts the edginess of Hart's lyrics. "Den of Iniquity" begins with a four-measure instrumental introduction, leading to the verse. The intro is first dominated by a crisp, sprightly figure in the high woodwinds (prefiguring the melody of the verse), followed by a saccharine sign gesture in the strings. These small instrumental gestures embody the comic contrast of the song: it is both feigningly proper and faux romantic in tone. The buttoned-up, jaunty affect of the piece imitates the innocent throwback feel of many cozy-cottage songs of the 1920s, which often featured short, snappy rhythmic gestures, dance-like tempos, and often a subtle backbeat. In this way, "Den of Iniquity" is cynically nostalgic, sonically capitalizing on the innocence of these early songs in the name of comic contrast. The humor of the song is heightened by its prim, proper dance-like character, which is made manifest in a character dance between Joey and Vera (sometimes called the "pillow dance," so named for the props) (see Figure 4.10). Lehman Engel said the song "suggests to me in feeling an eighteenth-century court dance."[53] The song certainly has the faux-restrained feeling of an aristocratic dance; one might consider it Rodgers and Hart's version of Gossec's "Gavotte," but with tongue planted firmly in cheek.

In alternating lines, Joey and Vera sing the first verse, mimicking the attitude of the winds in the introduction. The verse is a typical sixteen measures long, followed by a decidedly atypical chorus. The chorus is twenty-eight measures long, which repeats, and is arranged as two sets of twelve-measure phrases, followed by a four-measure tag (this form could alternately be seen as a twelve-measure phrase and a sixteen-measure phrase). While there is no larger contrasting B section, there are contrasting subphrases, and the feel is much like that of the parallel-period chorus seen in "I Could Write a Book" (rather than ABAB, though, "Den of Iniquity" reads more like AA'). The twelve-measure phrases are themselves broken down in uneven segments: the first four measures of the chorus are lilting, the following six are centered around a static, chromatically inflected figure, and the last two are elongations of the two-beat anacrusis to the chorus. The center six measures—the chromatically inflected figure—act as an extension of the expected four-measure response to the initial four measures. The elongation of this subphrase makes it musically prominent; it is also spiced by chromatic neighbors, making it one of the only musical ideas in the song that hints at anything other than total respectability. Importantly,

*Figure 4.10   Vivienne Segal (Vera) and Gene Kelly (Joey) pose during "Den of Iniquity";
NYPL Digital Collections, photo by Vandamm Studio, 1940*

this is also the section in which Vera and Joey, who sing in unison at the top of the chorus, alternate lyrics and egg each other on in acknowledgment of their tawdry relationship.

While the twelve-measure phrases of the chorus are unusual, Rodgers wrote a handful of songs with choruses that likewise use elongated phrases (both "Ship without a Sail" and "Nobody's Heart," for example, begin their choruses with twelve-measure phrases).[54] As Graham Wood has argued, it wasn't unusual for Rodgers to expand the typical eight-bar "limbs" of a chorus.[55] Rodgers and Hart's "Where or When" (whose chorus begins with a ten-measure phrase) also elongates an internal subphrase. Most of Rodgers's choruses, though, include a contrasting B section that, increasingly throughout their career, indicate psychological depth or narrative development. The lack of musical development might have been intentional on the part of Rodgers and Hart: the nature of Vera and Joey's relationship is blatantly transparent in this song, and requires no deeper insight.

## "TAKE HIM"

The duet "Take Him" was one of the more narratively significant moments in the show: it helped subvert the expectations of how a musical comedy should end. The song occurs near the end of act 2 (scene 4), right after Linda reveals to Vera that Ludlow and Gladys are planning to blackmail Joey and Vera. Sung by two women who are fed up with the messes that seem to follow Joey, the song is a musical rejection: "take him, you don't have to pay for him, take him, he's free." The song reverses the typical focus of female-female duets, which at that time usually depicted a pair of women pining over a specific man, the idea of a man, or even the same man. Rodgers and Hart's own song "Why Can't I?" (from *Spring Is Here*, 1929), for instance, depicts two women consoling each other over their lack of romance (or, as the character Mary-Jane says, their lack of "something in pants"). Other female-female duets, like the "Jealousy Duet" from Weill/Brecht's *Threepenny Opera* (which premiered on Broadway in English in 1933), feature women tearing each other apart because of a specific man. Like the cozy-cottage trope, the female-female duet became increasingly popular in the 1940s and 1950s, and at least on the surface, reinforced white, middle-class, heterosexual ideals in a musical.

As Stacy Wolf argues, however, the female-female duet "also troubles the integrated musical's heterosexual closure, at once signaling and perpetuating its failed heterosexuality."[56] According to Wolf's definition, "Take Him" could be classified as a "queer collaborative duet," in which "two women collude on a plan or support each other emotionally."[57] This duet is not queer because it holds some "erotic charge," but because it "displaces the heterosexual couple," late in the narrative, no less, through a song that is meaningfully homosocial.[58] Given that *Pal Joey*'s source material, songs, narrative, and lead characters all implicitly critique the conventions of musical theater, it follows that this iteration of the female-female duet would not only threaten the relationship between Vera and Joey, but would also finalize its destruction.

"Take Him" is a musical scene (see Table 4.2). The lead-in to the song is integrated in the same manner as the other book numbers. Vera asks Linda why she's helping Vera and Joey, and Linda responds, "Why? Because it's dishonest—that's all."[59] Vera presses her, resulting in the following dialogue which leads directly into the song.

*Table 4.2* Map of the form of "Take Him"

| Chorus (ABAB) | Verse (AA′) | Chorus | Chorus (half) | Dialogue (music stops) | Chorus (half) |
|---|---|---|---|---|---|
| Linda | Vera | Vera | Vera and Linda (in harmony) | Joey and Vera | Vera and Linda (in harmony) |

LINDA: Well I certainly hope you don't think it was what you think it was.

VERA: I think it was, though.

LINDA: Well, just don't think it was what you think it was. Take him.

## MUSIC CUE

Rather than begin singing an introductory verse, Linda begins with the chorus, connecting the title lyrics to her previous dialogue. Linda's chorus lists Joey's faults ("he has no head to think with / true that his heart is asleep"), while also pointing out his cheap charms ("But he has eyes to wink with / you can have him cheap"). Linda's last line of the chorus is the first hint that the interaction between the women is grounded in compassion: "Take him, but don't ever take him to heart." Vera enters on the verse, rejecting Linda's offer to "take" Joey ("Thanks, little mousie for the present and all that / But in this housey I would rather keep a rat"). After the verse, Vera sings her own chorus; like Linda, she lists Joey's faults, including his cheapness ("Last year his arm was busted / Reaching from a check") and his lack of intelligence ("I know a movie executive / Who's twice as bright"). Also like Linda, Vera concedes that Joey has his charms ("pajamas," after all, "look nice on him"), but that in the end, whatever woman ends up with Joey will "need aspirin." Like Linda's, Vera's last line is at its core based in kindness: "Take him, but don't ever let him take you." Now that the two women are on the same page, they sing another chorus in harmony, signifying a narrative unity based on the conventions of the love duet.

The surprising unity between the women—it is rare, certainly, to find a duet from this period sung between two women of very different social classes—upends the usual tension found between female characters who are interested in the same man. "Take Him" is a variation on the love-duet trope: Vera sings Linda's music (after a brief detour through a verse), and by the third chorus (a half-chorus) they're singing in harmony. The chorus melody is a syncopated, lively little tune, far from a lament for a lost man. Unlike "Den of Iniquity," the chorus is an even thirty-two measures, following the same parallel-period structure of "I Could Write a Book." Somewhere during Vera's iteration of the chorus, Joey enters, seemingly unable to grasp the meaning of the conversation between Linda and Vera. The music stops momentarily, and Vera and Joey have the following exchange:

JOEY: I was going to show you my dance. Who are you talking about?

VERA: Linda and I have discovered that we have a mutual friend.

JOEY: Yeah?

VERA: But I don't think you'd recognize him—even if we described him to you.[60]

After this exchange, Vera and Linda sing another half-chorus in harmony, reinforcing their united front. Although not indicated in the script, there's evidence that it was during this final half-chorus (and also possibly during the half-chorus that preceded the brief dialogue between Vera and Joey) that Joey dances his "strutty" "tap done in tango rhythm" (see Chapter 6 for an in-depth discussion of Joey's dance). The effect here is that Joey is oblivious to the women's complaints and has no idea that he's about to be thrown out on his rear. When Georgie Tapps took over the part of Joey after Kelly left for Hollywood, this dance was expanded—the original conductor score includes a score insert titled "Take Him: George Tapps Dance." The dance arranger (very likely Hans Spialek) transformed the duple-meter melody into a triple-meter waltz.

"Take Him" may have been the inspiration behind a handful of better-known female-female duets, most notably "Marry the Man Today" from *Guys and Dolls* (1950), sung by the characters Adelaide and Sarah Brown. Stacy Wolf notes that both "Take Him" and "Marry the Man Today" appeared near the end of each musical, and both were the last new song to be introduced in the show: they're both 11 o'clock numbers, occupying an important place in the story.[61] The impact of these songs, and the significance of these strong displays of female unity so late in the narrative, serve to take the focus off the heterosexual unions in the show and place it instead on the commiseration between the two women, who in both shows are character opposites (Sarah Brown and Adelaide are a variation on the virgin/whore dyad or, as Raymond Knapp states, one represents "religion" and the other "display," "a slightly more genteel parallel" to the former).[62] While "Marry the Man Today" is emphatically *not* a rejection of the men the two women are interested in (and the fact that each woman has her own love interest is a significant difference between the two shows), both duets are full of verbal wit, and both highlight the obvious flaws of the men they sing about. "Take Him," however, unsettles the heteronormativity of its show in a much more deliberate way: this song doesn't just signify the end of Vera and Joey's relationship, or the end of a potential relationship between Linda and Joey, but the end—or at least the beginning of the end—of the marriage trope in musical theater.[63]

While many of the book songs in *Pal Joey* are satirical, critiquing conventional stories and characters in musical comedy, they also support the critical perspective, expressed both then and now, that the show is "mature" (and thus revivable). Further, many of the books songs in *Pal Joey* are unusually sympathetic toward women; most of the characters whom Wolcott Gibbs called "living, three-dimensional figures" were, in fact, women. Yet they are often parodied, and certainly all of them are objectified. Nevertheless, these songs point toward the possibility of agency for women during this period, who were starting to see more realistic representations of themselves in literature and on stage. A deeper exploration of the female characters, as well as the lives of the actors who played them, will help address the question, and might clarify the role that Rodgers and Hart played in paving the way for more complex female characters on the Broadway stage.

# 5

## THE WOMEN OF *PAL JOEY*

• • •

If you really want to know it, I'm a little tired of sweet, sentimental roles. I'm weary of being the gooey, saccharine love interest of a play.[1]

—Vivienne Segal, 1933

Here is the only piece of straight advice: never forget that your girl or your wife is every damn bit as much a person as you are. [. . .] For you to attempt to dominate her, to pinch her personality, is some kind of sin.[2]

—John O'Hara, 1934

While Rodgers and Hart helped audiences see Vera in a more sympathetic light, the larger social commentary communicated through her character, and through the other women characters in the show, helps place the show, its creators, and Broadway of this period in a more complex light. By no means a progressive portrayal of gender roles, the show nonetheless worked to critique archetypes that had proliferated on the Broadway stage. Rodgers and Hart's (and O'Hara and Abbott's) formal innovations had repercussions beyond the unusual story and the critical reaction to the show. If conventional musical comedies of the period were defined by a white, middle-class, patriarchal, heterosexual perspective, then to challenge convention in musical comedy was to challenge the very structures that legitimized the most enduring societal institutions of the time, including marriage, the nuclear family, and class privilege. The particular way that O'Hara, Abbott, Rodgers, and Hart fashioned the female characters said much about conventions relating to women on Broadway; the performances, and influence, of the women who played these roles is perhaps even more significant.

*Pal Joey* features four markedly different types of female characters. The most prominent—Vera Simpson—is a wealthy woman of taste, sophistication, and hearty sexual appetite. Gladys, the crooked nightclub chorine, is working class, sexually experienced, and at home in the seedy environs of the act 1 nightclub. Linda, in form and outline the ingénue, is also a working-class woman, but of the secretarial type: she works as an assistant to a tailor, and is naive and sexually innocent. The last significant female character in *Pal Joey* (although she appears in only one scene) is Melba, a hard-boiled middle-class journalist—she went to

*Pal Joey*. Julianne Lindberg, Oxford University Press (2020). © Oxford University Press.
DOI: 10.1093/oso/9780190051204.001.0001

Mount Holyoke, after all—who immediately sees Joey for who he is. It is perhaps worth noting that none of these four women would have moved in the same social circles: they all approach Joey with a different set of manners, reflective of their social positions. The careful way that gender, inflected by class, functioned in *Pal Joey* was in large part the work of John O'Hara. As Fran Lebowitz said, "O'Hara understood better than any other American writer how class can both reveal and shape character."[3]

All four of these feminine archetypes had appeared on Broadway (and in film) before. In *Pal Joey* two of the types—the ingénue, Linda, and the nightclub singer, Gladys—are parodies. In reference to Linda, Rodgers said "There wasn't one decent character in the entire play except for the girl who briefly fell for Joey—her trouble was simply that she was stupid."[4] Linda serves as a foil to the typical ingénue trope, and doesn't develop as a character. Gladys, on the other hand, is a stereotype, albeit a funny one, of the tough-talking chorus girl (see Chapter 3 for more on Gladys, and June Havoc, who originated the role). Vera is, truly, the only female character in *Pal Joey* to be afforded a complex inner life. The character Melba, however, offers the audience shrewd commentary on the conventions that *Pal Joey* sends up. This chapter will look specifically at the character Vera, played by Vivienne Segal, and the song "Zip," sung by the character Melba and performed by Jean Casto (1940) and Elaine Stritch (1952).

## VIVIENNE SEGAL AS VERA SIMPSON

Vivienne Segal's performance of Vera Simpson was remarkable for a number of reasons. First, her character—the aging diva—was sexualized to an atypical degree. Even so, thanks to her performance (and to Abbott and O'Hara's dialogue and Rodgers and Hart's songs), the character retained her humanity. This can be seen in the critical reaction, which was almost unanimously complimentary. Burns Mantle (*New York Daily News*) said that she was "smartly cast" and that "her straight performance [is] creditable and helpful to the story."[5] Sidney B. Whipple (*New York World-Telegram*) commented that her "delightful personality, the loveliness of her voice and the perfection of her acting helped to make the comedy vivid and real."[6] Brooks Atkinson (*New York Times*) counted Segal as one of the show's "restricted blessings" and said further that Segal could "act with personal dignity and can sing with breeding."[7] As mentioned in Chapter 4, Richard Watts Jr. (*New York Herald Tribune*) found Segal/Vera "both believable and properly human."[8] These comments were a credit to Segal's acting, but also to her reputation: her turn as Vera was the culmination of a much-praised career change. By this point she had successfully transitioned from ingénue roles to those of sophisticated, witty, intelligent middle-aged women. The character Vera avoided censure for two reasons: despite her transgressions, Vera is a wealthy socialite, and, importantly, she was played by Vivienne Segal (see Figure 5.1).

*Figure 5.1  Vivienne Segal (Vera) looks down on Gene Kelly (Joey) in Pal Joey; NYPL Digital Collections, photo by Vandamm Studio, 1940*

In order to understand the significance of the character Vera, it is useful to trace the career of the woman who originated the role. Vivienne Segal's Broadway career spanned from 1915 to 1953, an unusually long stretch for an actor first type-cast as a sweet-faced ingénue. Although Segal initially gained fame for her roles in operettas, she later transformed her image by playing complex, world-wizened heroines in three musical comedies by Rodgers and Hart. Her skill as a singer was always remarked upon by critics, first aligned with naiveté, sweetness, and youth, and later with worldliness and elegance. Segal's career reflects how she navigated critical reactions to her age, and how she later worked to break free from typecasting.

Born in 1897 in Philadelphia, Segal first made her mark on Broadway in oper-etta. Blessed, or perhaps cursed, with a baby face and a small stature, she was most often cast as the naive, pure-of-heart female lead. Although she never took voice lessons, she made her stage debut in 1914 in a production of *Carmen* for the Philadelphia Operatic Society, starring in the title role; after she gained a bit of fame on Broadway, critics would say that she was the youngest singer to ever play the part. The following year she won the role of Mizzi in *The Blue Paradise*, Sigmund Romberg's adaptation of Edmund Eysler's German-language operetta. She went on to play in another Romberg adaptation (*My Lady's Glove*) and then in two Kern/Bolton/Wodehouse productions: *Miss 1917* (featuring a cast of over a hundred, including stars like Irene Castle and Lew Fields), and *Oh, Lady! Lady!* It was Segal who was slated to sing the eventually cut song "Bill" from the latter production, which famously made its way into *Show Boat* (performed by Helen Morgan).

In 1923 she won the title role in Albert Von Tilzer's *Adrienne*, and soon after featured in the *Follies* of 1924 and 1925. By this time she was married to matinee idol Robert Ames, with whom she soon had a very messy, and very public, divorce. It was during this period, in her late twenties, that Segal's public persona took on new depth—because she was a high-profile divorcée, her private life was in conflict with squeaky-clean ingénue image on stage. She got away with saying such things as the following: "I'm tired of a handsome husband who must have his imported cigarettes and his imported drinks and his $20 a pair silken pajamas, while he refuses to work or pay for them."[9] This new complexity in the press didn't extend to her roles. She continued to be cast as the artless ingénue, and referred to by critics as a romantic "prima donna," firmly connecting her to classical vocal styles and genres. She was described by different critics as "little," a reference to her small stature, "blessed with youth and grace," and "luscious of voice and a picture to look at."[10] She was lauded for her youth, skill, beauty, and grace, and generally in that order.

Segal continued to play ingénues well into her thirties. While this casting choice would perhaps be surprising on screen, there is a long history of women on stage, opera especially, playing roles that are "younger" than they are. This tradition relates to the voice cultivation involved in this type of singing—the debate over when a voice matures is a much-discussed topic in the operatic world, where many female vocalists *begin* their careers in their late twenties or early thirties. Consider Joan Sutherland, who recorded the role of Amina, an adolescent girl in Bellini's *La sonnambula*, when she was thirty-six years old (she later recorded the role when she was in her early fifties). Sutherland is, perhaps, in a category all her own, but the opera world has routinely cast older female singers in the roles of younger characters. While operetta often casts lighter voices—especially in the ingénue roles—these voices may still require many years to "mature." It was unusual that Segal began singing lead roles when she was still a teenager—critics certainly remarked on her age at both extremes of her career.

The fact that Segal's voice changed as she aged, even as she continued to play ingénues, was not discussed by critics (except to say, especially during the 1920s, that she was at her prime). There are few recordings of Segal from her early years on stage, so it is difficult to pinpoint the nature of those changes. Most of her work on film, however, is extant and reveals something about the very different conventions related to aging on stage, and aging on screen.

By the late 1920s, many Broadway stars had tried making it in Hollywood. Despite their star power, some of Broadway's most beloved actors—including Gertrude Lawrence, Fanny Brice, and Harry Richman—did not successfully transition from stage to screen. Comic stars, like Eddie Cantor and the Marx Brothers, found much more success, as did Fred Astaire, Irene Dunne, and, eventually, Ginger Rogers. The success of operetta stars from stage to screen was similarly mixed. Some of the beloved male stage stars like Dennis King (perhaps most famous for his roles in *Rose-Marie* [1924] and *The Vagabond King* [1925]) were thought to be too dramatic for the screen. Female operetta stars like Ethelind Terry (who played the title role in the hugely successful *Rio Rita* [1927]) were also unsuccessful on screen. Each case was different, but as Richard Barrios has speculated, "improper showcasing, weak stories, and unflattering photography" all played roles in their lack of success.[11]

Segal encountered similar disappointments. Although she played the part of Margot to great acclaim in the original stage version of the operetta *The Desert Song*, an actor named Carlotta King played the part in the screen transfer. Segal did, however, star in four films in 1930, all released by Warner Brothers in 1930 or 1931, who were clearly in the process of testing out her star power: these films include *Song of the West*, *Golden Dawn*, *Bride of the Regiment*, and *Viennese Nights*. *Song of the West*, Segal's first full-length film role, was the first "all-talking, all-color" picture to be filmed entirely outdoors. Based on Vincent Youmans and Oscar Hammerstein's stage musical *Rainbow* (1928), the film, unfortunately now lost, was moderately successful. Still, reviews like the following began to characterize critic's reaction to the Broadway star: "Vivienne Segal, who has charm on the musical comedy stage, but who, alas, sacrifices a good deal of it before the camera's merciless glare, is the picture's heroine."[12]

Her next role, in *The Bride of the Regiment*, was for another operetta based on a stage production. The film didn't fare well with critics or audiences—by this point, there was a short-lived critical and popular backlash against the opulent operettas that had done so well on stage in the 1910s and 1920s. One reviewer called the film a "pretentiously mounted, gaudily technicolored talkie-singie" that was "flat and tasteless—yes, even stupid."[13] The backlash against film operetta was related to new Depression-era aesthetics—for a period, audiences and critics saw a certain brand of over-the-top, Continentally inspired lavishness as distasteful. Segal's next film, *Golden Dawn*, was even less well received. Based on the 1927 stage musical by Kalman, Harbach, and Hammerstein, the film is an exoticist fantasy set in colonial Africa—Segal plays the part of Dawn, a white girl who is kidnapped as a baby and brought up by a black native mother. In typical fashion, Dawn falls in love with a white man and thus angers the jealous tribal leader. As one might imagine, sacrificial fires and white colonial intervention ensue; the tribal leader is killed by his own people, and Dawn (proven to be 100% white, of course) goes off with her love. The film is now terribly offensive, but it failed during its own time because it didn't satisfy the conventions of film exotica.[14] Segal too was a problem for many critics. Her character was written as a young adolescent girl, not a woman of thirty-three. Segal later commented on her involvement with the film, saying that "I was just a guinea pig for Technicolor [. . .] You felt like an ass, but what could you do? It was my livelihood."[15]

*Viennese Nights*, her final film from 1930, is considered by many to be her best. The narrative spans forty years, and she plays the role of Elsa—a woman who chooses financial security over love—in her youth, in mid-age, and finally at the end of her life. Critics commented on Segal's dramatic range, praising her ability to transform ages and still be convincing.[16] *Viennese Nights* was meant to be the first in a series of four original musicals written by Romberg and Hammerstein specifically for the screen. The early-Depression-era backlash against operetta stalled the project—only two films (*Viennese Nights* and *Children of Dreams* [1931]) were made.[17] The film wasn't very successful in the United States, but it enjoyed some popularity overseas. Although it is possible that the public (and the studios) tired of Segal because of her first two Hollywood flops, it seems more likely that her failure to succeed in Hollywood was related more to timing, both in terms of her age and the public reception of film operettas.[18]

After making these four films for Warner Brothers, Segal starred briefly in the 1931 stage revival of *The Chocolate Soldier*; after that, she began a respectable career in radio, and in 1934 came back to Hollywood to play a supporting part in her last film. Titled *The Cat and the Fiddle*, this film was Jeanette MacDonald's first for MGM, and rumor had it that Segal and MacDonald didn't get along.[19] Still, despite her small role, Segal shines in the film. Based on the Kern/Harbach musical of the same name, the film features MacDonald as Shirley Sheridan, a successful Tin Pan Alley composer, and Ramon Novarro as Victor Florescu, a struggling operetta composer.[20] Segal plays Odette, a prima donna who, as a favor to Victor, convinces her wealthy husband to fund Victor's operetta; she's also the star of his show. Segal's voice is better than ever in the film, demonstrated in her performance of "A New Love Is Old," and she is given the opportunity to dig into a different kind of role (see web example 5.1 ▶).[21] Odette is portrayed as predatory: she makes unwanted sexual advances, making clear to Victor that she expects her favor to be repaid. In many particulars this role seems to set Segal up for the role of Vera in *Pal Joey*: Odette is a wealthy middle-aged woman (Segal was nearly thirty-seven when the film premiered), she is unabashedly sexual, and she makes advances on a younger man (see web example 5.2 ▶). Unlike Vera, though, Odette is portrayed as a two-dimensional villain.[22] This is the first time, however, that a large audience saw Segal break free from her typical ingénue character. From this point in her career on, she changed direction.

In 1933 (a year before featuring in *The Cat and the Fiddle*) Segal did an interview with the *San Francisco Examiner* while performing in the Pacific Coast production of Jerome Kern and Oscar Hammerstein's *Music in the Air*; here she laments the types of roles that she was typically cast in: "if you really want to know it, I'm a little tired of sweet, sentimental roles. I'm weary of being the gooey, saccharine love interest of a play. That's why I'm having such a good time playing Frieda in 'Music in the Air.' It's a nice, catty role for a change and it's good exercise—keeps me on my toes."[23] The role of Frieda was hard won for Segal. Earlier in her career she began what would be a decades-long quarrel with Jerome Kern—when she was working on *Miss 1917*, she apparently declined to sing a song he had chosen for her to sing in favor of another song, chosen by Victor Herbert. Segal says she made an enemy out of him that day. Come 1932, Segal wanted to audition for the part of Frieda in Kern's *Music in the Air*. The part of Frieda—a German operatic diva; a comic role—would have been a departure for Segal. Kern, operating, according to Segal, on a decades-old grudge, refused to let her audition for the part. She jumped, however, at the chance to play Frieda in the Pacific Coast production of the show. Segal took a pay cut for it; she was used to receiving $1750 a week, and did the show for $500 a week. She would also only get $500 a week in her first role for Rodgers and Hart.

Her performance of Frieda helped shape the latter part of her career, which was crowned by roles in three successful Rodgers and Hart shows: *I Married an Angel* (1938), *Pal Joey* (1940), and the 1943 revival of *A Connecticut Yankee*. It was during her stint as Frieda in the Pacific Coast production of *Music in the Air* that Segal made her first connection with Rodgers and Hart. The songwriting team was stationed in Hollywood, working for MGM, and they came out to watch the show. Both Rodgers and Hart were impressed by Segal's comic performance, but Hart was especially enamored—Segal would become his favorite actress and a good friend. Hart was one of the first to recognize her comedic talent; he told her that someday he wanted to write a show for her.[24]

That role turned out to be Peggy in the musical comedy *I Married an Angel*, Segal's first Broadway role since 1931. The story follows a jaded banker (Willy), who declares that he's so weary of relationships that the only girl he could marry would have to be an angel. Lo, an angel comes to earth, and they get married. The angel is unfortunately unable to lie (even seemingly small, albeit important lies), and it wreaks havoc on Willy's life and on their relationship. Thankfully, his sister Peggy (played by Segal) is there to coach her through it: Segal's role was full of sharp wit in both lyrics and dialogue. Consider the song "A Twinkle in Your Eye," sung as a lesson from Peggy to Angel, which includes the following lines: "My sister Sue once took a swim without a stitch on. / The cop who caught her took her to the jail nearby. / The judge who tried her held her for examination. / Of course, it may have been the twinkle in her eye." Robert Francis, of *The Brooklyn Daily Eagle*, characterized Segal—now forty-one—as a "roistering, rollicking lady who carries the responsibility for most of the laugh lines in the play and does it with a fine sense of comedy. It's too bad that some one didn't discover this about her before. We've been missing a lot of fun."[25] Segal was deliberate in the way she framed this new phase of her career. Her playbill bio for the show reads thus:

> Her first professional debut was made in "The Blue Paradise" after a hasty four-day rehearsal period. She played the part of a sweet young maid in pink organdy and it seemed as though she were doomed to a life of saccharine ingenue and prima donna roles forever after [. . .] Then came the long vigil in which she decided she would not appear in any New York production until she could play a good roistering comedy role.[26]

Segal's Broadway comeback was a huge success. After playing Vera in *Pal Joey* a few years later, she played her next, and final, role for Rodgers and Hart in 1943. Playing the part of Queen Morgan Le Fay in an expanded revival of *A Connecticut Yankee*, she sang the comically homicidal song "To Keep My Love Alive," which Rodgers and Hart wrote especially for Segal (see web example 5.3 ▶). The wit and restraint of her performance of the song—the last that Larry Hart ever wrote—is a testament to the actor that Segal had become.[27]

The decision to cast Segal as Vera in *Pal Joey* was savvy. Segal was already a well-respected singer, had established herself as a comedienne, and was known for her grace and dignified bearing. These qualities helped soften the reaction to Vera. The appearance of Vera was not the first instance of a strong, self-possessed woman on either the Broadway stage or in film, but the degree to which she is sympathetic was unusual. Some reviewers compared Vera to the Marschallin from Richard Strauss's *Der Rosenkavalier* (1911); like Vera, the Marschallin is rich and largely sympathetic, and has a younger lover (Count Octavian Rofrano). The Marschallin tends, however, to revel more in her unhappiness. Her extended aria "Da geht er hin" is self-aware; in this piece the Marschallin thinks back to her naive youth, and reveals how unhappy she is in her marriage and in life. She also genuinely cares for Octavian. Vera tends not to wallow in such self-pity; she also moves between classes ("slumming," in the contemporary parlance), and her interest in Joey is purely carnal.

Vera doesn't fall into the trope of the older predatory socialite, as she had played in *The Cat and the Fiddle*, or the nonconformist but essentially comic rich woman (seen, for instance, in the Countess de Lage character from Clare Boothe Luce's *The Women*). Although the character Vera did not originate in O'Hara's original Joey stories, she has qualities in common with some of the women characters in his novels.[28] The character Gloria Wandrous from *BUtterfield 8*, for instance, is unapologetically sexual, though also tragic. This is partially because Wandrous lives her life like a man; the novel features an implicit critique of the rigidity of gender roles. Geoffrey Wolff, a biographer of John O'Hara, comments on O'Hara's approach to female characters: "He thought of women as fellow seducers, or accomplices in seduction. He surely thought of them as powerfully endowed with points of view, capable of commanding narratives as well as relationships."[29] This attitude can be seen in an excerpt of a letter (a portion of which is quoted at the beginning of this chapter) that O'Hara wrote to his brother, Tom, in 1934, mailed the day his first novel was published:

> Here is the only piece of straight advice: never forget that your girl or your wife is every damn bit as much a person as you are. She regards you as another person, just as you regard her as another person. She thinks the world revolves around her just as you do around yourself, just as anyone does. She has a vote in life as well as in politics, she eats and sleeps and suffers and loves and thinks (regardless of how badly you or I may think she thinks) like you and me. She was born, she lives, she's got to die; and for you to attempt to dominate her, to pinch her personality, is some kind of sin.[30]

John Updike, who was a strong promoter of O'Hara's work, remarked on the letter, "Rare advice for one man to be giving another in 1934."[31] Updike went on, "O'Hara's ability and willingness to portray women has not been often enough complimented [. . .] Throughout his fiction, women occupy the same merciless space his men do, with an equal toughness".[32] Vera, certainly, acts and lives according to her own self-interest; thus, in the end, she rejects Joey. The character—inflected as she is by realistic desires and motivations—is not so easy to plot on the traditional virgin-whore binary.

## MELBA AND "ZIP"

The character Melba, on the other hand, doesn't get anywhere near the inner life that Vera does. She is, however, the voice through which many of the show's anxieties—related to gender, sexuality, and class, in particular—are communicated. In her only scene in the show, Melba sings "Zip," one of *Pal Joey*'s biggest showstoppers, a mock striptease that takes place near the top of act 2. Melba Snyder is a smart, cynical journalist who interviews the cocky Joey about his newly opened nightclub Chez Joey; during the song she channels one of her most fascinating interviewees: Gypsy Rose Lee. Although this is Melba's only scene in the show, critics and audiences loved it, and after the opening of the Philadelphia tryout, Hart rushed to prepare extra verses for the inevitable encores to come.

Melba is witty (thanks to Hart's clever lyrics and John O'Hara's tough dialogue), portrayed as somewhat masculine, and knows what she wants in a drink. Her character further extends the deviance so purposely supplied by the creators of the show, particularly by O'Hara and Hart, who were intimately familiar with the world portrayed onstage. The song "Zip" is also at the heart of how women are represented in *Pal Joey*. Beyond the intentions of the creators, the song "Zip" reflects anxieties related to gender and class that were circulating during the 1930s, uniting the bored burlesque dancer and the tough female journalist, both elevated to archetypes in the prewar era.

The song, as well as *Pal Joey* itself, interacts with a series of gendered archetypes that developed in the 1930s, some a reaction to the economic crisis; the sexual division of labor, typified by the home/work split, was rocked by the entry of married women into the workforce.[33] While the "gold digger" trope dates back to the 1910s, it took on new meaning during the Depression; according to Margaret McFadden, the trope was often employed to "manage concerns about male economic responsibilities."[34] Pop culture of the period also saw the appearance of the "sissy" character, potentially a critique of the "old ruling-class," and marked as "effeminate, un-American, and parasitical."[35] Both of these archetypes implicitly critique the pre-crash association of money with masculinity, and made way for the newly idealized working-class masculinity tied to athleticism and virile sexuality, eventually typified by the first stage Joey, Gene Kelly, and the more hardboiled versions of this type, played by Humphrey Bogart and others.[36] This figuration occurred, inevitably, against a climate in which women were blamed for the economic crisis: for "taking" men's jobs, and for the assumption, embodied in the "gold digger" character, that men were valued and measured by the size of their wallets. Effeminacy in men was newly suspect, and was associated both with homosexuality and the decline of the American man, signaling a crisis in masculinity that arrived decades before the more commonly acknowledged "crisis" of the 1950s.[37] Throughout *Pal Joey*, Joey compensates for his financial instability by affecting a hypermasculine swagger.

The two archetypes seen in the character Melba were equally reflective of the period. Both the girl reporter and the burlesque entertainer (synonymous with the stripteaser by the 1930s) represented deviant forms of femininity. Although they might appear on the surface to be opposites, these character types were equally indicative of newly restructured labor forces. The girl reporter archetype—represented in popular film by fictional characters like Hildy Johnson from *His Girl Friday* and Torchy Blane from the Torchy Blane film series, and in real life by reporters like Adela Rogers St. Johns or Lorena "Hick" Hickok—is characterized as tough, self-reliant, career oriented, and often smarter than her male counterparts. This character is in some ways an outgrowth of the New Woman of the 1920s, though adapted to serve the needs—one of them being economic survival—of the 1930s. Although Hollywood softened its portrayals of these women (often by pairing her with a romantic lead who inevitably "domesticates" her), her more traditionally masculine traits were valued. As Philippa Gates puts it, "what is most interesting about the girl reporter [of the 1930s] is that she attracted her man, not because of her potential to be feminized [. . .] but because of her *masculinity*—her outspoken nature, her independence, her careerist ambition, drive, and success."[38] Still, pop-culture representations of the girl reporter were overwhelmingly portrayed as heterosexual, except for, occasionally, secondary comic characters. *Pal Joey*'s Melba is like the latter of these; she is impervious to Joey and interacts much more with the archetype of the "mannish woman," a trope often read as queer.[39]

As mentioned in Chapter 1, the character Melba originates in one of John O'Hara's "Joey" stories, titled "A Bit of a Shock," and in *Pal Joey* remains close to the original except for the ending.[40] Melba's appearance is focused on in both versions of the story, and relates directly to contemporary assumptions between outer appearance and sexual orientation. In O'Hara's story, which is written in the form of a letter from Joey to his "Pal Ted," Melba arrives during a rehearsal to cover a club act featuring Joey as emcee; she walks in shortly after Joey sits down in disgust, irritated at the amateur antics of the chorus girls. Joey is harsh in his appraisal of Melba's looks: her refers to her as a "something," rather than a woman, and later says "I tho't to myself Lesbo [. . .] I am all set to be m.c. in a crib where the Lesbos even come and watch the dress rehearsals."[41] His description of her appearance plays up her masculine qualities:

She is wearing this suit that you or I wd [sic] turn down because of being too masculine. Her hair is cut crew cut like the college blood. She is [sic] got on a pair of shoes without any heels and a pr. [sic] of glasses that make her look like she lost something but gave up the hope that she will ever find it.[42]

Joey underscores her appearance in order to set up Pal Ted for the plot twist at the end of his story. In the *New Yorker* story the joke is on Joey, who later finds out that Melba is in fact a conventionally beautiful woman. This last bit (the "shock") didn't make it into the final script of the show, although the rehearsal script kept the *New Yorker* ending.[43] Instead, Melba remains what she appears to be from the onset: tough, mannish, and impervious to Joey. The revision seen in the opening night script is curious, as the original twist is what eventually neutralizes Melba's deviance, which might be read as threatening to Joey. Joey's extended description also reveals how easily he aligns Melba's looks with her sexual orientation—an alignment, as George Chauncey and others have explored, that took on new significance during this period.[44]

Joey's focus on, and apparent disgust with, Melba's looks dovetails with descriptions made by contemporary critics and sexologists about perceptions of gay culture in New York.[45] In a pseudo-scientific article published in the December 1936 issue of *Current Psychology and Psychoanalysis*, titled "Degenerates of Greenwich Village," the author describes the physical appearance and sartorial choices of people the author diagnoses as lesbians:

> Often it is difficult to tell whether the creatures are boys or not. Clothed in mannish togs, flat-chested, hair slicked tightly back and closely cropped, seen in a restaurant or bar room, one often ponders before hazarding a guess to "its" sex. Faces then, often hard, voices low as a man's, their features have masculine characteristics, although few shave. Make-up is not used in an obvious fashion as it is by most women.[46]

This description is curiously close to O'Hara's/Joey's description of Melba, to the extent that one might wonder if O'Hara, whom some likened to an ethnographer, had read this sort of literature. It was certainly readily available, and its spirit was not only confined to medical circles—it was seen all over popular culture as well. The description of people the author perceives as lesbians, and Joey's description of Melba, reveal how destabilizing nontraditional expressions of gender were to traditional forms of masculinity and, by extension, to the newly unstable gender hierarchies in Depression-era New York. The song "Zip" encapsulates these anxieties, combining them with the image of the stripteaser, another archetype that confronts issues related to gender, class, expressions of sexuality, and the commodification of sex.

The song "Zip" depicts Melba's interview with the burlesque dancer Gypsy Rose Lee, perhaps the most famous stripper of the twentieth century. Singing from the perspective of Gypsy Rose, Melba paints her as an ironic intellectual, a quality Lee played up in her own acts. Like the character she sings about, Melba is transgressive in the way that she embodies femininity. Rather than playing up the "naturalness" of sex, Melba's performance, channeled through Gypsy Rose,

I've  in-ter-viewed Les - lie  How-ard  I've  in-ter-viewed No - el  Cow- ard

*Figure 5.2 "Zip," verse*

*Figure 5.3 "Zip," sketch*

promotes the idea that sex, or sex acts, might in fact be quite staged. This notion is reflected in the staging, the lyrics, and the music.

Rodgers's music is clever, and amplifies the disaffected, cynical personality of Melba and the fictional Gypsy Rose. The opening verse, for instance, is comprised of a broken Bb major chord, repeated three times (see Figure 5.2). This gesture is a sort of vamp—the figure doubles back on itself, and could continue on ad infinitum as Melba lists her illustrious interviewees. The repetition of the broken chord is comically singsong, and delivers the effect of someone "going through the motions"—the aural equivalent of boredom or possibly a childlike naiveté. Melba's inscrutable *ennui* is terribly intimidating to Joey, who is used to getting a rise out of everyone (for good or bad).

Rodgers's sketches reveal that he had originally thought of the opening melody more melodically. Instead of the broken chord, the melody in the sketch leads smoothly down in a scalar pattern (see Figure 5.3▶). The sketch is perhaps more musical, but it doesn't convey Melba's biting personality in the same way as the version that made its way into the show. In this way, Rodgers made the choice between composing something more conventionally musical, and creating a line that would best suit the character. Following many artistic choices made in *Pal Joey*, it seems that characterization and context in this scene mattered a great deal.

The lyrics for the verse are meant to set up a binary between the high-culture world that Melba's named interviewees represent, and the working-class world of burlesque (see Table 5.1). Hart drops the following names: Leslie Howard, Noel Coward, and Stravinsky. After naming Stravinsky, the orchestra plays a crunchy cluster chord, a clear nod to Stravinsky's bitonal writing in works like *The Rite of Spring*. This modernist high-art reference runs counter to the next name that Hart mentions, Minsky's, a reference to the theater owners whose name became synonymous with the striptease-focused variety of burlesque.[47] In contrast to the Stravinsky embellishment, the original drum part indicates a "bump" on "Minsky," though this "bump" doesn't appear on any of the recordings. This clear differentiation between classed cultural references is meant to be comic, but it also plays with the contrast between Melba and Joey—she is educated (earlier in the dialogue she indicates that she went to school at Mount Holyoke) and he is,

*Table 5.1* Pop culture references in "Zip," explained

| Line | Cultural Reference/Musical Effect |
| --- | --- |
| A countess named di Frasso[1] | Countess di Frasso (Dorothy Taylor) was an extravagantly wealthy American socialite, associated at different times of her life with British aviator Claude Grahame-White, Count Carlo Dentice di Frasso, Gary Cooper, and Benjamin "Bugsy" Siegel. |
| I've interviewed the great Stravinsky | Directly after Melba sings "Stravinsky," the orchestra plays a crunchy, dissonant cluster chord, a cheeky reference to the Russian composer's famed bitonal writing (i.e., Petrushka chord). |
| With a star who worked for Minsky. | In the 1930s, Lee was the Minsky's burlesque theater chain's biggest star. The Minsky brothers (Abe, Billy, Herbert, and Morton) had aspirations towards Ziegfeldian grandeur, but are now synonymous with the striptease-focused version of burlesque. |
| I met her at the Yankee Clipper | The *Yankee Clipper* was the name of a famous flying boat, manufactured by Boeing. The plane undertook a transatlantic journey in June 1939. Very likely a reference to Lee's position in a world of wealth. The term was also the nickname of Joe DiMaggio, whose graceful athleticism was associated with the flying sea vessel. Also the name of a DeMille film from 1927. |
| Zip! Walter Lippmann wasn't brilliant today. | American journalist and writer (1889–1974), famous for his political commentary. Cofounder of the *New Republic*, he also wrote for *World*, and the *New York Herald Tribune*, for which he wrote the syndicated column "Today and Tomorrow." Author of multiple books, including *Public Opinion* (1922), and the anti-socialist *The Good Society* (1937). |
| Zip! Will Saroyan ever write a great play? | William Saroyan was an Armenian-American writer, famous for his play *The Time of Your Life* (1939), which won both the Pulitzer Prize for drama, and the New York Drama Critics Circle Award. The premiere of the play featured Gene Kelly as "Harry the Hoofer," a performance that Rodgers said proved he'd be a perfect Joey.[2] |

*Table 5.1* Continued

| Line | Cultural Reference/Musical Effect |
| --- | --- |
| Zip! I was reading Schopenhauer last night. / Zip! And I think that Schopenhauer was right. | Reference to the German philosopher was very likely a nod to Lee's rumored intellectual prowess, and perhaps the popularity of pop psychology in the 1930s. |
| I don't want to see Zorina. | Cheeky reference to Vera Zorina, the Norwegian ballerina and actress who performed with the Ballet Russe de Monte Carlo, was married to George Balanchine, and starred in Rodgers and Hart's *I Married an Angel* (1938) (and the London version of *On Your Toes* in 1937), as well as a number of Hollywood films. |
| I don't want to meet Cobina. | Reference to Cobina Wright Jr., "it girl," actress, and model, famously wooed by Prince Philip of Greece in 1938, and named "Miss Manhattan" by the organizers of the New York World's Fair in 1939. |
| Who the hell is Margie Hart? | Burlesque star sometimes billed as "the poor man's Garbo"; rose to fame in the Minsky chain. From a *Life* magazine article from 1940: "In the sisterhood of strip-teasers redheaded Margie Hart is younger than Ann Corio, more queenly than Hinda Wausau and never resorts to speaking French like Gypsy Rose Lee."[3] |
| I consider Dali's paintings passé | Salvador Dali (1904–1989); In 1939 an exhibition by Dali, called *Dream of Venus*, showed at the New York World's Fair. The exhibition included surrealistic tableaux of nude women, some adorned with sea creatures. |
| Can they make the Metropolitan pay? | Potential reference to Dali's setting (with Massine) of the ballet *Bacchanale* (using music from Wagner's *Tannhäuser*), which premiered at the Metropolitan Opera House in 1939, to much fashionable scandal. |
| I don't care for Whistler's Mother | Famous painting by J. M. Whistler (1871). |

*(continued)*

*Table 5.1* Continued

| Line | Cultural Reference/Musical Effect |
| --- | --- |
| Charley's Aunt | A British farce (1892), revived multiple times; between 1915 and 1940, multiple silent and sound film versions were produced. The center of the farce is the cross-dressing lead, made to impersonate "Charley's Aunt." In 1948 a Loesser/Abbott musical adaptation premiered, titled *Where's Charley?*, featuring Ray Bolger. This musical was later adapted into a film, also starring Bolger. |
| Shubert's brother | Reference to the Shubert brothers, the powerful theater owners and producers. |
| Who the hell is Sally Rand? | (1904–1979); Burlesque star and actress; popularized the fan dance. Came up through vaudeville and found success in film. In her words: "I never really made any money until I took my pants off."[4] |
| That Stokowski leads the greatest of bands.[5] | Leopold Stokowski (1882–1977); famed conductor, most known for his tenure with the Philadelphia Orchestra, and a large number of recordings going all the way back to 1917. |
| Rip Van Winkle on the screen would be smart / Tyrone Power will be cast in the part. | Tyrone Power (1914–1958); American actor who gained fame in the late 1930s for his roles in a number of popular films, including *Day-Time Wife* (1937), opposite Linda Darnell; *Alexander's Ragtime Band* (1938), opposite Alice Faye and Dona Ameche; and *The Mark of Zorro* (1940), again opposite Linda Darnell. "Rip Van Winkle" might be a reference to his appearance in a number of period films. |
| Luscious Lucius | Lucius Beebe (1902–1966); widely read journalist who wrote for some of the most prestigious American papers, including the *New York Herald Tribune* and later on in the *San Francisco Chronicle*. His popular column "This New York" chronicled the club-going, upper echelon of New York society. Nicknamed "Luscious Lucius" for his smartly dressed, elegant figure. |

*Table 5.1* Continued

| Line | Cultural Reference/Musical Effect |
|---|---|
| I don't care for either Mickey—Mouse and Rooney make me sicky! | Mickey Rooney (1920–2014); at the time of *Pal Joey*, best known for playing Andy Hardy in a series of films devoted to the wholesome, all-American Hardy family; Judy Garland played opposite him in three films in the series as well as in the film adaptation of Rodgers and Hart's *Babes in Arms*. Rooney also played the part of Hart in *Words and Music* (1948), the biopic based on the career of Rodgers and Hart. |
| Who the hell's Lili St. Cyr?[6] | (1918–1999); famed burlesque entertainer; began her career in the late 1930s, and starred in a number of films in the 1950s. St. Cyr was known for her "bubble bath" stunt, in which she took baths on stage. |

1 Later lyric: "I've interviewed Leslie Howard / I've interviewed Noel Coward."

2 Richard Rodgers, *Richard Rodgers, Musical Stages: An Autobiography* (New York: Random House, 1975), 199.

3 "Margie Hart from Missouri Strips for 40c as the Poor Man's Garbo," *Life*, June 24, 1940, 49.

4 Sally Rand, in Rachel Shteir, *Striptease: The Untold History of the Girlie Show* (New York: Oxford University Press, 2004), 155.

5 Later replaced with "Toscanini."

6 According to Kimball, an earlier version of this lyric names "Rosita Royce" instead of St. Cyr. Royce was another famed stripteaser; her gimmick was live doves, which would alternately cover and uncover her. Dorothy Hart and Robert Kimball, eds., *The Complete Lyrics of Lorenz Hart* (New York: Da Capo Press, 1995), 274.

well, not. Like the "cheap" club numbers in *Pal Joey*, the audience is in on the joke because of their secure class position.

The mechanical, singsong nature of the introduction foreshadows the boredom of Gypsy Rose Lee at the chorus. In last two measures of the introduction, Melba shifts into the character of Lee. Like the highbrow/lowbrow contrast of the introduction, the chorus is marked by the contrast between a middle-class audience's perceptions of a stripper (and all of the classist baggage that went along with it), her actual labor, and her inner intellectual life. The performance of the song—in which the actor playing Melba mimes a striptease in tweed coat, glasses, and low heels—amplifies the disconnect between topic and execution.

The chorus is organized in the standard AABA songform—here, the A sections are typified by Lee's "contained" strip routine and her contrasting intellectual prowess, and the B sections are characterized by a more forward, confrontational delivery, in which she outlines her likes and dislikes. The final A section is each time capped off with a punch line when she dismisses other popular strippers of the period, including Margie Hart, Sally Rand, and Lili St. Cyr. Musically, the audience might expect the chorus to be somewhat raucous, reflecting the "hot" sounds of a typical Minsky strip routine. Rodgers instead goes for "buttoned up": the chorus is at the same moderate tempo as the introduction, and is characterized by woodwind flourishes, tasteful brushwork by the drummer, and pizzicato interjections by the strings.[48] It seems that Rodgers relished the opportunity to emphasize the comic contrast between our buttoned-up reporter and the unzipped chorus, using the innuendo-laden language of burlesque movement. Much of the commentary in *Pal Joey* concerns issues related to sexual containment and its alluring opposite. This song mocks both extremes.

Invoking the image of Lee was deliberate: her name highlighted not only the adult nature of the show, but also its inherent contradictions. Lee was one of the first burlesque stars to gain respect in mainstream venues, and by 1940 Gypsy Rose Lee was considered not only a stripteaser, but also an actor. By the time *Pal Joey* premiered, she had secured her place as an artist, albeit a slightly scandalous one, and appeared in both Minsky shows and on Broadway.[49] She first appeared in *Hot-Cha!* (1932), the Henderson/Brown comedy, then in the *Ziegfeld Follies of 1936*, and was Ethel Merman's replacement, and eventually took over the role, in Porter's *Du Barry Was a Lady* (1939). As far as her stage work goes, she is probably most remembered for her performance in Michael Todd's *Star and Garter* (1942). She never, however, shook her origins as a burlesque entertainer and capitalized on this association throughout her career: at the time of *Pal Joey*'s premiere, she was at work on her first book, *The G-String Murders*, successfully combining what one newspaper writer called her "literary laurels" with her famed stage work.[50]

Lee played up her intellectual prowess in her specialty act, "A Stripteaser's Education," which she performed in the *Ziegfeld Follies of 1936*. According to Rachel Shteir, "the number [. . .] made fun of the slumming literary audience clamoring to understand what she was thinking. Nothing endured like a working-class girl emulating the aristocracy, especially if she did it with style."[51] Here's a typical line from the act:

> And when I display my charms, in all their dazzling splendor
> And prove to you conclusively, I am of the female gender.
> I am really thinking of Elise de Wolff, and the bric-a-brac I saw.
> And that lovely letter I received from Mr. Bernard Shaw.

Lee's legacy disrupted preconceived attitudes toward strippers, and critiqued the traditional sexual mores of the day. Gypsy's act was a precarious dance between working- and middle-class aesthetics and their respective audiences. Though her acts played up her working-class roots via the strip, she did it in such a way to appeal to the "slumming literary audience."

## "ZIP" IN 1940

Jean Casto played the part of Melba in the premiere of *Pal Joey*. Casto, from Jackson Heights, Queens, graduated from the American Academy of Dramatic Arts in 1934, and enjoyed a relatively busy acting career, mostly in straight theater. She was a regular in Abbott productions, featuring in *Three Men and a Horse* (1935), written by Abbott, and *All That Glitters* (1938), produced by Abbott. *Pal Joey* was only one of two musicals that she featured in, the other the premiere of Rodgers and Hammerstein's *Carousel* (she played Mrs. Mullin). Later she went on to play Mrs. Mary Williams (long-suffering wife of crook-turned-good Monk, played by Lionel Stander, who incidentally played Ludlow Lowell in the 1952 revival of *Pal Joey*) in the film comedy *St. Benny the Dip* (1951), one of her only forays into Hollywood. Her film performance, one of the only audible remnants of Casto, reveals a rich alto speaking voice and an admirable acting range.

In an interview from 1941 with the *New York Post*, Casto somewhat sensationally chronicles her study of burlesque theater. She mentions that Abbott and Rodgers "initiated me into that form of recreation by taking me to a matinee around the corner from our rehearsal." She continued,

> My face was red when we entered the burlesque house, but I gradually calmed down watching the strip-teasers. That visit completely disillusioned me about the quality of burlesque humor, but it taught me a lot about torso twisting and the technique of disrobing publicly [. . .] I even began to enjoy my studies [. . .] but I consider my burlesque tour a course in sociology rather than in art.[52]

This interview serves a number of functions: it distances Casto from actual burlesque theater, it positions Casto as a once naive but now worldly character, and it capitalizes on the success of major burlesque stars, including Gypsy Rose Lee. In fact, the interview ends with remarks supposedly made to Casto by Lee (who was watching her sister in the show): "You may [be] all right, Miss Casto, in the legit, but you'd never make the grade for Minsky."[53]

A "legit" actor, Casto brought a "humorous condescension" (in the words of Brooks Atkinson) to the role. Although there are no recordings of her performance, Casto's tough wit remains a part of her legacy. In a review in *Billboard* (from 1949), for instance, the reviewer mentions that after replacing Shirley Booth in the play *Goodbye, My Fancy*, "no better substitute could have been found for her wry way with a caustic line than Jean Casto. The latter gets everything out of the cynical Washington secretary and contributes most of the play's top

*Figure 5.4  Jean Casto (Melba), Averell Harris (Max), and Gene Kelly (Joey), in Pal Joey;*
*NYPL Digital Collections, photo by Vandamm Studio, 1940*

chuckles."[54] Very much embodying the educated, cynical reporter, Casto partially
distances herself from the disreputable elements of burlesque, reaffirming the
class hierarchies emphasized in this scene (see Figure 5.4).

## "ZIP" IN 1952

Elaine Stritch, who played Melba in the 1952 revival and on the Capitol cast recording, emphasized the toughness of the character. At the time of the revival, Stritch
was not yet a name, though she'd featured in a number of Broadway productions.
She had signed the *Pal Joey* contract with the knowledge that Jule Styne, the
producer for the revival, and Rodgers weren't planning on having an out-of-town
tryout. This arrangement would have worked well for Stritch, because she was
at the time acting as Ethel Merman's standby for *Call Me Madam*. Stritch had

*Figure 5.5  Elaine Stritch as Melba Snyder, c. 1952; Museum of the City of New York*

planned on checking in with Merman before each show, then proceeding to the Broadhurst to play Melba Snyder in the second act of *Pal Joey* (she recounted the story many years later in her acclaimed one-woman show *Elaine Stritch at Liberty* [2001–2002], in which she says she figured it would all work out because Merman was such a famed workhorse, and no one thought she'd ever be off: "that'll be the day, right?"). When Stritch found out that *Pal Joey* would in fact have an out-of-town run, she panicked: this change meant that she had to rush between the Imperial Theatre in New York (leaving at 7:30 p.m.) and the Shubert in New Haven (arriving by 10 p.m. for her stage entrance in act 2 at 10:15); she had to drive out twice on matinee days. Thankfully for Stritch, the tryouts lasted only a week (see Figures 5.5 and 5.6).

Stritch's rendition of "Zip" is preserved on the 1952 Capitol cast recording. The orchestrations, by Don Walker, smack much less of "burly-q," compared to the Columbia studio recording sung by Jo Hurt. The reason for this difference is discussed in an amusing and insightful written exchange between Don Walker,

*Figure 5.6  Elaine Stritch as Melba Snyder, c. 1952; Museum of the City of New York*

orchestrator for the 1952 revival of *Pal Joey*, and a theatergoer named Fredrica Winters. In a letter written in January 1952, Winters bemoans the fact that the orchestrations for "Zip" on the revival, which she otherwise loved, are different from the those of the recording of "Zip" on the Columbia recording, which she considers "one of the greatest bits of musical satire I'd ever heard."[55] In response to Winters's query, Walkers apparently went out and bought a copy of the Columbia recording (which it seems, astonishingly, he had not heard), and after talking with musicians who "were on the Columbia date" came to the conclusion that the Columbia recording was a "'jam session.' What they played was never written down, and even the men themselves could never duplicate it exactly."[56] He goes on to say,

> When they started to record "Zip" they found that the arrangement was hopelessly square, and in desperation just told the boys to go ahead and fake anything they could think of. The musicians on the date were just about the finest and highest paid men in the business and they came through beautifully.[57]

His reference to the "hopelessly square" arrangement is a dig at Hans Spialek (the original orchestrator), who, Walker says, was "a very gifted legitimate arranger, who, however, is strictly from Vienna, if you know what I mean." Walker also muses on the different requirements of a song heard in the theater, and a song meant for a record:

> Let me add that I think that even if the arrangement could be duplicated in the theatre it would not be right under those conditions. Pit musicians are not of the calibre of recording men, and what you feel is satire on the record, in the theatre would become heavily obvious comment. You must admit that subtilty [sic] pays off in the present production. Miss Stritch stops the show with a number that has nothing to do with the plot. What more do you want? All this and Harry James too?[58]

Walker's detailed response might reveal a bit of defensiveness, but it also uncovers some interesting information about the intended effect of the song, and Walker's viewpoint on the orchestrations for the 1952 revival. Walker believed that the relatively "buttoned up" effect of the song—in which delicate high woodwind flourishes and understated, muted brass figures feature rather than the smeary brass interjections and bottom-heavy tom-tom patter included on the Columbia recording—was perfectly suitable to the satire implied in the song (see web example 5.4 ▶ for Jo Hurt's performance on the Columbia recording). It is worth noting that since Melba is miming a striptease, including "burly-q" interjections in a stage version would potentially influence the movement of the actor playing Melba. Much of the comic effect of this song is created through the hints toward burlesque, rather than the outright mimicking of it. This effect is much like burlesque itself—in any effective striptease, the audience is left wanting more, precisely because the performer pulls back on the obvious.

This characterization of Lee falls squarely in line with her reputation as, in the words of Stritch, a "piss-elegant stripper." Stritch's performance on the Capitol recording, aided by Walker's orchestrations (which follows the "buttoned up" affect of the original score), avoids overt sexualization in favor of tough cynicism (see web example 5.5 ▶).

The song "Zip," though seemingly just a rousing showstopper unconnected to the rest of the story, cleverly captures much of the anxiety underlying *Pal Joey*. Part of the appeal of "Zip" lies in the way that Melba channels both the deviance of the girl reporter—tied to labor, toughness, and seriousness—and the bored burlesque entertainer—often a glaring omission in discussions of labor, but equally tough. On the surface, one may be tempted to see the girl reporter and the burlesque entertainer as opposite sides of a gendered spectrum—serious versus frivolous; masculine versus feminine; work versus play; buttoned-up versus disrobed; asexual versus hypersexual; mind versus body. These archetypes, however, were equally deviant, and sensationalized a show that in the words of Richard Rodgers "forced the entire musical comedy theater to wear longs pants for the first time."[59] In contrast to the moralizing lessons seen in production-code censored film, the women in *Pal Joey* are not tamed, and our "hero" learns no lessons.

The song "Zip" is especially interesting as it relates to its lyricist. Hart was a closeted gay man, collaborating with one of the most strait-laced composers on Broadway. His lyrics have been read as autobiographical, especially those famously self-deprecating ones, like "your looks are laughable / unphotographable" from "My Funny Valentine," or the reference he makes to Joey as a "half-pint imitation" in "Bewitched, Bothered and Bewildered." Playwright Jerome Lawrence called him the "poet laureate of masochism." The following lyric from "Zip" captures a complex subject position:

> I don't like a deep contralto
> Or a man whose voice is alto
> Zip! I'm a heterosexual.

Though one might read this as an endorsement of gendered binaries, its sentiment is made unstable because of the ambiguous subject position of both the character and the lyricist. And perhaps these lines hide more than they reveal. Rather like the end of O'Hara's *New Yorker* story—where Melba reveals not only that she's conventionally attractive, but also that she's married, and that her husband used to "play football at Dartmouth" and is "satisfactory in every other way"—Melba's, and Gypsy Rose Lee's, toughness is undercut by their reliance on an imbalanced, gendered power structure.[60] The same can be said of Vera, who holds power over Joey only because she has a wealthy husband. Still, the popularity of the hard-boiled girl reporter and the ambivalent stripteaser, and the emergence of the sexually frank middle-aged woman, shows that this power structure was starting to erode.

Soon, however, these tough female characters were to be replaced by archetypes like the *femme fatale* and the love goddess of the 1940s and, eventually, by the *Playboy*-approved bombshell of the 1950s. Their mark, however, can be seen later on Broadway, in characters like Mame, or Charity, or even Sally Bowles. Ultimately, Vera and Melba both reflect a challenge to the typical, two-dimensional depictions of women on stage. The vibrancy of Vivienne Segal's, Jean Casto's, and Elaine Stritch's performances reveal the creative negotiations that women made while navigating masculine environments both within and outside of the entertainment industry.

# JOEY DANCES

• • •

The dancing in a musical often takes up more than half the time of the entire performance, it represents days of hard work and grueling rehearsals for the boys and girls and, nowadays, is an important asset to any show. But somehow recognition is slow in coming.[1]

—Robert Alton, 1940

If there is any virtue in being taken strictly for granted, the dancing in musical comedy and revue deserves some special crown. For there is no part of theatre today which at its own level and in its own way manages to be so finished in effect and at the same time so sparingly considered on the critic's page.[2]

—George Beiswanger, 1940

Alton and Beiswanger's comments reflect the state of dance criticism during their time. Not only did dance receive little attention from critics, but because of this neglect audiences didn't know how to talk in an informed way about the vibrant numbers that kept them coming back to the theater. Beiswanger, one of a small handful of dance critics commenting on Broadway shows, went on to say that the lack of attention to dance might have been "all to the good," for "there has been no superimposed and pretentious aesthetic to mix up the purposes of craftsmen selling their wares to a public which knew what it wanted only as it happened to like what it got."[3] Producers probably appreciated that dance appeared to be an organic expression of a show's spirit. Still, choreographers from the period—who most often identified as "dance directors"—deserve more attention paid to their craft, which was indispensable to the shows they worked on. Centering dance also helps resist the common practice of valuing live performance only by that which is tangible (i.e., the musical score and the script).

Referring to the typical theater critic's grasp of music, Richard Rodgers once said, "it would be helpful if the boys had a somewhat sharper musical perception which would enable them to tell the public what to expect from a score."[4] In the case of dance, the perception was even less sharp. From the late 1920s to the early 1940s John Martin, dance critic for the *New York Times*, was one of only two dance critics employed by a major newspaper in the United States.[5]

*Pal Joey*. Julianne Lindberg, Oxford University Press (2020). © Oxford University Press.
DOI: 10.1093/oso/9780190051204.001.0001

The previously mentioned Beiswanger wrote for the smaller publication *Theatre Arts*, and Edwin Denby, who went on to become a major figure in dance criticism, wrote for the magazine *Modern Music*. Martin's employment, which began in 1927, was precipitated by a new interest in dance in the United States, reflected in the burgeoning new schools of American dance that, like all branches of the arts in the United States, were part of a larger cultural project concerned with American identity and native artistic expression. Martin was particularly interested in modern dance, and was instrumental in furthering the career of Martha Graham. Although his focus at *The Times* was on classical dance, Martin also took time to comment on Broadway dance trends. As early as 1928, he was praising dancer directors such as Busby Berkeley, and later Albertina Rasch, for raising the standard of dance in musical comedies and revues.[6] When *Pal Joey* rolled around, Martin was one of a handful of critics to understand that Kelly's special way of characterizing Joey through dance was a big part of why the show worked:

> As a rule it is easy to separate the work of a Broadway dancer from the show in which he appears, for his numbers are generally to be classed as specialties which he has been hired specifically to do. It is quite simple to point out that his technique is good or bad, his style original or commonplace, his tricks brilliant or merely difficult, his manner suave or aggressive. Not so with Kelly and "Pal Joey," for here dancing and character are far more closely united than in the majority of ballets, and through both there runs a penetrating line of comment which makes it possible to laugh at Joey instead of shooting him forthwith.[7]

Martin's keen perception was rare, and is now rarer still.

In musical theater studies, the kinetic vibrancy of dance is too often considered secondary to the total effect of a show. When Broadway choreographers do get mentioned, they're usually praised for how well their dances characterize a mood or character, or for their role in a show's artistic vision; choreographers are certainly judged for how their dances propel or impede the dramatic action of a show. While these concerns are certainly worth discussing, and of central concern to some of the dances in *Pal Joey*, dance does so much more than tell a story. It can also viscerally engage an audience, reinforcing the interdependent nature of live performance. It can dynamize the space of the stage, the theater, and the diegetic world of the musical. Dance can also, quite literally, stop the show. In many shows from the 1920s and 1930s, this function was practical—showstopping numbers amplified the excitement of going to the theater and, through applause and standing ovations, almost certainly created in audiences feelings of mutual goodwill with the performers. While Oscar Hammerstein found showstoppers to be problematic, halting, he felt, the forward momentum of the story, Robert Alton and other dance directors from his time saw these moments as sure signs that they were doing their jobs.

The historical record shows that without Alton and Kelly, *Pal Joey* might well have been unpalatable for audiences. Dance saved the show from the danger of being too "straight" in regard to book, and too unpleasant in regard to character and situation. But due in large part to the lack of dance criticism during the period, many critics, and subsequently historians, have focused almost solely on the music and the book to explain its success and influence. This chapter will attempt to give dance its due.

## ROBERT ALTON (1897–1957)

> Bob never invented a new style of dance the way Jack Cole did or the way I always tried to do. What he did, the fusion of the styles that remained there, was so excellent, was so good, he should be given far more credit, I think.
>
> —Gene Kelly, on Robert Alton

Robert Alton was a veteran of Broadway dance well before he began his first job for Rodgers and Hart. While eventually known for his tenure as dance director at MGM during its heyday (represented by his work on *The Harvey Girls, Till the Clouds Roll By, Easter Parade, Show Boat* [1951], *The Pirate, Words and Music*, the film version of *Annie Get Your Gun, White Christmas*, and many others), Alton was for a time the most prolific and respected dance director on Broadway. In one season alone, Alton had "staged the dances for three hit musicals playing on Broadway [. . .], [had] a fourth on the road after months in New York, a fifth in rehearsal and [was] signed for a sixth and seventh in quick succession."[8] He became known for his ability to spot and cultivate talented dancers, for his upbeat, youthful dances, and, as was increasingly remarked upon by critics, for his ability to reflect character through movement and weave dance into the narrative of a story.

Trained in ballet, Alton studied in Springfield, Massachusetts with Ralph McKernan, whose other famous pupil was Eleanor Powell. He went on to study in New York with Mikhail Mordkin, formerly of the Bolshoi Ballet and the Ballets Russes and an early energizer of ballet in America. Through Mordkin Alton made his way to Broadway, first featuring in Mordkin's *Take It to Me* (1919), and then again with Mordkin's company in the *Greenwich Village Follies of 1924*. The latter production brought him into contact with both Cole Porter, whom he would work with extensively in the 1930s, and John Murray Anderson, whose penchant for lavish production numbers and eye for detail would influence Alton's approach toward Broadway dance. Alton would learn from Anderson the importance of staying focused on a show's commercial value: they were playing to a paying public who wanted showstoppers, and to producers who demanded them.

After touring with the *Greenwich Village Follies*, Alton began choreographing in earnest, first for a vaudeville show in a St. Louis movie house, and later in New York. There he acted as assistant to a number of workhorse choreographers, including the tap veterans Bobby Connolly and Sammy Lee, from whom he would learn popular dance styles that Alton, gifted with an ear for rhythm, would later integrate into his dance routines. During this time he assisted with the *Ziegfeld*

*Follies of 1927, 1931,* and *1933.* Since the nature of the revue is one of variety, Alton developed his eye and ear, becoming an expert in both dancing and choreographing tap, Latin dance styles (which were in vogue nearly the entire time he worked on Broadway), modern dance, acrobatic numbers, satiric dances, and character-driven dances. Alton choreographed his first Broadway show in 1933—the musical comedy *Hold Your Horses*—and quickly thereafter became known for his slick production numbers, his efficient rehearsal style, and his ability to get the audience up and out of their seats.

Alton's first big success came in 1934 with *Anything Goes*, his second collaboration with Cole Porter. The show was a huge success, and both Porter's and Alton's stars rose accordingly—reviews were nearly unanimously positive, with Atkinson calling it a "thundering good song-and-dance-show."[9] It is worth mentioning that Atkinson didn't reference Alton by name in his review—he does of course mention Porter, but generally focuses the review on the trio of leading stars: Victor Moore, Ethel Merman, and William Gaxton. Of Merman he says, "If Ethel Merman did not write 'I Get a Kick out of You' and also the title song of the show she has made them hers now by the swinging gusto of her platform style."[10] This statement gets right to the heart of the tension between authorship and collaboration in musical theater: who gets first credit? Atkinson does give credit to the "platoon of chorus girls whose dancing is also well planned," the "suite of [Donald] Oenslager settings," and the "wardrobe of gowns by Jenkins," but Alton goes unmentioned by name.

Regardless, the year 1934 was a good one for Alton: besides *Anything Goes*, he would cement his success with a string of other successful shows, including *Life Begins at 8:40, Thumbs Up,* and the *Ziegfeld Follies of 1934.* From that point on, he was considered one of the top dance directors on Broadway—although he experienced a few flops (including the leftist *Parade* in 1935 and Porter's *You Never Know* in 1938), he was generally connected with successful shows. And even in those shows that were flops, his dance routines were praised, sometimes referred to as the only saving grace of an otherwise tedious show. From 1938 to 1942, Alton's greatest successes were with Porter (*Leave It to Me, Du Barry Was a Lady,* and *Panama Hattie*), and Rodgers and Hart (*Too Many Girls, Pal Joey,* and *By Jupiter*).

Alton's working style was somewhat legendary: he was uncompromising, and demanded hard work from his dancers. His rehearsal style also reflected the quick, heady world of musical comedy. As Agnes de Mille put it,

> [He worked] at a speed suggestive of a radio sports commentator, with a whistle between his teeth. The dancers adored him. No time was wasted in his rehearsals. Slick, finished and speedy, the work went together. There were no great moments of dramatic revelation, but each routine was solidly built and effective.[11]

Alton and de Mille first met in 1937 when he was called in to "doctor" her choreography on *Hooray for What!*, de Mille's first—and disastrous—experience on Broadway. An antiwar satire, *Hooray for What!* failed at its preview in Boston, and de Mille was fired the next day.[12] Despite her terrible experience on the show—on top of her constant wrangling with Harry Kaufman, the business manager for the Shuberts, she remembers the way the chorus girls were treated like meat by management—she remembers her time with Alton fondly. De Mille states that "[t]he only pleasant episode connected with this experience was a conversation I had with Robert Alton," wherein he gave her some advice, which she took as an act of "true generosity": "[h]e was neither pompous nor boasting; he spoke out of friendly good will and a vast experience."[13] She lays out his advice for running rehearsals:

1. Begin with something technical and definite.
2. Begin on time. Be prompt.
3. Do not let the chorus sit down.
4. Never let them make a mistake. Do not pass over a fault. Stop them in the middle of a bar if necessary and correct.
5. Polish as you go along.
6. Never seem in doubt.
7. Never let the bosses see anything unfinished. If you have only eight bars to show them, show them this much and no more. If you have not this much, get up yourself and demonstrate.[14]

De Mille viewed numbers 6 and 7 as remnants of old Broadway, where the "old-style producer" reigned, and said that number 4 was necessary because Alton was working with chorus dancers, rather than "artists."[15] Still, de Mille took Alton's advice to heart, using most of it for the rest of her life.[16]

Alton's unique style was characterized by a kind of full-body tap foundation, wherein he united the attention to the torso of ballet with the footwork of tap, over which "elements of ballroom, ballet, folk, or ethnic dance could be grafted."[17] As Cecil Smith boldly stated, Alton represented "the truest and best representative in our time of the historic qualities of American popular theater dancing."[18] Alton was also known for the way he "broke up the chorus line," giving individualized parts to the dancers. *The Times* described his style this way:

Alton's style consists in following the identical technique of a dramatic sketch. Each of his dancers, male and female, dances an individual part. The old chorus line with twenty girls kicking precisely together, evolving every step in unison, all cogs in a dancing machine, is gone from Broadway. It remains in the Music Hall but not in musical shows. Instead, each dancer of Alton's is now an entity, doing different steps, the many blending into one whole pleasing unit. Many postures, many steps, many varying poses and effects—that is what an Alton dance number is made of.[19]

This descriptive language resonates with the ways that critics and scholars have discussed the term "integration." Here, individuating the chorus line is described as a technique in the service of creating a cohesive, total effect. Gene Kelly compared Alton's contributions in this area to George Balanchine's, a choreographer who was Alton's contemporary:

> What Bob Alton did was take a bunch of dancers who were trained—up to the point the dancers were trained at that time—and he amalgamated them into contrapuntal groups, very much with pop music the way that Balanchine did and does and always had with classical music. The girls would be the flutes and the other group would be the violins, and the boys would be the bass. [Balanchine would] have every instrument pretty much marked out, if you'd start to skeletalize the work. Being such a great musician himself, it seems such a natural thing for him to do. Well, Bob Alton did that very much. He was so successful and the proof was that every time he did a chorus number, it would stop the show.[20]

Alton's trick seemed to be his ability to fuse existing dance styles and pay heed to story and character without making any kind of grand statement about dance, musical comedy, and notions of "art"; in this way, he was the antithesis of Balanchine. John Martin put it this way:

> If Mr. Alton can lay out a nice tap routine or set his dancers jittering with the most frenetic, on the other hand the ballet is by no means unknown to him, nor are his eyes closed to the innovation in movement that the so-called modern dancers have revealed. He is innocent, however, of all taint of artiness, and can be chic without being chi-chi.[21]

The idea that Alton advanced Broadway dance from the precision drills typical of chorus lines of the 1910s and 1920s is sound. And yet his style captured the essence of musical comedy in the 1930s: quick-witted, sexy, youthful, full of variety, and energetic. Balanchine, especially in the last two decades, has been given the credit he is due in regard to his contributions to Broadway dance. Alton, who in many ways was the dance director most emblematic of Broadway during the period, has not.

## ALTON, BALANCHINE, AND BROADWAY DANCE

The relationship between Alton, Balanchine, and Rodgers and Hart is worth teasing out. Of the ten shows that Rodgers and Hart wrote after their return from Hollywood between 1935 and 1942—the most successful years of their partnership—only two of them were choreographed by someone other than Balanchine or Alton (see Table 6.1). Of the eight remaining shows, Balanchine choreographed four (*On Your Toes, Babes in Arms, I Married an Angel,* and *The Boys from Syracuse*), and Alton choreographed four (*Too Many Girls, Higher and Higher, Pal Joey,* and *By Jupiter*), splitting their contributions chronologically: Balanchine choreographed the shows between 1936 and 1938, and Alton the shows between 1939 and 1942.[22] Tellingly, the four unifying figures in Rodgers and Hart's

Table 6.1 Choreographer, producer, and run of Rodgers and Hart's post-Hollywood original book shows

| Production | Date of Premiere | Run of Show | Rank (Run of Performance) | Choreographer | Producer |
|---|---|---|---|---|---|
| Jumbo[1] | 11/16/1935 | 233 | 9[2] | Allan K. Foster[3] | Billy Rose |
| On Your Toes | 04/11/1936 | 315 | 4 | Balanchine | Wiman[4] |
| Babes in Arms | 04/14/1937 | 289 | 6 | Balanchine | Wiman |
| I'd Be Rather Be Right | 11/02/1937 | 290 | 5 | Charles Weidman | Sam Harris |
| I Married an Angel | c5/11/1938 | 338 | 3 | Balanchine | Wiman |
| The Boys from Syracuse | 11/23/1938 | 235 | 8 | Balanchine | Abbott[5] |
| Too Many Girls | 10/18/1939 | 249 | 7 | Alton | Abbott[6] |
| Higher and Higher | 04/4/1940 | 84[7] | 10 | Alton | Wiman |
| Pal Joey | 12/25/1940 | 374 | 2 | Alton | Abbott[8] |
| By Jupiter | 06/03/1942 | 427 | 1 | Alton | Wiman |

1 Abbott directed the book for Jumbo, his first collaboration with Rodgers and Hart.

2 While this ranking is based purely on number of performances, the venue for Jumbo—the Hippodrome—was far larger than any of the other theaters'(the seating capacity for Jumbo was 4300), and more tickets were sold for the show than for any other by Rodgers and Hart. See Geoffrey Block, "'Bigger Than a Show—Better Than a Circus': The Broadway Musical, Radio, and Billy Rose's Jumbo," Musical Quarterly 89, nos. 2–3 (2006): 168.

3 Jumbo was not a typical show, and the space of the Hippodrome called for more dramatic movement. Foster was credited with "equestrian, acrobatic and aerial ballets."

4 It should be noted that Abbott also wrote the bulk of the book for this show, marking his second collaboration with Rodgers and Hart.

5 Abbott also wrote and directed the show.

6 Abbott also directed the show.

7 The show returned that August for a short run of twenty performances.

8 Abbott also directed the show.

post-Hollywood period were Balanchine and Alton, and George Abbott and producer Dwight Deere Wiman. Rodgers and Hart effectively had one foot each in the world of musical comedy—full of flash and fun—and one foot each in the world of Broadway ballet. Three of Balanchine's shows were produced by Wiman, and the remaining one by Abbott. Alton worked with Wiman and Abbott on two shows, respectively. Abbott and Wiman were different men, and left their mark on their respective shows in individual ways. While Abbott was very hands-on and his influence often traceable, Wiman's contribution was "rather more difficult to quantify."[23]

While all of Rodgers and Hart's post-Hollywood shows were innovative in distinct ways, the shows they did with Balanchine tended to foreground dance as an integral part of the storytelling. Because of Balanchine's stature—a European dancer and choreographer who had worked with the forward-thinking Ballets Russes, who was at work founding an American school of ballet, and whose ballet company was in residence at the Metropolitan Opera—his contributions to *On Your Toes*, his first collaboration with Rodgers and Hart, were thought of in a different way from that of a "mere" dance director. Up to that point, Rodgers and Hart had worked with most of the great dance directors on Broadway, including Ned Wayburn (*Poor Little Ritz Girl*), Seymour Felix (*Peggy-Ann, Simple Simon*), Sammy Lee (*Betsy*), Busby Berkeley (*Connecticut Yankee, Present Arms*), Jack Haskell (*Chee-Chee*), and Bobby Connolly (*Spring Is Here, America's Sweetheart*). Felix was the innovative mind behind the dance sequences in the surrealistic *Peggy-Ann*; in the finale Felix was part of the team (including Rodgers, Hart, Herb Fields, and Lew Fields) that decided to opt out of a loud flashy finale in favor of something that better supported the book.[24] Despite having worked extensively with dance directors, Rodgers expressed that he felt a bit out of his depth with a "choreographer." As he later put it,

> I didn't know a thing about choreography and told Balanchine that I was unsure how we should go about it. Did he devise his steps first and expect me to alter tempos whenever necessary, or did he fit his steps to the music as written? Balanchine smiled and with that wonderful Russian accent of his said simply, "You write. I put on." And that was the way we worked. He used the music just the way I had written it and created his dance patterns to conform.[25]

Rodgers's comment reveals that he saw Balanchine as an equal creative collaborator, and was even open to following Balanchine's choreography, a concession he made for no other choreographer during his collaborations with Hart. In Rodgers's autobiography, and in interviews, Balanchine is the only choreographer whom Rodgers gives such deference to; in fact, he rarely mentions choreographers at all. We might speculate that the ubiquitous presence of dance directors, and their lowly position in the eyes of critics (who rarely mentioned them at any length), made Rodgers take them somewhat for granted. Certainly, the high-art credentials of Balanchine appealed to Rodgers, as did the idea that ballet could neatly contribute to the story. And this elite association was certainly in vogue at the time. The reference to ballet in *On Your Toes*—in story, choreographer, and dancers—was particularly effective because Russian ballet, which had made such a splash in Paris via the avant-garde Ballets Russes, had found an eager audience in America. As in Paris, American interest in all things Russian was rooted in an allure for the exotic as well as an interest in what ballet might contribute to American culture, both high and middlebrow. Incorporating Russian ballet into musical comedy contributed to a larger movement intent on elevating the musical. As James Steichen puts it, "'On Your Toes' is significant because it realizes the larger ambitions claimed by the musical as a whole. It was the prestige of ballet, and in particular modern Russian ballet, that helped elevate the musical."[26] Rodgers called Balanchine in whenever ballet was called for (as in "Peter's Journey" in *Babes in Arms* and the "At the Roxy Music Hall" number from *I Married an Angel*, the latter of which included an "arty underwater ballet" featuring the ballerina Vera Zorina). Balanchine also choreographed *The Boys from Syracuse*, which, like *On Your Toes*, lampooned "highbrow" art (this time Shakespeare) while also using it to boost its cultural credentials; this was Balanchine's only production with Abbott.

Rodgers's statement upon first working with Balanchine—"I didn't know a thing about choreography"—is either disingenuous, or simply a confirmation that he believed "choreography" was something altogether separate from Broadway dance. Abbott too, despite his mostly down-to-earth fare, was bitten by the Balanchine bug. Later, when accounting for the relative flop that was Rodgers and Hammerstein's *Me and Juliet* (which he directed), Abbott partially blamed its failure on the fact that Alton, whom he called a "routine, old-fashioned choreographer," was signed to stage the dances rather than someone like Balanchine.[27] While Broadway dance had surely shifted by 1953, the year *Me and Juliet* premiered, Alton's dances were never routine (critics always remarked upon the opposite effect), and he certainly was not an "old-fashioned choreographer." Alton was at that point working primarily for MGM; just a year later, he would choreograph the tongue-in-cheek number "Choreography," featuring Danny Kaye, in the film *White Christmas*. That number comments humorously on the divisions between so-called choreography and Broadway dance, a division Alton saw play out on Broadway in real time.

Alton's contributions to the musicals of Rodgers and Hart are of the youthful and exuberant variety. Alton's first collaboration with Rodgers and Hart—*Too Many Girls*—was symbolic of musical comedy. A collegiate "boy-and-girl" show, it was, according to Atkinson, "humorous, fresh and exhilarating," and he referred to the "vivacious dancing" as "especially jaunty."[28] It ran for a respectable 249 performances. Alton was praised by critics for the energetic act 1 closer ("an exciting bolero number danced infectiously and with mounting enthusiasm by the ensemble") and for the finale, a comic ensemble number titled "Give It Back to the Indians," a drag on New York City.[29] The youthfulness of the choreography—which required a great deal of talent and rehearsal on the part of the dancers—was typical of Alton's collaborations with Rodgers and Hart.

Alton's next show with the duo was not as successful. *Higher and Higher*—about a "maid who is passed off as a debutante," featuring Jack Haley, back from an extended stay in Hollywood, and a live trained seal on stage—closed after just eighty-four performances.[30] The book was weak, as most critics highlighted, and Vera Zorina, the star they had in mind for the title female role and who had done so well in *I Married an Angel*, was not available. As Rodgers later said, "If a trained seal steals your show, you don't have a show."[31] The saving grace of the musical, however, was the dancing. As Arthur Pollock put it in a feature titled "'Higher and Higher' Is Best When It's Dancing," "It is Robert Alton [. . .] who does most to make 'Higher and Higher' the swift and exciting thing it is at its best."[32] Atkinson, who said that "'Higher and Higher' may fall a bit short of the highest ranking," also praised Alton:

> Robert Alton, who stages dancing with extraordinary industry month after month, seems to have no end of ideas for stepping, skipping and whirling; and, as every one knows, the boys and girls of the chorus have ingenious feet.[33]

After *Higher and Higher* Alton was signed on for *Pal Joey*. By this time, Alton was one of the most respected dance directors on Broadway. In a feature from February 1940, John Martin stated that Alton had a virtual "monopoly" over Broadway choreography, and that he was a "young man of taste and ingenuity."[34] In an homage to Alton in *The Times* from March 1940, titled "Dances by Robert Alton" (a cheeky reference to his ubiquitous presence in playbills and reviews), he is credited for the precision of his choreography, and the perfection he expected from the dancers:

> Alton speaks with the quick, but quiet, authority born of years of handling groups of chorus girls, chorus boys, dancers, specialty artists, actors and temperamental principals. He demands instantaneous obedience in a profession notably disobedient. He demands obedience and gets it; and they like him for it. He knows his business, he can do the steps he demands and he has revolutionized musical comedy dancing in the past seven years.[35]

By the time of *By Jupiter* (1942), Alton was routinely being called the "best of the dance directors," or some variation on the same.[36]

So why has Alton been forgotten? One reason could be that he never wrote any of his dances down. As Zachary Dorsey explains, the word "choreography" literally means "dance writing"; the entrenched tradition of dividing and valuing cultural products along the oral versus literate binary is undoubtedly at play here.[37] Alton wasn't writing for posterity, but for the immediate making of a hit; he once said, "I have exactly six minutes in which to raise the customer out of his seat. If I cannot do it, I am no good."[38] Alton did, however, want Broadway dance to be recognized for the value it imparted to a show. To return to the comment that began this chapter, which Alton made in 1940 while working on the revue *Hellzapoppin*,

> [t]he dancing in a musical often takes up more than half the time of the entire performance, it represents days of hard work and grueling rehearsals for the

boys and girls and, nowadays, is an important asset to any show. But somehow recognition is slow in coming and I do believe straight-forward criticism and recognition of this work would help the dancers as well as the director.[39]

Just as theater critics are were often serious students of drama, "straight-forward criticism" would require a knowledge of the technical and creative elements of dance. Alton's practice of never writing anything down was part of his creative process: he believed that it kept him from repeating himself, and allowed for creative spontaneity. As he once said in an interview,

> First I study the book. Then I consult with the scenic designer and the costumer. We exchange ideas. With all this firmly in my mind I call a rehearsal. I say "Do this." And it's a step. I don't know why. It's always been that way.[40]

Later, while working on the revival of *Pal Joey*, he elaborated on this practice:

> I had forgotten the original *Pal Joey* choreography completely. I compose choreography spontaneously, and never make graphs or charts. I never do anything about choreography until I'm actually in rehearsal. I don't want to repeat myself so I forget it purposely. To my knowledge there is only one little step the girls do in *Pal Joey* now which was in the show originally.[41]

Alton's approach to staging dances is antithetical to the notion of withstanding "the test of time," a value that has been central to Western art ideals since the eighteenth century. The spontaneity of his practice, and his collaborative approach, defy typical discussions of dance on Broadway, which often include issues related to ownership, copyright, and creative credit. Thus, the work of dance pioneers like Alton is often forgotten.

## GENE KELLY: TOUGH, CHARMING, WORKING CLASS

Gene Kelly's contributions to *Pal Joey*, and to American dance in general, have been better documented. For John O'Hara, Gene Kelly *was* Joey. He felt this strongly enough that when Kelly left the show (he played from opening night until September 7, 1941), O'Hara wrote an op ed for *Newsweek*, warning audiences off the production.[42] O'Hara's appreciation for Kelly makes a great deal of sense: like O'Hara, Kelly was an Irish boy from Pennsylvania, and also like O'Hara, Kelly valued a kind of masculine toughness that came out in his characterization of Joey; this is reflected in *Time*'s review of the show: "As Joey, lean, dark Gene Kelly has a treacherous Irish charm, a sweet Irish tenor, a catlike dancing grace that makes vice almost as appealing as virtue."[43] Stanley Donen, who would go on to become a prominent director and celebrated collaborator with Kelly at MGM, met Kelly while working on *Pal Joey*. Just sixteen and a member of the chorus, Donen remembers that Kelly overshadowed everyone, including Vivienne Segal.

As Donen put it, "there are those moments on Broadway when people appear for the first time that are sort of sign posts."[44]

Kelly wasn't a singer, but a talented dancer who had also spent many hours in vaudeville houses and after-hours "cloops," learning tap steps from the great vaudevillians and street dancers in order to bring these steps back to his students at the Kelly family dance studio. Kelly's background and proficiencies were the perfect combination for the character Joey: his singing voice was fair but untutored, lending Joey a realistically working-class persona, and at the time he was deliberately working to communicate character through dance.[45] He would later use this talent to his advantage on screen. But before Kelly was Joey, he tested out a number of personas on the Broadway stage, including his iconic working-class Average Joe, which would directly impact his characterization of Joey.

Kelly's road to Broadway was smoothed over by his acquaintance with Robert Alton. Alton first met Kelly in Pittsburgh, when Kelly helped supply Alton with dancers from the Kelly family dance studio. Alton and Kelly hit it off; Kelly later called himself a "protégé of his on Broadway."[46] Alton helped him land his first job in the chorus for Porter's *Leave It to Me*, for which Alton directed the dances (and in which, coincidentally, Mary Martin had her big breakout role). Kelly then went on to feature in the intimate revue *One for the Money,* written by Nancy Hamilton and again choreographed by Robert Alton. Kelly's next performance—his penultimate show on Broadway—was his biggest break yet, and caught him the attention of Rodgers. The show was William Saroyan's *The Time of Your Life*, which premiered in October 1939. Billed as a straight play, *The Time of Your Life* nevertheless was saturated with mostly diegetic music, including "old country" harmonica tunes, a nostalgic recurrence of the song "The Missouri Waltz," and piano music played by the character Wesley, written and performed by Reginald Beane. Kelly played the part of Harry, a desperate hoofer with dreams of making it big as a dancing comedian; Harry and Wesley acted as a pair, with Harry dancing to Wesley's piano music. The pair reflected the tone of the action on stage: when things were going well, the pair danced and played exuberantly. When the villain (a vice cop named Blick) entered and bullied the lead character, the feel-good atmosphere was shattered: "Harry doesn't know what to do with his hands or feet. Wesley's arms hang at his sides."[47] Harry's working-class, melancholy affect—complemented by a suit that was slightly too big for him—was realized mostly through dance. Kelly would remark on this in subsequent interviews:

> I learned then that one can make dance fit a characterization, which was a revelation to me [. . .] I found out that I could dance as a trained dancer and make myself not look like a trained dancer.[48]

This attention to character was noticed by many critics, and perhaps piqued the interest of Rodgers and O'Hara, who both hoped to cast a lead that would take the edge off a hard-to-endure character. Kelly's rough-around-the-edges performance and his uncommon talent for dance revealed that he could be a good fit for Joey, who needed to be both charming and heelish.

Critical reactions to Kelly's Joey demonstrate that even when the reviewer disproved of the setting and situation, Kelly was impressive in the role. A particularly scathing review, published by the *Parents League Bulletin*, said that "[o]nly Gene Kelly's acting as Joey, the dances designed by Alton, and Mielziner's lighting come up to the standard of Rodgers' music, which deserves a far better story."[49] Another, by a staff correspondent at the *Christian Science Monitor*, said that "Mr. Kelly [. . .] proved in 'The Time of Your Life' what a charming young man he is. This charm is always present in his accomplished and graceful dancing. Otherwise, he is defeated—not by his own deficiencies but by the character Joey."[50] The most notorious review was of course given by Atkinson. Of Kelly, Atkinson said, "His cheap and flamboyant unction, his nervous cunning, his trickiness are qualities that Mr. Kelly catches without forgetting the fright and gaudiness of a petty fakir. Mr. Kelly is also a brilliant tap dancer—'makes with the feet,' as it goes in his vernacular—and his performance on both scores is triumphant. If Joey must be acted, Mr. Kelly can do it."[51]

Most reviews, including all the big New York papers save *The Times*, praised Kelly without reservation. Burns Mantle, of the *New York Daily News*, got right to the point, highlighting Kelly's essential likability:

> Happily young Mr. Kelly is able to give the part personal attractions that justify the O'Hara picture. He is likable as an individual and gifted as a dancer. Technically his range is wide without including any impulse toward the eccentric, which makes for an agreeable artistic balance.[52]

The loquacious Sidney B. Whipple, of the *New York World-Telegram*, similarly tied Kelly's appeal to his dancing ability:

> And, thanks to the expert direction of George Abbott and the aptitude of a young man named Gene Kelly, Mr. O'Hara's delightful sense of satire is unimpaired [. . .] Gene Kelly, who may be remembered as the dancing comedian of *The Time of Your Life*, is made for the part of Pal Joey. He brings out the amusing worthlessness of the young man, his cocky self-confidence, his magnificent pretensions. He maintains a certain amount of naivete even during his most ruthless chase after one of his mice. And he is extremely attractive. Mr. Kelly dances amazingly.[53]

Richard Watts, of the *New York Herald Tribune*, arrived at the same point as John Martin, astutely observing that Kelly preemptively saved a show that could have been disastrous with the wrong casting:

> It was a happy stroke of casting that placed Mr. Kelly in the title role. This young man, who was so good last season in "The Time of Your Life," is genuinely life-saving to "Pal Joey" for, if the chief part were not properly cast, the new musical show might have been too merciless for comfort. Mr. Kelly does nothing obvious about softening his characterization but he does manage to combine a certain amount of straightforward personal charm with the realism

of his portrait, so that Joey actually achieves the feat of being at once heel and hero.[54]

Although Watts didn't focus on Kelly's dancing in this passage, it is fair to say that his "straightforward personal charm" was telegraphed in large part through dance. And while Alton was credited with the dances, Kelly later said in an interview that Alton "would let me try things of my own." Kelly elaborated,

> When it came to certain things, Bob Alton would say, "Now what would you do there, Gene?" [. . .] He would chuckle when I would try things that nobody else was doing. He'd say, "My God! Where did you pick that up?" and I'd say, "Oh, I just made it up." And he'd say, "Now isn't that silly. That's great." And he'd incorporate it in the dance. That was very encouraging [. . .] Certain things happened dance-wise in that show that perhaps wouldn't have happened with any other choreographer.[55]

Alton's willingness to collaborate with Kelly disturbs the idea that Alton was a sole creative agent, and is perhaps another reason that historians don't tend to take him seriously as an artist. Really, though, the collaborative process—which is always central to musical theater—is just made more transparent because of Kelly and Alton's basic agreeableness.

While working on *Pal Joey*, Kelly encountered a problem that he needed to work out with Alton. He called it a "bit of a paradox":

> Just because [Joey] could only get a job in a fourth-rate nightclub, I couldn't then dance like a fourth-rate dancer. So I had to start thinking about that problem [. . .] So we combined, Mr. Alton and myself, some things like unusual and energetic steps that might be done in a kind of a cheap act, but would be exciting at the same time.[56]

Alton, Abbott, and Kelly agreed that a guy like Joey, who was constantly scheming and making passes at chorus girls ("taki[ing] them to bed one by one" when he could), would have endless amounts of energy. Alton and Kelly saw that this quality could be conveyed through dance:

> Some in just fast tap dancing, some of it was done with leaps, and some was done with good old-fashioned acrobatic tricks. But Alton and I worked that out very laboriously. That I think was difficult to do and I think maybe it was rare [. . .] I think it was unique to that production of *Pal Joey*.[57]

In this same interview, Kelly goes into detail about a scene in which dance was made to fit the character. In the act 2 song "Take Him," when Vera (Vivienne Segal) and Linda (Leila Ernst) finally decide to kick Joey to the curb, Kelly was positioned on one side of the stage, dancing and obliviously showing off as each woman lists his many faults. As Kelly described it,

> It was a strutty kind of dance. It was a tap done in tango rhythm, and it worked. It worked because it was a young male peacock doing this strut whereas if he had done a tap dance with bent knees, just done that, it wouldn't have had

that Spanish arrogant look that the good Spanish dancers get. We couldn't do a Spanish dance, of course, so we mixed it up with the tap.[58]

A portion of this dance sequence can be seen in the "La Cumparsita" sequence from the film *Anchors Aweigh* (1945); Kelly stated that "the first eight bars were the same" as the tap-tango from *Pal Joey*.[59] As Kelly tells it, "La Cumparsita" was based on the dance he did for "Take Him"—the dance was characterized by quick percussive footwork, based on tap dancing, paired with an erect upper body, in the way of a tango. The effect here is one of cockiness—Kelly and Alton combined the working-class association of tap with what might be read as the sensual machismo of the tango posture to characterize the young, cocky Joey. This dance was all about capturing the character. Martin praised Kelly's approach to characterization, simultaneously bemoaning the hierarchical divisions in the dance world:

> It has not been the habit of these definitely high-brow columns to consider the musical comedy field when annual awards are to be made, but when this field surreptitiously produces a work of art that is considerably better than most of the works that frankly admit to being art, all rules are off and all barriers down. A medal, by all means, for Mr. Kelly.[60]

## *PAL JOEY* AND ITS CHORUS

> Bob would take a group and always stop a show cold with a chorus [. . .] The choruses learned a lot from him, but they learned in a quasi-balletic way.[61]

—Gene Kelly

The dance numbers from *Pal Joey* that critics most often commented on were the jazzy chorus pieces. Four of the dance features, in particular, were meant to get the audience up and out of their seats: "You Mustn't Kick It Around" (from act 1), "Happy Hunting Horn" (act 1), "Plant You Now" (act 2), and "Do it the Hard Way" (act 2). These song-and-dance numbers are aesthetically related: they were fast paced, featured the dance chorus at their most virtuosic, and utilized the latest dance crazes and music. They exemplified youth, which was in turn personified by the chorus of "girls and boys" (see Figure 6.1). Unlike the nightclub burlesques (see Chapter 3), these songs are meant to be unironic showstoppers, engaging the audience in appreciation for the talented dancers on stage; the audience remains unbothered by the fact that the performers are meant to be hacks in the world of the musical. A more "integrated" approach to these dance numbers could have ruined the show.

The dancers were undoubtedly talented. The chorus—on opening night comprised of nineteen women and nine men—were mostly young, fresh-faced dancers who had already worked with Robert Alton, George Abbott, and/or Rodgers

*Figure 6.1 Gene Kelly and female chorus in Pal Joey; NYPL Digital Collections, photo by Vandamm Studio, 1940*

and Hart (see Table 6.2). Ten of the women (including Leila Ernst) and one of the men (Van Johnson) had worked the previous year on *Too Many Girls* with Alton, Abbott, Rodgers, and Hart. Of that show, one critic remarked in relation to the dancers that "Mr. Abbot knows about youth."[62] The ages of the dancers in *Pal Joey* confirm this: most of them were in their late teens or early twenties. Along with Stanley Donen, Shirley Paige was among the youngest—still a teenager—and was chaperoned by her mother while the company was out of town for previews.

Other members of the chorus had worked with Alton on shows that were not affiliated with Rodgers and Hart or Abbott, including *Anything Goes* (1934), *Hooray for What!* (1937), *Between the Devil* (1937), *You Never Know* (1938), *Leave It to Me* (1938), *Streets of Paris* (1939), and *Du Barry Was a Lady* (1939). Only a small handful of the dancers had not worked with Alton prior to *Pal Joey*. Alton reportedly wanted chorus dancers who knew "tap and ballet dancing" and, while he didn't insist on acrobatics, "four of the girls [could] do them."[63]

Competition for the show, as for all Broadway shows, was fierce (*PM* recounted that the chorus call "brought in between 400 and 500" dancers), and the grueling schedule that the dancers took on this dance-heavy show must have been exhausting.[64] Most made Chorus Equity minimum salary, which was $35 a week, and since youth was the aesthetic of choruses during this period their careers had expiration dates, unless they moved up to more theatrical parts (a rare occurrence

Table 6.2: The Opening Night Chorus of *Pal Joey*, and the number of shows they performed with Rodgers and Hart, Robert Alton, and/or George Abbott prior to *Pal Joey*. Names are in the order that they appeared in *Pal Joey*'s opening night program.

| Chorus members | # of shows done with Rodgers & Hart | # of shows done with Robert Alton | # of shows done with George Abbott | Broadway Debut |
|---|---|---|---|---|
| Sondra Barrett | 1 | 1 | 1 | |
| Diane Sinclair | 1 | 1 | 1 | |
| Amarilla Morris | 1 | 1 | 1 | |
| Jane Fraser | | | | |
| Claire Anderson | | | | x |
| Shirley Paige | | | | x |
| Alice Craig | 2 | 1 | 1 | |
| Louise de Forrest | 1 | 3 | 1 | |
| Enez Early | 1 | 4 | | |
| Tilda Getze | 1 | 3 | 1 | |
| Charlene Harkins | 1 | 1 | 1 | |
| Frances Krell | | 1 | | |
| Janet Lavis | | | | x |
| June Leroy | | | | |
| Olive Nicolson | | | | x |
| Mildred Patterson | 1 | 1 | 1 | |
| Dorothy Poplar | 1 | 1 | 1 | |
| Mildred Solly | 2 | 1 | 2 | |
| Jeanne Trybom | | | | x |
| Marie Vanneman | | 4 | | |
| Adrian Anthony | | 1 | | |
| John Benton | | | | |
| Milton Chisholm | | | | x |
| Stanley Donen | | | | x |
| Henning Irgens | | 2 | | |

| Chorus members | # of shows done with Rodgers & Hart | # of shows done with Robert Alton | # of shows done with George Abbott | Broadway Debut |
| --- | --- | --- | --- | --- |
| Van Johnson | 1 | 1 | 1 | |
| Howard Ledig | | | | x |
| Michael Moore | 1 | 2 | | |
| Albert Ruiz | | | | x |

indeed). The forced intimacy of the dancers sometimes created tension. Anna Mae Tesslo, a chorus dancer in *Too Many Girls*, described the petty backstage goings-on during that show to an interviewer for *The Pittsburgh Press*:

> [Tesslo] knows that a girl who is vastly hated by her sister hoofers is given the bum's rush—which means in this instance that the disliked girl is tossed out of the dressing room in her underwear to endure the jibes of the male ensemble until, after 10 minutes of frantic beating on the barred door, she is readmitted.[65]

A rosier portrait was painted in a feature for the *Brooklyn Citizen*, which described the extracurricular activities of *Pal Joey*'s chorus once the spring frost had thawed:

> By the number and variety of their activities, these energetic players in the O'Hara-Rodgers and Hart show disprove the old tale that chorus girls sleep all day and stay up all night. Bright and early every morning, eight of them, headed by blonde Jeanne Trybom and brunette Amarilla Morris, turn equestrienne [. . .] Two handball teams have been formed among the boys of the chorus.[66]

This interviewer plays up the "girls and boys" and their wholesomeness, which in turn underscored their ages. The youth of the chorus was essential to the aesthetic of the show and its demanding routines, enforced by the uncompromising Alton. To give a better sense of the taxing nature of the routines, consider this anecdote: when Alton was working in Hollywood just a year later (on the Astaire-Hayworth film *You'll Never Get Rich*), the chorus went on strike. As reporter Lucie Neville tells it,

> After the first day's rehearsal, the chorus went on strike, saying in sulky astonishment, "This is specialty stuff! We aren't going to work for chorus wages. No movie director ever asked us to do these steps." [. . .] But they appreciate Alton's driving energy and the fact that he can execute any step he expects them to do.[67]

The youthful, exuberant energy of the chorus was also often remarked upon in reference to the women of the chorus's weight. Sidney B. Whipple comments,

> Mr. Abbott's chorus girls are running a few pounds heavier this year and are not of the languid and undernourished type that has been the vogue. Their

plumpness in no way interfered with the acrobatic agility demanded in Robert Alton's vigorous and breathtaking choreography.[68]

Another described the female dancers as "the very veal trust of nourished girl-hood," anticipating the later association of the chorus with cattle.[69] One of the reviewers of the tryouts made a similar comment, remarking that *Pal Joey*'s "good-looking chorus" was a sign that "this year's crop of kisses is going to be built along healthy, curvaceous lines."[70] That weight was being connected to health is significant—it signals a shift in perceptions of what the ideal female body looked like. In the 1920s and into the 1930s, a thinner body type was associated with Ziegfeldian glamour, wealth, and a coy, demure brand of sexuality. During the same period fuller body types, especially when they were sexualized, were associated with burlesque theater, working-class audiences, and sexual availability. The pink-cheeked co-ed, on full display in *Too Many Girls* and *Pal Joey*, was a new, and popular, take on femininity.

## THE SHOWSTOPPERS

"You Mustn't Kick It Around" is the first chorus number in the show. The song and dance number occurs in act 1, scene 1, shortly after the show opens. The function of this number is to deliver what the very beginning of the show lacked: a visceral, smart, showstopping crowd-pleaser to draw the audience into the story. The scene is set up as a rehearsal number; Joey organizes the chorus girls in formation ("get in your places. Let's have some co-operation"). This song is preceded by dialogue that marks it explicitly as diegetic, but the music is less indicative of a tacky club number, and more in line with then current trends in music and dance. The song is a jazzy mid-tempo number featuring syncopated figures and a lengthy dance break.

In the premiere production Gene Kelly sang the first chorus, which was followed by a dance break featuring "Diane Sinclair, Sondra Barrett, Chorus Girls and Waiters." After the break June Havoc sang the final chorus of the song. "You Mustn't Kick It Around" is the "book" version—the polished, frankly unrealistic version—of what the audience observed when they first met Joey. Abbott's careful attention to narrative pacing is apparent in this scene—Abbott made sure to reveal Joey's faults early on (including his desperate, hackneyed performance style), and then drew the audience unwittingly into the paradox: sure, the characters are cut rate, but boy, can they dance!

In "Happy Hunting Horn," another showstopper, Joey crows over his success with Vera, whom he's about to go home with for the first time. Joey re-enters after exiting with her in order to lord his success over his fellow nightclub players (he has, after all, caught the attention of a wealthy potential benefactor). The song is not diegetic, but it's a backstage number, allowing for a kind of narrative overlap with the diegetic numbers. "Happy Hunting Horn" is an upbeat, mid-tempo song, capitalizing on popular musical and dance styles of the day—swing and jazz, primarily—and also includes a high-art Wagnerian reference, as the horn player quotes Siegfried's "horn call" from Wagner's *Ring* cycle.[71] The orchestration for "Happy Hunting Horn" features the French horn, which in this context evokes a hunting party (here, in a cringy twist, the "prey" are women). Rodgers's melodies for "Hunting Horn" feature open intervals, as would have been played by a natural horn, mimicking a hunting call.

After the opening chorus—in which Joey calls himself a "hunter" on the "chase," lying "in ambush" for the "beaut" that he's sure to catch—a dance break follows. Although Alton's original choreography has been lost, there exists a recording (featured on *The Ed Sullivan Show* on June 15, 1952) of his choreography for the revival—this version features Harold Lang, Norma Thornton, and chorus dancers. True to Alton's style, here the chorus line is broken up to feature individualized groups and soloists. First, as Lang sings the chorus, the chorus dancers walk out with linked arms, moving together. They aim their arms directly upward, creating a diagonal, angular shape, and flick their wrists and hands at the ends of phrases (which line up with the brass accents). At the bridge, the focus is on Joey, and the last eight measures of the chorus feature the women of the ensemble, circling Joey as he mimes the horn; the last line of the chorus ("happy little hunting horn") is punctuated by a "bang bang," after which a chorus girl comically (if morbidly) collapses. Throughout the dance, popular-style dance movement (involving the hips and lower body) are fused with balletic movements, including elegant leg lifts. In the finale, Lang performs a series of impressive fouetté turns ("whipped turns," in which Lang's raised leg, without touching the ground, whips in and out as he spins on his supporting leg). The effect is dizzying; Lang is virtuosic here. While "That Terrific Rainbow," "Chicago," and "Flower Garden" burlesqued both the music and dance of cheap clubs, "Happy Hunting Horn" (as well as "Do It the Hard Way," "You Mustn't Kick It Around," and "Plant You Now") are technically impressive, in line with the popular music of the day, and demonstrative of the latest dance crazes, in both 1940 and 1952 (see Figure 6.2).

Two songs in the show—"Plant You Now, Dig You Later" and "Do It the Hard Way"—featured Jack Durant as Ludlow Lowell, and Havoc as Gladys. Both were both called upon to use their comic vaudeville skills for these numbers. The most accomplished acrobat of the cast, undoubtedly, was Jack Durant. A stage and then film star known as one half of the vaudeville act Mitchell and Durant, Durant played the part of the con man Ludlow Lowell, Joey's crooked "agent," and Gladys's boyfriend. Durant started out in vaudeville at the age of nine, and, eventually recognized for his acrobatic abilities, became famous for an act in which he leapt backwards over seven chorus boys.[72] He reproduced this trick in "Do It the Hard Way," when he catapulted over a human bridge of at least four chorus girls. The climactic moment of "Plant You Now" is a sight gag during which Havoc carries Durant off the stage (see Figure 6.3).

*Figure 6.2 Van Johnson, Shirley Paige, and Gene Kelly, in "Happy Hunting Horn";*
*Photofest*

## DREAM BALLETS, BROADWAY, AND RODGERS AND HART

While showstoppers were exhilarating, critics adored dream ballets, and by the time of *Pal Joey* they were becoming something of a fad. Tim Carter, discussing the dream ballet in *Oklahoma!*, points out that Hammerstein, Kern, and Harbach, in addition to Rodgers and Hart, had all tried their hand at dream ballets in the 1930s.[73] While many remember George Balanchine as the pioneer of the dream ballet, Albertina Rasch, Madame Rasch to her dancers, had been staging them years earlier. There is also some evidence that the dream ballet, loosely defined, existed as far back as *Tillie's Nightmare* (1910), a play staged by the prominent dance director Ned Wayburn. Inspired in part by advances in

*Figure 6.3  Jack Durant and June Havoc from act 2, scene 2, "Plant You Now"; NYPL Digital Collections, photo by Vandamm Studios, 1940*

psychoanalysis—which influenced many art movements, perhaps most notably German expressionism—*Tillie's Nightmare* included an extended dream sequence, nearly the length of the entire play. The put-upon Tillie, played by the seasoned comedian Marie Dressler in a comic Cinderella role, falls asleep by the fireside and dreams of a life of wealth and luxury. What follows is a surrealistic dream, including a burlesque on the latest dance crazes (specifically targeting Gertrude Hoffman, a vaudevillian, and Ruth St. Denis, who would go on to cofound, along with Ted Shawn, the Denishawn School, a prominent influence on modern dance and American ballet). The show also featured Aaron's Dancing Dolls, a specialty dancing ensemble featured in many musical comedies of the period. While very little evidence of Wayburn's dance staging exists, dance certainly contributed to the effect of the dream sequences, even if only as parody.[74]

*Tillie's Nightmare* went on to form the basis of Rodgers and Hart's *Peggy-Ann* (1926), starring Helen Ford and choreographed by Seymour Felix. Felix worked alongside the producer and director (Lew Fields and Robert Milton) and the creators (Rodgers, Hart, and Herb Fields) to make sure the dance and staging contributed to a unifying effect. In fact, the closing scene, which nearly always in musical comedies of the period featured a big, rousing chorus number, was crafted according to story, rather than convention. After Peggy-Ann's fantastical dream, she returns to cold reality, and is a bit melancholy. A rousing chorus number would have made no sense, so Felix, encouraged to risk it by the elder Fields, put together an understated ending. It worked, and critics commented on this new emphasis on narrative. It also prompted Felix to speak publicly about dance, musical comedy, and narrative logic. In a feature with the *New York Herald Tribune*, Felix stated that in typical musical comedies, "the chorus interlude became a colorful but negative interruption to the action or comedy of the musical comedy book. It seldom aided development."[75] Felix worked against that convention in *Peggy-Ann*, and the show was successful. While this sort of dream-related dance number doesn't appear again in the work of Rodgers and Hart's until their collaborations with Balanchine, their other early work—including *Lido Lady* (both acted and choreographed by Jack Hulbert)—demonstrates their interest in how dance could reveal character and story.[76]

Despite these early dream sequences, Rasch and Balanchine's dream ballets are the true precursors to those that flourished during the "golden age" of the dream ballet (i.e., post *Oklahoma!*). While Balanchine's popular legacy is beginning to be recuperated, Rasch, as Kara Gardner has argued, tends be forgotten in Broadway histories.[77] Gardner puts it this way (using language that could also apply to Robert Alton):

> Because so much of her work was created in the years before Broadway dance was taken seriously, her contributions to the history of the musical have been largely overlooked. However, she was well known to Broadway audiences, composers, directors, and the choreographers from the 1920s through the 1940s.[78]

Rasch fused ballet with popular dance early in her career, blending jazz steps and ballet in the *Ziegfeld Follies of 1927*, and even choreographing a ballet based on Gershwin's *Rhapsody in Blue*.[79] In 1931, however, Rasch would stage her first dream ballets, first in the revue *The Bandwagon*, and then in Kern and Harbach's *The Cat and the Fiddle*. The dream ballet from *The Bandwagon* was called "The Beggar's Waltz," and featured Fred Astaire and the Austrian-born ballerina Tilly Losch. Although definitely a dream ballet, the sequence was part of a revue, and thus didn't connect to an overarching storyline of any kind. The dream ballet from *The Cat and the Fiddle*, titled "Dance in Phantasy," however, is much more in keeping with the dream ballets to come, focusing on the inner thoughts and desires of the protagonist, and moving the plot forward.[80] Rasch would go on to stage dream ballets in *Lady in the Dark* (1941), a show connected directly to psychoanalysis, which would, in Gardner's words, "be an important precedent that helped make the ballets of *Oklahoma!* and *Carousel* possible."[81]

Balanchine built upon the Broadway dance innovations of Rasch, creating ballets for the previously mentioned *On Your Toes* (1936), and then his first dream ballet, the "Peter's Journey" sequence from *Babes in Arms* (1937). It could also be argued that his "Aviator" ballet number from *I Married an Angel* (1938), as well as the surrealistic "At the Roxy Music Hall" number, were dream ballets. While Balanchine and, to a lesser degree, Rasch, have been acknowledged as pioneers of the dream ballet, Alton is rarely acknowledged for his contributions.

## "JOEY LOOKS INTO THE FUTURE": TELLING A STORY THROUGH DANCE

"Joey Looks into the Future" was the centerpiece of Alton's dances for *Pal Joey*. While this dream ballet was certainly not the first to appear on stage, it extended the possibilities of what a dream ballet could do in a narrative sense, and it, along with the dream ballets of Rasch and Balanchine, primed the way for the more recognizable ones to come. "Joey Looks into the Future" was the act 1 closer, giving the audience a brief glimpse into Joey's inner frustrations and desires. It also advanced the plot: during the ballet Joey and company's cheap club miraculously transforms (thanks to the stagecraft of Jo Mielziner) into Joey's dream club, the setting for act 2.

Gene Kelly thought that the idea for the dream ballet was Alton's: "I feel fairly sure it was Mr. Alton's because it was such a dance idea"; he later said that Alton wanted the ballet to show clearly that "Joey had bad taste."[82] Given that it would involve a set transformation, however, it was also very design oriented. Abbott, in contrast to Kelly, remembered that the ballet was Mielziner's idea:

> Jo Mielziner made a major contribution to the production by suggesting that the curtain of Act One be a scene in which Joey envisions his future in the magnificent club which his new girl friend is going to buy him. It cost ten thousand dollars to build the set, a good deal of money in those days when a musical had a budget of one hundred thousand dollars, but I accepted the suggestion unhesitatingly. This is a perfect illustration of how many collaborators there really are in a musical comedy.[83]

Regardless of whose idea it was, the dream ballet allowed Kelly to show off his considerable skill. As Kelly said, "the dancing all of a sudden got very balletic. And I was doing a *pas de deux* with a nice little ballet dancer."[84]

The dancer Kelly referred to was Shirley Paige, billed as a "specialty dancer." While not a prima ballerina in the way of Tamara Geva or Vera Zorina, she fit the part well. Paige, one of the youngest actors in the show, trained in her hometown ballet studio in Providence, where she "learned Russian ballet as well as tap dancing."[85] She started performing in nightclubs, including the Cocoanut Grove in Boston, the Samovar in Montreal, and Club Troika in Washington, DC, in the last of which she met Victor Moore. Moore reportedly then became a kind of mentor to her and, not too much later, her husband.[86] Paige met Robert Alton when she tried out for the chorus of *Du Barry Was a Lady* (she didn't get a part).

Alton apparently remembered her, though, and, according to one article, "went to great lengths to discover where Shirley Paige was living."[87] The rest of the creators were similarly impressed by Paige, who "[looked] well on the stage" with Kelly.[88]

The dream ballet was Paige's first featured entrance of the evening; she would come back at the top of act 2 to feature in "The Flower Garden of My Heart." Paige was, like Kelly, required to emphasize ballet technique, to play up the "class" aspirations of Joey, and to demonstrate that his vision was in bad taste. One way Alton did this was to have Paige frequently dance en pointe, performing the most difficult maneuvers in an attempt to show that she was trying too hard to be elegant. While none of the original choreography was written down—recall that Alton did this purposely—there are some clues as to the total effect of the ballet seen in the music, in Mielziner's prop lists, and in existing photos.

Production photos reveal that the set of Joey's dream club (which appears over the course of the dream ballet) is the same set that appears in act 2. This setting meant that Joey's delusions of grandeur were communicated primarily via costume, music, and dance, as the set turned out to be "real." John Koenig's costumes, to be sure, gave ample clues about character. The abbreviated length of the women dancer's rehearsal outfits, the spangles and sequins of the act 1 club numbers, and the overwrought frills of the act 2 club costumes tell the audience a great deal about the class of people they're observing. The costumes in the dream ballet number are equally revealing, so to speak: Joey danced this sequence with his coat off, affording an elegant view of his silhouette (this was in contrast to in his hoofer-like dances, including "You Mustn't Kick It Around," when he performed with his coat on). There were also yards and yards of a chiffon-like fabric featured in the dresses of the female chorus dancers, interspersed with more avant-garde and self-consciously exotic wear, including transparent harem pants and turbans. The men are besuited in white-tie tuxedos and Vivienne Segal, never the butt of the joke, wore an elegant chiffon-overlaid evening gown (probably designed by Helene Pons Studio).

Mielziner's prop list helps clarify the transformation of the old club into the new club, detailing what props were added, and by whom. One group of props on the list (listed under "Chez Joey," the new club), was a series of six open "dress shop boxes" containing blue dresses (all of the women's dresses were blue; Mielziner also lined the set walls with blue velour). These boxes might indicate that different members of the chorus put their Chez Joey dresses on during the ballet in full view of the audience (as seen in production photos, six of the chorus girls wore identical frothy confections; these might have been the dresses in the boxes). Another chorus member, Mildred Patterson, was given "practical kitchen matches" as well as "practical sandpaper" attached to her costume. Also on the prop list is a "crown of cigarettes," which Patterson wore atop her head: Paige and Kelly helped themselves to a cigarette each, and Patterson's "practical sandpaper," used to light the matches for the cigarettes, was affixed to her rear end (see Figure 6.4). Other props include menu cards, an evening stick, a monocle, autograph books, and large calling cards. One of the chorus boys—Michael Moore—holds onto a "news reporter's camera," equipped with flash bulbs, clearly meant for the

*Figure 6.4 Gene Kelly, Shirley Paige, and Mildred Patterson in the act 1 dream ballet: "Joey Looks into the Future"; photo by Ralph Morse, The LIFE Picture Collection/ Getty Images*

new club. The chorus was centrally involved in the visual transformation of this production number.

The music accompanying the dream ballet is similarly revealing. Although not indicated in the opening-night playbill, the ballet is preceded by the song "Pal Joey (What Do I Care for a Dame?)," which weaves seamlessly into the ballet.[89] It's an aggressive, unsophisticated character song, although not satirical in the way of "Chicago" or "That Terrific Rainbow." In this song Joey denigrates women in a classic case of projection, revealing his own insecurities. Joey's built-up frustrations, which stem from the preceding scene in the tailor shop (during which Vera bristles at his roving eye and Linda tells Joey off), are on full display. The lyrics to the song are deliberately brutish: "What do I care for a dame? / Every old dame is the same. / Every damn dame is the same." Later, they verge on violent: "What do I care for the skirts? / I'll make them pay till it hurts. / Let them put up till it hurts." The melodic line is almost recitational. Kelly sang first two lines on a repeated F, and the next two lines up a minor third. The brutishness of the song is in contrast to the hackneyed charm dance sequence that follows, a juxtaposition that was undoubtedly intentional. Eventually the lyrics point to Joey's aspirations: that he own his own nightclub, aimed at the "swell gentry," where he'll "wear top hat and cane." In true book fashion, the last lyric of the song—"I can see it plain"—sets up the dramatic transformation to follow.

When the ballet begins, the music is repetitive, inspired by the simple, determined energy of the "What Do I Care for a Dame?" theme. Patter-like, this continues for quite some time, presumably during the transition from one club to the next. After the opening, anxious introduction, a new musical section arrives, featuring the song "Bewitched," with the melody carried by a lilting solo violin. The audience would have related this song to the inner psychological state of Vera and not Joey; it's an interesting choice from a character perspective. The song, however, lends itself to dance, as can be heard when the theme transforms into a triple-meter waltz.

The waltz section is probably where the ballet movement really took off, perhaps brought on by Shirley Paige's entrance (see Figure 6.5). Undoubtedly, Paige and Kelly's pas de deux took place somewhere in this section of the ballet. Most

*Figure 6.5  Paige and Kelly pose during their pas de deux for the act 1 dream ballet: "Joey Looks into the Future"; NYPL Digital Collections, photo by Vandamm Studios, 1940*

of the remainder of the ballet features "Bewitched," save for a few "hot" breaks, and, surprisingly, a section from the cut song "I'm Talking to My Pal," complete with Lombardo-like saxophone harmonizing. Since the chorus to "Bewitched" is repeated so many times, Hans Spialek had fun with the orchestration: sometimes the melody featured the strings, sometimes a muted trumpet, sometimes dainty high winds (with a staccato articulation), sometimes saxophones (with a swing feel), and sometimes the full orchestra at a dramatic maestoso. Toward the end of the ballet, the theme shifts into triple meter, lying neatly with the melody; surely the Chez Joey patrons, and perhaps Kelly and Vera, were dancing a waltz here (although it isn't clear where Vera entered the scene, she features front and center in all of the photos of the finale of the ballet).

While Alton claims to have forgotten nearly all of the original choreography by the time he mounted the revival, there exists some interesting movement notation on what is presumably Max Meth's director score for the 1952 revival production.[90] Penciled-in annotations indicate where various members of the chorus entered and where the old club transitioned to the new club, a point well before the entrance of the "Bewitched" theme. The score also includes some specific movement notations, including terms like "bounce," "sissone," "jeté," "snap," "Spanish," and "turn." Meth's score also indicates where Helen Wood— the specialty dancer in the revival—entered, and when she began dancing with Harold Lang, who played Joey in the revival production.[91] "Vivienne entr" is annotated at the beginning of the bridge the second time through the chorus, and "Photo" is annotated soon after that. This note would help explain where the "news reporter's camera," included on the prop list for the original production, comes into play. In contrast to the original production, the revival included a new sung portion at the end of the ballet, featuring a choral rendition of "I Could Write a Book."

Whether or not it was originally Alton's idea, the dream ballet was a dramatic highpoint in the show. The message of the scene was reliant on the visual markers of ballet (i.e., dancers en pointe, a dramatic pas de deux) juxtaposed with "coarser" elements (like the previously mentioned "cigarette crown"), which were all referenced in order to send up Joey's hackneyed version of sophistication. The dance—commentary on technique and all—was so connected to character, and to story, that *Pal Joey*'s dream ballet marks a significant use of this now standard theatrical device well before the more commonly acknowledged dream ballets of the 1940s. As Martin put it, in retrospect upon reviewing the revival production in 1952,

> Though [Alton] could always handle a "routine" with the best of them, it was characteristic of his choreography then as now that it was beautifully integrated into the show itself. It is interesting, in light of the "Oklahoma!" revolution of Agnes de Mille, how plainly Alton's ballet, "Joey Looks into the Future," prepared the way for Miss de Mille's "Laurie [sic] Makes Up Her Mind." They are vastly different, of course, in content and form, but there is none the less an undeniable link between them in function.[92]

Alton's contributions to Broadway dance have not yet been properly acknowl-edged. His influence on Broadway dance can be seen in his interest in character-ization through movement, and in the sheer number of shows he choreographed during the flashy, sexy, exhilarating heyday of musical comedy. His influence on Gene Kelly has likewise not yet been properly recognized: they were both infa-mous workhorses, and they both took that energy to Hollywood when they worked for MGM. They also both became interested in how dance contributed to the total vision of a show. Kelly would turn to directing to satisfy this inter-est. Alton too took his turn at directing: he would go on to supervise, as well as choreograph, the celebrated revival of *Pal Joey* in 1952. His contribution to the success of the revival is almost invariably overlooked. A closer look at the revival not only illuminates the role of dance in the success of *Pal Joey*, but also the role that the revival played in its enduring legacy.

# REVIVING *PAL JOEY*

• • •

# HISTORY OF A HEEL

• • •

## THE 1952 REVIVAL

Those who recognized "Pal Joey" as a pioneer musical in 1940 were sound prophets.

—Brooks Atkinson, 1952

While the original *Pal Joey* marked a shift in the kinds of stories that could be told in a musical comedy, the 1952 revival has its own historical significance: it was the first Broadway revival to both involve members of the original production team and surpass the run of the original production.[1] Its popular success was reflected by its critical laurels: it won three Tony awards, including best choreographer (Robert Alton), best actress (Helen Gallagher as Gladys), and best musical director (Max Meth). It won fully eleven Donaldson awards, including best dancer in a musical (Harold Lang), best leading actress (Vivienne Segal), and best musical. It also won a Drama Critics' Circle Award for best musical. The critical and popular success of the revival made critics rethink the importance of the original show. Without the revival, and in the face of the Rodgers and Hammerstein revolution, the importance of the original production might well have remained obscured.

By the time the revival of *Pal Joey* rolled around, Richard Rodgers was a force to be reckoned with. Well into his partnership with Oscar Hammerstein, Rodgers was a much-lauded composer, having shown off his extensive and adaptive compositional chops with two very different partners; by this time he was also a successful businessman, teaming up with Hammerstein to produce a number of popular shows, both musical and straight (including John Van Druten's *I Remember Mama*, 1944, and Irving Berlin's *Annie Get Your Gun*, 1946).[2] When the revival of *Pal Joey* went into rehearsals, Rodgers had two long-running musicals playing in theaters on 44th Street: *South Pacific*, at the Majestic Theatre, and *The King and I*, across the street at the St. James. When the *Pal Joey* revival premiered at the Broadhurst on January 3, 1952, that would make three. This trio of hits provided a neat opportunity for critics, who were urged to compare the very different offerings provided by Rodgers with Hammerstein, and Rodgers with Hart, and to comment on the state of musical theater in the intervening years.

*Pal Joey*. Julianne Lindberg, Oxford University Press (2020). © Oxford University Press.
DOI: 10.1093/oso/9780190051204.001.0001

Richard Rodgers prepared for the critical reaction by publishing a piece in the *New York Times* in advance of the revival. Called "*Pal Joey*: History of a Heel," Rodgers's retrospective helped prep audiences for the show. He explained how to better sympathize with the character Joey ("Joey was not disreputable because he was mean, but because he had too much imagination to behave himself, and because he was a little weak"), outlined the major breakthroughs of the show ("nobody like Joey had ever been on the musical comedy stage before"), and reminded the viewer that this show helped propel both Gene Kelly and Van Johnson to fame.[3] Rodgers also set up the idea that the revival was a natural extension of new interest in the show, propelled by a series of recordings of the song "Bewitched," and a successful summer-stock run. He ended the piece by making a declarative statement: "While Joey himself may have been fairly adolescent in his thinking and his morality, the show bearing his name certainly wore long pants, and in many respects forced the entire musical comedy theater to wear long plants for the first time."[4]

Rodgers's article was in keeping with a narrative, encapsulated in the term "long pants" and concomitant with the idea of "maturity," that he and especially Hammerstein had crafted in relation to the two quite different phases of his career. It was no coincidence that near the beginning of his article Rodgers also mentioned the recent appearance of *The Rodgers and Hart Songbook*, published by Simon and Schuster in late 1951, which marked the first time that Rodgers and Hart's hit songs were collected in one volume. *The Rodgers and Hart Songbook* included a foreword by Oscar Hammerstein, who eloquently, if deliberately, placed Rodgers and Hart's career in the following terms:

> The essence of the work they did together was youth. They stayed young and adventurous and never lost an attractive impudence that was very much their own [. . .] In their extraordinary development as theatrical craftsmen, they never lost this gift of retaining their early character—a couple of lively New York kids, products of their town and their time.[5]

While stated in admiration, Hammerstein's use of the words "youth" and "theatrical craftsmen" are the inverse of terms that critics used to describe the work of Rodgers and Hammerstein: "mature" and "artistic." Even Hammerstein's reference to the topicality of Rodgers and Hart's shows—"a couple of lively New York kids, products of their town and their time"—is in opposition to the supposed "timelessness" of Rodgers and Hammerstein's shows, which by 1951 had affected a narrative shift on Broadway in relation to setting and atmosphere. Positioning Rodgers and Hart's shows as precursors to those Rodgers made with Hammerstein—and placing *Pal Joey* as the pivotal work that prepared the theatrical establishment for the "mature" period to follow—was an excellent public-relations move. Not only were fans of the original *Pal Joey* given the chance to be proven right, but also an old show—entertaining and flashy—was propped up as an exciting piece of living history. It was the show, perhaps, that started the Rodgers and Hammerstein "revolution."

This chapter will trace the history of the revival, from the Starlight Operetta production of *Pal Joey* in Dallas (1949), to a successful summer-stock tour, to the revival. Particular attention will be paid to records, recording technology, and the works-oriented model in cast recordings, all of which helped make these stage productions viable. The main creative forces behind the revival, in addition to Rodgers and O'Hara, were Jule Styne, producer, and Robert Alton, who supervised the production, as well as the boyish Harold Lang, who danced in the shadow of Gene Kelly as Joey. The critical reaction to the revival was, arguably, what made *Pal Joey* a subsequently durable show. It also revealed a good deal about the contemporary fidelities of musical theater, and how the discourse surrounding it reflected larger concerns about art during the period.

## FROM ASCAP BOYCOTT TO REVIVAL

In February of 1951 the Columbia recording of *Pal Joey*, conducted by Lehman Engel and under the supervision of Goddard Lieberson, was released to a public primed to consume it (the album was recorded in September of 1950). In 1948 Columbia had released their first long-playing (LP) record, which made it possible to listen to the music from an entire show without having to flip a record every few songs. Since cast recordings were typical from the time of the landmark Decca album of *Oklahoma!* (1943), which consisted of six 78s, each of which had to be flipped, the introduction of the LP changed the way that Broadway shows were listened to, providing a continuity that was in line with a new critical appreciation for dramatic unity.[6] The development of the LP and the standardization of the cast album went hand in hand with the critical elevation of musical theater as an art form, following a works-oriented model seen in classical music.

The *Pal Joey* record was part of a group of recordings, including *Anything Goes* and *Girl Crazy*, that were created with the purpose of providing complete, or nearly complete, recordings of shows that premiered before the standardization of cast recordings. The *Pal Joey* album was significant to the remounting of the revival for a few key reasons. First, it was released on the heels a series of popular recordings of the song "Bewitched," which had brought the song (and its show) back to public consciousness. During the time of its premiere, the songs hadn't heard airplay in any real way: the ASCAP boycott of early 1941 effectively kept the songs from being disseminated to a wider public. As Laurence Maslon discovered, however, during the summer of 1950—in June alone—six different recordings of the song made the Top 20 list of records most played on the radio.[7] These recordings featured Doris Day, Gordon Jenkins and His Orchestra, Mel Tormé and the Pete Rugolo Orchestra, Jan August and Jerry Murad's Harmonicats, Bill Snyder,

Larry Green and His Orchestra (featuring the Honeydreamers), and Roy Ross and His Orchestra. *Billboard* also reported that the sheet music single of "Bewitched," released by Chappell in 1950, was the best-selling sheet music for the week ending on May 26.[8]

Second, the Columbia recording included an original cast member, Vivienne Segal, singing the part she originated. Columbia's *Anything Goes* and *Girl Crazy* were Mary Martin vehicles, and as such retained very little of the original versions' particular style. The *Pal Joey* recording could boast a taste of Broadway. Playing opposite Segal as Joey was Harold Lang. Lang, a decent but not trained singer, was a gifted dancer who had just finished his run as Bill Calhoun/Lucentio in Porter's *Kiss Me, Kate*. Both Segal and Lang would go on to star in the Broadway revival, bringing a built-in audience with them. Lehman Engel, the musical director of the album (also a distinguished Broadway musical director), who worked with Lieberson on all of the pre-cast-album-era shows, was an avid fan of *Pal Joey*. Not only would he go on to cite it as the show that kicked off the "golden age" of musical theater, but he was also the musical director of the 1949 Dallas Starlight Operetta production of the show, featuring Segal, a casting choice that might have been the catalyst for the revival.[9]

In early 1949 Engel was offered—through Gus Schirmer Jr., who would go on to direct the summer stock *Pal Joey* featuring Bob Fosse and Carol Bruce—the musical directorship for the summer season of the Starlight Operetta. In Engel's biography he explains the grueling schedule:

> I had eight shows to prepare [. . .] We opened each show each Monday evening. Tuesday we began rehearsing the newly arrived principals for the next Monday night's opening. On Sunday night, after the final performance of that week's show, the scenery was changed, one set of costumes packed up, another set laid out, and by 2:00 A.M. we started dress rehearsals of the new show.[10]

In addition to Vivienne Segal, this production of *Pal Joey* also featured another actor—Georgie Tapps—who had been involved with the original production (Tapps took over the part of Joey in the original run when Kelly left the show). Engel called the production "the beginning of the revival that was to delight New York three years later."[11] The show wasn't very successful in Dallas; as John Rosenfield, arts critic for the *Dallas Morning News,* said, "As a presentation it was first-class. As a box-office item it was a whopping loss."[12] But, as Rosenfield continued, "Jule Styne and Leonard Key, in association with Anthony B. Farrell, were inspired, in their own admission, by the Dallas production of 1949."[13] While Rosenfield's comment is debatable (it was most likely the Fosse/Bruce summer stock performance that inspired Styne to produce the revival), it is nevertheless surprising that Engel wasn't involved with Styne's show. For a time he was involved in the production; he even wrote a nice note to Rodgers, dated September 11, 1951, saying how happy he was "that at long last PAL JOEY is to be done and, of course, I am happy to be associated with it."[14] In the end, for thus-far unknown reasons, Max Meth was signed.[15]

## A RISKY VENTURE: JULE STYNE'S GAMBLE

The link between Lehman Engel and the Dallas production and Jule Styne, the producer of the revival, was Gus Schirmer Jr., who directed the summer-stock production of *Pal Joey* that would eventually inspire Styne to mount the revival. Styne, one-time piano prodigy and eventual composer of some of the most beloved songs and shows on the Broadway stage and the Hollywood screen, was a devotee of Rodgers and Hart.[16] Like Rodgers and Hart, Styne had put his time in as a composer in Hollywood, and was disaffected by what he saw as a lack of creative agency there—his real love was the theater. His love for Rodgers and Hart went so far that at one point in his career, contemporaneous with the revival of *Pal Joey* and around the same time that he started to take on management positions on Broadway, Styne had planned to form a repertory company dedicated to the shows of Rodgers and Hart. Inspired by the D'Oyly Carte Opera Company, famous for its productions of Gilbert and Sullivan operettas, Styne had hoped to create an American counterpart, focusing its repertoire first on the shows of Rodgers and Hart's post-Hollywood years. An article from the *Post* reveals that set designer Oliver Smith and costumer Miles White (who both worked on the revival of *Pal Joey*) were working with Styne on the project:

> They are devising easy-to-transport paraphernalia for repertory around the world. Included in the Rodgers-Hart shows being planned for traveling are "Pal Joey," of course, "On Your Toes," "I Married an Angel" and "A Connecticut Yankee." [. . .] The producer-composer feels the repertory company can be formed, even in the face of present day costs, by the emphasis being placed on the writers rather than on elaborate backgrounds. The success of the Rodgers and Hart Song Book has proved this point to him.[17]

Unbeknownst to Styne, he would have no time to develop this project. Rather, Styne would spend the years after the *Pal Joey* revival—reportedly on the advice of Richard Rodgers—finding his voice on Broadway, culminating in his work on *Gypsy* (1959) and *Funny Girl* (1964).

In 1951, however, he was interested in the business end of Broadway. He had two successful Broadway shows in his pocket—*High Button Shoes* (1947) and *Gentlemen Prefer Blondes* (1949)—and would premiere the revue *Two on the Aisle*, starring Dolores Gray and Bert Lahr, who famously feuded throughout the production, in July 1951. Styne, who had up to this point produced only one show (the unsuccessful *Make a Wish*), had the idea for a revival while watching a summer-stock performance of *Pal Joey* in the summer of 1951 at the John Drew Theatre in East Hampton (the show ran at the John Drew from July 30 to August 4). The actors in the lead parts were Carol Bruce, who had played Julie La Verne in the

1946 revival of *Show Boat*, and a very young Bob Fosse, who had the previous year featured in the Wiman-produced revue *Dance Me a Song*. Both Bruce and Fosse would play their *Pal Joey* roles again, but not in Styne's revival.[18] The summer show, directed by Gus Schirmer Jr. (who would go on to direct City Center revivals of *Joey* with Fosse in 1961 and 1963), was well received by critics. Schirmer Jr., son of the famous music publisher, was also a prominent agent and had secured the 1949 Dallas engagement for Engel.[19] Further, Schirmer had reportedly personally invited Styne to the show.[20] While most accounts of Styne's revival of *Pal Joey* link it to the Columbia recording, Fosse, Bruce, Schirmer, Engel, and the 1949 Dallas production should get more credit. The announcement that a Broadway show was in the works happened while the summer production was still running; one critic, who had seen the show in Baltimore, linked the Bruce/Fosse/Schirmer production directly to the Broadway production-to-be: "After seeing the revival of "Pal Joey" at Olney this week, theatergoers will not be surprised to learn that a full-scale production has been announced for New York this winter."[21] While Fosse and Bruce would not be contracted for the Broadway run, Fosse would act as understudy to Lang; Lang, however, didn't miss a single one of the 542 performances. Fosse would have to wait until 1961 to play the role again.

After seeing the summer-stock show, Styne reportedly "immediately became convinced that the musical play was perfect for present-day Broadway."[22] He first approached Rodgers and O'Hara to secure the rights; both agreed, but Rodgers was skeptical about the project. Styne then visited film and theater director Elia Kazan, whose straight theater credits include the original productions of *A Streetcar Named Desire* (1947) and *Death of a Salesman* (1949), and whose films up to that point included Oscar winners *A Tree Grows in Brooklyn* (1945) and *Gentleman's Agreement* (1947), and the critically praised film adaptation of *A Streetcar Named Desire* (which would be released later that year). Kazan had two musical shows under his belt (Weill's *One Touch of Venus*, and Lerner and Weill's *Love Life*); Kazan was a "serious" director, and Styne must have thought that *Pal Joey*'s book would have piqued his interest. It did, but Kazan would act, as Styne tells it, only in an "advisory" position.[23] Kazan did suggest David Alexander as an acting coach for Lang, and Alexander went on to direct the scenes for the show. Still, Kazan's absence surely disappointed Rodgers; during the short period when it was rumored that Kazan was interested in directing the show, Rodgers sent him a wire with the following message: "I hear there is a possibility you may agree to direct book of Pal Joey. If you are trying to kill me with happiness this is the way to do it."[24]

Just a short time after approaching Rodgers, Styne had verbal agreements from Segal to play her original part, and Alton to again stage the dances. Segal hadn't had a Broadway hit since her last Rodgers and Hart show, starring as the comically murderous Queen Morgan Le Fay in the 1943 revival of *A Connecticut Yankee*; she had a brief encounter with Styne when she was signed to feature in his *High Button Shoes*, but, apparently through subterfuge on the part of Styne, the role eventually went to Nanette Fabray.[25] Alton hadn't choreographed a Broadway show since the John Murray Anderson revue *Laffing Room Only* (1944), as he was busy working as the dance director at MGM; his most recent film was the 1951 version of *Show Boat*. Next Styne found his Joey, the dancer Harold Lang; Styne knew that Joey had to be able to dance well, and he felt that Lang "look[ed] like Joey."[26]

Despite his tenacity, Styne had a terrible time raising funds for the revival. This makes some sense, as the revival of *Pal Joey* was to be the first to surpass the run of the original—at the time, investors saw revivals as risky business. The gossip columns chronicle numerous attempts by Styne to secure financing for the show. One of the first people rumored to be involved in the project was Ben Feiner, former television producer and brother to Dorothy Rodgers. Feiner was attached to the revival until early September, by which point permissions had been approved by Rodgers and O'Hara, the show was cast, and the production team secured (save for a few late additions, including the director of the book, David Alexander, who signed on in November). In an article from September 11, however, theater reporter Louis Calta revealed that because of "television commitments on the west coast," Feiner had stepped out as co-producer.[27]

As Styne later told *The Times*, who reported that he had approached "an estimated 500 potential investors,"

> I had people stop checks, back out and throw the word "revival" at me. [. . .] The day before we went into rehearsal, one of the investors, who had put up $40,000, died. I raised $15,000 in a hurry, but to get the additional $25,000 I put up $90,000 in collateral.[28]

Styne went back to Rodgers, hoping that he might invest in the project. Apparently Rodgers, who was scared off by the lack of investor, refused to invest until Styne raised the first $115,000 (over 90% of the total investment).[29] Rodgers later recounted in his autobiography, "At one point things looked so bleak that I pleaded with him to drop the project. But Jule had a stubborn faith for which I shall be eternally grateful, and eventually managed to get the show on."[30] Styne was able to entice Leonard Key, a producer-writer for NBC and CBS who was new to Broadway producing, and Anthony B. Farrell, a producer and theater owner with an impressive list of credits who had also worked with Styne on *Two on the Aisle*, to invest in *Pal Joey*. The budget for *Pal Joey* was $125,000, remarkably low for the time. In comparison, consider *Make a Wish*, the Hugh Martin piece that was Styne's only producing venture prior to *Joey*: the show had a $300,000 budget, and it ran for only just over a hundred performances. Since Styne had been burned before, he did all he could to keep costs low. He recalled one particular situation—when the costumes for the "Plant You Now, Dig You Later" sequence came in at $5000—for which he decided to cut the cost while also paying close attention to character and story:

> The girls were supposed to wear some fancy outfit that would have cost [$5000]. But this number is supposed to take place in Joey's night club. And we figured that Joey, as a supreme, egotistical bum, could logically like to have the girls wear sweaters with 'Chez Joey' printed on them in green—like a basketball team. With the sweaters they have white skating skirts. What they wear cost $400.[31]

After all was said and done, the show came in only $11,000 over budget and, judging by critical reactions, was none the worse for it.

Initially, Styne wanted to sidestep the out-of-town tryouts, instead opting for a series of previews in New York. The eventual date of the Broadway premiere, January 3, was set by November 27, around the same time that Lionel Stander was contracted to play the role of Ludlow Lowell.[32] Stander's involvement in the project proved tricky, as he'd been blacklisted in Hollywood, television, and radio because of his alleged Communist activities. He was called before the House Un-American Activities Committee (HUAC) back in 1940, and was dogged all the way into the 1960s. He became a counterculture hero of sorts when, while testifying before HUAC in 1953, he remarked,

> I know of a group of fanatics that are trying to deprive individuals of their civil rights and livelihood without due process of law. I was one of their first victims. They're former Bundists, America-Firsters and anti-Semites.[33]

While Stander's job wasn't in jeopardy—Broadway didn't react to the hysteria as Hollywood did—his name was certainly in the papers. According to Jule Styne's biographer, Styne's office was bombarded with callers, letter writers, and eventually picketers, once the news had spread that Stander was to appear in the show.[34] Rodgers, O'Hara, and Styne, however, refused to bow to pressure: Stander stayed in the show. To be sure, Stander's anti-censorship views worked nicely to promote a show that had had censorship issues of its own (and would continue to, up through the 1957 film adaptation).

Styne and Rodgers had not planned on having an out-of-town tryout, but sometime late in the rehearsal process (rehearsals began on November 28), they reconsidered. In a nice bit of symmetry, previews began at the Shubert Theatre in New Haven on December 25, 1951, eleven years to the day after the premiere of the original production.[35] One member of the cast—Elaine Stritch, who played Melba—found this new schedule a bit troubling, as she was acting as Ethel Merman's standby for Call Me Madam (see Chapter 5). The reviews for the tryout were overwhelmingly positive, although some critics mentioned that the second act needed a bit of "bolstering."[36] Interestingly, this was the same critique given of the original performance; critics worried that the second act was too "straight" in genre. Still, it was called "interesting and thrilling to watch from start to finish" by one critic, while another stated that "[i]f Gotham is looking for a tuneful book show with exceptional choreography, talented performers, shapely gams and an abundance of set and costume flash, this can well be it."[37]

## THE PRODUCTION

Two of the biggest differences between the 1940 and 1952 stage productions was the absence of George Abbott, and the new stature given to Robert Alton. Abbott was, at the time rehearsals began for *Pal Joey*, involved in at least three stage productions, including *Call Me Madam* (which was enjoying a return engagement at the Imperial), *A Tree Grows in Brooklyn* (which ran until December 1951), and *That Number*, a straight play that opened in October 1951. Abbott's hand, however, could still be seen in the script; the pace of the second act, for instance, was significantly "doctored" by him, and most of those changes remained in the 1952 book. Alton, who had returned for the revival of *Pal Joey* from Hollywood, was hired on not just to choreograph, but also to supervise the entire production. David Alexander, who directed the book, was below Alton in the production hierarchy. Still, Alexander was a respected acting coach, and according to Helen Gallagher, who won a Tony for her role as Gladys, he was able to clearly communicate with actors about character motivation: "it was not the usual linear language."[38] "He was very helpful to me," Gallagher recounted, "He turned me into a different kind of actor."[39] Alexander's involvement with the production reflects a different, older approach to putting a show together. Similarly to Alton's mentor, John Murray Anderson, who, despite being an accomplished dancer himself, staged shows and hired a dance director to do the dances, Alton wasn't interested in being an auteur. Yet Alton's previous experience on the show, his commitment to creating new dances, no matter if the show was a revival, and his ability to keep the pace of the show moving forward were significant to its success.

Act 1 of the revival script is not significantly different from the original opening-night script from 1940. Besides an added bit of dialogue between the chorus girls in act 1, scene 1—added between two iterations of the song "You Mustn't Kick It Around"—most of the revisions were minor, cutting now-obscure references (like that made to restaurateur Ernie Byfield), or adding lines, like the "skiddle-dee boo—yeah!" that caps off "That Terrific Rainbow." Act 2 included more significant revisions, principally because Lionel Stander, who played Ludlow Lowell, couldn't dance or otherwise throw himself about the stage as Jack Durant did in 1940–1941. The numbers that originally featured the nimble-limbed Durant—"Plant You Now, Dig You Later," and "Do It the Hard Way"—became, respectively, features for Helen Gallagher and Harold Lang. Since Gallagher's character, Gladys, had originally been part of "Plant You Now," it wasn't a big stretch to feature her, accompanied by the chorus. With this change, however, it became one of the least integrated of the dance numbers. Originally Ludlow, who had just scammed Joey into believing he was a legitimate agent, sang the song as he was exiting Chez Joey. The tone of the song is meant to be in contrast to the type of pretentious entertainment Joey had in mind for his club. The song is also a kind of roughly romantic number, in which Ludlow uses what one magazine called "jive talk" to bid farewell to Gladys.[40] Like many songs from *Pal Joey*, it's also a character number, and telegraphs what Pierre Bourdieu would have called Ludlow's "habitus": he's a crook, associated with the tough underbelly of Chicago, and uses slang to communicate his toughness. For instance, he refers to Gladys as a "hep-chick" and a "little potater," and the title of the song—"plant you now, dig you later"—is just another way of saying goodbye. When the song was transferred to Gallagher, the first refrain was cut entirely, and the number rings somewhat hollow. This is, of course, an observation made without the benefit of the choreography, which might well have distracted the audience from its relevance to the story.

The other Durant feature—"Do It the Hard Way"—was originally the most acrobatic of the show. As discussed in Chapter 6, Durant was meant to have catapulted himself over four chorus girls in the climax of the number. The difficulty of Durant's maneuvers were the main appeal of the song, and why it was given its title. In the revival, Alton tried to preserve some of the original intention of the dance by featuring Harold Lang, who did his fair share of acrobatic stunts during the song. The song originally featured in act 2, scene 3, also in Chez Joey, after Ludlow reveals to Gladys his plan to blackmail Joey. The song is precipitated by the exchange between Gladys and Ludlow, when Gladys says that their plan "might not be so easy."[41] Ludlow replies, "Did you ever see the time when I was afraid to do it the hard way? Don't answer."[42] The first line of the song plays up the "hard way" theme: "Fred Astaire once worked so hard / he often lost his breath. / And now he taps all other chaps to death."

When Lang took over the number, O'Hara/Alton/Styne moved the song to act 2, scene 4, which takes place in Joey's apartment, shortly before the song "Take Him." In order to integrate the song, O'Hara simply added a line to an exchange from the original show. Joey and Vera are talking, and at one point he mentions his father, who "always said I'd never amount to anything."[43] Uncharacteristically for their relationship, Vera asks what Joey's father is now doing; Joey responds by attempting one of his tall tales: "Dads—? Dads is in Palm Beach. . . ." As this point, the 1952 script is identical to the script from the original show. The last line of the next bit, however, was added: "Never mind. I'm sorry I asked. You always do things the hard way." Surprisingly, the lyrics to the song didn't need to be adjusted at all. Joey shared some things in common with Ludlow—primarily his arrogance and his use of slang—so the tone of the song was character appropriate. Still, John Martin, despite his praise of Alton and Lang, thought that the song and dance number seemed "less effective" than it was originally.[44]

Another change to the script—this time an addition—came in the form of a new diegetic number, performed in Chez Joey. The creators of the show must have believed that act 2, which had always been heavy on the dialogue, could use another club tune. The result was a reprise of sorts, but with a heavy tongue in cheek. Near the end of act 2, scene 3, the chorus rehearses another number, this time titled "Morocco." The costumes were orientalist stereotypes, with the men bare chested in turbans and spangled vests, and the women in very little. The comic punch line is that the song has the exact same melody and lyrics as the act 1 song "Chicago," except the word "Chicago" is replaced with "Morocco" (the underlying rhythm is a triplet-heavy bolero pattern). The original iteration of the song in 1940, a shallow chorus number, suggested that the featured locale could be replaced with any three-syllable place. This version of the song confirms that line of thinking. Beyond reworking Durant's features, the only other changes to act 2 involved tightening up Ludlow and Gladys's dialogue. Their dialogue was also the target of most of Abbot's "play doctoring" from the original production.

While the final version of the script is quite close to the original, the creative team behind the revival played around with other ideas, including adding even more diegetic club numbers to act 2, perhaps in an effort to make it less "straight." Don Walker, who was credited with "special orchestrations" for the show, was tasked with overseeing a reworked score. His papers include an annotated song list; under each song is an indication of whether or not the score for the piece was old (i.e., from the original production) or new (reworked by Walker). Most of the book songs used "old" scores, and most of the dance features had "new" scores; this approach makes a great deal of sense. Alton had devised entirely new dances, and the more popular-styled songs had to be updated for a more contemporary audience (Walker, for instance, changed the instrumentation slightly to match that of a 1950s big-band).

Walker's song list also reveals a preliminary idea that didn't make it to Broadway. For act 2, Walker's list includes songs that weren't included in the final score: the first is a reprise of "What Is a Man?," which follows "Den of Iniquity," presumably sung by Vera.[45] Later, after the song "Take Him" and the reprise of "Bewitched," is listed a "Tenor Specialty" based on the song "Do It the Hard Way" (with the penciled-in annotation "ballad"). Following that is a song titled "A Night in Morocco" (it is unclear whether or not this is the "Chicago" spoof), and then a number titled "Dance Music" with the description "Chorus of 'Plant You Now'— society dance style." These additions are indicative of a draft version of act 2 that played up Joey's bad taste in Chez Joey and addressed any potential concerns that the second act was too book heavy. In the end, these revisions were scrapped.

## ALTON

Robert Alton's contributions to *Pal Joey* are usually understated. His dances and staging were a major element in keeping the show fresh, young, and engaging, both in the original and revival productions. Many opening-night reviews for the revival credited Alton—who received very little credit the first time around—for the success of the show. John McClain, of the *New York Journal-American*, singled Alton out for his "incomparable talent," and for "pac[ing] the whole production to the tempo of a Texas twister."[46] McClain went on to praise his dances:

> Although confronted by the fact that many of the scenes take place in a night club not unlike the premises in "Guys and Dolls," he succeeded in making the new choreography equally furious and comical. His new ballet, "Joey's Dream," will match anything in town.[47]

William Hawkins, of the *New York World-Telegram and Sun*, also praised Alton's dances, saying that they were "Heaven sent, satirical but pretty, usually flavored with a suggestion of strip tease nonsense. They perfectly complement the salty humor of John O'Hara's book, and the late Lorenz Hart's brilliant lyrics."[48] Robert Coleman, of the *Daily Mirror*, likewise commented on the perfect union between dance and story: "Robert Alton, returned from Hollywood, has created fast, furious and funny ensembles, which skillfully further the action and serve as satiric comment on a dizzy era in American life."[49] One critic, commenting on the touring production, also remarked on the fast-paced, high-octane energy of Alton's staging, saying that the "dances are all supercharged, high-powered mementoes of the Thirties."[50] John Martin, dance critic for the *New York Times*, re-evaluated the dream ballet from the original *Pal Joey*, calling it a precursor to de Mille's dream ballet from *Oklahoma!* (see Chapter 6), and of Alton's work on the revival said, "The 'Pal Joey' club owes a big debt to Alton for saving its face. It is a pleasure to welcome an old master back into the field."[51] John Chapman, of the *Daily News*, made a provocative comment, relative to the changes that had taken place on Broadway in the decade prior to the revival: "There hasn't been a dancing chorus like this one around town in a long time—or dances like Alton's, either. Those high-stepping routines give today's artful ballet stuff a swift kick in the eye."[52]

Many critics, including Chapman, seemed to be refreshed by a show that both looked back to the quick-paced musical comedies of the thirties and paid attention to the story. Broadway ballet had definitely become a much welcomed staple of the stage, but Chapman's comment shows how much the dance directors of old were missed. Gallagher remembers Alton's special talents during rehearsals for the revival:

> He was a very unique man. He could sit in a chair and with different parts of his body simultaneously beat about eight rhythms. He could snap his fingers this way, he could move that toe, he'd use one hand, he could move his head. I mean, his coordination was—I mean, it was just mind-boggling. And it was a game, you know, and he'd show you what he could do. And he was a wonderful man. He was just a doll. But you'd never feel like you were working on something that was important, but he was important.[53]

Gallagher's last sentence is revealing—Alton was a master craftsman, not an auteur. Alton did what he did best—he got the audience up and out of their seats, cheering and begging for more. In an interview with *Dance Magazine*, Alton said,

> When I was assigned to the revival, I knew that people who had loved the show originally had built it up in their minds over the years, and probably believed that it was a much better show than it was. This became a challenge to me, and I staged it from the viewpoint of making it the great show they thought *Pal Joey* was.[54]

In order to make the revival live up to their expectations, he made the dance numbers "much bigger."[55] For instance, he added "about twelve more people" to the act 1 closer, the dream ballet, and "Happy Hunting Horn" featured thirty-two dancers, nearly double the number of the original. He also gave Lang more solo time, including on the aforementioned "Do it the Hard Way." Of Lang, Alton said, "Lang is basically a marvelous ballet dancer [. . .] [he] is certainly by far the best singing-actor who dances in the theater today."

Harold Lang, a dancer who won three Donaldson Awards for "Best Dancer on Broadway," was initially trained in classical dance.[56] Born in Daly City, California, Lang made his stage debut in 1939 with the San Francisco Ballet in a production of *Der Rosenkavalier* (although he was just a stand-in for that production). In 1941 he auditioned for Léonide Massine and was accepted into the Ballet Russe de Monte Carlo, and then later won a spot in Ballet Theatre (later known as American Ballet Theatre), where he met Jerome Robbins.[57] Lang's move from the Ballet Russe de Monte Carlo to Ballet Theatre was intentional:

> Ballet Russe had *Rodeo*, which is an American saga, but Ballet Theatre was doing really new things, more psychological pieces. With Ballet Russe, the dominant pattern, as far as I was concerned, was too much corps, not enough solo. Ballet Theater promised a greater variety of roles, wherein I would be called upon to act, as well as have fine technique.[58]

He expanded on this idea by critiquing Balanchine's choreography, whom he had worked with in the Ballet Russe de Monte Carlo and later on Broadway:

> I was amazed at Balanchine's preference for orchestrating bodies. Rather than make a statement about a person in a given situation, Balanchine says: "Body, come on, move to this music, do this movement, this beautiful movement." Balanchine has his place, a huge place, in ballet history; but I miss the fact that dancers are human beings.[59]

While at Ballet Theatre Lang helped make dance history as one of the three sailors in Robbins's *Fancy Free,* which premiered at the Metropolitan Opera House in 1944. The show was a major success, and was "performed over 160 times in its first season."[60] The now-classic show, scored by a young Leonard Bernstein, told the story of three sailors on leave who happen upon two girls; the lack of a third woman provides the central conflict of this narratively driven ballet. Jerome Robbins, John Kriza, and Lang played the sailors, while Muriel Bentley and Janet Reed played the two women. In order to impress them, the sailors each takes a solo dance turn, expressing both his personality and his method for captivating women. Lang's dance revealed a cocky, bold character, while Kriza's was more romantic, and Robbins's more intensely seductive. The ballet would go on to inspire Leonard Bernstein's *On the Town.*

Of his performance in *Fancy Free,* Robbins praised Lang's technique, saying:

> The first sailor was this extroverted, bravura boy—Harold Lang danced that. He had a formidable technique. Not a classical, *danseur noble* technique, but still a very strong one, and yet he was unusually limber. No one has been able to do that double air turn into the split the way Harold Lang did it. Which was straight down with the feet—one in front and one in back, and the arms out to the side. When he landed he looked like a jack.[61]

Many of these acrobatic elements can be seen in the production photos from *Pal Joey* (see Figure 7.1). Lang's performance in *Fancy Free* inspired a number of admirers, Arthur Laurents among them. Laurents, who had an on-and-off affair with Lang up until the time of *Pal Joey*, said of him in *Fancy Free,* "He was the sailor with the ingratiating boyish grin and the white pants molded to Nobel-worthy buttocks."[62]

Lang's technique was also commented upon by the much respected dance critic Edwin Denby, who considered Lang's dance the most effective of the three: "Harold Lang's brilliant acrobatic turn [included] splits like those of the Berry Brothers. It was in this number that the house took fire, and from there on the ballet was a smash."[63] Elsewhere in his review, he calls the ballet a "direct, manly piece." Further,

Figure 7.1  *Harold Lang's acrobatic tricks in the act 1 dream ballet; Photofest*

[t]here isn't any of that coy showing off of "folk" material that dancers are doing so much nowadays. The whole number is as sound as a superb vaudeville turn; in ballet terminology it is perfect American character ballet [. . .] If you want to be technical you can find in the steps all sorts of references to our normal dance-hall steps, as they are done from Roseland to the Savoy; trucking, the boogie, kneedrops, even a round-the-back done in slow motion.[64]

Denby's comment points out a debt that has yet to be fully paid to vaudeville, popular dance, and, especially, African American dance acts like the Berry Brothers. The Berry Brothers and the Nicholas Brothers—the latter of whom worked with Balanchine and Alton on the Ziegfeld *Follies of 1936*, and with Balanchine again in *Babes in Arms*—don't get nearly enough credit for their contributions to Broadway dance.[65] Beyond the shows these two acts did on Broadway, they were frequent performers in clubs, including the famous Cotton Club in Harlem, where white patrons and artists were inspired to "borrow" their steps. This trend, of course, is part of the long history of co-opting black creativity for white mainstream audiences. Lang's particular style—rooted in classical training, but infused with the steps, attitude, and music of popular dance—is what made him such a good fit for Broadway.

Lang, an active member with Ballet Theatre, was exhausted from the touring schedule, and decided to try his hand at Broadway, another avenue where his dancing could help express character. He secured a role in the short-lived *Mr. Strauss Goes to Boston* (1945), which was choreographed by Balanchine. Lang's reviews were good, but the show closed so quickly—it only ran for twelve performances—that his brother, who came right out to see Lang in his first Broadway role, arrived too late. Lang's next Broadway role was a featured part in the Nancy Hamilton revue *Three to Make Ready* (1946), followed by a lead role in *Look, Ma, I'm Dancin'!* (1948)—for which he would win a Donaldson—choreographed and co-directed, with George Abbott, by Jerome Robbins, with a score by Hugh Martin. The cast record for that show, released by Decca, +was Lang's first of an eventual eight.[66] That same year Lang would get his biggest break yet, featuring as Bill Calhoun/Lucentio in Porter's *Kiss Me, Kate*, choreographed by Hanya Holm, in which he sang the hit "Bianca" (where Porter cheekily rhymed "Bianca" with "spank-a" and "Sanka"). The show was an enormous hit, and Lang's reviews were generally good, though one from John Martin, who praised Holm, must have stung: "[Lang] is an excellent dancer, of course [. . .] but here he seems to find it difficult to fit himself into the general style of the piece, and his dances have the quality of interpolations. One wonders, indeed, if Miss Holm has choreographed them for him."[67] As in his previous role, Lang can be heard on the cast recording of *Kiss Me, Kate* alongside Alfred Drake and Patricia Morison. *Make a Wish*, with a Hugh Martin score, was not well reviewed, but Lang's performance alongside Helen Gallagher, whom he had great onstage chemistry with, and whom he would meet again in *Pal Joey*, was viewed favorably.[68] His time on this show also put him in the way of Styne.

While *Kiss Me, Kate* was the most successful show Lang would star in, *Pal Joey* provided him with a title role—for many critics Lang met or even surpassed the expectations set by Gene Kelly in the original. Given that Kelly's star was by this point a secure fixture in the firmament of Hollywood—*An American in Paris* was released about a month before *Pal Joey*'s rehearsals began, and *Singin' in the Rain* would be released during the run of the show—his shoes were, to put it mildly, hard to fill. Lang's take on the character, however, was not a replica of Kelly's; he made the part his own, playing up the boyish, naive charm that he had become known for in his stage roles.

The critical reactions to Lang supports this point. Brooks Atkinson, who famously made an about-face in relation to his negative review of the original production, said of Lang,

> It would be hard to improve upon Harold Lang's performance as the heel of Chicago night life. He acts with the cheap guile that Mr. O'Hara caught in his pitiless portrait of one of the most revolting characters in current letters— plausible, clever, superficially ingratiating, but consistently odious when the balance is struck. Mr. Lang is pleasant as a singer. As a dancer he is superb; he is light, swift, gay and inventive.[69]

Richard Watts Jr., of the *New York Post*, said that "Mr. Lang registers a very complete personal triumph as singer, actor and dancer."[70] John Martin said, in contrast to his mostly negative review of Lang's dancing in *Kiss Me, Kate*,

> He is a much more experienced dancer (and a much better one) than Gene Kelly was when he played Joey at the start of his career. If he takes an altogether different approach to the character, it is a thoroughly convincing one. Where Kelly played him always with half an eye winking at the audience in devastating comment, Lang plays him straight. But both characterizations stem from authentic types of low-life dancers on the make. It is barely possibly (if memory can be relied upon) that Alton was happier in his choreography for Kelly's hoofer than for Lang's, but that is not important. Lang does him proud at every turn.[71]

Martin's review, coupled with his praise for Alton, was indicative of how much Joey's character (and our sympathy toward him) depended on dance.

There were a handful of mixed and negative reactions to Lang's portrayal of Joey. McClain, who conceded that "Harold Lang works like a maniac all evening," felt that the shadow of Kelly left Lang's performance wanting:

> He is a most engaging performer and a dancer of rare ability, but it is impossible not to compare him, somewhat to his disadvantage, to the great Kelly. Kelly was somehow a much more attractive heel and a more skillful dancer, or my memory fails me.[72]

The most negative review, made by Walter Kerr of the *New York Herald Tribune*, felt everything is the show was perfect except for the portrayal of the central character:

> [Lang] is a lightweight in heavyweight company, a lamb in wolf's clothing. He still looks as though he would be just a shade under-age for the part of Willie Baxter in "Seventeen." Nor is his physical slightness and eternally juvenile appearance all that is wrong here. His heart is pure, too, though he has learned how to throw a line out of the side of his mouth, and how to ape the shellacked toughness of O'Hara's night-club crowd, he must force the mannerisms all the way, and I, at least, didn't believe a dirty word of it. Mr. Lang can be engaging, and he works like a demon; but he cannot escape looking like a puss in boots much too big for him.[73]

Kerr's language just barely hides his doubt that Lang—a man who was rumored to have had affairs with Gore Vidal, Leonard Bernstein, Jerome Robbins, and John Kriza, and a confirmed affair with Arthur Laurents—could effectively portray an archetypically straight womanizer. While potentially homophobic, this argument is also misguided. Lang was potentially the perfect fit for Joey; as Laurents remembers, Lang was desired and had by as many as he wanted—and he wanted hordes, but he only wanted them sexually. Emotionally, he gave himself to no one which, as the night follows the day, made him more desirable.[74]Whatever the root of Kerr's doubts, he was in the minority.

## PAL JOEY VERSUS GUYS AND DOLLS: ANTIHEROES AND SHIFTING CONVENTIONS ON BROADWAY

While some critics were busy comparing Lang to Kelly, even more were occupied with the similarities between *Pal Joey* and *Guys and Dolls*. The comparison was inevitable: both dealt with underworld types whose flaws were on display. *Guys and Dolls*, the Frank Loesser–Jo Swerling–Abe Burrows comedy, adapted from stories by Damon Runyon, premiered in November 1950, a little over year before *Pal Joey*. It was a huge success, running for 1200 performances. The show is about a couple of gamblers (Sky Masterson and Nathan Detroit) who, through schemes and weak natures, get into trouble that ultimately threatens their romantic relationships. The sexual politics of the show—in which men express a desire for freedom while women, seen especially the character Adelaide, desire domestic stability—replicate the sexual politics of the 1950s. Despite its flawed male characters, *Guys and Dolls*, as opposed to *Pal Joey*, is fairly conservative.

Critics were interested in the different ways that these two popular shows focused on underworld characters and settings. The authors of the source material for the shows—O'Hara and Runyon—had been compared before, usually in reference to the types of people these writers focused in on. One major difference, however, was in how each author characterized these flawed types. Runyon had what John Chapman of the *Daily News* called a "father's fondness for his characters"; ultimately, "he forgave their frailties."[75] Chapman went on to say that "O'Hara has only contempt for his."[76] This opinion is borne out in the moral logic of their respective universes. In *Pal Joey*, characters are not so much sympathetic as tolerable; in *Guys and Dolls*, the audience roots for the gangsters and gamblers. As John Mason Brown put it, "Grandly tough and superbly gaudy as they are, the touts and tinhorns in 'Guys and Dolls' have hearts as large as valentines."[77] McClain ended his piece with a clear description of the show's differences:

> There is plenty of humor and wit in "Pal Joey," all of it sharp or brittle; the wit and humor in "Guys and Dolls" is more soundly based on human frailty, instead of human rascality. "Joey" is brilliant; "Guys" is heart-warming—and each show is the best of its kind.

The comparison between these two shows is significant, inasmuch as it attempts to answer another question: were audiences more ready to accept Joey, Vera, and the residents of Chez Joey in 1952 than they were in 1940?

The answer to this question was both yes and no. Despite the "good many people" who were shocked by the original production, Wolcott Gibbs had apparently not met anyone "who found anything embarrassing in the goings on at the Broadhurst."[78] In fact, Gibbs went on, "a few [. . .] said they considered the whole thing a little quaint, but the chances are they were just showing off."[79] Certainly, by 1950 sexual politics in the United States had been hugely affected by World War II; the reality of women in the workforce during the war, and the subsequent effort to get men back to work after the war ended, would put new focus on motherhood, domesticity, and clearly defined gender roles for both men and women. Various gendered archetypes developed out of this focus, some of which are reinforced in *Guys and Dolls*, in which the narrative trajectory for both female leads, despite their seemingly nonconforming partners, leads directly to marriage. Compared to 1940, *Pal Joey*'s message was not so different in 1952, but its critiques were now part of a national conversation. The Kinsey reports, for instance, were released in 1948 (*Sexual Behavior in the Human Male*) and 1953 (*Sexual Behavior in the Human Female*), and both suggested that human sexuality was far more complex than previously thought. Just a year after the revival of *Pal Joey*, *Playboy* released its inaugural issue, and at around the same time Frank Sinatra began his extraordinary career comeback: both *Playboy* and Sinatra would contribute significantly to the "swingin' bachelor" archetype. In this way, *Pal Joey* was more relevant than ever.


## CRITICAL REACTIONS: MYTHMAKING

The critical reactions to the show as a whole parallel the legacy that *Pal Joey* now holds; critics has been honing their phraseology—and their ideology—since the critical shift after *Oklahoma!* As James O'Leary has pointed out, in the early days of its premiere it wasn't so much *Oklahoma!*'s formal integration, but the cultural moment, the "tonal shift" of its setting, and the concerted efforts of its creators and producers to guide the narrative, that prompted such strong critical reactions.[80] The revival of *Pal Joey* contributed to this discourse; just as with *Oklahoma!*, critics of the original production of *Pal Joey* commented mostly on its unusual story and, to be sure, on a tonal shift of a very different sort than that of *Oklahoma!* In 1952, as critics were looking back for models in an attempt to form a lineage related to the "integrated" ideal, the idea of a "literate" book and the concept of theatrical "artistry" was valued. The notion of "standing the test of time" was undoubtedly at play in the opening-night reviews, reinforcing the idea that musical theater works are (1) essentially about the work, not the particular performance and (2) meant to be revived. John McClain remarked that the book "seems to have withstood the ravages of time," while Robert Coleman compared it to a fine wine that had "grown better with age."[81] Richard Watts Jr. called the show "every bit as brilliant, fresh and delightful as it seemed when it set new standards for its field over ten years ago"; Walter Kerr, despite being critical of Lang, felt that "[n]othing of what John O'Hara or Richard Rodgers or Lorenz Hart wrote in 1940 has dated the least bit."[82]

Other critics felt that the opportunity to see it again helped clarify *Pal Joey*'s role in theater history. In the same review, Watts Jr. said, "I hate to inflict on it so seemingly serious-minded a label, but 'Pal Joey' is very definitely an authentic work of art."[83] In Brooks Atkinson's opening-night review, he stated that "'Pal Joey' was a pioneer in the moving back of musical frontiers, for it tells an integrated story with a knowing point of view."[84] One critic said, of the touring production, that "seeing it again, which is an endlessly pleasant experience, one is reminded that it is 'Pal Joey,' not 'Oklahoma!' that initiated the era of great musicals in the American theater."[85] In another piece by Atkinson, written about a week after his opening-night review, he declared,

> The reappearance of "Pal Joey" provides an opportunity to see what has happened to Mr. Rodgers' conception of the musical play in the last twelve years. Most people regard "Pal Joey" as the musical play that broke the trite formula of insipid romance. Although this assumption overlooks the originality of "Of Thee I Sing" and "Porgy and Bess" it is a tenable thesis. The pioneering of "Pal Joey" did open the way to "Oklahoma!", "Carousel," "South Pacific" and "The King and I." [. . .] "Pal Joey" is the epitome of Broadway and as exhilarating as though it had just been written.

These comments were bellwethers of the discourse to come, which looked back to the 1940s and 1950s, especially, as a golden age existing between the "frivolous" 1920s and 1930s, and the supposed decline that came after (one might notice that this discourse is also reflected in most jazz histories, roughly contemporaneously).[86] As with J. S. Bach, whose legacy was recuperated well after his death, *Pal Joey*'s contemporary legacy rests on a latter-day effort to form a serious, artistic lineage in musical theater. Had Styne not worked so hard to remount the revival, it is probable that the original production would have remained a historical event. Instead, the revival of the show made musical theater history, and, perhaps, reminded audiences that messy endings, unrepentant antiheroes, and exhilarating, showstopping dance numbers still had their place on Broadway.

# PAL JOEY GOES TO HOLLYWOOD

• • •

The 1957 screen adaptation of Rodgers and Hart's *Pal Joey* (1940)—starring Frank Sinatra as Joey, Rita Hayworth as Vera, and Kim Novak as Linda—redeems Joey.[1] Now a singer rather than a dancer, Joey genuinely falls in love with the ingénue Linda, and makes seemingly selfless decisions that the stage Joey would have scorned. The film praises Joey's vulnerability and laughs conspiratorially at his self-seeking behavior; in the end Joey gets the girl. The 1957 screen version of *Pal Joey* promotes a set of emerging gender archetypes that defy traditional, middle-class, suburban constructions of masculinity and femininity. Joey's stage-to-screen evolution—from heel to swinging bachelor—is mirrored by Linda's transformation from stenographer to sex kitten.

Both of these archetypes are responses to what cultural theorists have called the postwar "crisis" in masculinity, and both reject traditional constructions of gender and domesticity in favor of something more sexually deviant, even potentially "progressive." Vera's character presents a foil to these seemingly uncomplicated archetypes. Vera, as played by Segal, was selfish and sexually experienced. As played by Rita Hayworth, however, she is tamed by Joey in the end. The anxiety over contested gender roles is reflected in the alteration of the original score, which is reworked, repurposed, and in some cases eviscerated in order to promote the ethos of the film.

## ADAPTING *JOEY*

The film adaptation of *Pal Joey* was released by Columbia, headed by the irascible Harry Cohn. Directed by George Sidney, the film featured a heavily revised screenplay by Dorothy Kingsley (both veterans of Broadway-to-Hollywood adaptations).[2] Columbia had secured the rights to *Pal Joey* in early 1941, but they had a notoriously difficult time with casting. Early on they had considered casting Gene Kelly, again in the title role, with Rita Hayworth as Linda (their partnership had already proven successful in *Cover Girl*, from 1944).[3] MGM, however, refused to loan out Kelly. Other considerations for the title role included Marlon Brando, Kirk Douglas, and Jack Lemmon. At other points Marlene Dietrich, Ethel Merman, and Mary Martin were considered for the role of Vera.[4]

*Pal Joey*. Julianne Lindberg, Oxford University Press (2020). © Oxford University Press.
DOI: 10.1093/oso/9780190051204.001.0001

Although the basic outline of the original story remains, except for the Hollywood ending, much of the book was adjusted to satisfy a more conventional love triangle and the trio of stars who made it up. In the film, the story is set in San Francisco rather than Chicago, Vera is now a widow rather than an adulterer, Linda is a chorus girl rather than a secretary, the character Gladys is reduced to almost nothing, and many subplots and characters are cut altogether, including Ludlow Lowell and Melba. Another major revision is the medium through which Joey's charms are communicated: instead of a third-rate nightclub dancer, Joey is now a third-rate nightclub singer.[5] The irony, of course, is that both Kelly and Sinatra were masters of their respective crafts, and part of Joey's charm is that, at least from the nondiegetic perspective of the audience, he is *not* in fact a hack.

The score was also radically altered. Although some of Rodgers and Hart's songs from *Pal Joey* remain—including "I Could Write a Book," "Bewitched, Bothered and Bewildered," and "Zip"—many are cut or reduced to orchestral underscore, the latter skillfully arranged by Nelson Riddle. A handful of songs from earlier Rodgers and Hart shows are also strategically incorporated into the film, including "There's a Small Hotel" (from *On Your Toes*, 1936), "The Lady Is a Tramp" and "My Funny Valentine" (from *Babes in Arms*, 1937), and "I Didn't Know What Time It Was" (from *Too Many Girls*, 1939). As much as a vehicle for the lead stars, the show was also a Rodgers and Hart showcase, even though censors from the PCA office ruthlessly purged much of Hart's lyrical wit. Joseph Breen's initial report on the script (from February 14, 1941) states that the lyrics to "Happy Hunting Horn," "Bewitched, Bothered and Bewildered," and "In Our Little Den" are "entirely unacceptable," and goes on to say that "a number of the others contain unacceptable lines, which will have to be changed." [6] Breen's report officially rejected the script for its inclusion of "blackmail, sex perversion, adultery, [and] offensive dialogue."[7] Between 1941 and the release of the film in 1957, Columbia engaged in a back-and-forth with the PCA office in regard to the "unacceptable" elements of the film; the censored aspects of the film were often the result of concessions made on the part of Columbia, while some of its racier elements were included because of a PCA policy that had relaxed, to a certain degree, by 1957. Still, Dorothy Kingsley recalls that it was Cohn who favored the Hollywood ending, in which Sinatra and Novak literally walked off into the sunset: "Well, the story should have stopped with Pal Joey walking away, just alone, with the girl telling him, 'That's all, brother,' you know. But Harry Cohn insisted that we put on the traditional happy ending, that Kim and Frank must get together. And we fought and we fought but it didn't do any good."[8]

For those critics who were expecting a true-to-the-original revival of *Pal Joey*, the film was a disappointment. Film critic Daniel O'Brien, in a book dedicated to the films of Frank Sinatra, said, "If the 1950s revival had toned down some of the show's more controversial elements, Columbia's ultra-safe adaptation went for total emasculation."[9]

O'Brien's critique is ironically relevant, as the film reacts in various ways to anxieties surrounding masculinity. As countless studies have outlined, attitudes toward gender and sexuality were shifting in the 1950s. Numerous publications in the popular press addressed what many saw as a "crisis" in masculinity.[10] Not only were women in the workforce in unprecedented numbers, but many social critics saw the rise of corporate America (and office culture specifically) as emasculating, as well. Contemporary novels like *The Man in the Gray Flannel Suit* (1955) addressed these issues, questioning whether or not one could be personally fulfilled (or optimally masculine) in such an environment. For many, corporate environments went hand in hand with the "feminization" of mass culture. The civil rights struggle offered yet another critique of white, patriarchal culture. Historian James Gilbert argues that there was a "relentless and self-conscious preoccupation with masculinity," and that this preoccupation led to new and varied masculine archetypes.[11] The official image of the cheerful 1950s housewife, standing behind her corporate, besuited husband, was challenged by the reality of women in the workforce, and new attitudes toward sex and sexuality.

Karen McNally, in a consideration of Frank Sinatra's film roles, traces new attitudes toward sex in the postwar era to ambivalent feelings regarding white, middle-class, suburban constructions of gender roles, and to the infamous Kinsey reports (released in 1948 and 1953), which revealed that the sex lives of average Americans were far more varied than most publicly admitted to.[12] In 1953 (the same year the Kinsey report on female sexuality was released) the first issue of *Playboy* was launched, providing an antidote to the seemingly emasculated environment of corporate, suburban culture.[13] Early issues of *Playboy* were sophomorically misogynistic, blaming women for denying men their full masculine potential by trapping them in restrictive marriages.[14] Arguably the strongest proponent of the new "swinging bachelor" archetype, *Playboy* carved a space out for a non-normative form of virile heterosexuality, inextricably tied to material pop culture. By the mid-1950s, Frank Sinatra was their poster boy (see Figure 8.1).[15]

Sinatra's hipness was signaled through pop-culture references (especially urban slang), snappy dressing (with his hat tilted cockily to the side), and a disregard for traditional postwar views concerning marriage and domesticity. Joey's slang, which originated in O'Hara's libretto and was updated for the film adaptation, is rooted in the vernacular of urban African American culture, especially that associated with jazz and jazz musicians. The preface to Wentworth and Flexner's *Dictionary of American Slang* (1967) explains, in part, why Sinatra (or Joey, for that matter) might have adopted the vernacular of a minority social group: " For self defense, and to create an aura (but not the fact) of modernity and individuality, much of our slang purposely expresses amorality, cynicism, and 'toughness.'"[16] The history of slang runs parallel to the history of American popular song: the so-called deviance of the material culture of marginalized groups is seen as both dangerous and desirable. When pulled into the mainstream, the dangerous qualities

*Figure 8.1: Hayworth, Sinatra, and Novak in a publicity still for Pal Joey; Photofest*

of a given cultural signifier are eventually neutralized, though they still retain the thrill of nonconformity.

One of the early trailers to *Pal Joey* plays up his use of slang, conflating Sinatra, the star, with Joey, the "heel." In the trailer, Sinatra/Joey gives us a crash course in Joey's "slanguage," and, incidentally, the film's attitude toward women. The trailer opens with Sinatra introducing himself to the audience as "your pal Joey."[17] He goes on to describe Joey's "slanguage," which is made up, according to Sinatra, of "Joey-isms." In particular, he outlines four terms: "mouse" (a beautiful woman), "gasser" (the "very best," typified by Rita Hayworth's figure), "loose" (Joey's unattached attitude toward life), and "poppin'" (demonstrated in a clip from the film, when Sinatra/Joey is peeping through a keyhole at a bathing Novak/Linda). He goes on to say that his philosophy in life is this: "treat a dame like a lady, and a lady like a dame" (in *Pal Joey* the "mouse" is the dame, and the "gasser" is the lady). Some of the language Sinatra introduces was already a part of O'Hara's Joey stories from the late 1930s (principally, the term "mouse" to describe the various women that Joey encounters), and some of it shows up in jazz lexographies.[18] Joey/Sinatra's slang marks him as an outsider—he is socially deviant, but also "hip," and in line with the masculine archetype promoted by *Playboy*. His deviance was tied to signifiers that were in conflict with middle-class respectability.

*Playboy* also challenged dominant views of femininity, especially where sex was concerned. *Playboy*, whose playmates appeared each month as centerfolds, rejected the idea that women couldn't be both sexual and wholesome (the early centerfold features, for instance, were accompanied by other photos of the play-mate, cooking, horseback riding, or even having dinner with her parents).[19] Although most studies of *Playboy* play up the misogynistic qualities of the maga-zine, which undoubtedly existed and persist today, the magazine also carved out a space (in an admittedly heteronormative, heavily conditioned universe) for the wholesome sex kitten, termed by *Playboy* as a "playmate." The sex kit-ten/playmate—naturally sexual, and perceived as somewhat innocent—helps complicate the virgin-whore dichotomy. To an extent, both Novak/Linda and Hayworth/Vera take on the role of the sex kitten in *Pal Joey*, though, undoubt-edly, Hayworth's role is a bit more complex.

Clearly, the appearance of the sex-kitten archetype is less illustrative of how women experienced their own sexuality, and more indicative of how sexuality is embodied. The sex kitten/playmate is the counterpart to the swingin' bachelor/playboy, and perhaps says more about constructions of masculinity than about actual feminine desire. And yet, the 1950s discourse on sexuality was complex; in a discussion of the cultural discourse surrounding Marilyn Monroe, Richard Dyer states that "the image of the desirable playmate, which Monroe so exactly incar-nated, is an image of female sexuality for men. Yet so much does it insist on the equation women = sexuality, that it also raises the question, or spectre, of female sexuality for women."[20] Dyer's insight might help us better understand the film versions of both Linda and Vera, who, to varying degrees, are cast as playmates.

## THE PLAYMATE

Kim Novak's Linda is much more central to the narrative than the original stage role was. To ensure that the audience knows she is ingénue material, Ned, the bandleader, describes Linda as "a nice kid" and goes on to say that "[s]he has ambition, too—she wants to be a singer." Still, this observation occurs as Joey is sizing her up, appreciating her figure as she performs in the abbreviated costume of a nightclub dancer (see Figure 8.2). The visual portrayal of Linda is in direct contrast to the Linda of 1940, who is modest, reserved, and primly dressed, and the antithesis of the nightclub dancer Gladys (see Figure 8.3). Still, Novak's Linda is characterized as innocent, and even wholesome.

Novak's star image during this period—reflective of the sexual politics of the day—was dictated by her contract at Columbia, under the direction of Harry Cohn. As many accounts document, Cohn was cruelly controlling of his stars—especially his female stars—and both Hayworth and Novak's relationship with Cohn were among the most publicly fraught. As Hayworth's career began to decline—and as she pushed against the strictures of her contract—Cohn sought out another star to replace her. Marylin Monroe was contracted to 20th Century Fox, and in the early 1950s, Novak was regularly compared to her and to other famous blondes. It is likely that Cohn sought to reproduce the most marketable aspect of Monroe—her

*Figure 8.2: Still from Pal Joey (1957), Columbia Pictures: "That Terrific Rainbow" dance sequence*

"sexual readiness"—in Novak. He tried to do so by dictating what roles she played, how she behaved in public (and whom she dated), and, crucially, how she looked. To differentiate her from other famous studio blondes, including Marilyn Monroe and later Jayne Mansfield, she was dubbed, and made into, "the lavender blonde." The studio also sought to create an air of relatability; as Sumiko Higashi observes, "since most *Photoplay* readers could not aspire to become a voluptuous blonde, stories continued to stress the star's awkward and gawky girlhood," emphasized, for instance, in a story titled "How to Be Good and Popular."[21]

The song that introduces Linda/Novak—and, perhaps, best demonstrates her "naturally sexy," *Playboy*-approved side—is "That Terrific Rainbow," a tune that was originally performed by Gladys and the nightclub dancers. In the stage musical, this song is meant to reveal the depraved state of a cheap club in the South Side of Chicago. On stage, the tune not only creates an aura of tackiness, but also brings into question the true attitudes of the nightclub chorines toward sex: perhaps they're bored with it. The playmate archetype is at odds with sexual boredom, for she is, seemingly, always "ready." In this way, the embodied sexuality of some of the nightclub dancers (and their calculated attitude toward it) sets them apart from the *Playboy* ideal.

*Figure 8.3  Jack Durant (as Ludlow Lowell), Leila Ernst (as Linda English), and June Havoc (as Gladys Bumps); NYPL Digital Collections, photo by Vandamm Studio, 1940*

The scene plays out differently in the film: the introduction is thrown out—flattening out the characterization of the women—and each line of the chorus is given to a new dancer. All of the girls, except Linda, are either characterized as world-weary dancers, or empty-headed bimbos. None of them can sing, and many of them overact, to comic effect. When Linda eventually enters, appropriately on the lyric "Doncha know your mama / has a heart of gold," the aim is to set her apart from the other nightclub dancers. Her voice, dubbed by Trudy Erwin—a crooner known for her collaborations with Bing Crosby, and for dubbing vocals for other Hollywood starlets, including Lucille Ball and Lana Turner—is much more polished than that of her colleagues, and she moves naturally, without overacting. So, while the audience is encouraged to gaze upon the "mouse with the built" (the words of Joey/Sinatra uses when he sees her for the first time), they are also encouraged to view her as somewhat innocent of her sexuality. Although she does appear in full dress in the film, Linda/Kim Novak is often seen in short, strapless club numbers, or form-fitting gowns with severe slits up the skirt. A conspicuous bathtub scene is also included, which was played up in early promotional material (see Figure 8.4). But, in the words of Ned, the bandleader, we are assured that "she's a nice kid." The notion that women should be "naturally" sexual (implying an innocence and a continual "readiness"), while also exuding a niceness, or a wholesomeness, is in line with the fraught sexual politics of the 1950s, as well as the popular discourse surrounding Kim Novak herself.

*Figure 8.4 Still from Pal Joey (1957), Columbia Pictures: Linda bathing at the Hotel*

Linda's wholesome side is exemplified by her performance of "My Funny Valentine," originally from Rodgers and Hart's *Babes in Arms*, and here performed in the aspirational Chez Joey (this club, bankrolled by Vera, debuts in act 2 of the stage version of *Pal Joey*). "My Funny Valentine" is both a gift to Linda (Joey allows her to sing the feature), and a love song to Joey who, as even the film concedes, is terribly flawed. Through the combination of soft-focus close-ups, string accompaniment, and the sultry, dark tones of Erwin's voice, this song is the true love ballad of the film (see Figure 8.5). The tune begins with a solo guitar—played by Bobby Sherwood—outlining a broken f-minor chord, which sets the stage for the string orchestra's sotto voce entrance. Dominated by lushly orchestrated strings, "My Funny Valentine" creates a romantic sensibility not yet heard in the film. While relatively short (Novak/Erwin sings through the form only one and a half times [the bridge and final chorus is repeated]), the song carries narrative weight. It brings out Vera's jealous side, and she subsequently makes Joey fire Linda. It also convinces Joey, as well as the audience, that he is capable of a kind of selfless love not consistent with his stage persona.

Significantly, the original stage production of *Pal Joey* did not include a sincere love song. "My Funny Valentine," however, transforms Linda from a cheap dancer into a romantic lead. By playing up the "natural," innocent sexiness of Kim Novak, the film reinforces the idea that a more calculated relationship to one's sexuality (as typified by the other dancers in the nightclub shows and Vera) is undesirable. The distinction between these two versions of sexualized femininity is demonstrated throughout the film.

Linda's performance of "My Funny Valentine" signals the softening and taming of a kind of sexuality that, a decade prior, would have been considered dangerous.

*Figure 8.5 Still from Pal Joey (1957), Columbia Pictures: "My Funny Valentine"*

Consider the words of historian Elaine Tyler May, who argues that during the postwar era, "knockouts and bombshells could be tamed, after all, into harmless *chicks, kittens,* and the most famous sexual pet of them all, the Playboy bunny."[22] Surely we can add to this list Joey's term "mouse," his pet name for Linda.

## FEMME FATALE?

Novak's image in the film is deliberately set against Hayworth's. Significantly, this tension was also being played out in real life: Cohn was both goading Hayworth and paving the way for her replacement as Columbia's "love goddess" when he helped cast Novak as Linda against Hayworth's Vera, originally a character decades older than the young ingénue. The press, predictably, saw the potential for scandal, and played up what they saw as a certain rivalry between the two actors. The contrast between Hayworth and Novak was, at Cohn's hands, at the expense of Hayworth. In a cruel bit of symmetry, a comparison between the two actors has also been played up in scholarly literature, but to the opposite effect: Hayworth is often "rescued" from her cruel treatment at the hands of Columbia and Cohn, but usually at the expense of Novak, who is characterized as vacant, against Hayworth's complexity, and lacking, against Hayworth's talent. Film scholar Adrienne McLean, in her illuminating study of Hayworth, admits in her conclusion that she set out to rescue Hayworth, too, at the expense of Novak. Through research, however, she found that Novak was not, in reality, the "blank" (or, in the words of a 1956 *Time* cover story, the "pudding-faced, undistinguished girl") that the press made her out to be.[23] Novak, in fact, received good reviews for many of her films, *Pal Joey* included. As McLean puts it, "Novak (like Hayworth) did have something more than a face and body, as it is probably not mere nostalgia that leads headline writers to refer now to Novak with epithets reminding us of her 'enduring magnificence.'"[24] Further, the two women were, in fact, friendly on the set of *Pal Joey*: Hayworth sympathized with Novak (who was just a few years into her contract at Columbia), and Novak admired the film veteran.

*Pal Joey* was Hayworth's last film with Columbia and marked the end of a bitter relationship with Cohn and with the studio. Her last performance with Columbia is indicative of the kind of image Cohn tried to project, even as Hayworth "rejected the binding stereotype that the Love Goddess represented."[25] Hayworth's Vera undergoes a similar sort of "softening" as Novak's Linda, though, for plot purposes, she remains the foil to the relationship between Linda and Joey. Vera can't quite achieve "playmate" status, because she is a bit too smart, and a bit too ruthless: she "owns" Joey for a good part of the film (despite Joey's insistence that "nobody owns Joey but Joey"). Her age is also a barrier to "bunny" or "mouse" status, although Rita Hayworth was in fact a few years younger than Sinatra. And yet any power she has—whether it is through status, money, or sex—is consistently neutralized. The song "Zip" demonstrates her lack of agency well.

"Zip" presents perhaps the biggest alteration to an existing song in the screen version of *Pay Joey*. Melba, who originally sang the song, doesn't exist in the film; instead, Vera sings "Zip." This change marks a clear distinction between the stage and screen Veras: in the film, it is revealed that our sophisticated society dame was actually once a stripper known as "Vanessa the Undresser." Joey outs Vera at a society party (where he's performing, and where he first meets her), and, somewhat against her will, convinces her to perform the song. This maneuver effectively takes Vera off her gilt pedestal—the audience is made aware that she was once part of the same working class that Joey now occupies, and the power dynamics between the two shift considerably. As in the original, the tune is performed as a mock striptease, but now Vera sings the song in the first person, about her own mind/body disconnect when stripping. The bulk of Hayworth's version is dubbed over by Jo Ann Greer (as are the rest of her songs in the film), but Hayworth herself recites the introduction as a monologue, in a posh, affected manner, which, given her origins, the audience now knows is a ruse. Some of the humor of the original introduction is lost, but Hayworth's version brings out the sultry side—the sexually experienced side—of Vera's character, which is amplified by Greer's lush, teasing, warm voice, a stark contrast to the bright timbres of most of the actors who played Melba on stage. Joey appreciates the performance, and we can see that her sexual charms are not lost on him.

The lyrics of the screen version are also significantly altered. Given the references to contemporary pop culture (some that were out of date by that point), these edits are partially understandable, and certainly the PCA office flagged some of the original lyrics.[26] But it seems that one of the primary purposes of changing the lyrics was to transform the irreverent, critical, somewhat "masculine" Melba (and by extension, Gypsy Rose Lee) into our screen Vera, who has lost her claws in favor of a more *Playboy*-approved performance. What is lost is the bulk of Hart's lyrical brilliance.[27] Instead, the jokes are transparent, and not nearly as funny. Take Hart's caustic, culminating line: "Zip! It took intellect to master my art / Who the hell is Margie Hart?" With each iteration of the chorus, the fictionalized Gypsy Rose references her stripteaser rivals: Margie Hart, Sally Rand, and Lili St. Cyr. In the film, Hayworth sings "Zip! It took intellect to master my art / Every movement from the heart."

Hayworth's performance is also self-reflexive—this scene immediately brings to mind another famous mock-strip performed by Rita Hayworth: "Put the Blame on Mame" from her iconic *Gilda*, from 1946 (see Figure 8.6). Although performed by one of the most famous femmes fatales of the 1940s, the lyrics to "Put the Blame on Mame" also comment on the way that women function as scapegoats in film noir. Richard Dyer argues that this song—in addition to Hayworth's star status, the film's objectification of the character Johnny, and the fact that Hayworth is given a number of non-partnered dance features (perhaps as a form of self-expression)—might allow for a reading in which *Gilda* allows Hayworth a degree of agency.[28] *Pal Joey*, I argue, undercuts Hayworth's agency. "Zip" comments not only on the character Vera, but also on the star playing her, whose own status as a femme fatale was established by Columbia, a studio she was now on rocky terms with.[29] Linking Vera to Gilda provides the subtext that characters who use sex as a tool/weapon are necessarily punished. It also places Vera in the position of being objectified by Joey, a relationship that was reversed in the original (Vera refers to Joey somewhat condescendingly as "beauty" in both the stage and film versions). As Karen McNally has noted, Joey "forces her to revisit her relinquished identity as an erotic object and puts in place the power plays that will define their relationship."[30] This scene helps Joey regain power over Vera, while Vera makes

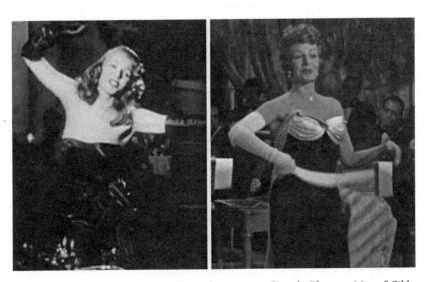

*Figure 8.6 Stills from Rita Hayworth's mock stripteases: "Put the Blame on Mame," Gilda (1946); "Zip," Pal Joey (1957); Columbia Pictures*

herself vulnerable to both Joey and to the viewer. It's a little hard to reconcile this difference, given our knowledge of the original character.

The film Vera is made even more vulnerable through her performance of "Bewitched." In its stage life, this song humanizes a hard-to-like character. The original Vera is a married woman, an experienced adulterer, and, at heart, a cynic where men are concerned. Rita Hayworth's performance of the tune, however, dispenses with Vera's characteristic self-awareness, and instead relies on her own "love goddess" star image, which was cultivated, and exploited, by Columbia. Numerous scholars and critics have noticed that her costume in this scene—a yellow silk and lace negligee—is reminiscent of the outfit featured in her famous "pinup" photo from 1941, published in *Life* magazine. Other references to the star's glory days are also made. Karen McNally makes the case that Hayworth's strategic hairstyling in *Pal Joey* was in contrast to her typical image: "by tying up and taming the star's trademark long, flowing hair, the film suggests that Hayworth's days as a misunderstood femme fatale may be behind her."[31] And yet in the beginning of this scene, her hair flows freely: here she is much more "love goddess" than "society matron," and more easily fits the *Playboy* ideal.

What's particularly telling about the scene is that while many of the lyrics are censored, Hayworth's performance is overtly sexual, as communicated through Hayworth and Greer's vocals, Hayworth's gestures, and strategic film cuts. The tune begins with a sultry, spoken introduction (spoken by Hayworth, as in "Zip"), as Vera rolls atop her bed, stretching suggestively for the camera: "He's a fool and don't I know it / But a fool can have his charms / I'm in love and don't I show it / Like a babe in arms." This morning-after scene is full of innuendo, even without the original lyrics. Jo Ann Greer's voice enters on the lyric "Men are not a new sensation," and Vera begins her morning routine: putting on her dressing gown, brushing her hair, pinning it up, taking tea, and eventually disrobing (on the line "the way to my heart is unzipped again") before entering the shower. Here the sexual thrill is played up by mirrors, and quick camera cuts that barely avoid any nudity.[32] Since the original scene from the stage show doesn't include any of the aforementioned visual cues (it was originally set in a tailor shop), this scene was not altered to satisfy the censors.

On the contrary, Hayworth's performance of "Bewitched" is meant to satisfy the typical sorts of roles Columbia afforded her. Although Vera seemingly expresses her own sexual desire, a scene like this undercuts her agency. As Dyer has said of Marilyn Monroe, her image reinforces a *Playboy*-approved attitude that women's sexuality is for men: the discourse on Monroe's body "is not referring to a body she experiences but rather to a body that is experienced by others . . . by embodying the desired sexual playmate she, a woman, becomes the vehicle for securing a male sexuality free of guilt."[33] Ultimately, Vera's three-dimensional inner life—conveyed partly through a worldly-wise cynicism and her unexpected affection for Joey—is reduced to a clichéd, two-dimensional portrayal of feminine desire.

The sexual power dynamics of Hayworth's scenes are fascinating when compared to Sinatra's performance of "The Lady Is a Tramp," when Joey willingly objectifies himself. Like "My Funny Valentine," "The Lady Is a Tramp" is from *Babes in Arms* (1937). In *Babes in Arms* the song was sung by the character Billie (Mitzi Green), a young girl who proudly rejects typical constructions of middle- and upper-class femininity.

Sinatra's version of the song transforms the gender dynamic by exploiting the two meanings of the term "tramp." His performance reveals yet another way that Joey's working-class identity is linked to Vera's (a clever pairing to "Zip"). Dorothy Kingsley, the screenwriter, claimed that this song was chosen to advance the plot: "we wanted Rita to get together with Joey and have him tell her that he knew the type of dame she was, I happened to think of this Rodgers and Hart song, 'That's Why the Lady is a Tramp.' And when he looked at Rita and said, 'that's why the lady is a tramp,' I think the audience got the whole picture."[34]

Though central to the film Joey's philosophy –"treat a dame like a lady and a lady like a dame"—his performance of this tune is a risk. Having already been snubbed by Vera, and prior to this performance, Joey goes to her estate to let her know that the only reason he was originally interested in her was her money; he rightly assumes that this atypical disregard for her social position will intrigue her. (There is a parallel to this encounter in the original stage production, though instead of coming to her house, he calls Vera on the telephone and tells her to "go to hell.") When she arrives at the club after hours and requests a song, it is a way of both exerting her power over Joey, and letting him know that his earlier behavior intrigued her.

The two uses of the term "tramp"—associated both with overt sexuality and/ or prostitution and with the free-spirited hobo—reveal a great deal about Joey's relationship with Vera: he is clearly offering her his sexual favors in return for her funding of his club, but he is also aligning himself with her working-class roots, which the lyrics regard as virtues (both of them like the "free, fresh wind in [their] hair"). The careful balance with which Joey expresses his own freedom, while simultaneously offering it to Vera, is indicative of the power relations of the film, which are much more straightforward in the stage version (Rita Hayworth, after all, was a major, if aging, sex idol). The performance of the song, despite the lyrics, emphasize that he is offering himself—namely his body—to Vera. This offer is underscored when, at the bridge, he leaves the piano bench, and displays himself at the front of the stage, eventually leaning over her table, circling her, and, as Karen McNally observes, approaching her "in a style similar to a flirtatious striptease act."[35] At one point he spreads his arms wide (as a gestural articulation of the lyrics, which he leaves out), offering himself. After the performance, she accepts his proposal, saying, "Come now, beauty," and takes him to her yacht. Despite the lyrics, it is Joey who plays the part of the "tramp." The parallel scene on stage happens entirely through dialogue; after he insults her she slaps him, but soon after says, "Come on." He replies, "Where to?" and her answer is pure, self-aware Vera: "Oh, you know where to. You knew it last night. Get your hat and coat. I'll be waiting in the car."

* * *

Though not otherwise addressed in this chapter, it would be worth further considering, as Karen McNally has, the inconsistencies in Joey's "swinging bachelor" character, an interesting counterpoint to characterizations of the female leads (there are many inconsistencies. For one, he is securely working class, and conspicuously without the bachelor pad. For another, he is routinely objectified).[36] What is clear, however, is that by 1957 Joey was not nearly as subversive as he was in 1940.

# CONCLUSION

• • •

## ADAPTING *JOEY*

I often find myself trying to reconstruct what the world "felt" like in 1940. (Borrowing from Mr. Sondheim, "I was younger then . . . I was only ten.") A family, a city, I suppose a whole nation trying to stand tall after a long depression. A president who had occupied the White House most of my life. Grover Whalen welcoming us to the World of Tomorrow out in Flushing. Swing bands on hotels rooftops across the country. Hollywood planting impossible dreams in our heads on Saturday afternoons for eleven cents. The whole globe teetering on the brink of one more great war. And Larry Hart in the wings at the Barrymore jotting down encore stanzas to "Zip" and "Bewitched." If I could charter a time machine, 1940 would be the first stop of my tour.[1]

—Richard Rodgers

Rodgers's letter, to Theodore Mann in 1976, captures the distance that one, even one who was there, might have felt about a time nearly four decades past. The gap between 1940 and what came after—the US engagement in World War II, the baby boom, the Cold War, McCarthyism, the space race, the Civil Rights Act, and Vietnam, as well as Rodgers's more personal tragedies and triumphs, including his storied golden age with Hammerstein and the death of both of his long-time collaborators—must have seemed vast to Rodgers, let alone anyone trying to revive his early shows. Mann, who was set to direct the 1976 revival of *Pal Joey* for Circle in the Square, had written to Rodgers, asking him to provide any additional information he could about the origins of *Pal Joey*. Feeling inadequate to the task—Rodgers said he felt his thoughts would be "little more than a thick mixture of nostalgia and conjecture"—Rodgers instead sent Mann copies of O'Hara's original Joey stories.[2] O'Hara, to be sure, was a keen documentarian of a time, and his stories are perhaps one of the clearest lenses through which to view that particular time and place.

*Pal Joey*'s acclaimed revival helped cement its place in the canon, and because of its success, a number of productions were subsequently mounted. Some were successful, especially in the decade or so following the revival, and many were

*Pal Joey.* Julianne Lindberg, Oxford University Press (2020). © Oxford University Press.
DOI: 10.1093/oso/9780190051204.001.0001

flops. Attempts to revive *Pal Joey* have had to grapple with its setting—it was a tough environment, though not set during Prohibition; it was scrappy, though set before the onset of the US involvement in World War II; it was often mean, though set after the country had partially recovered from the Depression. Communicating the specific feel of the late 1930s and the specific flavor of post-Repeal nightlife is undoubtedly a challenge. O'Hara communicated these things through fine detail, some of which is beyond what an audience can now relate to (consider O'Hara's references to Alice Faye, Ernie Byfield, and other now mostly forgotten names). Some revival productions have tried to stay true to its era, but imaginations can falter—some productions' over-the-top wise-guy vernaculars come off as stilted and labored, more Prohibition-gangster than anything else.

The casting for Joey, in particular, can make or break the show; most revivals have called for Joey to be an excellent dancer; the character also has to be uncommonly charming. The book too posed a problem: many productions have significantly reworked the book, making, for instance, Joey more likable, Linda more three-dimensional, or the setting more contemporary. While songs have rarely been taken out of the production, many have added songs (some have added the cut "I'm Talking to My Pal" back in, while others have added songs from other Rodgers and Hart shows). As with all revivals, the question of relevance has always been an issue. This chapter considers the afterlife of *Pal Joey*, exploring the reasons for the success of some productions, and for the failure of a host of others. More recent critiques of *Pal Joey*—of the script, and the use of slang, in particular—frequently point out how dated the show is. John O'Hara's writing is so specific to time and place that it can appear outmoded, or, to use a term supplied by a number of critics, tacky. This particular face of American identity has also been copied, parodied, and overplayed in both foreign and domestic film and theater. *Joey* is slippery, and has beguiled and bewildered producers and directors since its premiere.

## THE LONDON PRODUCTION: *JOEY* GOES ABROAD

Jack Hylton, an English bandleader-turned-impresario, brought *Pal Joey* to London in 1954. Hylton was known for bringing high-quality shows to the West End; also in 1954, he had produced *Ring Out the Bells* (an English revue), as well as two American imports, including Lerner and Loewe's *Paint Your Wagon*, and Harold Rome's *Wish You Were Here*. *Pal Joey* started its preview run in Oxford on March 16, and came to the Prince's Theatre in London on March 31. The show featured two Americans who were already well acquainted with their roles: Carol Bruce as Vera, and Harold Lang as Joey.[3] Lang of course featured in the celebrated revival, and both Lang and Bruce, the latter stepping in for Segal, played the touring production. George Martin, who had danced in the 1952 revival and also acted as Robert Alton's assistant, was credited with recreating Alton's dances. While the show opened to generally excellent reviews, the production didn't recoup its costs. Bruce, however, was praised by critics; some compared her cool, dignified bearing to that of Marlene Dietrich, and one besotted critic said, "Miss Bruce gives a poise, a dignity altogether her own, so that it is a vivid pleasure merely to see her walk about the stage [. . .] [S]he has the most precious of stage gifts, which is personality."[4] Lang was described as "bold and crude [. . .] Thanks to him, I saw that this originally must have been one of the most ruthless and unpleasant shows ever put on."[5]

Although Pal Joey would meet with much harsher censorship in Hollywood, the Lord Chamberlain's Office had a fair number of complaints that had to be addressed before the show could be licensed for performance. The first read-through of the script was on July 4, 1952, during the run of the revival (on behalf of Tom Arnold, another English theater producer); the reader for the Lord Chamberlain, C. D. Heriot, referred to the show as "the brashest, sourest, most cynical and certainly the most amusing American musical I have read for some time [. . .] there must be a few cuts: America is less sensitive than we are!"[6] Most of the complaints objected to the sexual puns, innuendos, and jokes in the show, specifically those that referred to homosexuality (seen especially in the first act), and prostitution. The song "Bewitched" was specifically targeted, and the following lines had to be removed:

"and worship the trousers that cling to him"
"Horizontally speaking / He's at his very best"
"Horizontally speaking is not the whole thing now"[7]

When the show was finally licensed, Heriot made the comment that offensiveness aside, it was still "perhaps a little too dry for the sweet tooths of English musical comedy audiences."[8] Papers reported that when Princess Margaret saw the show in Oxford, the song "Den of Iniquity" had to be cut entirely.[9] Another critic called the lyrics to that particular song "as frank a lyric as London has ever been offered."[10] In a comment that echoes some American reviews of the 1952 revival, one critic found it to be a nice change from then typical American fare: "After the bracing prairie breezes of 'Oklahoma,' 'Annie Get Your Gun' and the rest of the American folksy shows, it is refreshing to take a deep breath of the smoky city atmosphere of 'Pal Joey.'"[11]

The reaction of London critics to Pal Joey is telling: just as the "folksy" shows of Rodgers and Hammerstein came to define a particular brand of American identity, Pal Joey—full as it was of both the vibrant energy and seedy environs of the United State's major metropolitan areas—was seen as another side of the American character.[12] Much more rough-and-tumble, and rooted in outsider communities, images of the American nightclub had been broadcast to the world since the days of the first talking pictures. One reviewer put it this way: "At first I felt I was watching an early talkie. Period: Chicago, 1935. Behind the scenes in a night-club. Tough guys and prancing showgirls. Wisecracks and hullabaloo."[13]

## BOB FOSSE AS JOEY

In the summer of 1950, Bob Fosse won his first starring role in Gus Schirmer's touring summer-stock production of *Pal Joey*. Kevin Winkler called Joey Fosse's "acting summit"; he was the understudy for Lang in 1952, and he would go on to play Joey in the City Center revivals of 1961 and 1963. Winkler points out a connection between Fosse's and Joey's biographies:

> Fosse's background and personal status held similarities with the character of Joey. Like Fosse, Joey was an experienced hoofer, ingratiating and glib on a nightclub floor and expert in the byways of backstage life, particularly with women. Joey and Fosse, both show business veterans by an early age and surrounded by beautiful women, shared the drive to score with as many of them as possible.[14]

Winkler goes on to compare Fosse's relationship with his second wife, Joan McCracken (who was ten years his senior), to Joey's relationship with Vera; McCracken gave Fosse "entrée to a luxury world," in the same way that Joey hoped Vera would.[15]

The production was generally well received although, as Winkler notes, Fosse's own reviews were mixed. Joan Mann choreographed the show, and also starred as Gladys (Mann had also played Gladys in the 1949 Dallas production). Bruce, whom one critic described as possessing a "fascinating personality," reportedly "performed with an ease and polish that was delightful to behold."[16] Fosse, the same critic commented, was "a slight young man with ice blue eyes, a shock of corn-colored hair and nimble dancing feet [who] makes one think of 'Skeets' Gallagher, when that star was in his prime."[17] The show was minimalist out of financial necessity (it was accompanied by two pianists), but as most critics commented, the book held up and Bruce and Fosse seemed to embody, respectively, the cool sophistication of Vera, and the cheap, big-headed, sometimes-charming appeal of Joey.

When Schirmer directed the City Center revival in 1961, he brought back Bruce and Fosse, the latter of whom had, in the interim since his performance in the summer stock tour as Joey, made a name on Broadway as the choreographer for *The Pajama Game* (1954), *Bells are Ringing* (1956), and director/choreographer for the Gwen Verdon show *Redhead* (1959). Schirmer hired Ralph Beaumont (who had danced with Verdon, now Fosse's wife, in *Can-Can*) to do the dances.[18] As Winkler notes, however, "in dance terms, Fosse was 'the Muscle' and staged his own numbers."[19] The show ran for the expected two weeks, and then was given a three-week extension because of "tremendous public demand."[20] One critic called Fosse "probably its best ever Joey [. . .] and is just about perfection as the two-timing, low-down hero of the piece."[21] Verdon dubbed one of Fosse's dances from the show "The Narcissistic Tango," when he "affected a Spanish dancer's rigid upper body and tight wrists above the head but eventually retreated into his comfort zone with leap turns and knee work."[22] It seems plausible that this dance would have occurred during the song "Take Him," which was the same placement of Gene Kelly's cocky tap-tango (see Chapter 6). Schirmer again called on Fosse, this time opposite the Swedish-born Viveca Lindfors, to play Joey in the 1963 City Center revival. Jack Durant, who played Ludlow Lowell in 1940, was back in his role as the acrobatic con man, and so was George Martin as choreographer (his last *Pal Joey* was the London production, in which he recreated Alton's dances), this time paired with his wife, Ethel. Both George and Ethel Martin were Jack Cole dancers and had, as a team, choreographed summer-stock musicals. As in the 1961 production, however, critics remarked that "it is difficult to tell where he leaves off and the Martins begin."[23]

## THE FLOPS: CIRCLE IN THE SQUARE, 1976, AND *PAL JOEY '78*

While the revivals produced between 1954 and 1963 were all critical successes, the next decade wasn't so kind to *Joey*. The first major flop was the Circle in the Square production from 1976. Intended to be a fairly faithful recreation of the original production (the creative team used the 1952 script), personnel issues tainted the entire show: between the previews and the opening of the show, the show lost its two lead actors. Produced by Paul Libin and Theodore Mann, Mann, who also directed, had convinced Edward Villella, a principal dancer at the New York City Ballet, to play the part of Joey. Villella had no background as a singer or actor, but Mann felt sure he could pull it off. In the part of Vera was Eleanor Parker, the Academy Award–nominated film star probably most popularly known for her role as the Baroness in the film adaptation of *The Sound of Music* (1965). Just a few days before the opening of the show, however, Villella pulled out, citing "artistic differences," and Parker followed shortly after, citing the same.

As it turns out, there were major problems backstage. The biggest was that Villella never felt confident in his role, and he clashed seriously with the show's choreographer, Margo Sappington. According to a lengthy *New York Times* article, which was published the day the show opened, Villella had been taking voice lessons, working day in and out to become a confident singer, but he wasn't satisfied with his progress.[24] Villella's "definite lack of rapport" with Sappington led to him threatening to quit unless Mann let George Balanchine, his mentor, rechoreograph some of his dances.[25] Mann allowed it, and Balanchine reworked the act 1 dream ballet, as well as Villella's "Happy Hunting Horn" solo. This move, predictably, infuriated Sappington. Still not confident, Villella again threatened to quit if Mann didn't let his other mentor, Jerome Robbins, come observe the rehearsals. Mann again relented, and Robbins agreed to "make a few suggestions" (he was paid $1000 for it).[26] Meanwhile, the music director, Gene Palumbo, felt that Mann's direction was lacking, and that the show lacked focus because of "a lack of communication between himself, Mann and Miss Sappington."[27] Further, Parker was feeling neglected, and, by June 4, refused to go on stage. In the end, Sappington felt that Balanchine's new dances clashed with hers, and called for her original dances to be reinstated. This demand infuriated Villella, and Mann had to make the decision to keep either Villella or Sappington. He chose Sappington. Thus, the understudies for Villella and Parker—Christopher Chadman and Joan Copeland—performed on opening night. The *Times* feature probably drove some interest, but in the end the show closed after seventy-three performances. Chadman was panned by critics. One said "there is good news and bad news about 'Pal Joey'"; the "good news" was Joan Copeland, and the "bad news" was Chadman, who was "there in person, but any resemblance to the slick lady killer with too many hands and no heart is merely coincidental."[28] Copeland, Arthur Miller's sister, had experience in both straight and musical theater, and was generally praised.

Like the Circle in the Square production, *Pal Joey '78* was a flop with a similarly fraught backstage life. Lena Horne's triumphant return to Broadway, over two decades following her last appearance in *Jamaica* (1957), didn't happen according to plan. According to Horne, an updated, all-black cast version of *Pal Joey* had been in the works for years:

> First they wanted me to do it as a 90-minute TV show opposite Sammy Davis, but the deal fell through. Then Gene Kelly came to Vegas to see me and ask about doing it for the stage. I said great, if they could get a dynamite Joey like Ben Vereen; but nothing came of that either.[29]

The version of *Pal Joey* that eventually materialized at the Ahmanson Theatre in Los Angeles in April 1978, produced by the Los Angeles Civic Light Opera, was heavily reworked by Jerome Chodorov and Mark Bramble.[30] Originally slated to be choreographed and directed by Gower Champion, Michael Kidd (as director) and Claude Thompson (as choreographer) took over after differences were reported between Champion and Horne.[31] Touting a disco-inspired score, with orchestrations by Motown veteran Gil Askey, the production featured Clifton Davis as Joey and Josephine Premice as Melba, whose role was expanded. In *Pal Joey '78*, as it was titled, Horne plays the part of an older singer (Horne was sixty-one) who has gained wealth and fame, all of her own doing. Melba plays her press agent; "Zip" became a duet sung between the two women. Joey is a similar type as in the original, but Davis's role was cut back considerably. Rather than feature Vera in four songs, like the original production, Horne sang in eight. Two earlier Rodgers and Hart songs—"A Lady Must Live" from *America's Sweetheart*, 1931, and "This Can't Be Love," from *The Boys from Syracuse*, 1938, both sung by Horne—were interpolated into the score. A rumor started that Horne was behaving like a prima donna, demanding all of the show's attention and requesting that Premice's scenes be cut.[32] Claude Thompson, in an interview with one of Horne's biographers, supported this claim, adding that he was personally hurt when Horne, whom he had been friends with for decades, didn't intervene when he was fired from the show.[33] Horne denied all allegations that she had "insisted on doing things her way" (the allegations also held her responsible for suggesting that the show be set in the 1970s), responding thus:

> I have kept silent until now from defending myself against the many innu-endoes that have been printed about my influence on the production of "'Pal Joey' '78" [. . .] My management and I had conferences with the producers regarding my appearance in 'Pal Joey' before Mr. Gower Champion was con-tracted to direct the production. Our suggestion was that this 'Pal Joey' would take place in the '30s or '40s and located in Kansas City, where many black men and women had money and where Joey's songs would have been marvelous in the Count Basie style of that period.[34]

Although *Pal Joey '78* was never recorded, there are some hints as to what it might have sounded like. Gil Askey, the orchestrator for the production, was also a producer and musical director at Motown Records, and had been Diana Ross's musical director for thirteen years. In 1967 Askey and Berry Gordy released *The Supremes Sing Rodgers and Hart*, which features the song "I Could Write a Book."[35] While some of the songs on this crossover record have mid-century, hard-swinging big-band orchestrations, "I Could Write a Book" is a more contemporary take on a girl-group sound, anticipating the forward-moving groove of disco, and perhaps anticipating the sound of *Pal Joey '78*. Horne, despite the unsuccessful run of *Pal Joey '78*, featured a few years later in her own one-woman show on Broadway called *Lena Horne: "The Lady and Her Music."* During this show Horne sang "Bewitched" and "A Lady Must Live," among other jazz standards; the live performance was subsequently released on record, produced by Quincy Jones. Horne captures the audience through comic monologues and dramatic perfor-mances: she begins "Bewitched" by saying "I'm gonna sing a sad song about an old broad . . . with money. She falls in love with a young, *young* stud [. . .] She permit-ted herself to get weak once in a while."

*Pal Joey '78* was panned. Most critics commented on how beautiful Horne appeared and sounded, but criticized the book, which seemed to be adapted only to showcase Horne. A particularly scathing review, based on the show after it had moved from Los Angeles to San Francisco, captures the worst criticisms of the show:

> Not even a living legend can save "Pal Joey '78." The show just might create a kind of "cult" legend of its own. It's that bad—a disaster unworthy of the label professional entertainment. [. . .] Horne plays Vera like a girlish Mae West lost in Harlem—lots of throaty "Ya! Babys" with accompanying pelvic thrusts [. . .] Clifton Davis [. . .] portrays Joey with all the warmth, vitality and charm of a pick pocket at a funeral [. . .] There is no pacing. The staging is clumsy. The sets—when they work—are tacky. The costumes lack style [. . .] But the most offensive element in "Pal Joey '78" is the outrageous black stereotyping.[36]

The criticism of the black stereotyping in the show, from a white critic in this instance, was a common complaint. What was not remarked upon is the entrenched history that led to this moment; like most all-black cast musicals of the twentieth century, this one had a mostly white creative team. For most of the twentieth century, to be sure, stereotyped depictions of African Americans were not only welcomed, but expected. Things were changing during this period (*The Wiz*, for instance, which had premiered on Broadway the previous year, was directed by Geoffrey Holder and choreographed by George Faison); it was a sign of the times that this particular criticism was widespread. An all-black-cast version of *Guys and Dolls*, directed by Billy Wilson (who had, like Premice and Thompson, also performed with Horne on *Jamaica*), also premiered on Broadway in 1976. Although similarly set in the seedy environs of a night club, it resisted the caricatures of *Pal Joey '78*. Despite the producer's intentions, *Pal Joey '78* never made it to Broadway.

## *JOEY* LOOKS INTO THE FUTURE

After the failures of the 1970s, *Pal Joey* wouldn't have a full Broadway revival for over thirty years. *Joey* did, to be fair, play frequently, if not regularly, in regional productions, and there was a successful London revival in 1980 (starring Sian Phillips and Denis Lawson), as well as a few off-Broadway productions with limited runs. Most successful was an *Encores!* production from 1995, featuring Patti Lupone and Peter Gallagher, which used as much of the original score as was possible, and which produced an album ("I'm Talking to My Pal," the number cut from the original production, is the last song on the album).[37] Lupone's Vera was much different from Segal's, but she embodied the worldly, sexually experienced woman-of-a-certain-age that Lupone herself would help standardize on Broadway. Bebe Neuwirth, as Melba, and Vicki Lewis, as Gladys, also give effective, character-driven performances on the album.

The more recent history of *Pal Joey* has been fairly uneven. Roundabout Theatre's Broadway revival from 2008, directed by Joe Mantello, was choreographed by Graciela Daniele and featured a new book by Richard Greenberg, freely adapted from O'Hara's original. The revival featured Stockard Channing and Matthew Risch, the latter of whom stepped in at the last minute for Christian Hoff, who had reportedly injured his foot (though there were rumors that Hoff wasn't a strong enough dancer). A *New York Times* story on the show claimed "key members of the production said that [. . .] Joe Mantello had originally wanted a major, bankable star—Harry Connick Jr. in particular, or Hugh Jackman—in the role of Joey."[38] The show opened to mixed reviews, and only ran for eighty-five performances. Channing received generally good notices and Martha Plimpton, who played Gladys (and who performed the number "Zip"), was nearly universally praised. Risch was given mixed reviews—he was often criticized for seeming green (he was, indeed, a relative novice), or simply not charming enough.

Robert Hofler, of *Variety*, found the revival "gutsy enough to warrant attention," and found it "bizarre to see Mantello's staging pejoratively described as 'ruthless,' 'joyless' and 'unhappy'—as if such qualities don't compute in musical theater."[39] Hofler found Risch "tough and uncompromising," avoiding a more ingratiating approach to Joey. He ends his piece by musing on an issue that relates back to the critical reception of the original production (and to Wolcott Gibb's wry comment that "amoral people are all right on the stage so long as they're not accompanied by popular music"): "As one prominent Broadway talent put it to me not long ago, 'The New York critics are, for the most part, a depressed lot who have no problem being challenged by plays but look to the musicals to cheer themselves up.'"[40]

Since then, a number of Broadway revivals have been rumored, but none have materialized. The latest of these was a projected revival to be directed by Tony Goldwyn, grandson of Samuel Goldwyn and star of the television series *Scandal*. In December 2017 Goldwyn, who has a handful of performing credits on Broadway but thus far no production credits, announced the projected revival with a revised book by screenwriter and off-Broadway playwright Richard LaGravenese. Goldwyn had done a read-through of the show in 2016, but nothing had developed. In September 2018, an Equity casting announcement went out for a developmental lab of the show. The acting call specified that Joey was to be in his "late 20s-late30s" and that

> [t]his character is African-American. Jazz singer, with big ambitions to be a star performer in 1930s Chicago. Confident, charming, amoral, Joey can be a romantic heel who uses women to his own advantage (until he falls in love for the first time). At heart, Joey is an artist—devoted to a jazz sound ahead of its time. Fighting uphill battles of racism and the Depression, Joey will let nothing stop him to be on top. Baritone—Baritenor with ability to understand the idiom of jazz and its idiosyncrasies.[41]

The lab was unfortunately canceled, and no further plans have been made to stage the show.

Goldwyn/LaGravenese's casting call emphasizes another angle on Joey—the outsider status that seemed to have been central to O'Hara's conception of the character. A number of summer-stock and off-Broadway productions have played with the significance of being an outsider, both in terms of race and sexual identity. One production from 2012, directed by Peter Schneider, updated the setting to 1948 and featured a bisexual, African American Joey in a love triangle with a white Vera, an African American Linda, and a white male pianist.[42] Like other revivals, the score interpolated a handful of Rodgers and Hart songs from other productions, including "The Lady Is a Tramp," "Sing for Your Supper," and "Glad to be Unhappy."

As seen in *Pal Joey '78*, an African American Joey was not new, nor was a gay or bisexual Joey. Although not seen in mainstream venues, a rich history exists of *Pal Joey* being performed in gay venues, sometimes as all-male productions. The earliest of these that I am aware of (there are very likely earlier examples), dates to 1967, and was put on by the Society for Individual Rights (S.I.R.), an early gay political organization; in 1967 they called themselves the "largest homophile group in the country."[43] S.I.R. was based in San Francisco, hosted community gatherings, and published a monthly magazine (called *Vector*). The production of *Pal Joey* was held at the S.I.R. community center, and ran for a week. *Vector* published a review of the production, and in true community theater spirit remarked that "it may have not been the greatest smash in San Francisco, but it was nevertheless very entertaining."[44]

In addition to a playful take on 1930s glamour and smut, all of these productions played up the gendered archetypes offered in the show, including the diva-like "Red Hot Mama," and the swaggering, hyper-masculine working-class entertainer, personified by Joey. While the canonic legacy of *Pal Joey* relies almost entirely upon its premiere and first successful revival, the show has remained significant in less traditional venues, morphing and adapting to whatever best serves the interests of its audience, just as, one might imagine, Joey himself would. Despite its critical accolades, *Pal Joey* has retained the scrappiness of the underdog. We like him that way. As Vera said, in her Joey-inspired words, "If you started dressing like a gentleman you might begin behaving like one, and that I but never could take."[45]

# APPENDIX 1 THE CAST

The cast in the order in which they appeared on opening night

| The Principals | |
| --- | --- |
| Joey Evans | small-time, womanizing nightclub performer |
| Linda English | secretary to a tailor and one of Joey's love interests |
| Vera Simpson | wealthy, older married woman; funds Joey's dream club |

| Significant Supporting Characters | |
| --- | --- |
| Mike Spears | owner of a cheap club in Chicago |
| Gladys | featured dancer at a cheap club in Chicago |
| Max | manager of act 2 club |
| The Tenor | featured performer at act 2 club |
| Melba Snyder | hard-boiled reporter |
| Ludlow Lowell | con man |
| Commissioner O'Brien | police commissioner in Chicago |

A number of score sources exist for *Pal Joey*. The most widely available source is the piano-vocal edition by Chappell & Co., published in 1962. This score includes all of the songs performed in the initial run with the exception of "I'm Talking to My Pal," which was dropped during the Philadelphia tryouts. The Chappell score includes, as in the original, encores for the dance features, as well as a short encore for "Bewitched."

Rodgers and Hammerstein: An Imagem Company (formerly The Rodgers and Hammerstein Organization) now licenses the score and orchestral parts for *Pal Joey*, although the license was previously owned, like all songs by Rodgers and Hart, by Tams-Witmark. The journey from premiere to licensed score appears not to have been a straightforward one. The original full-orchestral partiturs, for one, are lost. Hans Spialek was the principal orchestrator for the show; evidence suggests that Ted Royal also helped.[1]

A bound piano-conductor score that appears to have been used by musical director Harry Levant in the original production (1940–1941), and George Hirst in the touring production, is held by the Rodgers and Organization, and is the basis of the licensed conductor score. There is much evidence, however, to suggest that the individual stand parts (in the absence of full orchestral scores), were copied incorrectly in the licensed parts. Paul Christman, Director of Musical Theatre at the Weitzenhoffer School of Musical Theatre at the University of Oklahoma, recently completed a restoration and reconstruction of the orchestrations. Christman was interested in working on a restored version of the score because, he asserts, "those who have produced or studied *Pal Joey* know there are significant errors in the score that have gone uncorrected since its premiere," and, therefore, professional productions have been forced to "change or reduce the instrumentation upon discovering problems with these parts."[2] There is evidence to support these claims. In an interview with Bruce Pomohac, an account confirmed by Wayne Blood and others at the R&H Organization, Christman found that it wasn't until the mid-1990s that the R&H Organization had in its archives all of the original stand parts. In the 1950s Tams-Witmark had given the R&H Organization what was originally thought to be all of the production materials it had related to *Pal Joey*. According to Pomohac, "Rodgers had to rely on copies of the orchestration obtained from Tams-Witmark and his memory when putting together the licensed orchestrations and published score in 1962."[3] But one day before the New York City Center Encores! recording was made in 1995, a box containing the bound stand parts (very likely used in the original production) was dropped off at the R&H Organization offices. Apparently because of time

constraints, only some of this material was incorporated into the Encores! recording. Still, that recording is probably closest to the original orchestration of the
premiere. Christman's restored and reconstructed score is based on these bound
parts, as well as on orchestrations of nine pieces prepared by John McGlinn in the
1980s in collaboration with Hans Spialek (unfinished due to Spialek's unfortunate
passing in 1983). McGlinn's full scores and Spialek's annotations are held by the
R&H Organization. Christman's restored score has now been digitized; his next
step is to perform the restored score in concert.

What appear to be the original stand parts (held by the R&H Organization)
are loose, and sometimes out of order in each book. There is evidence (including markings within the music) that these parts were used in the 1940/1941
original run. The "Overture" part for Trumpets 1 and 2, for instance, includes a
penciled-in annotation with a list of the brass players' names, with "1940-1941"
indicated.[4] The Trumpet I/II part seems to be in the hand of copyist Guido
Tutrinoli, who worked with the Chappell orchestrators during this period and
into the 1950s—most of the pit parts, and a set of conductor cue sheets, are in
this hand.[5] "That Terrific Rainbow" is in the hand of another copyist, and anec-
dotal evidence suggests that it was added to the show after rehearsals began.[6]
Levant's score (and the conductor cue sheets) also often include penciled-in
annotations referring to actors from the original run, including June Havoc,
Gene Kelly, Shirley Paige (the specialty dancer), and Vivienne Segal.

The woodwinds for the original orchestration are as follows: Reed 1 (first alto
sax, doubling flute), Reed 2 (oboe/English horn/alto sax), Reed 3 (clarinet/bass
clarinet/tenor sax), Reed 4 (flute/clarinet/tenor sax), and Reed 5 (bassoon/clari-
net/tenor sax). Rather than typical big-band orchestration, the reed parts appear
to be true pit doubles, even though certain songs require the reeds to assume
the sound of a swing band. When the 1952 revival was mounted (orchestrations
by Don Walker, who worked on nine shows with Rodgers, with both Hart and
Hammerstein), the original orchestrations were still missing. In any case, Walker
went for a hotter arrangement, approximating the hard-swinging bands popular
in the 1950s. He rearranged the original five reed books to set up a traditional big-
band arrangement: Alto I, Alto II, Tenor I, Tenor II, and Baritone (an added part).
His orchestrations can be heard on the revival "cast" recording (omitting most of
the revival cast, excepting Helen Gallagher) recorded by Capitol in 1952.

Throughout this book, when I refer to the "original score" or the score from the
"original production," I'm referring to Levant's conductor score and cue sheets,
and/or the original stand parts (all held by the R&H Organization). When I reference the piano-vocal score, I am referring to the published Chappell & Co. score
(1962), unless otherwise indicated.

Three of O'Hara's draft typescripts are extant; the earliest of these, and what
was very likely O'Hara's first draft of the script, is housed at the R&H Organization;
copies of the second, potentially a rehearsal script (written after Rodgers and
Hart began writing the music), are housed both at the R&H Organization and
in John O'Hara's Papers at Penn State. The R&H Organization also owns a typescript that appears to reflect what was heard on opening night. The licensed script

is based on both the opening-night typescript and the drafts, and includes the following note:

> This edition of *Pal Joey* has been prepared from the original 1940 libretto and earlier drafts by John O'Hara. Since the *Pal Joey* vocal score was prepared for the 1952 revival, it differs somewhat from this edition. The musical numbers in this libretto coincide with the numbers in the vocal score, although certain incidental numbers that appeared in the 1952 revival have now been deleted. Songs have been reassigned to the characters who originally sang them, so certain cues and stage directions in the vocal score are no longer applicable. The lyrics in this libretto should be considered definitive.

In 2014 Laurence Maslon edited a version of the libretto for the Library of America edition. This script differs in parts from the licensed script, and reflects, mostly, the opening-night script, edited for clarity. When I refer to the "preliminary script" I am referencing O'Hara's earliest draft; when I refer to the "rehearsal script" I'm referencing what appears to be a working draft, used during rehearsal; when I refer to the "opening-night script" I am almost always referring to the opening night script held by the R&H Organization and Penn State.

Although some of O'Hara's typescripts include Hart's lyrics, none are complete. The best source for Hart's lyrics remains *The Complete Lyrics of Lorenz Hart*, edited by Dorothy Hart and Robert Kimball; the second edition (1995) includes the original lyrics to "What Is a Man?" (originally "Love Is My Friend"), which were for decades thought to be lost.


## SOURCES

### O'Hara's Pal Joey Stories

| | |
|---|---|
| 1939–1940 | John O'Hara's original Joey stories, published in installments in the *New Yorker* |
| 1940 | *Pal Joey*, published by Duell, Sloan & Pearce; includes fourteen of John O'Hara's Joey stories, including the twelve published in the *New Yorker* and an additional two, previously unpublished, stories |

### Score Sources

| | |
|---|---|
| 1940 | Rodgers's holograph piano-vocal scores; includes the dropped "I'm Talking to My Pal" (Richard Rodgers Collection, Library of Congress) |
| 1940 | Rodgers' sketches (Richard Rodgers Collection, Library of Congress) |
| 1940 | Conductor score, conductor cue sheets, and stand parts from the 1940/1941 production (R&H Organization) |
| 1940/1980s | Full orchestral score for "Bewitched" in John McGlinn's hand, with assistance by the original orchestrator, Hans Spialek (John McGlinn Collection, Library of Congress) |
| 1940/1980s | A reconstruction of Spialek's orchestrations (of nine pieces), prepared by John McGlinn in the 1980s in collaboration with Hans Spialek (unfinished); includes Spialek's annotations (R&H Organization) |

| 1952 | Stand parts and conductor score from the revival (R&H Organization) |
|---|---|
| 1952 | Piano-vocal score for the revival (Don Walker Collection, Library of Congress) |
| 1962 | Published piano-vocal score, Chappell & Co (commercially available) |
| 1995 | City Center *Encores!* parts and conductor score (R&H Organization) |
| 2018 | Paul Christman's reconstructed score, based on the McGlinn/Spialek collaboration, and other archival evidence (forthcoming) |

## Libretti sources

| 1940 | Preliminary draft script: O'Hara's earliest draft typescript, very likely written in the spring or summer (R&H Organization) |
|---|---|
| 1940 | Rehearsal script: Updated draft typescript, very likely revised in the Fall (O'Hara Papers, Penn State) |
| 1940 | Opening-night typescript (R&H Organization and Penn State) |
| 1940/2014 | Library of America edition, based on the opening-night script with additional notes and annotations, ed. Laurence Maslon |
| 1952 | Published libretto, based on the 1952 revival (Random House, Fireside Theatre edition) |

## Lyrics

| 1940 | Complete lyrics, including encores and alternate verses, published with annotations in *The Complete Lyrics of Lorenz Hart* (eds. Dorothy Hart and Robert Kimball); includes the lyrics to "Love Is My Friend" |
|---|---|
| 1940 | Library of America edition, based on the opening-night script with additional notes and annotations, ed. Laurence Maslon |
| 1952 | Published libretto, based on the 1952 revival (Random House, Fireside Theatre edition) |
| 1962 | Published piano-vocal score, Chappell & Co; incomplete lyrics |

## Audio Recordings

| 1951 | Columbia Records session (featuring Harold Lang and Vivienne Segal); Recorded in September, 1950, and released in February, 1951 |
|---|---|
| 1952 | Capitol Records Revival "Cast" recording; featuring Jane Froman and Dick Beavers (Helen Gallagher, singing the part of Gladys, and Elaine Stritch, singing the part of Melba, are the only singers on the recording who remain from the 1952 stage revival) |
| 1980 | London Cast Recording (featuring Sian Phillips and Denis Lawson) |
| 1995 | City Center *Encores!* Recording (featuring Patti Lupone and Peter Gallagher) |

## Recorded Live Performances:

| 1940/1941 | 8 mm footage (no sound) from the original production; some of the clips are filmed from the house, and some from the stage wings; property of Rosemarie Sibilio, friend of June Havoc (June Havoc Collection, Boston University) |
|---|---|

| 1945 | November 18; Gene Kelly on Paul Whiteman's "Your Radio Hall of Fame"; Kelly and Martha Tilton (as Linda) perform the dialogue from the "Pet Shop" scene; the dialogue is adapted from O'Hara's short story "Bow Wow" rather than the musical, and includes no songs |
| 1952 | June 15; Harold Lang featured on *The Ed Sullivan Show*, performing Robert Alton's "Happy Hunting Horn" routine with Norma Thornton and chorus dancers (New York Public Library for the Performing Arts) |
| 2008 | Bootleg of the live performance of the 2008 revival, featuring Stockard Channing and Matthew Risch (currently available on YouTube) |

# APPENDIX 3

## DETAILED DIFFERENCES BETWEEN REHEARSAL SCRIPT AND OPENING-NIGHT SCRIPT

| ACT I | Rehearsal script | Opening-night script |
|---|---|---|
| Scene 1: Club | Begins with Joey auditioning on the song "You Mustn't Kick it Around" (1-1-1) | The song that Joey auditions on is not indicated in the script (1-1-1) |
| | Includes opening dialogue between Joey and a piano player (1-1-1) | Dialogue between Joey and piano player is cut |
| | | Noel Coward line is cut; |
| | Joey declares that emcees who wear tails think they're "some poor man's Noel Coward" (1-1-4) | Dialogue added between Joey and the chorus girls (1-1-5) |
| | | Dialogue added to introduce "Kick It Around," which closes the scene (JOEY: "Now get your places, and let's have some cooperation" (1-1-7) |
| Scene 2: Pet Shop | Joey tells Linda a tall tale about his high-class upbringing. In this version of the script, the word "chauffeur" is spelled "shofer," as O'Hara would have spelled it in the original stories. Joey also refers to the Chauffeur as "Abbott," a likely reference by O'Hara to George Abbott (1-2-8) | In this script, the word "chauffeur" is spelled correctly, and "Abbott" is changed to "Chadwick." This might have been Abbott's edit, but it would have, at some point, passed through O'Hara's hands (1-2-11) |
| | The lead-in dialogue, as well as the cue for the music, to "I Could Write a Book" is already present in the rehearsal script (JOEY: "You inspire me. You know what I mean" (1-2-12) | Lead-in dialogue remains the same (1-2-9) |

| ACT I | Rehearsal script | Opening-night script |
|---|---|---|
| Scene 3: Club | The stage directions indicate that "A GIRL is singing 'I'M BLUE' song and JOEY walks on during song" (1-3-10) | Stage directions indicate the song "Chicago": "GIRLS do Chicago Number." (1-3-15) |
| | The scene begins with Joey flirting with Linda. Over a page of dialogue is included (and subsequently cut from the opening-night script), and includes lines that strengthen their relationship (i.e., "JOEY: I have some more stuff to do but I can steal a little minute with you. How's the dog situation?" Etc.), and performance directions that indicate that Joey sees Linda's true worth (i.e., "[it is obvious to us that he has been surprised by her frankness and the naïve interest in him that she has revealed]") (1-3-11, 1-3-12) | The scene begins with Mike telling Joey that Vera has arrived: "Mrs. Prentiss Simpson. Mrs. Chicago Society" (1-3-15) |
| | | All of Doane's lines are cut |
| | | Linda is hurt that Joey snubs her, but he doesn't give her as much attention here (1-3-17) |
| | | Much of Joey's club patter (which reads as O'Hara showing off) is cut (1-3-15; 1-3-16) |
| | A character named "DOAN" (Linda's "boyfriend," played by Stanley Donen; the name was very likely derived from his name) has a few lines (this character is listed in the original playbill as "Albert Doane") (1-3-11; 1-3-12) | Joey interacts with Vera in the way that he does *because* he knows who she is (1-3-15) |
| | | "Rainbow" indicated (1-3-19) |
| | Linda is hurt that Joey snubs her, which makes more sense in this version of the script (1-3-14) | |

| ACT I | Rehearsal script | Opening-night script |
| --- | --- | --- |

Joey's club patter, which occurs after his conversation with Linda (which occurs in reverse order in the opening-night script) includes a lot more tongue-in-cheek name-dropping, and other wordy banter (i.e., "In addition to that Bennie Goodman and Artie Shaw will be here with their clarinets [. . .] Beatie and Clifton and Gertie and Noel, and Bennie and Artie will be here directly") (1-3-12; 1-3-13)

Stage directions indicate that he notices, and appreciates, Vera, and vice versa ("VERA [. . .] is studying Joey—and he is not unaware of it—pretty much as he usually studies a girl. In other words, with more than a casual thought to the Hay department" (1-3-14)

Joey finds out who Vera is only after he interacts with her (1-3-16)

No mention of "That Terrific Rainbow," or any other song (1-3-17)

| ACT I | Rehearsal script | Opening-night script |
|---|---|---|
| Scene 4: Joey and Vera's rooms | Shows Joey calling many more women than just Linda and Vera (though, in this script, that part is crossed out); Linda hangs up on him, and her hurt makes sense, because of previous scene (1-4-18) | Calls Linda, but she isn't seen on stage; she hangs up on him; not as much back-story to explain her offense (1-4-21) |
| | After Joey tells Vera to "go to hell" she says to the maid, "If Mr. Evans calls, I'm not in" (1-4-20) | The latter line is cut (the song cue, included in the original conductor cue sheets, is Joey's final line: "go to hell," etc.) |
| | Vera sings "Bewitched" after their exchange (1-4-20) | Vera sings "Hello Love/Love Is My Friend" These lyrics are much more sentimental than the eventual "What Is a Man?" (1-4-23; 1-4-24) |
| Scene 5: Night Club, after hours | In this draft, the chorus's parts aren't yet named ("Kid" "Second Kid," etc.) | The parts are given the actor's names: "Sandra" (Sondra Barrett, The Kid) "Fraser" (Jane Fraser, playing Terry), "Diane" (Diane Sinclair, playing Agnes), "Amarilla" (Amarilla Morris, playing Valerie) (1-5-25; 1-5-26) |
| | Joey's insult to Vera (that he saw her name on the 1919 social register; there's a "1910" typo, a holdover from the preliminary script) (1-5-24) | A bit of dialogue added for Vera's entrance (1-5-26) |
| | "Hunting" indicated after Joey's line "[a]wfully sorry, folks but I've got to leave you." Right after, the script says, "[S]uggested spot for number— JOEY and GIRLS—where he's highhatting them")— potentially a new number? | Dialogue added to show that Vera is perceptive, and understood the nature ($) of Joey's initial interest (1-5-28; 1-5-29) |
| | | Year remains 1919 |
| | | Dialogue between the girls and Mike added (in prep for "Happy Hunting Horn"— "he says he's going hunting," etc.) (1-5-30) |

| ACT I | Rehearsal script | Opening-night script |
|---|---|---|
| Scene 6: Tailor shop | There's indication of the pretense on Vera's part, for the benefit of the Tailor, that they aren't carrying on an affair, which Joey doesn't catch ("so glad I was in town when you called" said at the same time Joey says, "[D]id you lock the door? I don't trust the elevator boys") (1-6-26) | These lines are cut, perhaps because they aren't realistic—Vera wouldn't try to hide this from a *tailor*, right? |
| | No indication of "Bewitched" (remember: in this script it happens after the phone call when he tells her to go to hell); instead, there's a suggestion for a "[d]uet about jealousy?," presumably sung by Linda, and maybe Vera? (1-6-27)—is this the precursor to "Take Him"? | Added bit of dialogue (to precede "Bewitched")—in which Joey vocalizes that he appreciates that she pampers him: "That's the way to do it. / Do what? / Keep me as sweet as I am—pamper me a little. / Somebody started that a long time ago. / Well, it got results."—CUE for song (1-6-33); **3 choruses are included |
| | Joey imagines himself in his soon-to-be-opened club; this scene includes some lines when he says how he's different from guys like Harry Richman: "No. I guess not an opera hat. Richman and guys like that, they work with canes and opera hats. They even wear dinner coats. But not me. I come out in white tie and tails . . ." (1-6-29) | Added dialogue between Joey and Vera—he's talking about clothing, she thinks he's talking about a girl ("mouse") (1-6-39; 1-6-40) |
| | | This bit gets cut |
| | | "[S]scratch" (1-6-40) |
| | | In this version, Joey says to Ernest, after Linda storms out, "Ah—let it alone. [Ernest exits] She can't bother me; nobody can" MUSIC CUE: "what do I care for a dame" |
| | | ALSO, an interesting note: "LIVE MIC OF F.R." |
| | | Notes on the dream ballet (personnel, props/costumes—old versus new club) (1-6-45) |

| ACT I | Rehearsal script | Opening-night script |
|---|---|---|
| | "[M]oola" (1-6-29) | |
| | After the Linda/Vera scene, Linda is upset, and ends the scene with the line "I'd rather sleep on the living room couch. . . ." Right after Joey says, "[W]hat the hell?" This is followed by the annotation (<u>FINALE</u>—PRODUCTION NUMBER TO BE DECIDED) (1-6-32) | |

**ACT II**

| Scene 1: Chez Joey | O'Hara describes the scenario for "Flower Garden," but does not include dialogue; directly after the description of "Flower" Melba enters | The dialogue that opens the act is close to what O'Hara describes in the rehearsal script (the character names are haphazardly replaced with the names of the actors—Whyte, Rice—FYI, "Whyte" is Jerry Whyte, the actual stagehand for *Joey*, playing the part of a stagehand; "Rice" is Edison Rice, playing the light guy, Scholtz [character is not in the opening-night program]; "Victor" is played by Van Johnson; "Mickey" doesn't appear in the opening-night program, either) (2-1-1 to 2-1-6) |
|---|---|---|
| | Little bit of dialogue [gets cut] (some of the Dartmouth bit; some of the name-dropping, which was a lot even for Joey!) (2-1-4) | |
| | No lead-in/integrated dialogue in prep for "Reporter Song" (2-1-5) | |
| | The "shock" (that Melba is conventionally attractive) remains in this version of the script (2-1-6) | |
| | Large section of dialogue between Max and Ludlow; Max name-drops known mobsters, including "O'Hara"; Max shows he's onto him: "Well, sit down and get drunk and tell our star here how you're gonna make him not Vallee exactly not Crosby exactly, but a combination of the two. Sure." This all occurs in front of Joey. Big section between Lowell and Joey gets cut, too—lots of detail related to voice versus dancing, etc.) gets cut (2-1-8 to 2-1-9) | Short bit of dialogue added to introduce Melba scene (2-1-6)

Dialogue added leading to "Zip" (2-1-11)

Instead of Joey's appreciation for her looks, Melba offends him, and he gets brutal: "I'd like to interview you some day. / You'd get some information" (2-1-11) |

| ACT II | Rehearsal script | Opening-night script |
|---|---|---|
| | Lots of dialogue (mostly Lowell's), including name-dropping (Freddie Astaire, Ty Power, details of all the money Joey will make, etc.) (2-1-10, 11, 12,13) | Bit of dialogue added to introduce Ludlow. |
| | | Max's extraneous dialogue is cut; cutting the dialogue makes Joey even stupider to accept Ludlow's "services." |
| | "Plant You Now" indicated, but with no dialogue lead-in | In the previous version Lowell tries too hard to convince Joey when he doesn't need to (perhaps the reason that all of this is cut). |
| | | Nearly a page of dialogue added to integrate the rehearsal number ("Plant You Now") (2-1-19) |
| Scene 2: Joey's Apartment | Stage directions show that the creators are still working out some things: "VERA comes in, maybe rubbing her hands with a lotion. Anyway doing something to show she has spent the night there" (2-2-15) | Dialogue between Joey and Vera added to integrate "Den of Iniquity" and reinforce the "cozy-cottage" trope ("maybe not any place else—but here it's just you and I. While we're here I can be reasonably sure of you. That's why I'm really beginning to like this terrible apartment") (2-2-23) |
| | Some dialogue between Joey and Vera (later gets cut) (2-2-15) | |
| | Almost two pages of dialogue (later cut) between Joey and Vera (Vera is jealous of Gladys, and tells Joey to cut her out of the show. He resists, in an uncharacteristically virtuous gesture); what follows is the lead-in to "Den of Iniquity," eventually cut: "Vera: "You adorable, darling heel. I think I might be going to cry. But I'm not! Just remember. Don't ever let me catch you" (2-2-16 to 2-2-18) | |

| ACT II | Rehearsal script | Opening-night script |
|---|---|---|
| Scene 3: Chez Joey | Some interesting dialogue between Linda and Gladys (later cut): Linda admits that she knows Joey is flawed; she also makes an interesting statement about "cynical people": "It's awfully easy to be cynical. In a way being cynical is a kind of feeling sorry for yourself." Gladys follows with the tough line "[y]ou figure that way? I'd like to be around when you get alone with Max. If I heard any screams I'd be cynical and feel sorry for myself." Linda, even more surprisingly, says, "Oh, bushwa! I'm a pretty girl and I'm 20 years old. I always had to take care of myself" (2-3-19 to 2-3-20) | Since the dialogue in the rehearsal script is cut, Linda's character is flattened out here; she is more naive, and more Pollyanna-ish.

Section added to integrate "Do It the Hard Way" (2-3-29 to 2-3-30) |
| | Section (later cut) between Lowell and Gladys. Gladys's "gangster talk" gets cut: "Ear-y-sipelas" (a kind of pig latin); joke (later cut), involving the mispronunciation of "argot" (2-3-22) | |
| | Bits of dialogue between Gladys and Lowell (later cut) mostly related to their blackmail scheme (2-3-23 to 2-3-25) | |
| | "Hard Way" indicated, but with no integrated dialogue (Linda simply leaves, saying goodbye to Lowell and Gladys) | |

| ACT II | Rehearsal script | Opening-night script |
|---|---|---|
| Scene 4: Joey's apartment | Lengthy section of dialogue (later cut) between Ernest (the Tailor), Joey, Vera, a car sales-man (here O'Hara revels in his detailed knowledge of cars). This section also includes a bit about vernacular and class: Joey, to salesman: "Laid down? What the hell? As soon as you start getting into the big chips do you have to start learning a new language?" VERA: "YES! And I'm glad you're finding that out" (2-4-30) (2-4-27 to 2-4-31) | "Take Him" is a musical scene—Joey comes in part way to talk to Linda and Joey (added: 2-4-36); the song continues after this exchange, while Joey dances. |
| | | Some added dialogue between Joey and Lowell (2-4-40) |
| | | SCENE 5 added: |
| | A bit of dialogue (later cut) between Vera and Linda (about how Linda recognized Vera from the society pages, etc); some additional dialogue leading to "Take Him" (2-4-32 to 2-4-34) | A page of dialogue between Linda and Joey is added here (following an off-stage din-ner with Linda's sister); the two say goodbye, leaving the fate of their relationship in doubt. It's clear, however, that Joey is leaving (Linda says, "[I]f you ever come back to Chicago, you must come again"). Joey's final line, "And thanks—thanks a million," might indicate a bit of redemption for Joey. |
| | "Take Him" is already integrated (2-4-34); after Vera's dialogue with Joey, however, the song ends (Vera checks to see if Joey was listening in, and he wasn't) (2-4-35) | |
| | | Added song: |
| | Dialogue included after "Take Him," eventually cut (2-4-36) | JOEY *sings reprise of "I Could Write a Book"* |
| | Dialogue with Lowell and Gladys, eventually cut (2-4-40, 2-4-41) | |
| | Lots of dialogue, eventually cut, in the final pages (2-4-42, 43); this material demonstrates Joey's jealousy (he refers to Mr. Simpson as a "rumb-dumb old man"; to Vera, Joey says "[B]low, mother" rather than the even-tual "blow") (2-4-43) | |

| ACT II | Rehearsal script | Opening-night script |
| --- | --- | --- |
| | Performance directions read, "[S]ings a reprise and exits"— not clear if "Bewitched" was chosen at this point—(2-4-43) | |
| | 2-4-44: Joey refers to Vera as "That bitch" (in this draft, the line is crossed out); Large section of dialogue between Assistant Manager and Joey, eventually cut (2-4-43) | |
| | A section that references a real life William Morris agent (Square Deal Grady), eventually cut (2-4-45) | |
| | ENDING: Joey and Linda walk off together, indicating that, at least for the moment, they are together (no mention of music, or an ending beyond this moment) (2-4-47) | |

# NOTES

• • •

## TIMELINE: FROM SHORT STORY TO MUSICAL COMEDY

1. John O'Hara, letter to Gus Lobrano, March 20, 1940 (John O'Hara Papers, Pennsylvania State University, Box 1, folder 22).
2. Robert Rice, "How a Musical Is Made," *PM Weekly*, December 22, 1940.

## INTRODUCTION

1. "Pal Joey," Inter-office report from the PCA to the Motion Picture Producers and Distributors of America, December 27, 1940. Motion Picture Association of America, Production Code Administration records, Margaret Herrick Library, Academy of Motion Picture Arts and Sciences, Beverly Hills, CA.
2. Letter from Joseph Breen to Harry Cohn, February 14, 1941. Motion Picture Association of America, Production Code Administration records, Margaret Herrick Library, Academy of Motion Picture Arts and Sciences, Beverly Hills, CA.
3. John O'Hara, "Foreword," in *The Farmers Hotel* (Random House, 1951), ix–x.
4. Sidney B. Whipple, "Pal Joey Is a Bright, Gay, Tuneful, Novel Work," *New York World-Telegram*, December 26, 1940; Richard Watts Jr., "The Theatres: Night Club Portrait," *New York Herald Tribune*, December 26, 1940; Wolcott Gibbs, "Upturn," *New Yorker*, January 4, 1941.
5. Brooks Atkinson, "Christmas Night Adds *Pal Joey* and *Meet the People* to the Musical Stage," *New York Times*, December 26, 1940.
6. Ibid.
7. Sidney B. Whipple, "Pal Joey a Comedy-Coated Indictment," *New York World-Telegram*, March 15, 1941. *Tobacco Road* played on Broadway for an astounding 3182 performances. Burns Mantle described the character Jeeter Lester as "a hard chewing, spitting, cursing son of the soil who sleeps in his clothes as long as they will stand the strain and approaches the responsibilities of husbandry and domestic service with the intelligence and enthusiasm of a Belgian hare." Burns Mantle, "*Tobacco Road* Story of Georgia," *New York Daily News*, December 6, 1933. It's worth noting the Erskine's sympathy and advocacy for working-class white people, seen in his fiction, is complicated by his support of eugenics; both inform his characters. For more, see Karen Keely, "Poverty, Sterilization, and Eugenics in Erskine Caldwell's *Tobacco Road*," *Journal of American Studies* 36, no. 1 (2002): 23–42.
8. Louis Kronenberger, "*Pal Joey* Shocked 'Em," *PM Weekly*, December 29, 1940.
9. Ibid.
10. In Weill/Brecht's version, however, the act 3 deus ex machina is intended to be viewed critically by the audience.
11. Henry T. Murdock, "*Pal Joey* Scores Hit at Forrest," *Public Ledger* (Philadelphia), December 12, 1940.

12. Gibbs, "Upturn."
13. Alisa Roost, "Before *Oklahoma!* A Reappraisal of Musical Theatre during the 1930s," *Journal of American Drama and Theatre* 16, no. 1 (2004): 1–35.
14. Scholarship emerged in the 2000s to counter these narratives. See, for instance, Allison Robbins's research on how Busby Berkeley's stage work affected his work in film, Dominic Symonds's work on the early shows of Rodgers and Hart, and Geoffrey Block's consideration of Depression-era musicals. Allison Robbins, "Busby Berkeley, Broken Rhythms and Dance Direction on the Stage and Screen," *Studies in Musical Theatre* 7, no. 1 (2013): 75–93; Dominic Symonds, *We'll Have Manhattan: The Early Works of Rodgers and Hart* (New York: Oxford University Press, 2015); Geoffrey Block, "Revisiting the Glorious and Problematic Legacy of the Jazz Age and Depression Musical," *Studies in Musical Theatre* 2, no. 2 (2008): 127–146.
15. Waters, *"Pal Joey"* (Philadelphia), December 12, 1940, clipping from unidentified newspaper, in John O'Hara Papers, Box 20, folder 2.
16. Robert Sensenderfer, *"PAL JOEY*—George Abbott Musical about Night Club Life Has Premiere," *Evening Bulletin* (Philadelphia), December 12, 1940.
17. Louis Kronenberger, *"Pal Joey* Brings Holiday Cheer," *Time*, December 26, 1940.
18. Gibbs, "Upturn."
19. In his monograph on *Lady in the Dark*, Bruce McClung gives a useful overview of the impact of the Depression on Broadway. McClung, *Lady in the Dark: Biography of a Musical* (New York: Oxford University Press, 2007), 154–155.
20. Laurence Maslon, *Broadway to Main Street: How Show Tunes Enchanted America* (New York: Oxford University Press, 2018), 60
21. Ibid.
22. John O'Hara in Lucius Beebe, "Concerning the Author of *Pal Joey*, John O'Hara, Product of a Forgotten Age and Yale Man Who Never Went There," *New York Herald Tribune*, January 12, 1941.
23. Lehman Engel, *The American Musical Theater* (New York: Collier, [1967] 1975), 35.
24. Engel considered all of the Gershwin's shows, except for *Porgy and Bess*, to be similarly "unrevivable." Ibid., 15.
25. Ibid., 35. Engel's full list includes the following shows: *Pal Joey* (1940), *Oklahoma!* (1943), *Carousel* (1945), *Annie Get Your Gun* (1946), *Brigadoon* (1947), *Kiss Me, Kate* (1948), *South Pacific* (1949), *Guys and Dolls* (1950), *The King and I* (1951), *My Fair Lady* (1956), *West Side Story* (1957), *Gypsy* (1959), *Fiddler on the Roof* (1964), *Company* (1970), and *A Little Night Music* (1973).
26. Engel, *American Musical Theater*, 35 and 37.
27. Geoffrey Block, "The Broadway Canon from Show Boat to West Side Story and the European Operatic Idea," *Journal of Musicology* 11, no. 4 (Autumn 1993): 529.
28. Laurence Maslon, ed., *American Musicals: The Complete Books and Lyrics of 16 Broadway Classics, 1927–1969* (Boone, IA: Library of America, 2014). The collection includes the librettos for *Show Boat* (1927), *As Thousands Cheer* (1933), *Pal Joey* (1940), *Oklahoma!* (1943), *On the Town* (1944), *Finian's Rainbow* (1947), *Kiss Me, Kate* (1948), *South Pacific* (1949), *Guys and Dolls* (1950), *The Pajama Game* (1954), *My Fair Lady* (1956), *Gypsy* (1959), *A Funny Thing Happened on the Way to the Forum* (1962), *Fiddler on the Roof* (1964), *Cabaret* (1966), and *1776* (1969).

Library of America, "About," https://www.loa.org/about (accessed January 4, 2018).

29. See Laurence Maslon, "Curtains Up! Get the Rights! Choosing the 16 Greatest Musicals of Broadway's Golden Age," *Salon*, October 31, 2014. https://slate.com/culture/2014/10/what-are-the-best-musicals-of-broadways-golden-age-behind-the-library-of-america-selections.html (accessed January 4, 2019).

30. In the following pages I refer to the "preliminary script" (O'Hara's earliest draft of *Pal Joey*), the "rehearsal script" (what appears to be a working draft, used during rehearsal), and the "opening-night script" (currently held by the Rodgers and Hammerstein Organization and Penn State). Please refer to Appendix 2 for more on score and libretto sources.

## CHAPTER 1 O'Hara the Heel: From Short Story to Script

1. VPH, "O'Hara Died Unforgiven by Critics Who Hated His Success, Personality," *World Herald*, May 3, 1970; B. A. Bergman, "O'Hara Never Forgot a Friend, or an Insult," *Philadelphia Bulletin*, April 19, 1970.

2. Richard Rodgers, letter to John O'Hara, June 14, 1951 (Richard Rodgers Papers, NYPL for the Performing Arts, Box 4).

3. For a fascinating look at the "drunk narrative" and constructions of gender in American literature of the early twentieth century, which examines the work of O'Hara and others, see John W. Crowley, *The White Logic: Alcoholism and Gender in American Modernist Fiction* (Amherst: University of Massachusetts Press, 1994).

4. The term "bender" is particularly apt in this case, as it reminds the reader of Milton "Doc" Bender, perhaps the most notorious, and many say destructive, influence on the life of Larry Hart. Some of Hart's early biographers even state that the term "bender" was based on Doc Bender (this is incorrect, as the term dates to at least the mid-nineteenth century).

5. John O'Hara in Earl Wilson, "It Happened Last Night," *New York Post* (March 28, 1948); reprinted in Matthew J. Bruccoli, *The O'Hara Concern* (Pittsburgh: University of Pittsburgh Press, 1975), 150.

6. John O'Hara, letter to William Maxwell, c. 1940 (O'Hara Papers, Box 1, folder 23); O'Hara in Earl Wilson, "It Happened Last Night."

7. O'Hara in Wilson, "It Happened Last Night," *New York Post* (March 28, 1948).

8. Bruccoli, *O'Hara Concern*, 44.

9. Richard L. Coe, "*Joey* Is Tuneful, Tart, and Terrific," *Washington Post*, April 21, 1953.

10. Rodgers, *Musical Stages*, 199.

11. O'Hara's letter is reprinted in a *PM Weekly* feature written before the premiere of the show in early December 1940, and subsequently on the record sleeve of the 1951 Columbia recording of *Pal Joey*.

12. John O'Hara, letter to Richard Rodgers, c. 1950 (Richard Rodgers Papers, Box 4).

13. This letter is undated, but must have been written before the premiere of the film, in May 1950; the "big moving picture company" was MGM.

14. O'Hara, undated letter, c. May 1950.

15. Ibid.
16. O'Hara, letter to Rodgers, June 10, 1951 (Richard Rodgers Papers, Box 4).
17. Rodgers, letter to O'Hara, June 14, 1951.
18. Ibid.
19. O'Hara, letter to George Cukor, May 2, 1954 (George Cukor Papers, Academy of Motion Picture Archives).
20. George Cukor, letter to Harry Cohn, May 5, 1954 (George Cukor Papers, AMPA).
21. Waters, "*Pal Joey*"; Watts, "Night Club Portrait."
22. John O'Hara, "Some Fond Recollections of Larry Hart," *New York Times*, February 27, 1944..
23. Ibid.
24. Ibid.
25. O'Hara also never won the Gold Medal for Fiction, awarded by the National Institute of Arts and Letters, and in 1961 resigned from the organization in hurt. In a letter to Glenway Wescott, president of the agency, he said, "Twice in the past six years I have been passed over for the Nobel prize—twice that I know of, and I don't know how many other times. But the Nobel people take in the world; the Institute-Academy people take in the work of U.S. citizens only. Not even to be nominated for the fiction prize is a judgment that, considering my work since 1948, I cannot accept with any grace." O'Hara, in Bruccoli, *O'Hara Concern*, 276.
26. John O'Hara, in "A Writer's Look at His Town, Career and Future," *Princeton Packet* (November 23, 1961).
27. Though O'Hara himself never categorized his work this way, Bruccoli makes the case that his work has much in common with the genre: "the novel of manners may be defined as a novel in which the essential elements are the customs and conventions of a social class in a particular time and place. The word *manners* is not intended in the narrow meaning of etiquette or deportment, but in the sense of values and codes of conduct." Bruccoli, *O'Hara Concern*, 253.
28. Julian and his wife, Caroline English, share a surname with the Linda English, the naive ingénue from *Pal Joey,* the musical. It's rather unlikely that O'Hara meant to draw a connection between the characters, as Julian and Caroline are of the social elite (Caroline is Bryn Mawr educated), and Linda is a working-class secretary, first charmed by Joey precisely because she isn't aware of the social codes of people like the Englishes. Given O'Hara's attention to detail, however, there might be a less obvious reason for their connection.
29. Charles Champlin, "Literary Scene: The Time of John O'Hara," *New York Post*, April 20, 1970.
30. O'Hara in Bruccoli, *The O'Hara Concern*, 95.
31. John O'Hara, "Foreword" to *Appointment in Samarra*, quoted in Bruccoli, *the O'Hara Concern*, 74.
32. Bruccoli, *O'Hara Concern*, 151.
33. For a chronology of O'Hara's life and work experience, see Bruccoli, *O'Hara Concern*, xxiii–xxix.
34. O'Hara, in Harvey Breit, "Talk with John O'Hara," *New York Times Book Review* (September 4, 1949).

35. Bruccoli, *O'Hara Concern,* 281. In a retrospective on O'Hara's death, Richard Boeth comments on how prolific he was in the genre of the short story. See Boeth, "Appointment in Samarra," in *Newsweek,* April 20, 1970.

36. Champlin, " Literary Scene: The Time of John O'Hara."

37. This number doesn't include the over 200 stories that he wrote, but were rejected by various editors at the *New Yorker.* For more information on the number and nature of the rejection letters, see Bruccoli, *O'Hara Concern,* 403–421.

38. O'Hara, letter to William Maxwell, c. early 1940 (John O'Hara Papers, Penn State, Box 1, folder 23).

39. To be fair, O'Hara was first discovered by the "literary people" after publishing *Appointment in Samarra,* in 1934. The Joey stories, however, were popular in the mainstream. The "O'Brien" comment is in reference to another columnist employed by the *New Yorker.* Ibid.

40. Quotation from Duell, Sloan & Pearce, quoted in book review for *Pal Joey, Enterprise* (High Point, North Carolina), August 4, 1940.

41. "Mr. O'Hara," in *New York Herald Tribune,* October 31, 1940.

42. Ibid.

43. For instance, Joey abbreviates "week" to "wk," "although" to "altho," and "assistant manager" to "asst mgr," and he spells "negotiate" as "negosiate," "verge" as "vurge," and "in error" as "an error."

44. O'Hara, "The Erloff," *Pal Joey* (New York: Duell, Sloan & Pearce, 1940), 118.

45. H. L. Mencken, in Richard McRae, "'What Is Hip?' and Other Inquiries in Jazz Slang Lexicography," *Notes* 57, no. 3 (2001), 574. This quotation first appeared in H. L. Menken, *The American Language: An Inquiry into the Development of English in the United States* (New York: Knopf, 1962), 704.

46. McRae, "What Is Hip?" 575.

47. Until 1938, Katherine Angell White was O'Hara's editor; William Maxwell, who would become a good friend of O'Hara, took over in 1938, and stayed on through the period when O'Hara wrote most of his *Joey* stories.

48. O'Hara, in letter to William Maxwell, March 14, 1939 (O'Hara Papers, Box 1, folder 23).

49. One also might quibble with O'Hara's definition of "crib" in this letter. The now more common use of the term—to mean "house," or "domicile"—seems to be rooted in the 1950s use of the term. Still, the connection to "nightclub" doesn't appear in any of the major jazz lexicons. See, for instance, Robert Gold's *A Jazz Lexicon,* which traces the term back to the early 1930s: *"Thieves' slang:* a dwelling-house, shop, public-house, etc." *Jazz Lexicon,* 72.

50. Phil Ford, "Somewhere/Nowhere: Hipness as an Aesthetic," *Musical Quarterly* 86, no. 1 (January 2002), 54.

51. O'Hara, letter to Joseph Bryan, May 3 or 4, 1937 (O'Hara Papers, Box 1, folder 10).

52. O'Hara, "How I Am Now in Chi," *Pal Joey* (novel), 36.

53. Ibid, 49.

54. Harris, who would go on to be a prominent voice actor, was first associated with Jack Benny (he was musical director for the then-named Jello-O Program,

starring Jack Benny), and was known for his comic caricatures and song-speech style of delivery. Harris is perhaps now best known for his portrayals of Baloo and Little John in Disney's animated films *The Jungle Book* (1967) and *Robin Hood* (1973).

55. See Appendix 2 (213) for more information on the extant scripts.

56. O'Hara, "Joey and the Calcutta Club," *Pal Joey* (novel), 131.

57. O'Hara, "A New Career," *Pal Joey* (novel), 166.

58. O'Hara, "Reminiss?" *Pal Joey* (novel), 192.

59. Of Lombardo he said, "the first time I heard Guy Lombardo I liked him [. . .]. The second time, the second record of his, made me want to smash the phonograph." O'Hara, letter to William Maxwell, c. late 1939 (O'Hara Papers, Box 1, folder 23).

60. These articles include "Saxophonic Fever," *New York Herald Tribune* (February 17, 1929); "The Decline of Jazz," *New York Herald Tribune* (September 14, 1930); "Jazz Artists," *New York Herald Tribune* (December 14, 1930); "A Jazz Leader," *New York Herald Tribune* (January 25, 1931); "Jazz from the West," *New York Herald Tribune* (March 1, 1931); and "Sing Us the Old Songs," *New York Herald Tribune* (August 9, 1931).

61. This very scene plays out in O'Hara's first novel, *An Appointment in Samarra* (1934), when Julian English and his date (and soon to be wife) Caroline are dancing along to a local dance band: he's quiet, and since they are in the middle of an argument, Caroline accuses him of sulking. He reveals to her chagrin that, on the contrary, "I was thinking what a lousy band this is. Does that make you sore?" O'Hara, *Appointment in Samarra*, 90.

62. O'Hara, "Saxophonic Fever." The reference to the "trick" ending on Paul Whiteman's recording of "Lady of the Evening" is also mentioned in *Appointment in Samarra* ("the fanciest trick ending ever put on a record"); the protagonist Julian English eventually breaks the record—some scholars have connected this act to his subsequent, and shocking, suicide. O'Hara, *Appointment in Samarra*, 203.

63. The Prince of Wales was frequently in the American press during this time; he later famously abdicated his throne to his younger brother in order to marry the sophisticated divorcee Wallis Simpson. Their relationship featured in the gossip pages of many American magazines and newspapers.

64. John O'Hara, "Entertainment Week: Introduction to Tosca," *Newsweek*, December 29, 1941.

65. I am not the first to observe that O'Hara's journalistic writings tend to be less critically aware than his novels and short stories. The writer and critic Harvey Breit once lamented, "As good a novelist and short-story writer as Mr. O'Hara is, that is how poor a journalist he is. His prose, though appearing casual, is in fact careless; his facts go unchecked; his biases are so rampant that contradictory arguments under his nose are overlooked [. . .] Yet the novelist has the crucial qualities of a first-class journalist: the savage eye, the sure ear, the economical prose." Breit, *The Writer Observed* (World Publishing, 1956), 20.

66. John Howland, "Jazz with Strings: Between Jazz and the Great American Songbook," in *Jazz/Not Jazz: The Music and Its Boundaries* (Berkeley: University of California Press, 2012), 111–147.

67. O'Hara, "Sing Us the Old Songs," *New York Herald Tribune*, August 9, 1931. He does admit that there were three standouts in the last year, but only three, which include "Body and Soul," "The Wind in the Willows," and "Stardust."

68. O'Hara inconsistently uses the term "jazzophile" to describe himself. Though he says he is "not quite" one in "The Decline of Jazz" (written in 1930), in a letter to William Maxwell from 1939, he reclaims the term: "There are things which, as a jazzophile, I know, probably as well as Gene Buck." His ambivalence surrounding this term might be related to contemporary debates around the use and meaning of the term "jazz." O'Hara, letter to William Maxwell, 1939 (O'Hara Papers, Box 1, folder 23).

69. In another connection to his own characters, O'Hara describes Julian English (from *Appointment in Samarra*, 1934) as a person "whose ear for jazz was superb." O'Hara, *Appointment in Samarra,* 90.

70. O'Hara, "Saxophonic Fever."

71. O'Hara, "Entertainment Week: An American in Memoriam," *Newsweek,* July 15, 1940.

72. Ibid.

73. Ibid.

74. Joan Peyser, *The Memory of All That: The Life of George Gershwin* (Milwaukee: Hal Leonard, 2006), 155.

75. O'Hara, "Entertainment Week: Notes on Notes," *Newsweek,* May 5, 1941.

76. O'Hara goes on to express his opinion on the ASCAP boycott: "The awful music that drives you away from your radio these nights is the fault of the creature of the broadcasters. They have taken the stand that they don't want to pay ASCAP as much as ASCAP thinks it deserves, and so the broadcasters institute what is in effect a public-be-damned policy. The argument that the public doesn't know the difference doesn't hold good with me. I'm a member of the public, and I know the difference, and what's more, I know what the public is missing, and would not be missing if it were not for the stubbornness of the broadcasters. Stubbornness, and I might add, an unwillingness to pay up. Now, especially, we could be using some good songs. We're going to need them. We've got them, but you're not hearing them on the big networks. It's a disgrace." Ibid.

77. O'Hara was an avid fan of the theater; in 1957 he contributed to *Theatre Arts* magazine's regular feature, "My Ten Favorite Plays." O'Hara named *Pal Joey; Chee-Chee* (also by Rodgers and Hart); Weill, Hughes, and Rice's *Street Scene;* and the Gershwins' *Of Thee I Sing* as his favorite musicals.

78. *Times,* October 26, 1941; *Times,* November 18, 1949; *Times,* August 7, 1953.

79. John O'Hara, "Foreword" to *Five Plays* (Random House, 1961), xii.

80. O'Hara, in Bruccoli, *O'Hara Concern,* 274–275.

81. Irving Berlin, interview with the author, in Bruccoli, *O'Hara Concern,* 275.

CHAPTER 2 Rodgers and Hart's Boldest Venture

1. John O'Hara, letter to Richard Rodgers, reprinted in Mary Morris and Robert Rice, "How a Musical Is Made," *PM Weekly*, December 22, 1940. O'Hara's letter is also printed on the back of the album cover for Columbia's recording of *Pal Joey* (1951), and in Rodgers's autobiography, *Musical Stages,* 198.

2. In his autobiography, Rodgers recalls that he was in Boston while trying out *Too Many Girls* (in October 1939) when he received the letter, but O'Hara sent the letter from Los Angeles (and he wasn't in L.A. working for 20th Century Fox until January 1940). Further, O'Hara stated that an encounter with George Oppenheimer in early 1940 (Oppenheimer was interested in securing the stage rights for the Joey stories) put O'Hara in mind of a potential Rodgers and Hart collaboration. Matthew Bruccoli states that Rodgers and Hart were trying out *Higher and Higher* (also in Boston) when they received the letter. Given that O'Hara refers to "a commitment with Dwight Wiman for a show this Spring," it's unlikely that *Higher and Higher*, which must have been the show O'Hara refers to, was already in its tryouts. Rodgers, *Musical Stages*, 198. Bruccoli, *O'Hara Concern*, 161.
3. Rodgers, *Musical Stages*, 198.
4. Ibid.
5. Rodgers, *Musical Stages,* 202. Rodgers, "*Pal Joey*: History of a Heel," *New York Times*, December 30, 1951.
6. Atkinson, "Christmas Night Adds *Pal Joey*.
7. Henry T. Murdock, "*Pal Joey* Scores Hit at Forrest," *Public Ledger* (Philadelphia), December 12, 1940.
8. Sidney B. Whipple, "*Pal Joey* is a Bright, Gay, Tuneful, Novel Work," *New York World-Telegram*, December 26, 1940.
9. Watts, "Night Club Portrait."
10. The year 1941 was the only one during this period when Rodgers and Hart didn't premiere a new show, but *Pal Joey* ran for the bulk of the year. Geoffrey Block, *Richard Rodgers* (New Haven & London: Yale University Press, 2003), 76–77.
11. Their most well-received work on film was undoubtedly heard in *Love Me Tonight* (1932), their collaboration with Rouben Mamoulian.
12. Dominic Symonds, *We'll Have Manhattan: The Early Works of Rodgers and Hart* (New York: Oxford University Press, 2015).
13. Rodgers, *Musical Stages*, 97.
14. Ibid.
15. "The Boys from Columbia," *Time*, September 26, 1938. Reprinted in *The Richard Rodgers Reader*, ed. Geoffrey Block (New York: Oxford University Press, 2002), 47–53.
16. "Boys from Columbus."
17. George Abbott, *Mister Abbott* (New York: Random House, 1963), 176.
18. Dominic McHugh, "'I'll Never Know Exactly Who Did What': Broadway Composers as Musical Collaborators," *Journal of the American Musicological Society* 68, no. 3, Fall 2015, 605–652.
19. Rodgers, "How to Write Music in No Easy Lessons: *A Self Interview*," in *Theatre Arts*, October 1939, reprinted in *The Richard Rodgers Reader*, ed. Block, 262.
20. Ibid.
21. Geoffrey Block, *Richard Rodgers*, 26.
22. Ibid.
23. Richard Rodgers, *The Rodgers and Hart Songbook* (New York: Simon and Schuster, 1951), 3.

24. Richard Rodgers "A Composer Looks at His Lyricists," *Dramatists Guild Quarterly* (1967), reprinted in *The Richard Rodgers Reader*, ed. Block, 301.

25. Robert Rice, "How a Musical Is Made," *PM Weekly*, December 22, 1940.

26. On April 30, the *Pittsburgh Post-Gazette* called *Pal Joey* one of Abbott's "contemplated projects." Harold W. Cohen, "The Drama Desk," *Pittsburgh Post-Gazette*, April 30, 1940.

27. "Set for Lead," *Brooklyn Citizen*, November 9, 2910.

28. Rodgers, *Musical Stages*, 199.

29. Alvin Yudkoff, *Gene Kelly: A Life of Dance and Dreams* (New York: Stage Books, 1999), 76.

30. Gene Kelly in Clive Hirschhorn, *Gene Kelly: A Biography* (New York: St. Martin's Press, 1984), 72–73.

31. Ibid, 73.

32. Although not directly connected to Ernst, the first of the Aldrich films, *What a Life* (1939), was based on the stage play of the same name, produced and directed by Abbott in 1938.

33. "Wants Leila," *Daily News*, June 23, 1940; "*Off the Grass* Off till Aug. 15; Barrymore Hit," *Daily News*, June 29, 1940.

34. "About Costumes; 4th *Father* Cast," *Daily News*, September 29, 1940.

35. In a letter from March 1940 O'Hara mentions to his friend Gus Lobrano (an editor at the *New Yorker*) that he plans "to write the book for a musical comedy." John O'Hara, letter to Gus Lobrano, March 20, 1940 (O'Hara Papers, Box 1, folder 22). *PM Weekly* reports that he began writing in May. Rice, "How a Musical Is Made."

36. "The Stage," *Chicago Tribune*, September 3, 1940; "Helen Morgan's Daughter Plans Theatrical Career," *Los Angeles Times*, September 17, 1940.

37. Rice, "How a Musical Is Made."

38. "Mielziner Draws Sets for New Abbott Show," *Courier-Post* (Camden, NJ), November 13, 1940.

39. June Havoc, *More Havoc* (New York: Harper & Row, 1980), 205.

40. Rice, "How a Musical Is Made."

41. "The White-Haired Boy," *Boston Globe*, October 29, 1940.

42. Ibid.

43. Rodgers, *Musical Stages*, 199.

44. Ibid, 200.

45. Ibid, 200.

46. Richard Rodgers, "The Reminiscences of Richard Rodgers," interview with Kenneth Leish, Oral History Research Office, Columbia University, 212.

47. Abbott, *Mister Abbott*, 194–195.

48. Ibid, 194.

49. "George Abbott, Master of the Revels," *Brooklyn Daily Eagle*, March 12, 1939.

50. Abbott, *Mister Abbott*, 89. The musicals he refers to are *Where's Charley?* (1948), with music and lyrics by Frank Loesser, based on the much-adapted British farce *Charley's Aunt* (1892), written by Brandon Thomas; Abbott also famously adapted Shakespeare's *The Comedy of Errors* for Rodgers and Hart's *The Boys from Syracuse* (1938).

51. Advertisement, *Hartford Courant*, September 15, 1926; "Philip Dunning Gets the Break: After Years of Struggle Former Meriden and Hartford Man Attains Fame as Author of *Broadway*," *Hartford Courant*, September 26, 1926.
52. Abbott, *Mister Abbott*, 177. I borrow the term "circus-musical" from Geoffrey Block; the term encapsulates the hybrid nature of the show. Geoffrey Block, "'Bigger Than a Show—Better Than a Circus': The Broadway Musical, Radio, and Billy Rose's *Jumbo*," *Musical Quarterly* 89, nos. 2–3 (2006): 164.
53. Nancy Randolph, "Jumbo Circus Gives Preview for Charity," *New York Daily News*, October 13, 1935.
54. Billy Rose, the producer, actually convinced Actor's Equity to classify the show as a circus, which meant he could, in the words of Block, "rehearse his performers ten weeks beyond the legal schedule without paying them in hard cash. In exchange, Rose would have to feed a large number of human and animal carnivores in keeping with circus protocol." Block, "'Bigger Than a Show,'" 167–168.
55. Abbott, *Mister Abbott*, 177.
56. Arthur Pollock, "Hoofer Goes Russian!" *Brooklyn Daily Eagle*, May 10, 1936.
57. "Living Statistics: Where Do George Abbott's Actors Come from and Why Do They Get Jobs with Him, Young and Old?" *Brooklyn Daily Eagle*, April 23, 1939.
58. "George Abbott, Master of the Revels." Besides *The Boys from Syracuse* (which was playing at the Alvin), *What a Life* (at the Mansfield Theater), *The Primrose Path* (across the street at the Biltmore), and *Mrs. O'Brien Entertains* (at the Lyceum Theatre) were playing simultaneously during February and early March 1939. *What a Life*, which ran for 538 performances, was the longest running of the bunch.
59. Waters, unknown publication, Philadelphia, December 12, 1940 (clippings, O'Hara Papers, Box 20).
60. Linton Martin, "The Call Boy's Chat: Heel and Hoofer Is Now a Musical Comedy Hero," *Philadelphia Inquirer*, December 15, 1940.
61. Abbott, *Mister Abbott*, 195.
62. Rodgers, "Reminiscences of Richard Rodgers," 213.
63. John Martin, "The Dance: Pal Kelly," *New York Times*, June 8, 1941.
64. Jack Gaver, "*Pal Joey* Returns as 'Dancingest Show in Town,'" *Arizona Republic*, December 16, 1951.
65. Rice, "How a Musical Is Made."
66. Ibid.
67. J. H. Keen, "*Pal Joey*: And What a Pal for Abbott," *Philadelphia's Pictorial*, December 12, 1940.
68. Havoc, *More Havoc*, 213.
69. Ibid.
70. O'Hara in Lucius Beebe, "Concerning the Author of *Pal Joey*, John O'Hara, Product of a Forgotten Age and Yale Man Who Never Went There," *New York Herald Tribune*, January 12, 1941.
71. O'Hara, "Foreword," *Farmer's Hotel*, ix–x.
72. Arthur Bronson, "The Stage: *Pal Joey* Full of Snap and Sting" *Philadelphia Record*, December 12, 1940; Keen, "*Pal Joey*."

73. Henry T. Murdock, "*Pal Joey* Scores Hit at Forrest," *Public Ledger* (Philadelphia), December 12, 1940.

74. Sensenderfer, "PAL JOEY—George Abbott Musical about Night Club Life Has Premiere."

75. Murdock, "*Pal Joey*."

76. Abbott, *Mister Abbott*, 195.

77. O'Hara, "Some Fond Recollections of Larry Hart."

78. Beebe, "Concerning the Author of *Pal Joey*."

79. John O'Hara, *Pal Joey*, Rehearsal script, act 1, scene 3, lines 12–14.

80. These references appear on the following pages in the script: Noel Coward (1-1-4), Harry Richman (1-6-29), Al Jolson (2-1-10), Fred Astaire, Tyrone Power (2-1-11), a series of mobsters (2-1-8–9), and Billy "Square Deal" Grady (2-4-45). True to O'Hara's eye for detail, nearly all of the mobsters mentioned were real-life Chicago mobsters (or people associated with the mob)—"Big Jim" Colosimo, Dean O'Banion, Al Capone, George "Bugs" Moran, and Alfred "Jake" Lingle. "O'Hara" was probably a deliberate self-reference, but may also laterally refer to Edward J. O'Hare, the crooked Chicago lawyer who worked for Capone and later turned on him (and was murdered, likely, because of it).

81. Rehearsal script, 2-4-29–31. Like all of his pop-culture reference, O'Hara had strong feelings about what cars said about the men who owned them: "In the twenties if you said a man owned a Franklin you would not be talking about the kind of man who owned a Buick, although some Buicks cost the same amount of money as some Franklins. The Franklin-owner would not be wearing an Elks tooth nor a Rotary Club button. He might wear a Masonic pin, but not a Shriner's. The Franklin-owner was more likely to be a tennis player than a golfer, a doctor than a real estate agent, a college man than a non-college man, and a much more independent thinker than the Buick owner. He would also be likely to own more securities than the Buick owner, whose money would be tied up in personal enterprises." Quoted in Matthew Bruccoli's preface to an unidentified collection of John O'Hara's essays. O'Hara Papers, Box 18, folder 24.

82. Rehearsal script, 1-3-11.

83. Rehearsal script, 1-3-12.

84. This passage also cut Stanley Donen's one line in the play (Donen plays the character "Doane," obviously a play on his name, the boyfriend of Linda).

85. Rehearsal script, 1-3-14.

86. Ethan Mordden, *Anything Goes: A History of American Musical Theatre* (New York: Oxford University Press, 2013), 251.

87. Andrea Most, *Theatrical Liberalism: Jews and Popular Entertainment in America* (New York: New York University Press, 2013), 107–108.

88. Mandy Patinkin's recording of the song, included on his album *Dress Casual* (Masterworks Broadway, 1990), however, is full of pathos. His interpretation is much more in line with Most's reading of the song.

89. Geoffrey Block, *Enchanted Evenings: The Broadway Musical from "Show Boat" to Sondheim and Lloyd Webber* (New York: Oxford University Press, 2009), 109–110.

90. The finding aid for the Richard Rodgers Papers does note that Rodgers's business correspondence includes "both complimentary and uncomplimentary letters,

indicating that Rodgers did not edit the collection or eliminate unfavorable information." Finding Aid, Richard Rodgers Papers (1914–1989), New York Public Library for the Performing Arts (accessible at http://archives.nypl.org/the/21252#overview).

91. These full scores include *Allegro, Carousel, Flower Drum Song, The King and I, Oklahoma!, Pipe Dream, The Sound of Music,* and *South Pacific.* See the finding aid for the Richard Rodgers Collection, prepared by Mark Eden Horowitz in 1995: http://findingaids.loc.gov/exist_collections/service/music/eadxmlmusic/eadpdfmusic/2002/mu002002.pdf

92. There are prominent exceptions to this rule, including Block's work on Richard Rodgers with Hart (including his books on Rodgers—*Richard Rodgers* and *The Richard Rodgers Reader*—the sections on *On Your Toes* and *Pal Joey* in *Enchanted Evenings,* and his prominent article on *Jumbo,* Block, "'Bigger Than a Show"), and Dominic Symonds's work on the early career of Rodgers and Hart (*We'll Have Manhattan*). Symonds is planning a second installment of his project, covering the post-Hollywood years of Rodgers and Hart (1935–1943).

CHAPTER 3  Digging for Dirt: Inside the Club

1. John O'Hara, to William Maxwell, c. 1938 (O'Hara Papers, Box 1, folder 23).
2. John O'Hara, *Pal Joey,* opening-night script, 1940, 1-1-1.
3. Stage equipment estimate, M. Weiss, of Weiss and Sons (Makers of Curtains, Draperies, Stage Equipment), sent to Carl Fisher (general manager for *Pal Joey* and nephew of George Abbott), December 5, 1940 (Jo Mielziner Papers, NYPL, Box 47, folder 3).
4. Armond Fields and L. Marc Fields, *From the Bowery to Broadway: Lew Fields and the Roots of American Popular Theater* (New York: Oxford University Press, 1993), xiii.
5. For a useful discussion on the concept and historical practice of musical and theatrical integration, see Geoffrey Block, "Integration," in *The Oxford Handbook of the American Musical* (Oxford and New York: Oxford University Press, 2011), 97–110.
6. Ethan Mordden, *Beautiful Mornin': The Broadway Musical in the 1940s* (New York: Oxford University Press, 1995), 54.
7. Richard Rodgers, *Musical Stages: An Autobiography* (New York: Random House, 1975), 198.
8. Rodgers, *Musical Stages,* 201.
9. Rodgers, "How to Write Music in No Easy Lessons: A Self Interview," *Theatre Arts* (October 1939), included in *The Richard Rodgers Reader,* Block, ed., 263.
10. Watts, "Night Club Portrait."
11. Burns Mantle, "*Pal Joey* Smart and Novel," *New York Daily News,* December 26, 1940.
12. Sidney B. Whipple, "*Pal Joey* is a Bright, Gay, Tuneful, Novel Work," *New York World-Telegram,* December 26, 1940.
13. Bosley Crowther, "Hi-De-Ho! The Night Clubs Turn 'Em Away," *New York Times,* March 21, 1937.

14. O'Hara, *Pal Joey* (the novel), 80, 49–50, 80–81.
15. See Dominic Symonds's discussion of the *Fifth Avenue Follies* in Symonds, *We'll Have Manhattan*, 74–76.
16. Lorenz Hart, in *The Complete Lyrics of Lorenz Hart*, eds. Dorothy Hart and Robert Kimball (New York: De Capo Press, 1995), 60. The lyric is incomplete; as stated by Hart/Kimball, "the music is missing. Only a portion of the lyrics survive." Ibid.
17. The song was originally referred to as "Big Town" or "A Great Big Town" (in the original script, conductor score, and orchestral parts, and later in the piano-vocal score published by Chappell), but appears as "Chicago" in all the playbills for the original production, and the revival of 1952.
18. Lehman Engel, *The American Musical Theater* (New York: Macmillan, 1975), 129.
19. Laurence Maslon, ed. *American Musicals 1927–1949: The Complete Books and Lyrics of Eight Broadway Classics* (New York: Library of America, 2014), 675.
20. O'Hara, *Pal Joey*, opening-night script, 1940, 1-1-1.
21. O'Hara, *Pal Joey: The Libretto and Lyrics* (New York: Random House, 1952), 3; Lorenz Hart, John O'Hara, and Richard Rodgers, *Pal Joey* (New York: Chappell, 1962), 39.
22. For more on the chronology of sources, see "A Note Regarding Score and Libretto Sources" (Appendix 2).
23. A dialogue between Joey and the rehearsal pianist (later cut) appears at the beginning of act 1, scene 1 in O'Hara's earliest draft script—here Joey tries to convince the pianist of his value:

    JOEY: Now listen, brother, I'll do the leading. You just play nice, and softly the first chorus. The second chorus—
    PIANO PLAYER: (*sarcastically*) What second chorus?
    JOEY: Be nice, now. Last four bars of the SECOND chorus you watch my heel, my right heel, and then you can come in as loud as you like. I get the job, maybe I'll take you all over the country with me.

24. Joe Mantello's 2008 revival follows the 1957 film version, beginning with Joey's arrival in Chicago, as he gets kicked off a train; the scene continues with a choreographed sequence depicting his hard luck trying to find employment in club after club (underscored by "Plant You Now," "Bewitched," "I Could Write a Book" and others). The scene abruptly shifts into his audition for Mike, as Joey sings "Chicago," accompanied, as in the original, by solo piano.
25. Preliminary draft script.
26. Although "Blue Moon" was originally composed for Jean Harlow for the film *Hollywood Party*, Shirley Ross first performed the song in the 1934 film *Manhattan Melodrama*; it was popularized, with new lyrics by Hart, by Connie Boswell in 1935. Although O'Hara very likely used the song as a stand-in in the script for something yet to be written, Rodgers would have very likely objected had the suggestion been serious. Consider Rodgers's comments on the interpolation—against his will—of the song "Mountain Greenery" (from *The Garrick Gaieties* of 1926) into his and Hammerstein's show *Allegro* (1947), a song that was used to place a scene in the mid-1920s: "I hated the idea of dredging up something from the past for its obvious applause-catching effect." Rodgers, *Musical Stages*, 252.

27. In the draft the title is abbreviated to "Kick It Around"; rehearsal script, 1940, 1-1-1.
28. Preliminary script.
29. Ibid.
30. Scott Miller, *Rebels with Applause: Broadway's Groundbreaking Musicals* (Portsmouth, NH: Heinemann, 2001), 27.
31. Symonds, *We'll Have Manhattan*, 6.
32. In referencing "Ten Cents a Dance," Hart might have been connecting the desperate, tired energy of the character who first sang the song (Sal, a taxi dancer) to the dancers in the chorus line. The America First Committee was a short-lived antiwar, isolationist organization—accused by many of furthering anti-Semitic rhetoric—that vocally aimed to keep the United States out of World War II; it was established just a few months before the premiere of *Pal Joey*. Although short-lived, the political stance of the organization has remained a forceful part of American politics; the Trump Administration's use of the term "America First"—in reference to both domestic spending and foreign policy—is just the latest example of its relevance.
33. O'Hara, *Pal Joey* (novel), 173–174.
34. The original size of her part can be confirmed by looking at O'Hara's preliminary draft script. Havoc, *More Havoc*, 205.
35. Ibid., 205
36. Ibid., 206.
37. Ibid. Havoc's account is supported by the version of the song that appears in the original production's orchestra books. What seem to be the earliest copies of any parts are in the hand of the copyist referred to as "Guido" by musical director Harry Levant (likely Guido Tutrinoli)—"That Terrific Rainbow" appears in the hand of another, unidentified, copyist.
38. Mantle, "*Pal Joey* Smart and Novel"; Watts, "Night Club Portrait"; Atkinson, "Christmas Night Adds *Pal Joey*."
39. "The Theatre: New Plays in Manhattan" *Time*, January 6, 1941
40. O'Hara, rehearsal draft script, 1-3-10.
41. The Chappell score changes the word "weakened" to "lowered," rendering the word painting that much more obvious. It is unclear who changed the lyric.
42. Rodgers, *Musical Stages*, 201.
43. This expressive indication does not appear in Levant's conductor score or the original stand parts, but it does appear in an undated packet of "cue sheets," held at the Rodgers and Hammerstein Organization, which very likely date to the original production.
44. While Rodgers never wrote an actual blues number—in the standard twelve-bar form, at least—he and Hart followed a popular practice in the 1920s and did reference the blues in some of their song titles. These include "Chorus Girl Blues" (originally in the amateur show *Say Mama* [1921]) and "Atlantic Blues" (from *Lido Lady* [1926]). "Atlantic Blues" isn't in a blues form, but the chorus melody is based on a pentatonic collection (B-C#-D#-F#-G#).
45. Jonathon Green, *Cassell's Dictionary of Slang* (London: Weidenfeld & Nicolson, 2005), 746.

46. The "red hot mama" trope can also be seen in other forms of popular culture of the period. Consider, for instance, the Betty Boop short "Red Hot Mamma," from 1934, in which Betty Boop dreams she's in hell, only to give the demons there the "cold shoulder" (a literal ice cube emerges from her shoulder).

47. Sidney B. Whipple, *New York World-Telegram*, December 26, 1940.

48. Depending on the recording, the word "weakened" is replaced with "lowered" (as in the 1952 Capitol cast recording, and the 1962 Chappell piano-vocal score), reflecting the contour of the melody; the 1951 Columbia recording and *The Complete Lyrics of Lorenz Hart* uses the word "weakened." Hart, *Complete Lyrics of Lorenz Hart*, 271.

49. Vernon Macfarlane was a well-known interior designer, famous for adding "exotic" elements to his designs, inspired by the designs and textiles of various locales in Africa, Latin America, and elsewhere. His work included the interior of the chi-chi restaurant Montparnasse (originally located on E, 79th), as well as one of the toniest nightclubs in Manhattan, El Morocco, where Macfarlane's blue and white zebra-striped seat cushions became iconic. O'Hara's "Richman corn" comment is a reference to Harry Richman, who made his fame in revues, became internationally famous for performing the title song in the 1930 film *Puttin' on the Ritz* (in top hat and tails), and eventually married a Ziegfeld girl. O'Hara, *Pal Joey*, preliminary draft script.

50. Cecil A. Smith and Glenn Litton, *Musical Comedy in America: From "The Black Crook" to "South Pacific"; from "The King and I" to "Sweeney Todd"* (New York: Routledge, 1987), 176.

51. Prop list, "PAL JOEY—PROPS—complete as of Nov 26," Jo Mielziner Papers, NYPL for the Performing Arts, Box 47, folder 4.

52. Nelson Rae was a young operatic singer with no musical theater experience, who at one time sang with the St. Louis Municipal Opera Company.

53. The last few measures of the original conductor cue sheet pinpoint where Gladys finally "liberated" her high B♭; right after the high note, the cue sheet has the following line penciled in: "this number is much too high for me." This line doesn't appear in any of the scripts for the show, drafts or otherwise, and may have been ad libbed by Havoc.

54. Havoc, *More Havoc*, 206.

55. Both the 1952 cast recording and the 1995 City Center Encores! recording begin at the Maestoso.

56. There is also a possibility that the instrumental introduction in D major was nondiegetic underscore, though this point seems unlikely because the cue that precedes it, spoken by the character Victor (the director of the number), sets up the rehearsal to follow and reads "and try to get it right just once." (2-1-3; Penn draft)

57. Steel, the tenor to introduce Irving Berlin's "A Pretty Girl Is like a Melody" in the *Ziegfeld Follies of 1919*, went on to record Rudolf Friml's "Bring Back My Blushing Rose," and Berlin's "Little Butterfly."

58. Hart, "American Beauty Rose," in *Complete Lyrics of Lorenz Hart*, 72.

59. Rodgers, *Musical Stages*, 83. Another song featured in *The Rose of Arizona* portion of the *Gaieties* of 1926 was "It May Rain," which included the lines "It may rain

when the sun stops shining. / It may rain when the sky is gray. / But after clouds will go, / You'll see a bright rainbow." Dominic Symonds calls "It May Rain" a "parody of the trite moon-June song Rodgers and Hart so vehemently disliked." "Flower Garden," and the verse to "That Terrific Rainbow," include exactly this type of clichéd, overeager lyric. Symonds, *We'll Have Manhattan*, 83.

60. Apparently the satirical elements of the number were lost on many, as the lavish set design, featuring tons of rhinestones, instead impressed them. As Magee puts it, "the scenic wonders inspired more awe than laughter. Although some of the in-the-know revue regulars chuckled at the number's satirical intent, many audience members simply murmured admiration and offered sincere applause for an opulence that appeared more ravishing than foolish." Jeffrey Magee, *Irving Berlin's American Musical Theater* (New York: Oxford University Press, 2012), 169.

61. Ibid. Magee makes a nod to "Flower Garden of My Heart" and "Springtime for Hitler," from *The Producers*, both production numbers that are in the same mold as "My Beautiful Rhinestone Girl."

62. O'Hara, in Bruccoli, *O'Hara Concern*, 150.

63. Samuel Marx and Jan Clayton, *Rodgers and Hart: Bewitched, Bothered and Bedeviled* (New York: G. P. Putman's Sons, 1976), 39.

64. Gene Kelly in Frederick W. Nolan, *Lorenz Hart: A Poet on Broadway* (New York: Oxford University Press, 1994) 273.

65. Rodgers, *Musical Stages*, 198.

66. Sidney B. Whipple, "*Pal Joey* a Comedy-Coated Indictment: Entertainment Is Satirical Exposure of Vicious Café Factors," *New York World-Telegram*, March 15, 1941.

67. Frank Vreeland, "The Great Neon Way," *Rob Wagner's Script*, Beverly Hills, May 3, 1941.

CHAPTER 4  I Could Write a Book (Musical): The Book Numbers

1. Wolcott Gibbs, "Upturn," *New Yorker*, January 4, 1941.

2. Gibbs was the inspiration for the name of O'Hara's fictional town Gibbsville (a riff on his hometown, Pottsville, Pennsylvania), which is where his first novel, *Appointment in Samarra* (1934), as well as some of his short stories, was set.

3. Gibbs, "Upturn."

4. See Chapter 1, Table 1.1, for a summary of the original *New Yorker* story.

5. In an era-appropriate bit of dialogue, Joey also reveals that his father killed himself after the crash: "Daddy. He was never brought up to work. He never did a day's work in his life, so when the crash came he took the only way out, for him. I don't think he was a coward. That way Mother got some insurance." Linda predictably replies, "Oh, how awful." Opening-night script, 1-2-12.

6. Opening-night script, 1-2-12.

7. John O'Hara, "Bow Wow," *New Yorker*, May 13, 1939.

8. O'Hara, 1-2-12.

9. The use of repeated pitches in a verse wasn't foreign to the songs of Rodgers and Hart. On the verse for "It Never Entered My Mind" (from *Higher and Higher*), for

instance, the same pitch is repeated twenty-seven times (five measures) before moving up a whole step. In this instance, however, the repetition serves to create the feel of a dazed, lonely person (the character Sandy Moore, played by Shirley Ross), pining for her love.

10. Block also notes other examples of textual realism in *Pal Joey*: the use of the word "blue" on a "blue" note in the chorus to that "Terrific Rainbow," and the "horn-like fifths" that mimic a hunting call, paired with lyrics that evoke a hunt in "Happy Hunting Horn." Block, *Enchanted Evenings*, 107.

11. Mark N. Grant, *The Rise and Fall of the Broadway Musical* (Lebanon, NH: Northeastern University Press, 2004), 141.

12. The only difference between this sketch and the final version of the melody is the dotted quarter note on the first beat of the second measure of the chorus; the dotted quarter, followed by an eighth note, lends a jaunty affect to the melody. Rodgers eventually straightened this rhythm out into two quarter notes, perhaps to create a smoother, more effortless line.

13. Note: these sketches, held in the Richard Rodgers Collection at the Library of Congress, aren't labeled as "I Could Write a Book" (in the finding aid, or in the sketch itself); Richard Rodgers Collection, Box 12, folder 40, p. 8.

14. Graham Wood, "The Development of Song Forms in the Broadway and Hollywood Musicals of Richard Rodgers, 1919-1943," (PhD diss., The University of Minnesota, 2000), 112.

15. Ibid.

16. Alec Wilder, *American Popular Song: The Great Innovators, 1900–1950* (New York: Oxford University Press, 1972), 216.

17. Kelly was at the time on leave from the Navy; he entered the Navy on January 9, 1945, and despite the end of the war, didn't complete his active service until May 13, 1946. In the first part of Whiteman's program, Kelly playfully slips into the character Chip from *On the Town* (1944): Whiteman explains that Kelly is on a forty-eight-hour pass, and Tilton comments, "I've always wanted to know how a Navy man spends his leave." Kelly follows up with "My first stop is the Museum of Natural History, then Grant's Tomb, then the Art Institute," and so on. Kelly would go on to direct and star in the successful film version of *On the Town* (1949). In the film, Kelly played Gabey, and Frank Sinatra played Chip.

18. Rice, "How a Musical is Made," *PM Weekly*, December 22, 1940.

19. O'Hara, 1-4-22.

20. The lyrics to "Love Is My Friend" are printed in the opening-night script, held in both John O'Hara's papers at Penn State, and in the Rodgers and Hammerstein library.

21. Hart and Kimball, *Complete Lyrics of Lorenz Hart*, 272.

22. Dorothy Hart apparently communicated with them both on the subject. Ibid.

23. "Gossip of the Rialto," *New York Times*, March 30, 1941.

24. For a more in-depth look at the gender archetypes presented in *Pal Joey*, see Chapter 5.

25. Graham Wood calls this particular form a "double chorus" with "intervening interlude." He notes that Rodgers used this form frequently, though he didn't always call the patter section by that name. Wood notes other songs by

Rodgers and Hart that include an interlude: "On a Desert Island with Thee" (*A Connecticut Yankee*), "What Do You Want with Money" (from the film *Halleluiah, I'm a Bum*), "Over and Over Again," "The Circus on Parade," and "Little Girl Blue" (*Jumbo*), "There's a Small Hotel" (*On Your Toes*), "Johnny One Note" (*Babes in Arms*), "Come with Me" (*The Boys from Syracuse*), and "Nobody's Heart" (*By Jupiter*). Wood, "The Development of Song Forms," 158 n. 96.

26. Block, *Enchanted Evenings*, 108.

27. Carol Bruce, who played Vera opposite Harold Lang's Joey in the 1954 London production, remembers singing the following lyric (on closing night, despite the Lord Chamberlain's previous censorship of the line), for instance: "I've tripped again / I've slipped again / My chastity belt is unzipped again." See Carol Bruce, interview with Skip Lowe, 1993 (https://www.youtube.com/watch?v=Yym7Uk6Wd2U)

    There are also a number of parody versions of the song. Samuel Marx and Jan Clayton note that William Bowers, a Hollywood screenwriter who is credited with "additional dialogue" in the film version of *Higher and Higher*, wrote his own parody of the chorus: "I'm wild again, with child again, / You might even say I'm defiled again, / Betrayed, bothered, and be-pregnant am I." Clayton and Marx, *Rodgers and Hart: Bewitched, Bothered and Bedeviled*, 245. The three-part rhyme must have been irresistible for some: one fan wrote to Rodgers, after watching the revival production, suggesting the following lines (he mentions in the letter, "there was an insistent demand for encores, and it seemed a pity that there were no more verses"):

    > Bruised again,
    > Bemused again,
    > Just getting used to being used again,
    > Bewitched, Bothered, and Bewildered am I.
    > Blind again,
    > Inclined again,
    > Could be arrested for what's on my mind again.
    > Bewitched, Bothered, and Bewildered am I.
    > I have dreams, they're theatric, full of arms and legs and necks.
    > I need help—not psychiatric—just plain old-fashioned sex.
    > Aglow again,
    > I know again,
    > My hormones are starting to grow again,
    > Bewitched, Bothered, and Bewildered am I.

    The fan, a lawyer named Pearson Neaman, offered the lyrics "for free"; Rodgers was gracious in his response. Pearson E. Neaman, letter to Richard Rodgers, February 15, 1952.

28. Rehearsal script, 1-6-27.

29. Opening-night script, 1-6-33.

30. These lyrics appear in the rehearsal conductor score, with the warning "I just wanted to tell you to go to hell before I leave," indicating that this version appeared when "Bewitched" was placed in act 1, scene 4. This lyric also appears in *Complete Lyrics of Lorenz Hart*, 272.

31. Opening-night script, 1-6-34.
32. There is some evidence to indicate that first two bars of the introduction were cut in performance: in the original flute part (included in the Reed 1 book), and the original violin part, the first two bars are crossed out. There is no way of verifying, however, when those markings were made.
33. Watts, "Night Club Portrait."
34. Sensenderfer, "PAL JOEY—George Abbott Musical about Night Club Life Has Premiere"; Bronson, "The Stage: Pal Joey Full of Snap and Sting."
35. Kronenberger, "Pal Joey Brings Holiday Cheer."
36. The song was originally performed and eventually published in C major. Lupone's version of the song was lowered to A♭. An interesting letter from Max Meth (the musical director in the revival production) reveals that for the revival Rodgers wanted to lower Segal's songs by a half step, but she refused: "Following your request to have the keys lowered in Vivian Siegal's numbers, I [. . .] presented the idea to Vivian [. . .] In speaking to her, I made it appear that the consensus of opinion was that during the inclement winter weather and the strain of performing eight times a week, it would be wise for her to sing a half tone lower, in order to conserve her voice. Much to my amazement, she flatly refused to have any keys changed, since in her opinion, the present keys are absolutely perfect in her voice range. She seems rather annoyed, so I dropped the subject." Max Meth, letter to Richard Rodgers, November 30, 1952.
37. Block, Enchanted Evenings, 107.
38. Rodgers, "How to Write Music," 262.
39. Rodgers, Musical Stages, 201.
40. Engel observes that the "sequence of the jokes is determined here by their comparative strength." He argues that the placement of the line "Bewitched, Bothered and Bewildered" at the end of each "punchline" gives viewers the opportunity to laugh "while assuring the audience that it is missing nothing." Engel, American Musical Theatre, 107.
41. Stockard Channing's version of the reprise, for Joe Mantello's 2008 Broadway revival, managed to be both comic and tragic (she got a laugh on the line "the ants that invaded my pants" but left out the final "Bewitched, bothered and bewildered," instead appearing somewhat shattered). Channing's performance (of the song and its reprise) is much more heartrending than either Segal or Lupone's.
42. Rehearsal script, 2-2-15.
43. Opening-night script, 2-2-22.
44. In the 1952 script, Vera doesn't specify her age, simply saying that she's "over twenty-one." Segal was forty-three when Pal Joey premiered. See Chapter 5 for a more in-depth discussion of Vera/Segal's age. 1952 Fireside script, 100.
45. Ibid, 2-2-23.
46. Surprisingly, this storyline was picked up by the producers of the film version of Pal Joey. See Julianne Lindberg, "Adapting Pal Joey: Postwar Anxieties and the Playmate," in The Oxford Handbook of Musical Theatre Screen Adaptation, ed. Dominic McHughs (New York: Oxford University Press, 2019).

47. Rehearsal script, 2-2-17. This idea was transferred to the plot of the 1957 film; in the film, Vera forces Joey to fire Linda, though (who is a chorus girl in the film).
48. Waters, "*Pal Joey.*"
49. Jeffrey Magee, "From Flatbush to Fun Home: Broadway's Cozy Cottage Trope," in *Rethinking American Music,* eds. Tara Browner and Thomas L. Riis (Urbana: University of Illinois Press, 2019).
50. Beyond "Den of Iniquity," Rodgers and Hart wrote other parodies on the cozy-cottage trope. One is the song "Come with Me" from *The Boys from Syracuse* (1938). This song upends the heteronormative aspect of the trope by describing a "house of rest" with "lots of friends": a "strictly male house" that, fittingly, ends up being a "jailhouse."
51. Magee, "From Flatbush to Fun Home."
52. Stanley Donen, outtake from interview for the PBS documentary *Broadway: The American Musical.* Available to view at the New York Public Library.
53. Lehman Engel, *Their Words Are Music: The Great Theatre Lyricists and Their Lyrics* (New York: Crown, 1975), 36.
54. See Graham Wood, "The Development of Song Forms," 144.
55. Ibid, 152.
56. Stacy Wolf, "'We'll Always Be Bosom Buddies': Female Duets and the Queering of Broadway Musical Theater," *GLQ: A Journal of Lesbian and Gay Studies* 12, no. 3, 2006, 353.
57. Ibid, 354.
58. Ibid, 354.
59. Opening-night script, 2-4-34
60. Opening-night script, 2-4-36.
61. Wolf, "Female Duets," 375 n. 53.
62. Raymond Knapp, *The American Musical and the Formation of National Identity* (Princeton, NJ: Princeton University Press, 2005), 139. Quoted in Wolf, "Female Duets," 374 n. 44.
63. In light of this point, it is interesting to note that in 1943 *Oklahoma!,* which for many signaled a new era in musical theater, reinforces the old marriage trope with new, wartime fervor through its own 11 o'clock number, the song "Oklahoma."

CHAPTER 5 The Women of *Pal Joey*

1. Vivienne Segal, in Lloyd S. Thompson, "Vivienne Segal Looked It Up to Make Sure—Yep, She's Original *Desert Song* Star," *San Francisco Examiner,* July 23, 1933.
2. John O'Hara, letter to Tom O'Hara, August 16, 1934. Reprinted in *Selected Letters of John O'Hara,* ed. Matthew Bruccoli (New York: Random House, 1978), 96.
3. Fran Lebowitz, "Introduction," in *BUtterfield 8,* by John O'Hara (New York: Modern Library, 2003), xiii.
4. Rodgers, *Musical Stages,* 200.
5. Mantle, "*Pal Joey* Smart and Novel."
6. Whipple, "*Pal Joey* Is a Bright, Gay, Tuneful, Novel Work."
7. Atkinson, "Christmas Night Adds *Pal Joey.*"'

8. Watts, "Night Club Portrait."

9. "How Mr. Ames Lost His High Salaried Wife," *Courier-Journal* (Louisville, KY), August 8, 1926.

10. Burns Mantle, "The Yankee Princess," *New York Daily News*, October 22, 1922; "*My Lady's Glove* Comes from Vienna: Operetta by Straus Adapted for Us Differs Little from Many Others Made Over," *New York Times*, 1917; "Ziegfeld Follies Bloom for Summer: Latest Edition Has Talented Newcomers and Old Favorites," *New York Times*, July 1925; "*Castles in the Air*" Has Colorful Dances: Capable Singers in a Highly Pleasing Mixture of Musical Comedy and Operetta," *New York Times*, September 1926.

11. Richard Barrios, *A Song in the Dark: The Birth of the Film Musical* (Oxford and New York: Oxford University Press, 2010), 135.

12. Irene Thirer, "*Song of the West*, a Single, Brings Prairies to Warner," *New York Daily News*, March 1, 1930.

13. "*Bride of the Regiment*, a Vitaphone Operetta 2ith Vivienne Segal and Allan Prior, Opens at the Hollywood Theater," *Brooklyn Daily Eagle*, May 22, 1930.

14. Consider this quotation by Lloyd Acuff, writing for the *Daily News*: "If you like your Africa stark and merciless, a la "Trader Horn,' or fantastic and exciting, like the adventures of 'Tarzan,' 'Golden Dawn' is scarcely the film for you. Ray Enright, apparently given the task of linking plenty of song and dance sequences with what is fundamentally a rather grim story of savage life, did so effectively. But the result is an operetta—not the tense, tomtom thumping variety of African drama one might be led to expect by the lobby posters." Lloyd Acuff, "*Golden Dawn* Cast Sings and Dances Ably," *New York Daily News*, July 28, 1930.

15. Vivienne Segal, interview with Anthony Slide, *Film Fan Monthly*, October 1972.

16. This was not the first time she had made this transformation—the stage musical *The Blue Paradise*, which she starred in at just eighteen years old, required her to play a young woman and that same woman twenty-four years later.

17. The only known copy of *Viennese Nights* is currently held at the Film and Television Archive at UCLA.

18. By the time Jeanette MacDonald and Nelson Eddy entered the business, the backlash against film operettas had ended, and the duo enjoyed a lucrative association.

19. As Segal tells it, MacDonald schemed to cut her already supporting role down to almost nothing. Apparently, MacDonald's first words to Segal once on set were "'Hello, Viv, have you seen your part? It stinks!'" Vivienne Segal, interview with Anthony Slide, *Film Fan Monthly*, October 1972.

20. The film preserved the score from the 1931 stage musical, but changed the book considerably.

21. In the stage version of the show, the character Victor sings the song.

22. While Segal starred in only two Broadway shows after *Pal Joey*, she later featured in a handful of television spots. Two of these appearances were in the series *Alfred Hitchcock Presents* (these include the episodes "Hooked," which aired September 25, 1960, and "Apex," which aired March 20, 1962). In both of these episodes, Segal plays the part of an older woman whose husband wants to kill her (spoiler: it doesn't go well for either husband). It seems that after *Pal Joey*, Segal experienced typecasting of a different kind than that of her early career.

23. Vivienne Segal, in Lloyd S. Thompson, "Vivienne Segal Looked It Up to Make Sure—Yep, She's Original 'Desert Song' Star," *San Francisco Examiner*, July 23, 1933.

24. Samuel Marx and Jan Clayton, *Rodgers and Hart: Bewitched, Bothered, and Bedeviled; A Dual Biography* (New York: G. P. Putnam's Sons, 1976), 209.

25. Robert Francis, "Vivienne Segal, Minus Romantic Frills and Pink Organdy, Wisecracks Her Way through *I Married an Angel*," *Brooklyn Daily Eagle*, December 4, 1938.

26. Program for *I Married an Angel*, directed by Joshua Logan, produced by Dwight Deere Wiman, Shubert Theatre, May 11, 1938.

27. Segal's rendition of the song can be heard on the recording of *A Connecticut Yankee* by Decca, featuring Segal and Dick Foran.

28. John Harrison sees hints of Vera in the character Mavis Ketchall, from the Joey story "Joey and Mavis" (published in the *New Yorker* on May 4, 1940). In the story, Mavis is indeed a wealthy middle-aged woman (Joey guesses thirty-two or thirty-three), but she is a widow, and although she enters Joey's club with an entourage, as she does in the musical, that's pretty much where the similarities end. Mavis is, in personality, nothing like Vera.

29. Geoffrey Wolff, *The Art of Burning Bridges: A Life of John O'Hara* (New York: Knopf, 2003), 184.

30. O'Hara counters this progressive-sounding statement with a more timely sentiment: "I speak of conscious domination. Inevitably the man will dominate in the right ways. The woman will dominate by influence and suggestion; the man by being a man." O'Hara, letter to Tom O'Hara, *Selected Letters of John O'Hara*, 96.

31. John Updike, *Hugging the Shore: Essays and Criticism* (New York: Knopf, 1983), 185.

32. Updike makes the dubious claim that O'Hara became "virtually a feminist writer," but the point stands that O'Hara hasn't been given enough credit for his portrayal of women with complex inner lives. Ibid.

33. While most associate the surge of women in the workforce with the onset of World War II, the economic effects of the Depression meant that women, even married women, had begun working out of necessity years earlier. To be fair, the numbers were far more dramatic during the war. Denning notes that by 1950, the number of women in the workforce was double what it had been in 1930. Michael Denning, *The Cultural Front: The Laboring of American Culture in the Twentieth Century* (London: Verso, 1997), 30.

34. Margaret McFadden, "'Anything Goes': Gender and Knowledge in the Comic Popular Culture of the 1930s" (PhD diss., Yale University, 1996), 13.

35. Ibid, 257.

36. For more on this point, see Julianne Lindberg, "*The Time of Your Life*: Gene Kelly, Working-Class Masculinity, and Music," *Studies in Musical Theatre* 10, no. 2 (Fall 2016), 177–193..

37. George Chauncey, *Gay New York: Gender, Urban Culture, and the Making of the Gay World, 1890–1940* (New York: Basic Books, 1995).

38. Philippa Gates, *Detecting Women: Gender and the Hollywood Detective Film* (Albany: State University of New York Press, 2011), 133.

39. David Lugowski, "Queering the (New) Deal: Lesbian and Gay Representation and the Depression-Era Cultural Politics of Hollywood's Production Code," *Cinema Journal* 38, no. 2 (Winter 1999), 4.

40. John O'Hara, "A Bit of a Shock," in *Pal Joey* (New York: Duell, Sloan & Pearce, 1940), 171–181.

41. O'Hara, *Pal Joey*, 175.

42. Ibid.

43. Rehearsal script, 2-1-6.

44. Chauncey, *Gay New York*.

45. During the 1930s, especially after 1934 (after La Guardia became mayor of New York), police began to crack down more on gay establishments or establishments that catered to gay clientele. This crackdown was part of a larger anti-vice effort under La Guardia, but it disproportionately affected queer communities.

46. Bruce Rogers, "Degenerates of Greenwich Village," in Neil Miller, *Out of the Past: Gay and Lesbian History from 1869 to the Present* (New York: Vintage Books, 1995), 146–147.

47. Surprisingly, this was not the first time Hart rhymed Stravinsky with Minsky. In the song "The Three Bs" (from *On Your Toes* [1936]), which takes place during a classroom lesson in which hopeless students confuse the object of their study (classical music) with popular culture, one student answers the question "And what did Shostakovich write?" with "Lady Macbeth from Minsky." The word "Minsky" rhymes with the previous line, "Tchaikovsky, Moszkowski, Mussorgsky, Stravinsky"; the correct name of Shostakovich's opera is, incidentally, *Lady Macbeth of the Mtsensk District*.

48. While the 1951 Columbia record includes "hot" accents at the ends of phrases—including brass growls and suggestive tom-tom "bumps"—there's no indication of such in the original score.

49. Lee is now most prominently associated with Styne/Sondheim/Laurents's *Gypsy* (1959), which was inspired by her memoirs. June Havoc was initially vehemently against the project, but eventually relented when she realized that it would provide her sister with much-needed income.

50. Tom Wolf, "Gypsy Rose Lee Is Exposed Again in Quest of Literary Laurels," *Anniston Star* (Alabama), August 15, 1941.

51. Rachel Shteir, *Striptease: The Untold History of the Girlie Show* (New York: Oxford University Press, 2004), 179.

52. Jean Casto, "'Zip'—It's a Strip Tease, but All She Takes Off Is a Heavy Tweed Coat," *New York Post*, March 29, 1941.

53. Ibid.

54. Bob Francis, "Broadway Reviews: *Goodbye, My Fancy*," *Billboard*, July 2, 1949, 54.

55. The Columbia recording features Jo Hurt at Melba. She excels at bringing out the humorous mind/body disconnect through a distinction between timbres on the word "Zip!" (which are alternately flat and bored, or nasal and flirtatious) and the rest of the lyrics (which she performs in a broad belt). The orchestral accompaniment also emphasizes the distinction, including muted trumpet "wha-whas," a clear reference to burlesque houses, at the ends of phrases. Frederica Winters, letter to Don Walker, January 20, 1952.

56. Ibid.
57. Ibid.
58. Ibid.
59. Rodgers, "*Pal Joey*: History of a 'Heel,'" *New York Times* (December 30, 1951).
60. O'Hara, *Pal Joey*, 71.

CHAPTER 6  *Joey* Dances

1. Robert Alton, c. 1940, as quoted in Richard Kislan, *Hoofing on Broadway: A History of Show Dancing* (New York: Prentice Hall, 1987), 67.
2. George Beiswanger, "Broadway on Its Toes," *Theatre Arts*, February 1940, 107.
3. Ibid.
4. Rodgers, "How to Write Music in No Easy Lesson," 264.
5. The other was Mary Watkins, of the *New York Herald Tribune*. Other critics, including Edwin Denby, wrote for smaller publications (in his case, the magazine *Modern Music*), and George Beiswanger, who wrote for the magazine *Theatre Arts*.
6. Martin singles out how Berkeley used the "rhythmic structure of jazz" as a foundation for his dances in Rodgers and Hart's *Present Arms*. John Martin, "The Dance: New Musical Comedy Talent," *New York Times*, July 22, 1928; Martin, "The Dance: Numbers for Our Revues," *New York Times*, October 18, 1931.
7. John Martin, "The Dance: Pal Kelly," *New York Times*, June 8, 1941
8. "Dances by Robert Alton," *New York Times*, March 3, 1940. The author is referring to the 1939–1940 season, and the three "hit" musicals mentioned are Rodgers and Hart's *Too Many Girls*, Cole Porter's *Du Barry Was a Lady*, and Nancy Hamilton's revue *Two for the Show*. The touring show mentioned was the Shuberts-produced revue *Streets of Paris*, the show in rehearsal was Rodgers and Hart's *Higher and Higher*, and one of the two shows under contract was, presumably, Porter's *Panama Hattie*, while it was speculated that he was going to commence work on *Louisiana Purchase* (in the end, Balanchine choreographed the ballets for this show, while Carl Randall staged the rest of the dances). Alton had certainly not yet signed to direct dances for *Pal Joey* by March, the date of this article.
9. Brooks Atkinson, "*Anything Goes* as Long as Victor Moore, Ethel Merman and William Gaxton Are Present," *New York Times*, November 22, 1934.
10. Ibid.
11. The whistle between Alton's teeth reminds the reader of the early days of Broadway dance, when precision kick lines performed demanding drills, never a leg out of place. Ned Wayburn, one of great early dance directors, was also purported to always have a whistle at the ready. This may have been an intentional reference by de Mille. Agnes de Mille, *Dance to the Piper* (Boston: Little, Brown, 1951), 184.
12. For more on this story, see Carol Easton, *No Intermissions: The Life of Agnes de Mille*, 144–145; despite its rough start, the revised show went on to have a respectable run of 200 performances.
13. De Mille, *Dance to the Piper*, 183.
14. Ibid, 183–184.
15. Ibid, 184.

16. For more on Alton's contributions, and his brush with de Mille, see Raphael Francis Miller, "The Contributions of Selected Broadway Musical Theatre Choreographers: Connolly, Rasch, Balanchine, Holm, and Alton," PhD Dissertation, University of Oregon, 1984, 259–263.

17. Kislan, *Hoofing on Broadway*, 64.

18. Cecil Smith, quoted in Kislan, *Hoofing on Broadway*, 64.

19. "Dances by Robert Alton," *New York Times*, March 3, 1940.

20. Gene Kelly, interview with Marilyn Hunt, oral history project, NYPL, March 10–14, 1975.

21. John Martin, "The Dance: Revue Style," *New York Times*, February 18, 1940.

22. Balanchine's and Alton's careers collided in other ways, too: in 1936, before either of them had worked with Rodgers and Hart, they both worked on the *Ziegfeld Follies of 1936* (which famously featured Josephine Baker, as well as the Nicholas Brothers, Bob Hope, and Eve Arden). In the playbill, they're credited this way: "Modern Dances by Robert Alton" and "Ballets by George Balanchine." This credit reflects a distinction seen in the programs of many earlier revues, between ballet and modern and popular dance.

23. Dominic Symonds, quoted from his paper "Laughter on Tenth Avenue: Rodgers and Hart, Dwight Deere Wiman, and *On Your Toes* (1936)," presented at Song, Stage and Screen XI, June 2016, City College of New York. Symonds has argued that Wiman's calm, generous nature, and his ability act as a "father figure" to those he worked with made him exceedingly valuable: "In bringing together a family, Wiman showed very different, though just as important skills to George Abbott, and it was these that clearly made him much-loved and highly-regarded within the industry."

24. See Armond Fields and L. Marc Fields, *From the Bowery to Broadway: Lew Fields and the Roots of American Popular Theater* (New York: Oxford University Press, 1993), 452–457.

25. Rodgers, *Musical Stages*, 175.

26. James Steichen, "Balanchine's 'Bach Ballet' and the Dances of Rodgers and Hart's *On Your Toes*" *Journal of Musicology* 35, no. 2 (2018), 286.

27. Abbott, *Mister Abbott*, 243.

28. Brooks Atkinson, "The Play: *Too Many Girls* Opens with a Score by Rodgers and Hart under George Abbott's Direction," *New York Times*, October 19, 1939.

29. Burns Mantle, "Bring Out the Cheer Section for the Hit, *Too Many Girls*," *New York Daily News*, October 19, 1939

30. Although it did come back for a brief return engagement that August.

31. Rodgers, *Musical Stages*, 195.

32. Arthur Pollock, "*Higher and Higher* Is Best When It's Dancing," *Brooklyn Daily Eagle*, April 5, 1940.

33. Brooks Atkinson, "The Play: Jack Haley Renews Broadway Acquaintances in Rodgers and Hart's *Higher and Higher*," *New York Times*, April 5, 1940.

34. John Martin, "'The Dance: Revue Style; Robert Alton and Two for the Show'—Recitals of the Week and After," *New York Times*, February18, 1940.

35. "Dances by Robert Alton," *New York Times*, March 3, 1940

36. Arthur Pollock, "*By Jupiter* Stages Battle of the Sexes," *Brooklyn Daily Eagle*, June 4, 1942.
37. Zachary Dorsey, "Choreography," in the *Oxford Handbook of the American Musical*, 337.
38. Robert Long, *Broadway, the Golden Years: Jerome Robbins and the Great Choreographer-Directors, 1940 to the Present* (New York: Continuum, 2003), 16.
39. Alton, as quoted in Kislan, *Hoofing on Broadway*, 67.
40. Ibid, 62–63.
41. Alton, in Nelson Lansdale, "A Revival Improves on the Original *Pal Joey*," *Dance Magazine*, June, 1952, 13.
42. O'Hara had a regular entertainment column in *Newsweek*. He wrote, "OK, so I wrote 'Pal Joey.' But I am not recommending it. Gene Kelly is no longer in it. Neither is Leila Ernst, nor June Havoc, nor Jack Durant. Vivienne Segal's still in it and God knows she does all she can, which is a lot, but not even Miss Segal can surmount a lot of people named Throckett."
43. "The Theatre: New Plays in Manhattan" *Time*, January 6, 1941.
44. Stanley Donen, outtake from interview for the PBS documentary *Broadway: The American Musical*. Available to view at the New York Public Library.
45. Kelly, in fact, was always self-conscious about his singing and speaking voice. He took elocution lessons for a time (to rid himself of his native Pittsburgh accent), and around the time of *Leave It to Me* (1938) took voice lessons for a few weeks. He took voice lessons again in preparation for his *Pal Joey* audition. Gene Kelly, interview with Marilyn Hunt.
46. Ibid.
47. William Saroyan, *The Time of Your Life* (London: Methuen Drama, [1939] 2008), 28.
48. Kelly, interview with Marilyn Hunt.
49. *Parents League Bulletin*, January 1941.
50. Staff correspondent of *Christian Science Monitor*, December 26, 1940.
51. Atkinson, "Christmas Night Adds *Pal Joey*."
52. Burns Mantle, *New York Daily News*, December 26, 1940.
53. Sidney B. Whipple, *New York World-Telegram*, December 26, 1940.
54. Richard Watts, Jr., *New York Herald Tribune*, December 26, 1940.
55. Kelly, interview with Marilyn Hunt.
56. Ibid.
57. Ibid.
58. Ibid.
59. Ibid.
60. John Martin, "The Dance: Pal Kelly," *New York Times*, June 8, 1941
61. Kelly, interview with Marilyn Hunt.
62. Arthur Pollock, " 'Too Many Girls' Hasn't Too Many," *Brooklyn Eagle*, October 19, 1939.
63. Rice, "How to Make a Musical," *PM Weekly*.
64. Robert Rice, "How a Musical Is Made," *PM Weekly*, December 22, 1940.
65. Douglas Gilbert, "This 'Line Girl' Satisfied with Her Job, Doesn't Yearn to Be Great Star," *Pittsburgh Press*, March 16, 1940.

66. Phyllis Perlman, "Times Have Changed," *Brooklyn Citizen*, June 14, 1941.

67. Apparently after the SAG officials watched the routines, they upped their salaries to that received by specialty dancers. Lucie Necille, "Screen Chats," *Shamokin News-Dispatch* (PA), May 9, 1941.

68. Whipple, *New York World-Telegram*, December 26, 1940.

69. Ashton Stevens, "'Heel' Show Is a Quick Click," *Chicago Herald American*, January 13, 1942.

70. Henry T. Murdock, "*Pal Joey* Scores Hit at Forrest," *Public Ledger* (Philadelphia), December 12, 1940.

71. Originally played by Morris Speinson—at one time a member of the Cleveland Symphony Orchestra and later a member of the Paul Whiteman Orchestra— the horn call plays up the hunting tableau, and cheekily mixes "high art" with a decidedly earthy topic. The quotation was penciled in, indicating that it was added later.

72. See Bill Smith, *The Vaudevillians* (New York: Macmillan, 1976), 105–106.

73. Tim Carter, *Oklahoma! The Making of an American Musical* (New Haven and London: Yale University Press, 2007), 128.

74. Fields and Fields, *From the Bowery to Broadway*.

75. Seymour Felix, *New York Herald Tribune*, January 16, 1927.

76. See Dominic Symonds's discussion of *Lido Lady* in *We'll Have Manhattan*, 126–139.

77. The George Balanchine Foundation, for instance, has received significant funding to document Balanchine's popular legacy (the project is called Popular Balanchine); the NYPL for the Performing Arts holds multiple dossiers containing archival material from the project (for catalog information, see http://catnyp.nypl.org/record=b89221070).

78. Kara Anne Gardner, *Agnes de Mille: Telling Stories in Broadway Dance* (New York: Oxford University Press, 2016), 16.

79. Ibid., 13.

80. In fact, as Gardner points out, Kern "intended [*The Cat and the Fiddle*] to follow *Show Boat's* model of integration between story and song." Gardner, *Agnes de Mille*, 14.

81. Ibid., 16.

82. Kelly, interview with Marilyn Hunt.

83. Abbott, *Mister Abbott*, 195.

84. Ibid.

85. "Better Start Early, Says Shirley: That Is, if You Intend to Be a Ballet Dancer in *Pal Joey*," *Brooklyn Daily Eagle*, May 4, 1941.

86. Moore and Paige would go on to both feature in the vaudeville revue *Keep 'Em Laughing* (1942); that same year, they secretly married. She was reportedly twenty-two and he was sixty-seven when they made the announcement a year and a half later.

87. "Better Start Early, Says Shirley."

88. Ibid.

89. This title is published in the piano-vocal score by Chappell, 78.

90. The score is held, in an uncatalogued box with stand parts and director scores, at the Rodgers and Hammerstein Organization.

91. According to the annotation, Wood entered during the bridge of the first iteration of "Bewitched"; "H&H twirl" is annotated (presumably meaning "Harold" and "Helen") on the last eight bars of the chorus.

92. John Martin, "The Dance: *Pal Joey*; Robert Alton, Harold Lang and a Masterpiece," *New York Times*, February 17, 1952.

CHAPTER 7  History of a Heel: The 1952 Revival

1. Most call *Pal Joey* the first Broadway revival to surpass the run of the original, period, but *The Red Mill*, a Victor Herbert show produced by Charles Dillingham in 1906 (which ran for 274 shows) was surpassed by its revival in 1945, running for 531 performances.

2. He would use the play *I Remember Mama* as the source material for his last original musical, with lyrics by Martin Charnin.

3. Rodgers, "*Pal Joey*: History of a Heel."

4. Ibid.

5. Oscar Hammerstein, "Foreword," *Rodgers and Hart Songbook*, x.

6. George Reddick notes that when Wagner's *Ring* Cycle was eventually released by Decca, in installments, it took 19 LPs. The producer of the project, John Culshaw, "estimated that the same recording would have required 112 records on 78s." Reddick, "The Evolution of the Original Cast Album" in *Media and Performance in the Musical: An Oxford Handbook of the American Musical*, vol. 2 (New York: Oxford, 2018), 108.

7. These statistics apply to the week ending on June 2, 1950. Maslon, *Broadway to Main Street*, 24.

8. *Billboard*, June 3, 1950, 22.

9. Engel, *American Musical Theatre*

10. Lehman Engel, *This Bright Day: An Autobiography* (New York: Macmillan, 1974), 173.

11. Ibid.

12. John Rosenfield, "The Passing Show: Two Hits That Dallas Didn't Like," *Dallas Morning News*, January 29, 1952.

13. Ibid.

14. Lehman Engel, letter to Richard Rodgers, September 11, 1951.

15. An announcement in the *New York Times* from September 1951 stated that Engel was going to conduct the show. Louis Calta, *New York Times*, September 11, 1951.

16. Prior to *Pal Joey*, Styne's stage credits included *High Button Shoes* (1947), *Gentlemen Prefer Blondes* (1949), *Make a Wish* (1951), and *Two on the Aisle* (1951). He wrote the scores for all but *Make a Wish* (music and lyrics by Hugh Martin), which he produced. If based on the Broadway run, his most successful future musical would be *Funny Girl* (1964), which ran for 1348 performances. His most defining success was, arguably, *Gypsy* (1959).

17. *The Rodgers and Hart Songbook*, featuring a foreword by Oscar Hammerstein and an introduction by Richard Rodgers, was published by Simon and Schuster in late 1951 and was a bestseller. Vernon Rice, "Curtain Cues: A D'Oyly Carte for Rodgers and Hart," *New York Post*, January 2, 1952.

18. Bruce would play Vera again in the 1954 London production with Lang, and both Bruce and Fosse would again play the leads in the 1961 City Center revival. Fosse went on to play Joey in the 1963 City Center revival with the Swedish-born Viveca Lindfors in the role of Vera.

19. Schirmer worked as an agent to an impressive list of stars, including Shirley Jones, Ethel Merman, and Carol Channing.

20. See Martin Gottfried, *All His Jazz: The Life and Death of Bob Fosse* (Cambridge, MA: Da Capo Press, 2003), 63.

21. Donald Kirkley, "*Pal Joey* Has Olney Revival," *Baltimore Sun*, September 13, 1951.

22. *Pal Joey* souvenir program, 1952.

23. The nature of his involvement is unclear, although Styne's biographer, presumably on the basis of a conversation with Styne, says that Kazan "promised to come in after one week of work, take a look at the first-act run-through and render an opinion." Theodore Taylor, *Jule: The Story of Composer Jule Styne* (New York: Random House, 1979), 158.

24. Richard Rodgers, telegram to Elia Kazan, October 4, 1951. A few weeks before Rodgers sent this telegram, Styne contacted him to say that he had "made every effort to get a top director for 'Pal Joey,' and although they are all excited about the project and love the show, they seem to feel that they can't garner any new laurels by directing it." Jule Styne, letter to Richard Rodgers, September 18, 1951.

25. As Theodore Taylor, who purportedly learned this event in an interview with Styne, reports, Styne felt, after signing Segal for the part of Mama Longstreet in *High Button Shoes*, that Nanette Fabray would be better for the role. Apparently during an "angel" audition (for potential backers), Styne purposely left out Segal's big numbers, saying that they were being cut. Segal supposedly left the show because of it. If this story is in fact true, Segal luckily never learned about the trick. Taylor, *Jule*, 119.

26. Taylor, *Jule*, 158.

27. Louis Calta, "*Pal Joey* to Begin Return Run Dec. 25: Jule Styne Expects to Offer Musical Revival on 11th Anniversary of Its Bow," *New York Times*, September 11, 1951.

28. Styne's collateral involved his projected royalties on the shows *Gentlemen Prefer Blondes* (1949) and *Two on the Aisle* (1951), the latter of which was still playing when *Pal Joey* premiered. J. P. Shanley, "Balancing *Joey*'s Budget: Jule Styne Talks about Cutting Costs for Musical Hit," *New York Times*, February 17, 1952. The investor who had died was named George Pollack, a Chicago attorney and friend of Styne's. See Taylor, *Jule*, 159.

29. Taylor, *Jule*, 159.

30. Rodgers, *Musical Stages*, 201–202.

31. Shanley, "Balancing *Joey*'s Budget."

32. Louis Calta, "*Pal Joey* Revival Delayed for a Week: Rodgers-Hart-O'Hara Musical Will Open Here Jan. 3—Lionel Stander Signed," *New York Times*, November 27, 1951.

33. This same article contrasts Stander's fiery response with Jay Gorney's testimony: "Like Stander—but much more politely—he requested that the TV lights be turned off. He was not an actor, just a songwriter, he said, and

the lights disturbed him." His calm demeanor was a ploy, apparently, because soon afterward, "bouncing in his chair and with no warning, Gorney began auditioning from the First Amendment. He sang with an odd rhythm: '. . . Congress shall make no laws respecting an establishment of religion—' That was as far as he got before the surprised chairman's gavel banged. Lots of leftists have enjoyed quoting the Bill of Rights, etc., to law officials. Nobody else, so far as is known, ever got away with serenading the House Un-American Activities Committee." Lionel Stander and Jay Gorney, quoted in "Red Probe Has Actor Yelling—But Not Telling," *Daily News*, May 7, 1953.

34. Taylor, *Jule*, 162.
35. Styne had hoped to give the Broadway premiere on December 25, but had to settle with the previews.
36. "Plays Out of Town: *Pal Joey*," *Variety*, January 2, 1952.
37. F.R.J., "Last Night's Play: *Pal Joey* Opens Run at Shubert," *New Haven Journal Courier*, December 26, 1951; "Plays Out of Town: *Pal Joey*," *Variety*, January 2, 1952.
38. Helen Gallagher, interview with Liza Gennaro, New York Public Library, March 22, 2006.
39. Helen Gallagher, interview with the author, May 15, 2019.
40. Staff, "'Pal Joey' Opens With Everything it Takes to Make a Hit," *P.M. Weekly*, December 26, 1940.
41. Opening-night script, 2-3-30.
42. Ibid.
43. 1952 script, 114
44. Martin, "*Pal Joey*; Robert Alton, Harold Lang and a Masterpiece."
45. Don Walker Papers, the Library of Congress.
46. John McClain, "Fast, Funny, Feasible and Still a Great Hit," *New York Journal-American*, January 4, 1952. Another critic, commenting on the touring production, referred to the pace as moving with "the speed and force of a tornado." Jay Carmody, "The Passing Show: Brilliant *Pal Joey* Opens Fortnight at the Shubert [D.C.]," *Evening Star* (Washington, DC), April 21, 1953.
47. McClain, "Fast, Funny, Feasible."
48. William Hawkins, "*Joey* Just What Stem Needed," *New York World-Telegram and Sun*, January 4, 1952.
49. Robert Coleman, "*Pal Joey* Better Than Ever in Comeback," *Daily Mirror*, January 4, 1952.
50. Ernie Schier, "*Pal Joey*, at Shubert [DC] Is Still a Bewitching, Beguiling Production." *Times-Herald* (Washington, DC), [probably] April 21, 1953.
51. Martin, "*Pal Joey*; Robert Alton, Harold Lang and a Masterpiece."
52. John Chapman, "*Pal Joey* Returns, Still a Smart, Swift and Well-Cast Music Show," *Daily News*, January 4, 1952
53. Gallagher, interview with Liza Gennaro, March 22 and April 3, 2006.
54. Robert Alton, quoted in Nelson Lansdale, "A Revival Improves on the Original *PAL JOEY*," *Dance Magazine*, June 1952.
55. Ibid.
56. He won Best Dancer for his performances in *Look Ma, I'm Dancin'* (1948), *Make a Wish* (1951), and *Pal Joey* (1952).

57. The Ballet Russe de Monte Carlo formed after the Ballets Russes folded, and was to premiere such highly regarded ballets as DeMille's *Rodeo* (1942).

58. Harold Lang, interview with Helene Vandenplas, "Harold Lang Footnotes." Harold Lang Papers, NYPL.

59. Ibid.

60. *Fancy Free* marked Robbins's first professional show in which he was to receive credit for choreography. For an excellent overview of the production and its relevance to Robbins's career, see Robert Emmet Long, *Broadway, the Golden Years: Jerome Robbins and the Great Choreographer-Directors, 1940 to the Present* (New York: Continuum, 2003), 66–70.

61. Jerome Robbins, "Bringing Back Robbins's 'Fancy,'" *Dance Magazine*, January 1980, 71.

62. Gore Vidal, with whom Lang also had an affair, said further that "Harold had a very nice ass [. . .] Lenny Bernstein called it the seventh or maybe the eighth wonder of the world." Arthur Laurents, *Original Story By: A Memoir of Broadway and Hollywood* (New York: Applause, 2000), 47. Gore Vidal, in Jay Parini, *Empire of Self: A Life of Gore Vidal* (New York: Anchor Books, 2015), 70.

63. Edwin Denby, "Superb Super-Vaudeville," *New York Herald Tribune*, April 19, 1944.

64. Ibid.

65. While the Nicholas Brothers had a fruitful association with Balanchine, the Russian choreographer never credited the duo, and dance scholars are just beginning to focus in on the debt he owed to African American dance and dancers. As for Alton, the only mention the brothers gave was to say that one of their dances in the Ziegfeld *Follies*, which also featured Josephine Baker in a number titled "Maharanee," was credited to Alton but, in the words of Fayard Nicholas, "He didn't show us what to do. In fact, nobody did [. . .] we did our own steps, our own choreography." Fayard Nicholas, interview with the author, in Constance Valis Hill, *Brotherhood in Rhythm: The Jazz Tap Dancing of the Nicholas Brothers* (New York: Cooper Square Press, 2000), 110. For more on "Africanisms" in Balanchine's choreography, see chap. 5 in Brenda Dixon Gottschild, *Digging the Africanist Presence in American Performance: Dance and Other Contexts* (Westport, CT: Praeger, 1996). For a look on how race has impacted notions of ownership in dance, see Anthea Kraut, *Choreographing Copyright: Race, Gender, and Intellectual Property Rights in American Dance* (New York: Oxford, 2015).

66. His album credits include *Look, Ma, I'm Dancin'* (Decca), *Make a Wish* (RCA Victor), *Kiss Me, Kate* (Columbia), *Pal Joey* (Columbia), *The Bandwagon* (1953 recording; RCA Victor), *I Can Get It For You Wholesale* (Columbia), Ben Bagley's *The Decline and Fall of the Entire World as Seen through the Eyes of Cole Porter* (Columbia), and Bagley's *Jerome Kern Revisited* (Columbia).

67. John Martin, "The Dance: Debut; Hanya Holm in Bow as Choreographer for *Kiss Me, Kate*," *New York Times*, January 20, 1949.

68. Gallagher first met Lang on the show *Mr. Strauss Goes to Boston*: "I had sort of been promoted to be Harold's partner in one little place because Harold was short and all the girls were tall, and he wanted a short partner, and he thought I was it. So Balanchine said to him, 'Well, who do you want to dance

with?' He says, 'Her.' So I got to be his partner in my second show. I was crazy about Harold Lang, because I remember seeing *Fancy Free* and *Graduation Ball*, thinking, 'Oh, I want to dance with that man,' and the next show I danced with him." Gallagher, interview with Liza Gennaro, New York Public Library, March 22, 2006.

69. Brooks Atkinson, *New York Times*, January 4, 1952.
70. Richard Watts Jr., "The Happy Brilliance of *Pal Joey*," *New York Post*, January 4, 1952.
71. Martin, "*Pal Joey*; Robert Alton, Harold Lang and a Masterpiece."
72. McClain, "Fast, Funny, Feasible."
73. Walter Kerr, *New York Herald Tribune*, January 4, 1952.
74. Laurents, *Original Story By: A Memoir of Broadway and Hollywood*, 47.
75. John Chapman, "*Pal Joey* versus *Guys and Dolls*," *Daily News*, January 13, 1952.
76. See Chapter 1 for more on O'Hara's writing style, and his approach to the literary "antihero."
77. John Mason Brown, "In a Class by Itself," *Saturday Review*, February 2, 1952.
78. Wolcott Gibbs, "The Theatre," *New Yorker*, January 12, 1952.
79. Ibid.
80. James O'Leary, "*Oklahoma!*, 'Lousy Publicity,' and the Politics of Formal Integration in the American Musical Theater," *Journal of Musicology* 31, no. 1, 2014, 139–182.
81. McClain, "Fast, Funny, Feasible," 1952; Coleman, "*Pal Joey* Better Than Ever," 1952.
82. Watts, "Happy Brilliance of *Pal Joey*"; Kerr, 1952.
83. Watts, "Happy Brilliance of *Pal Joey*."
84. Brooks Atkinson, *New York Times*, January 4, 1952.
85. Jay Carmody, "The Passing Show: Brilliant "Pal Joey" Opens Fortnight at the Shubert [D.C.]," *Evening Star* (Washington, DC), April 21, 1953.
86. See, for instance, Mark N. Grant, *The Rise and Fall of the Broadway Musical* (Lebanon, NH: Northeastern University Press, 2004), for a nuanced, opinionated take on musical theater history in decline. For a fair counter to this narrative, see Jessica Sternfeld and Elizabeth L. Wollman, "After the 'Golden Age,'" in *The Oxford Handbook of the American Musical* (New York: Oxford University Press, 2011.

CHAPTER 8 *Pal Joey* goes to Hollywood

1. A version of this chapter first appeared in *Oxford Handbook of Musical Theatre Screen Adaptations*. I thank Norm Hirschy and Oxford for permission to reprint.
2. Before he worked on *Pal Joey*, Sidney's stage-to-screen musicals included *Annie Get Your Gun* (1950), *Show Boat* (1951), and *Kiss Me, Kate* (1953); Kingsley's included *Girl Crazy* (1943), *Kiss Me, Kate* (1953; with Sidney), and the screen-to- (eventually) stage *Seven Brides for Seven Brothers* (1954).
3. Daniel O'Brien, *The Frank Sinatra Film Guide* (London: Batsford, 1998), 102,
4. In a letter from Harry Cohn to George Cukor, who was slated to direct the film as early as 1954, Cohn notes that he met with Brando: "He was forthright,

friendly and simple . . . I had a very friendly and helpful talk with Richard Rodgers this morning. He is enthusiastic about the notion of Brando playing the part. He did make the observation that he hoped Brando could be light enough." This is an interesting comment, in light of the fact that Brando would play Sky Masterson in the MGM film version of *Guys and Dolls* the following year (1955). Cohn goes on to say that he also heard back from Mary Martin, who was considered for the role of Vera: "She could not imagine herself playing it." Harry Cohn, letter from Cohn to George Cuckor, May 2, 1954, Margaret Herrick Library, Academy of Motion Picture Arts and Sciences.

5. Though Hermes Pan choreographed the diegetic club numbers and the "dream" sequence at the end of the film (loosely tied to the dream ballet that closed the first act of the stage show), none of Bob Alton's original choreography remains.

6. Joseph Breen, letter to Harry Cohn, February 14, 1941, Motion Picture Association of America, Production Code Administration records, Margaret Herrick Library, Academy of Motion Picture Arts and Sciences.

7. Ibid.

8. Dorothy Kingsley, interview with Leonard Spiegelgass, in "Fade in . . . Fade Out: A Writer's Retrospective" (1970). Transcript held at the Margaret Herrick Library, Academy of Motion Picture Arts and Sciences.

9. O'Brien, *Frank Sinatra Film Guide*, 104.

10. Three of the most visible, by the decade's end, were William Atwood, George B. Leonard, and J. Robert Moskin's *The Decline of the American Male* (New York: Random House, 1958); Arthur Schlesinger Jr.'s "The Crisis of American Masculinity" in *Esquire*, November 1958; and Philip Wylie's "The Womanization of America" in *Playboy*, October 1958.

11. James Gilbert, *Men in the Middle: Searching for Masculinity in the 1950s* (Chicago: University of Chicago Press, 2005), 2.

12. Karen McNally, *When Frankie Went to Hollywood: Frank Sinatra and American Male Identity* (Urbana and Chicago: University of Illinois Press, 2008), 133–169.

13. For a thorough, enlightening exploration of the gender roles promoted by *Playboy*, see Carrie Pitzulo, *Bachelors and Bunnies: The Sexual Politics of Playboy* (Chicago and London: University of Chicago Press, 2011).

14. An article from *Playboy*'s inaugural issue, titled "Miss Gold-Digger of 1953," criticized alimony laws; another, titled "Open Season on Bachelors," warns men off of marriage. For more, see Pitzulo, *Bachelors and Bunnies*, 23–24.

15. McNally makes the important point that Sinatra's persona didn't always line up easily with *Playboy*'s "swingin' bachelor" archetype; her chapter on *The Tender Trap* and *Pal Joey* aims to reveal the contradictions in Sinatra's *Playboy* persona, principally his unstable class status (in contrast to the middle-class aspirations of *Playboy*) and his routine objectification in film. McNally, *When Frankie Went to Hollywood*, 133–169.

16. Harold Wentworth and Stuart Berg Flexner, eds., *Dictionary of American Slang* (New York: T. Y. Crowell, 1967), xi–xii. This passage is quoted in Rick McRae's informative "'What Is Hip?' and Other Inquiries in Jazz Slang Lexicography," in *Notes* 57, no. 3, 575.

17. Frank Sinatra, "*Pal Joey* Trailer."

18. The term "gasser," for instance, is defined in Robert S. Gold's *A Jazz Lexicon*: "by analogy with the immobilizing effects of being, literally, gassed," and is cited as "current since c. 1942." References for the term include *The New Cab Calloway's Hepster's Dictionary* (1944), and *Down Beat* (July 28, 1948). *A Jazz Lexicon* (Knopf, 1964), 119–120.

19. For more on the normalization of the "girl next door," see "Inventing the Girl-Next-Door: The Pulchritudinous Playmates," in Pitzulo's *Bachelors and Bunnies*, 35–70.

20. Richard Dyer, "Monroe and Sexuality," in *Heavenly Bodies*, 2nd edition (London and New York: Routledge 2004), 50.

21. Sumiko Higashi, *Stars, Fans, and Consumption in the 1950s: Reading "Photoplay"* (New York: Palgrave, 2014), 78.

22. Elaine Tyler May, *Homeward Bound: American Families in the Cold War Era* (New York: Basic Books, 1990), 108.

23. Adrienne McLean, *Being Rita Hayworth: Labor, Identity, and Hollywood Stardom* (New Brunswick, NJ: Rutgers University Press, 2004), 202.

24. Ibid., 203.

25. Ibid., 203.

26. In a letter to Harry Cohn contained in the Production Code files, Joseph Breen reveals that an early script had Linda perform "Zip": "it will be absolutely essential that there be no objectionable movements where Linda is pantomiming a strip tease." Joseph Breen, letter to Harry Cohn, May 4, 1954, Production Code Administration records, Margaret Herrick Library, Academy of Motion Picture Arts and Sciences.

27. According to the Production Code file, Stanley Styne, son of Jule Styne, wrote the revised lyrics. Styne, in PCA note dated February 12, 1957. Production Code Administration records, Margaret Herrick Library, Academy of Motion Picture Arts and Sciences.

28. Richard Dyer, "Resistance through Charisma: Rita Hayworth and *Gilda*," in *Women in Film Noir*, 2nd edition, ed. E. Ann Kaplan (London: British Film Institute, 1998) 115–122.

29. Hayworth's rocky relationship with Columbia studio head Harry Cohn is well documented. *Pal Joey* was her last film as a contracted actor with the studio.

30. McNally, *When Frankie Went to Hollywood*, 163.

31. McNally also notes that this was Hayworth's last film with Columbia under contract. Other scholars and critics have noted Hayworth's uneasy relationship with Columbia's head, Harry Cohn, which, in addition to life circumstances, very likely resulted in Hayworth's exodus from Columbia. McNally, 165.

32. The Production Code note from February of 1957 warns that "care will be needed in this scene where Vera takes a shower, to avoid any undue exposure." In the end, the studio just barely heeded this recommendation.

33. Richard Dyer, "Monroe and Sexuality" from *Heavenly Bodies*, 2nd edition (London and New York: Routledge 2004), 39.

34. Dorothy Kingsley, interview with Leonard Spiegelgass.

35. McNally, *When Frankie Went to Hollywood*, 166.

36. Ibid., 133–169.

# CONCLUSION

1. Richard Rodgers, letter to Theodore Mann, May 10, 1976.
2. Ibid.
3. While Lang was always slated for the role, for a time the English actress Adele Dixon was considered for Vera.
4. Harold Hobson, "Black Musical," *Sunday Times* (London), April 4, 1954.
5. John Barber, "That Guy Joey is in Town," *Daily Express* (London), April 1, 1954.
6. C. D. Heriot, review for *Pal Joey* for the Lord Chamberlain's Office, April 7, 1952.
7. Ibid., April 7, 1952.
8. Ibid., March 10, 1954.
9. Barber, "That Guy Joey."
10. John Balfour, "Pal Joey's a Low Down Hero," *Daily Sketch* (London), April 1, 1954.
11. Peter Senn, "America Sends Us Another Hit Show," *Oxford Mail* (Oxford, UK), March 17, 1954.
12. The next successful production of *Pal Joey* to come to London would arrive in 1980, starring British stars Sian Phillips, in her first musical, and Denis Lawson; it was a success. The show produced a cast album; Phillips's gravelly alto is full of world-weary character.
13. Barber, "That Guy Joey."
14. Kevin Winkler, *Big Deal: Bob Fosse and Dance in the American Musical* (New York: Oxford University Press, 2018), 26.
15. Of course, as Winkler points out, "Where Joey was opportunistic and self-deceiving, Fosse was grateful and clear-eyed: 'Joan was incredible to me. She really helped me to believe in myself, and she told me honestly what I had to do.'" Ibid, 26–27.
16. "Summer Theatre," *Republican and Herald* (Pottsville, PA), July 10, 1951.
17. Ibid.
18. Jule Style was originally going to direct the production, but he was too wrapped up in his upcoming production, *Subways Are for Sleeping*. Since Schirmer was to be Styne's "associate director" anyway, he took over the assignment altogether.
19. Winkler, *Big Deal*, 87.
20. Louis Calta, "*Pal Joey* a Hit; Run Is Extended," *New York Times*, June 2, 1961.
21. "*Pal Joey* Revived: Again It's a Hit," *Show Pictorial*, June 17, 1961.
22. Winkler, *Big Deal*, chap. 4.
23. John McClain, "A Happy Revival of *Joey*," *New York Journal-American*, May 30, 1963.
24. Patricia Bosworth, "Why Edward Villella Won't Star in *Pal Joey* Tonight," *New York Times*, June 27, 1976.
25. Ibid.
26. Ibid.
27. Ibid.
28. Majorie Gunner, "On and Off Broadway," *Floral Park Bulletin* (Queens, NY), July 15, 1976.
29. Lena Horne in Leonard Feather, "Everything's Coming Up Roses," *Los Angeles Times*, April 16, 1978.

30. Chodorov is best known for writing *My Sister Eileen* (1940), and its adaptation *Wonderful Town* (1953), the latter of which won the Tony for best book in 1953. Bramble would go on to write the books for *Barnum* (1980) and the stage adaptation of *42nd Street* (1980); he was nominated for a Tony for both productions (as well as for directing the revival of *42nd Street* in 2001).

31. Thompson had starred in some of the most well-received black-cast musicals of the earlier era, including *Jamaica* with Horne and Premice, and *House of Flowers*, with Pearl Bailey. He also featured alongside Eartha Kitt in *Shinbone Alley*, and *Mr. Wonderful* with Sammy Davis Jr. "Gower Champion, the director, and Lena Horne, the singer and actress, have not seen things the same on 'Pal Joey.'" Liz Smith, "There's Been a Change in Direction," *New York Daily News*, March 6, 1978.

32. Like Claude Thompson, Premice had worked with Horne on *Jamaica* in 1957.

33. Claude Thompson, in James Gavin, *Stormy Weather: The Life of Lena Horne* (New York: Atria, 2009), 410.

34. Lena Horne, in Stanley Eichelbaum, "Lena on How *Joey* Moved to '78," *San Francisco Examiner*, September 28, 1978.

35. Some of the songs on the album, including "The Lady Is a Tramp," "Blue Room," and "Bewitched," are underpinned by a heavy-swinging, mid-century big-band sound. Others, including "Mountain Greenery" and "Lover," are reminiscent of the backbeat-heavy sound of Motown girl groups; still others, including "Spring Is Here," represent the "jazz with strings" sound popular in the 1950s and 1960s.

36. Jack Neal, "Lena Can't Save *Joey*," *Reno Evening Gazette*, August 29, 1978.

37. See "A Note Regarding Score and Libretto Sources," Appendix 2, for more information on the orchestration for the *Encores!* album.

38. Harry Connick Jr. had done a reading of the part in 1998, with a book by Terrence McNally, who had adapted the *Encores!* version in 1995.

39. Robert Hofler, "*Pal Joey* Gets Mixed Response," *Variety*, January 9, 2008.

40. Ibid.

41. Equity casting announcement, posted on Broadwayworld.com. https://www.broadwayworld.com/equity-audition/PAL-JOEY-REDUX-Developmental-Lab-2018-19288 (accessed January 8, 2018).

42. Michael Gioia, "Peter Schneider, Patrick Pacheco, Michael Reno Will Debut Re-Envisioned *Pal* Joey, with Interracial and Gay Themes," *Playbill*, August 9, 2013. http://www.playbill.com/article/peter-schneider-patrick-pacheco-michael-reno-will-debut-re-envisioned-pal-joey-with-interracial-and-gay-themes-com-208368 (accessed January 8, 2019).

43. *New York Times*, November, 1967.

44. C. Thayer, "*Joey* . . . A Hit or a Miss!" *Vector*, September 1967.

45. Opening-night script, 1-6-33.

APPENDIX 2  A Note Regarding Score and Libretto Sources

1. This would make a great deal of sense, given Royal's experience with and in dance bands, and the dance band sound: from the early 1930s Royal was a member of the Ted Weems orchestra, and he wrote big-band charts for Weems, Tommy Dorsey, Paul Whiteman, and Harry James. See Steven Suskin, *The Sound of*

*Broadway Music: A Book of Orchestrators and Orchestrations* (New York: Oxford University Press, 2011), 505.

2. Paul Christman, "*Pal Joey*: Reconstructing a Classic Rodgers and Hart Score," *Studies in Musical Theatre* 3, no. 2 (2009), 174–175.

3. Bruce Pomohac in ibid., 175.

4. Since the names survive, I was able to ascertain that nearly all of these players had big-band experience, and some performed with symphonic orchestras, including Morris Speinson (the horn player who was featured and performed the cheeky *Siegfried* horn call in "Happy Hunting Horn"), who was also in the Cleveland Orchestra in the early 1920s. Significantly, these players were all in the "sweeter," more commercial white bands, including Paul Whiteman's orchestra, the Original Memphis Five (who were, indeed, mostly born in New York), Tommy Dorsey's orchestra, Al Katz's orchestra, and Charlie Davis's orchestra. Vincent Grande, trombonist for The Original Memphis Five (also called The Cotton Pickers), was even best man in fellow trombonist Glenn Miller's wedding (see George Thomas Simon, *Glenn Miller and His Orchestra*, 32). The players (in the order listed) are as follows: Harry Bloom, Ricky Trent, Arthur Gianone, Vincent Grande, Morris Speinson, Irving Solow, Eddie Kooden, and Ralph Hayes (the last three names were written in a different hand, and were all trumpet players, probably indicating that they were substitutes).

5. In a note on one of the instrumental parts, Harry Levant (the musical director for the first run, from opening night until November 29, 1941) asks a "Guido" to rewrite a portion of the score, thus indicating that Guido [likely Guido Tutrinoli] was copyist during the first run, and his hand is reflected in the orchestra parts, the conductor cue scores, and the piano-conductor scores.

6. See Havoc, *More Havoc*, 205.

# RECOMMENDED READING LIST

• • •

## Selected Primary Sources

Abbott, George. *Mister Abbott*. New York: Random House, 1963.

Atkinson, Brooks. "Christmas Night Adds *Pal Joey* and *Meet the People* to the Musical Stage." *New York Times*, December 26, 1940.

Beiswanger, George. "Broadway on Its Toes." *Theatre Arts*, February 1940.

Gibbs, Wolcott. "Upturn." *New Yorker*, January 4, 1941.

Hart, Lorenz. *The Complete Lyrics of Lorenz Hart*. Dorothy Hart and Robert Kimball, eds. New York: De Capo Press, 1995.

Hart, Lorenz and Richard Rodgers. *The Rodgers and Hart Songbook*. Oscar Hammerstein and Richard Rodgers, eds. New York: Simon and Schuster, 1951.

Havoc, June. *More Havoc*. New York: Harper & Row, 1980.

Martin, John. "The Dance: Pal Kelly." *New York Times*, June 8, 1941.

Martin, John. "The Dance: *Pal Joey*; Robert Alton, Harold Lang and a Masterpiece." *New York Times*, February 17, 1952.

O'Hara, John. "Entertainment Week: An American in Memoriam." *Newsweek,* July 15, 1940a.

O'Hara, John. *Pal Joey* [the novel]. New York: Duell, Sloan & Pearce, 1940b.

O'Hara, John. *Pal Joey: The Libretto and Lyrics*. New York: Random House, 1952.

O'Hara, John. "Some Fond Recollections of Larry Hart." *New York Times*, February 27, 1944.

Rice, Robert. "How a Musical Is Made." *PM Weekly*, December 22, 1940.

Rodgers, Richard. *Musical Stages: An Autobiography*. New York: Random House, 1975.

Rodgers, Richard. *"Pal Joey*: History of a Heel." *New York Times*, December 30, 1951.

Segal, Vivienne. Interview with Anthony Slide. *Film Fan Monthly,* October 1972.

## Selected Secondary Sources

Block, Geoffrey. *Enchanted Evenings: The Broadway Musical from "Show Boat" to Sondheim and Lloyd Webber*. 2nd ed. New York: Oxford University Press, 2009.

Block, Geoffrey. *Richard Rodgers*. New Haven and London: Yale University Press, 2003.

Block, Geoffrey, ed. *The Richard Rodgers Reader*. New York: Oxford University Press, 2002.

Bruccoli, Matthew J. *The O'Hara Concern*. Pittsburgh: University of Pittsburgh Press, 1975.

Bruccoli, Matthew J., ed. *Selected Letters of John O'Hara*. New York: Random House, 1978.

Chauncey, George. *Gay New York: Gender, Urban Culture, and the Making of the Gay World, 1890–1940*. New York: Basic Books, 1995.

Christman, Paul. "*Pal Joey*: Reconstructing a Classic Rodgers and Hart Score." *Studies in Musical Theatre* 3, no. 2 (2009): 171–183.

Clayton, Jan and Samuel Marx. *Rodgers and Hart: Bewitched, Bothered and Bedeviled.* New York: G. P. Putman's Sons, 1976.

Engel, Lehman. *The American Musical Theater.* New York: Collier, (1967) 1975.

Engel, Lehman. *Their Words Are Music: The Great Theatre Lyricists and Their Lyrics.* New York: Crown, 1975.

Fields, Armond and L. Marc Fields. *From the Bowery to Broadway: Lew Fields and the Roots of American Popular Theater.* New York: Oxford University Press, 1993.

Ford, Phil. "Somewhere/Nowhere: Hipness as an Aesthetic." *Musical Quarterly* 86, no. 1 (January 2002): 48–81.

Gilbert, James. *Men in the Middle: Searching for Masculinity in the 1950s.* Chicago: University of Chicago Press, 2005.

Hirschhorn, Clive. *Gene Kelly: A Biography.* New York: St. Martin's Press, 1984.

Kislan, Richard. *Hoofing on Broadway: A History of Show Dancing.* New York: Prentice Hall, 1987.

Knapp, Raymond. *The American Musical and the Formation of National Identity.* Princeton, NJ: Princeton University Press, 2005.

Kraut, Anthea. *Choreographing Copyright: Race, Gender, and Intellectual Property Rights in American Dance.* New York: Oxford University Press, 2015.

Lindberg, Julianne. "Adapting *Pal Joey*: Postwar Anxieties and the Playmate." In *The Oxford Handbook of Musical Theatre Screen Adaptation,* ed. Dominic McHugh. New York: Oxford University Press, 2019.

Lindberg, Julianne. "*The Time of Your Life:* Gene Kelly, Working-Class Masculinity, and Music." *Studies in Musical Theatre* 10, no. 2 (Fall 2016): 177–193.

Magee, Jeffrey. "From Flatbush to Fun Home: Broadway's Cozy Cottage Trope." *Rethinking American Music,* eds. Tara Browner and Thomas L. Riis. Urbana: University of Illinois Press, 2019.

Maslon, Laurence, ed. *American Musicals: The Complete Books and Lyrics of 16 Broadway Classics, 1927–1969.* Boone, IA: Library of America, 2014.

Maslon, Laurence. *Broadway to Main Street: How Show Tunes Enchanted America.* New York: Oxford University Press, 2018.

McHugh, Dominic. "'I'll Never Know Exactly Who Did What': Broadway Composers as Musical Collaborators." *Journal of the American Musicological Society* 68, no. 3 (Fall 2015): 605–652.

McLean, Adrienne. *Being Rita Hayworth: Labor, Identity, and Hollywood Stardom.* New Brunswick, NJ: Rutgers University Press, 2004.

McNally, Karen. *When Frankie Went to Hollywood: Frank Sinatra and American Male Identity.* Urbana and Chicago: University of Illinois Press, 2008.

Miller, Scott. *Rebels with Applause: Broadway's Groundbreaking Musicals.* Portsmouth, NH: Heinemann, 2001.

Mordden, Ethan. *Beautiful Mornin': The Broadway Musical in the 1940s.* New York: Oxford University Press, 1995.

Nolan, Frederick W. *Lorenz Hart: A Poet on Broadway.* New York: Oxford University Press, 1994.

Shteir, Rachel. *Striptease: The Untold History of the Girlie Show*. New York: Oxford University Press, 2004.

Suskin, Steven. *The Sound of Broadway Music: A Book of Orchestrators and Orchestrations*. New York: Oxford University Press, 2011.

Symonds, Dominic. *We'll Have Manhattan: The Early Works of Rodgers and Hart*. New York: Oxford University Press, 2015.

Taylor, Theodore. *Jule: The Story of Composer Jule Styne*. New York: Random House, 1979.

Winkler, Kevin. *Big Deal: Bob Fosse and Dance in the American Musical*. New York: Oxford University Press, 2018.

Wolf, Stacy. "'We'll Always Be Bosom Buddies': Female Duets and the Queering of Broadway Musical Theater." *GLQ: A Journal of Lesbian and Gay Studies* 12, no. 3 (2006): 351–376.

Wolff, Geoffrey. *The Art of Burning Bridges: A Life of John O'Hara*. New York: Knopf, 2003.

Wood, Graham. "The Development of Song Forms in the Broadway and Hollywood Musicals of Richard Rodgers, 1919–1943." PhD diss., University of Minnesota, 2000.

## Selected Archives

Circle in the Square Papers. New York Public Library for the Performing Arts, New York, NY.

Don Walker Collection. Library of Congress, Washington, DC.

Gallagher, Helen. Interview with Liza Gennaro, March 22, 2006. New York Public Library for the Performing Arts, New York, NY.

Harold Lang Papers. New York Public Library for the Performing Arts, New York, NY.

Jo Mielziner Papers. New York Public Library for the Performing Arts, New York, NY.

John O'Hara Papers. Special Collections Library, Pennsylvania State University.

Lord Chamberlain's Plays. British Library, London.

Motion Picture Association of America Production Code Administration Records. Margaret Herrick Library. Academy of Motion Picture Arts and Sciences, Beverly Hills, CA.

Richard Rodgers Collection. Library of Congress, Washington, DC.

Richard Rodgers Papers. New York Public Library for the Performing Arts, New York, NY.

Rodgers, Richard. "The Reminiscences of Richard Rodgers." Interview with Kenneth Leish. Oral History Research Office, Columbia University.

Rodgers and Hammerstein Organization, New York, NY.

# INDEX

• • •

*For the benefit of digital users, indexed terms that span two pages (e.g., 52–53) may, on occasion, appear on only one of those pages.*
Tables and figures are indicated by *t* and *f* following the page number